Envisioning Effective Ministry:
Evangelism in a Muslim Context

Envisioning
EFFECTIVE
Ministry:

*Evangelism
in a Muslim
Context*

Laurie Fortunak Nichols
and Gary R. Corwin, eds.

emis

Evangelism and Missions Information Service
P.O. Box 794, Wheaton, IL 60187
Website: www.emisdirect.com

BILLY GRAHAM CENTER
WHEATON COLLEGE

Envisioning Effective Ministry:
Evangelism in a Muslim Context
(An *EMQ* Monograph)

Edited by Laurie Fortunak Nichols & Gary R. Corwin
Layout & Design by Dona Diehl

Published by EMIS, a division of the Billy Graham Center at Wheaton College, 500 College Ave., Wheaton, IL 60187.

Printed in the United States of America.

For information about other resources or publications of EMIS or the Billy Graham Center:
Phone: 630.752.7158
Email: emis@wheaton.edu
Online: www.emisdirect.com

ISBN: 978-1-879089-50-1

Table of Contents

SECTION 5

Evangelistic Methods & Church Planting   203

Endorsements

Nichols and Corwin have done an outstanding job of gathering in this one volume articles which reflect a wide spectrum of missiological views on the contextualization of the gospel in Muslim work. In it, the reader's attention will be drawn to the growing fault lines developing between the C4 and C5 "Insider Movement," fault lines that are now emerging inside of mission agencies, supporting churches, and even seminaries. The reader would do well to read, ponder, pray, and test these views in the light of scripture. Above all else, read Corwin's epilogue on "Muslim Ministry in the Days Ahead."

— **Dr. Don McCurry**, *president of Ministries to Muslims; founder and former director of The Zwemer Institute of Muslim Studies*

EMQ has been my staple reading since I entered missions in 1972. Therefore, most of the articles in this compilation I had already read, but the scope and depth of the collection is breathtaking once you read them all together. Doing so gave me renewed hope for substantial spiritual breakthroughs among Muslim peoples and a thankfulness to God for the great people he has called to take the gospel to them for such a time as this! Whether for inspiration or insight, this book is must-reading for mission pastors, prospective missionaries, and those excited to see least reached peoples discover their Savior.

— **David Lundy**, *international director of Arab World Ministries*

What you hold in your hands is a treasure of wisdom. Written by academics and practitioners who have labored in the Muslim context for years, it is inspiring, instructive, and challenging. The editors have done a phenomenal job in compiling this volume, which offers not only a breadth of approaches to Muslim ministry, but also presents a balanced look at many of the current controversial issues. As a South Asian Christian and the son of a Muslim Background Believer who is committed to reaching Muslims, I recommend this book to all who are serious in sharing Christ with Muslims.

— **Dr. Samuel Naaman**, *professor in the Missions Department at Moody Bible Institute; president of the South Asian Friendship Center in Chicago*

It is evident that God is moving in remarkable ways to fulfill his mission of being exalted among the nations. Creative mission strategies have engaged unreached people groups and resulted in an accelerating global harvest. Yet a remaining formidable barrier to global evangelization seems to be the Muslim world across the 10/40 Window, but even this barrier is beginning to crumble. Laurie Fortunak Nichols and Gary Corwin have provided a service to the Great Commission community with this volume. Representing the diversity of views, strategies, and insights that are both contemporary and dated, *Envisioning Effective Ministry: Evangelism in a Muslim Context* will be a valuable resource for those devoted to bring Muslim Background Believers into the Kingdom of God.

— **Jerry Rankin**, *president of the International Mission Board, SBC*

I give my highest recommendation to this volume, which should be on the bookshelf of every lover of Muslims. Most of the significant evangelical missions leaders focused on the Muslim world have articles represented in this volume. As such, it is both a historical and thematic document that saves one all the trouble of digging through past issues of *EMQ* looking for significant articles on Islam. I have already passed it on to some of my research students. The articles are short and take one through the many significant debates, such as the C5 Muslim evangelism controversy, that evangelicals have wrestled with concerning missions to Muslims. You get to see how this debate, and many others like it, had its beginning in the pages of *EMQ*. It is also a book with heart—the heart of those who burn with passion for Muslims to finally have a chance to hear of a Savior.

— **Dr. David Cashin**, *professor of intercultural studies at Columbia International University*

This is a brilliant idea: create an *EMQ* anthology of the most stimulating ministry-to-Muslim articles spanning the post-Lausanne (1974) era in Anglophone missiology. The fifty selected articles focus critically on evangelism/contextualization issues among Muslims and the 300-page work reads like a "who's who" of North American evangelical Islamic missiologists. This anthology is also a splendid companion to Keith Swartley's *Encountering the World of Islam* (2006), which together will amply cover all contemporary primary-source material for a university/college level course on outreach to Muslims. This work is an answer to prayer for my "Engaging the Muslim World" course at Houghton College. *Shukran EMQ!*

— **Rev. Dr. Benjamin Lee Hegeman**, *academic dean of école biblique en langue baatonou, SIM-Bénin/Togo; SIM lecturer on the history of Christian-Muslim relations at Houghton College*

Are you looking for the best of the best on Islam? Here it is packed in one volume. The most contemporary thinking on Islam done by those who know it best is found in this compilation by EMIS. These articles on one of the greatest eternal challenges to Christianity—Islam—are much too valuable and useful to be relegated to the archives. A big thanks to EMIS for repackaging and reissuing them here. This book can readily serve as a text for the classroom, small groups, Sunday school, or mission orientation classes. No one serious about learning about Islam should ignore this book, and no one going to the Muslim world should go without it.

— **Marvin Newell**, *executive director of CrossGlobal Link*

In *Envisioning Effective Ministry*, the reader discovers that reaching Muslims with the good news of Jesus Christ is both thrilling and complex. The voices and experiences of missionaries from the past, challenges swirling around contextualization methodologies, central theological issues of the present, and timely questions about future direction are well presented. This book provides vast information, wisdom, and prophetic warnings to edify and strengthen the Church—and the bright hope that our Triune God has surely been at work and will continue to build his Church among Muslims.

— **Joy Loewen**, *author of* Woman to Woman: Sharing Jesus with a Muslim Friend

When Paul and Barnabas returned to Jerusalem with a report of church growth among the Gentiles, it produced some controversy. *Envisioning Effective Ministry* reveals to the reader the progress of God's kingdom among the Muslim peoples of the world. The growth of Christ's body is often accompanied by both controversy and complexity. The Muslim world is no exception. Thankfully, editors Nichols and Corwin have not spared us. Dare to read this only if you're willing to be made uncomfortable. Here you will find the tension of controversy alongside the joyful progress of the kingdom. But this is controversy the Church needs—the kind that takes us outside our walls seeking to incarnate the gospel among the world's cultures and peoples.

— **Mike Kuhn**, *author of* Fresh Vision for the Muslim World; *pastor for adults/Christian education at Cedar Springs Presbyterian Church in Knoxville, Tennessee*

I praise God that a passion for his glory has spawned a wide array of ideas and approaches for reaching Muslims—along with valid concerns that some approaches are less biblically sound than others. This volume brings together a rich overview of these perspectives. Open discussion of these issues is bearing good fruit in sharpening efforts to see Muslims come to true faith and maturity in Christ. Important issues still remain to be tackled, as noted by Corwin in his epilogue. Although the process is not yet complete, this compilation brings us many good steps forward.

— **L. D. Waterman** *(pseudonym) oversees church-planting teams with Pioneers; has worked among Muslims in Southeast Asia for fourteen years*

Envisioning Effective Ministry is a practical and powerful compilation of insights from cutting-edge thought leaders and grassroots practitioners. In reading these articles I was reminded of a statement I heard from a seasoned leader who said: "I don't have all the answers. Some of the answers I do have are wrong. If I knew which ones, I'd change them." Read this incredible resource with that spirit of humility and I believe you will find a treasure chest of wisdom that stimulates fresh thinking and God-honoring action.

— **Steve Moore**, *president/CEO of The Mission Exchange*

Laurie Fortunak Nichols and Gary Corwin have done a monumental service for the church universal and to those interested in ministering to Muslims by assembling together the wisdom of many great servants of God who are on the leading edge of missions. These articles that first appeared in *EMQ* are foundational to the discussion of ministry to Muslims. Particularly helpful is compiling the current discussion into five thematic categories for easy reference. I would highly recommend *Envisioning Effective Ministry* to anyone seeking to understand the current discussion of missions to Muslims and best practices.

— **Roy Oksnevad**, *director of Muslim Ministries at the Billy Graham Center at Wheaton College*

Editors

Gary R. Corwin is associate editor of *EMQ* and staff missiologist with the international office of Serving in Mission (SIM).

Laurie Fortunak Nichols is managing editor of *EMQ* and editorial coordinator at the Billy Graham Center at Wheaton College. She is also editorial coordinator of *Lausanne World Pulse*.

Article Contributors

P. J. Anderson (pseudonym) is a missionary in a Muslim nation.

Nur Armagan (pseudonym) is a Turkish Christian who is a trained sociologist and theologian.

Clive Beestand (pseudonym) has been living in and observing the Arab culture since 1964.

Bruce Bradshaw is a graduate of Bridgewater, Virginia, State College and Gordon-Conwell Theological Seminary.

Dan Brown served as field director in the international headquarters of Frontiers in England. Previously, he was a church planter for ten years in the Middle East.

Ralph E. Brown served with the Conservative Baptist Foreign Missionary Society in West Pakistan. He has completed multiple terms in the Sind area.

Patrick O. Cate, president and general director of International Missions, began his ministry in the Middle East in 1974. He is a graduate of Wheaton College, Dallas Theological Seminary, and Hartford Seminary Foundation.

Gary R. Corwin is associate editor of *EMQ* and staff missiologist with the international office of Serving in Mission (SIM).

H. M. Dard (pseudonym) is a missionary serving in a Muslim country.

Carlos Diaz (pseudonym) serves with TEAM, where he trains and coaches Latino missionaries working among Muslims. He and his wife have worked with Muslims for over twenty years in Central Asia and Europe. Previously, Diaz was academic director of IIbET (Iberoamerican Institute of Cross-Culture Studies) in southern Spain.

Steven Downey is head of communications at an intergovernmental organization. He worked for twenty years at various Christian mission agencies.

Don Eenigenburg is director of church planting for Christar. He and his wife, Sue, have served with Christar since 1986. They have four children, all married, and three grandchildren.

Sue Eenigenburg is director of women's ministry in Christar. She and her husband, Don, have been involved in missions for twenty-three years. Sue is the author of *Screams in the Desert: Hope and Humor for Women in Cross-Cultural Ministry*.

Dean S. Gilliland is professor of contextual theology and African studies at the School of World Mission at Fuller Theological Seminary. He was a missionary to Nigeria for twenty-one years before joining the Fuller faculty in 1977. Dean's Ph.D. is in West African Islam.

David Greenlee serves as international research associate with Operation Mobilization.

Bradford Greer (pseudonym) has been working in the Muslim world since the mid-1980s.

Richard Heldenbrand has been a missionary to Muslims for many years.

Rev. Dr. Herbert Hoefer is the mission chair at Concordia University in Portland, Oregon. He is also Lutheran Church-Missouri Synod (LCMS) area director for South Asia. Herbert was a missionary of the LCMS to India for fifteen years.

Erik Hyatt is associate pastor for global outreach at Bethlehem Baptist Church in Minneapolis, Minnesota. He has a M.Div. in intercultural studies from Western Seminary in Portland, Oregon, and is currently working on a D.Miss. from Fuller Seminary.

Merlin W. Inniger has served with International Christian Fellowship in Pakistan since 1954, in evangelism and Bible teaching.

Warren Larson is the academic program director and associate professor of Muslim Studies at Columbia International University (CIU). He served as a missionary in Pakistan for twenty-three years and has written extensively on Islam, including a book on Islam in Pakistan. Larson is also director of the Zwemer Center for Muslim Studies at CIU.

Greg Livingstone has been focused on the Muslim world since his call to Libya in 1959. He assisted George Verwer in founding Operation Mobilization, and led OM's first team to India in 1963. Later, as the North American director of Arab World Ministries (AWM, then NAM), Greg recruited ninety-five new disciple-makers to take up residence in Morocco, Algeria, Tunisia, and France. In 1982, AWM encouraged Greg to launch a "separate sister mission": Frontiers.

Tony Lynn has been a pastor or a missionary since 1977. Tony earned a D.Min. from Mid-American Baptist Theological Seminary.

Joshua Massey is a cultural anthropologist, linguist, and missiologist, laboring among Muslims in Asia and the Middle East since 1985. He presently works with Muslim reformers and Muslim followers of Jesus to disciple nations and alleviate human suffering.

Jerry Otis has served in the Philippines with the Christian and Missionary Alliance since 1967. A former engineer, he is a graduate of the University of Kentucky, and studied at Jeffray School of Missions.

Phil Parshall is missionary-at-large with SIM (Serving in Mission). He served for forty-four years among Muslims in Bangladesh and the Philippines. Parshall has authored nine books on Islam. His Ph.D. is from Fuller Seminary and he has had fellowships at Harvard and Yale Universities.

Ken Peters got his appetite whetted for future missionary service during his one-year stint in 1987 in a Muslim desert village in northern Sudan.

Randal Scott (Scott Breslin) has lived in the Middle East for over twenty-five years. As a field director with Frontiers, Randal supervised teams doing ministry among Muslim peoples. He is currently on assignment with Operation Mobilization.

Jay Smith (pseudonym) is an American missionary with Brethren in Christ World Missions. Formerly a missionary in a North African country, he has participated in debates with Muslims throughout England.

John Speers, a Christian (Plymouth) Brethren missionary in Manila, sent his article to *EMQ* on May 18, 1991. On June 11, 1991, he was killed on a street in Cotabato City, Mindanao, the Philippines, where he had gone for a month to brush up on local language and culture. Authorities said he was killed on an apparent whim by a drug addict.

David Teague served in the Middle East under Interserve from 1983 to 1992. Presently, he leads seminars on the spiritual formation of mission leaders.

Mark Terry is professor of missions at a seminary in the Pacific Rim and visiting professor of missions at The Southern Baptist Theological Seminary in Louisville, Kentucky. He holds a Ph.D. in missions from Southwestern Baptist Theological Seminary and previously served as a missionary in the Philippines from 1976 to 1989.

Bruce Thomas (pseudonym) is a former U.S. Army officer, Columbia International University graduate, and teacher of English at a private university in southeast Asia since 1989.

John Travis (pseudonym) and his family have lived in Muslim communities in Asia for more than twenty years. John holds a Ph.D. and frequently teaches and trains field workers throughout the Muslim world.

Gerald Wiens (pseudonym) works in Central Asia.

J. Dudley Woodberry is dean emeritus and senior professor of Islamic studies at the School of Intercultural Studies at Fuller Theological Seminary. He has served on the staff of the Christian Study Centre in Rawalpindi, Pakistan, and as a pastor in Kabul, Afghanistan, and Riyadh, Saudi Arabia.

Scott Woods is a missionary in Southeast Asia. He has been engaged in C4 church planting for many years.

The Story of *Evangelical Missions Quarterly*

EVANGELICAL **MISSIONS** **QUARTERLY** was conceived in an ice cream shop called the Eskimo Inn in Winona Lake, Indiana. After the day's evening session at the first joint meeting of the Evangelical Foreign Missions Association (EFMA, now The Mission Exchange) and the Interdenominational Foreign Mission Association (IFMA, now CrossGlobal Link) in October 1963, a small group sat around the table talking about what they would like to see as lasting outcomes of the historic gathering. Someone tossed out the idea that the two associations should join hands and produce a journal that would cross the lines between them and stand as a joint evangelical testimony to what they believed about world missions.

Out of the Winona Lake conference came the Joint EFMA-IFMA Committee on Missions Quarterly. Meeting on December 4, 1963, at the Christian Literature Crusade in Fort Washington, Pennsylvania, it included Horace L. Fenton Jr., Kenneth Adams, and Wade T. Coggins (substituting for Clyde W. Taylor) representing the EFMA, and Edwin L. Frizen Jr., Ralph B. Odman, and Jim Reapsome representing the IFMA. It was decided that the proposed quarterly would be supervised by a board of directors, four from EFMA and four from IFMA.

The purpose of the journal was (and still is) to glorify God through the encouragement and inspiration of evangelical Christians who are dedicated to the command of Jesus Christ to proclaim the gospel to the whole world. *EMQ* pledges loyalty to the Bible, the inspired word of God, and to the truth it proclaims.

There were (and still are) six editorial components to *EMQ*:

1. Reporting. The journal should inform of events and trends vital to the cause of missions, interpreting them in the light of the evangelical position.

2. Stimulating. The journal should stimulate evangelical leaders of missions and national churches to write, expressing their views on problems vital to the ongoing evangelical witness. It should stimulate and encourage the total missionary force in the application of effective strategy and methodology to their work.

3. Linking. The journal should be a channel of communication linking the missionary force and the church constituency in a better understanding of basic problems and victories.

4. Edifying. The journal should not overlook the possibility of having a devotional ministry to its readers.

5. Helping. There should be practical helps giving clear instruction on how to undertake certain projects—a workshop or how-to-do-it page.

6. Reviewing. The journal should review current books of importance in the field of evangelism and missions.

By the end of 1964, two major goals had been accomplished: *Evangelical Missions Quarterly* had been born and a new corporation had been established to publish it: Evangelical Missions Information Service (EMIS). In 1998, Jim Reapsome retired as director and EMIS came under the umbrella of the Billy Graham Center (BGC) at Wheaton College. The name was changed to the Evangelism and Missions Information Service to encompass the BGC's focus on evangelism, but *EMQ* remained the same, that is until 2006. In 2006, EMQonline.com was launched. EMQonline contains all forty-five years of *EMQ* archives, plus current mission news from around the world.

To read *EMQ* writer's guidelines, go to page 286.

(Portions of this appeared in Jim Reapsome's 2004 article, "Forty Years: The Story of *EMQ*." Reapsome served as editor of *EMQ* from 1964-1997. He was executive director of EMIS from 1982-1997.)

FOREWORD

Ministry to 1/4 of the World's People
Greg Livingstone

"One generation will commend your works to another; they will tell of your mighty acts."—Psalm 145:4

WELCOME TO THE WORLD OF 2010. You may not get "turned on" by statistics, but stop and realize that statistics are about real people for whom God sacrificed himself.

Soon, one of every four men, women, and children in this world will be Muslim. If God "so loves the world," that means twenty-five percent of "the compassion the Lord Jesus feels for the multitudes" is focused on Muslim people. Have you ever said that you wanted to be like Jesus? If this is true, twenty-five percent of your caring should logically be for Muslims.

I doubt you would be reading this book unless you were already a Great Commission Christian. You have already "lifted up your eyes" and do care deeply. However, you may be asking:

- What *does* God have in mind for Muslims?
- How *do* I go about caring for them?
- Why *are* Muslims the exception to the fruitfulness the Church of Jesus Christ is experiencing worldwide?
- How *will* it be possible to establish the first communities of people who have switched their loyalties from their community's version of Islam to loving obedience to the Lord Jesus?
- Why *is* it that even when evangelical, Spirit-filled messengers of Christ do have the opportunity to explain what the Messiah accomplished on the cross, very few Muslims want to hear about it? Why do the friendliest Muslims simply change the subject?

Well, read on! You will find the answers to many of these questions in this compilation.

When we look at the hot topic of contextualization among Muslims, it is often as if we are dealing with two street gangs convinced the other is on the wrong turf. It might be amusing if it weren't so deadly serious. Envision an army that has such dissension its soldiers are shooting at each other instead of the enemy. The veterans fear the new recruits aren't "going by the book." The more recently trained cadets fear the old veterans are more focused on keeping tradition than "winning the war."

Is Satan laughing? Is there a well-planned Satanic scheme being implement-ed to "divide and conquer" (or at least divert) God's appointed ambassadors to the Muslim world?

It seems the enemy has three schemes to deceive the sending churches and yet a fourth to divert the practitioners who are laying down their lives to see Muslims "transferred from the domain of darkness into the Kingdom of God's beloved Son" (Col. 1:13).

Deception 1. Muslims are too difficult and resistant and are enemies of the gospel; therefore, all Christians should ignore them. Why waste time and money sending expensive missionaries to evangelize them? They are not going to believe in Christ.

Deception 2. Muslims are "coming to the Lord" by the millions through dreams, healings, and satellite television; therefore, there is little need to send expensive missionaries to those dangerous countries. The Lord is doing it by himself.

Deception 3. "Let the nationals do it. They know the language and the culture, and they are much cheaper to support." Of course that isn't a bad idea if you can find Muslim Background Believers (MBBs) or citizens who will take the risks. Often, the citizens are a different culture and deeply hurt by Muslim domination, and are therefore very slow to be "moved with compassion" for the Muslims.

As if these three issues aren't creating enough difficulty, Satan is using yet another way to divide and conquer. These include the beliefs that:

"Some left-wing missionaries and agency leaders are ignoring the scriptures and are more interested in applying anthropology than biblical theology!"

"Some right-wing evangelicals are missiological *jihadists*, more focused on criticizing fellow missionaries than winning Muslims to Christ."

It is a foundational premise of New Testament teaching that Christ's adherents are to establish an *ekklesia* (church/community) of fellow believers among every *ethnos* (people group) on earth. But how to do that is what the writers in this book are wrestling with.

And for reasons only God knows, he has chosen to utilize human instruments while he "builds his Church." Historically, there is little evidence of God creating communities like the church in Ephesus, Rome, Niger, or New Guinea without human instruments. So shouldn't we, by now, know the right way to do ministry to Muslims? Apparently not. However, in these pages you will read how various Christian workers are utilizing local culture and Islamic forms. Even when these workers don't, you will see that the Father is revealing to Muslims that the Lord Jesus really is the way (path), the truth, and the only source who can provide righteousness and eternal life.

How do we explain the thousands of Kabyles in North Africa deciding to become "Christians"? Some estimate we may have 100,000+ new brothers and sisters from Muslim families in a certain nation in southeast Asia. No one can accurately assess the response among the multiple Muslim people groups in parts of the Middle East and Asia who love the Lord Jesus as their Savior and Lord. Indeed, the angels are leaping with joy!

Who is doing this ministry right? If you examine where there are churches of MBBs, you'll see some worship in English and look pretty Western (C1), while others seem to be "invisible" (C6), while still others might look more Muslim than any "Christian church" you've ever experienced (C4), or even identify themselves as Muslims who follow Jesus (C5).

Some of the most vivacious, multiplying congregations look and sound just like your church back home, except that they worship in French, Arabic, or Indonesian. Is that okay? Or do they run the risk of so greatly turning off the vast majority of Muslim on-lookers that those churches will go on for generations as an extracted handful?

On the other hand, some Jesus followers function so completely within the mosque system, identifying themselves as Muslims, that either (1) communication of the real Jesus may be compromised or (2) Muslim on-lookers may ultimately conclude they that are nothing but deceivers. Is that okay? Compli-

Perhaps we should look at the differently gifted ambassadors called to Muslims like differently gifted members of a football team. Some concentrate on offense; others on defense.

cating things still further, some estimate that eighty percent of Muslims who profess Christ turn back to Islam, especially when they get married.

Some of the writers herein are so concerned about where the Church isn't, in any form, that certain other things take on less importance. Where the resistance is great, the Church is not birthed. She has been aborted, if ever conceived at all. That bothers some of us greatly! We feel some of what the Apostle Paul was feeling when he penned Romans 9:2-3. To paraphrase, "I have great sorrow and unceasing anguish in my heart. For I could wish that I myself were cursed and cut off from Christ for the sake of my [Muslim] brothers [getting adopted into God's family]."

People with that much burden, who care *that* much for Muslim peoples, just might, at times, try too hard. They might experiment beyond biblical parameters because they find it anguishing to see Muslims whom they've come to love pass into a Christ-less eternity year after year after year.

Others, whose burden for Muslim people may be equally great, feel constrained by scripture to be more cautious, desiring to contextualize the gospel to the full extent possible culturally, but unwilling to confuse the issue of who Christ is and what he expects of his people.

Food for Thought

Our Lord warned, "A house divided against itself will collapse." Perhaps we should look at the differently gifted ambassadors called to Muslims like the differently gifted members of a football team. Some concentrate on offense; others on defense. We are called to love the Lord our God with our minds as well as our hearts. So as you listen to Christ's ambassadors present their deeply-felt views in the following pages, ask yourself:

1. Does anyone want to go back to the 1960s? What articles would one find back then on how to win Muslims? Who was wrestling with the issues on how to rescue Muslims from Satan's kingdom? Where could one go back then to prepare for becoming an effective disciple-maker among Muslims?

2. During the 1960s hardly any of us had ever seen a Muslim, much less met one, and even more remote was the idea of having one for a friend. Yet, is it not usually necessary to make a Muslim my friend before he or she is likely to become Christ's friend? Didn't most of us become believers because someone who we felt cared for us shared him with us?

3. Would any missionaries leave his or her home, extended family, raise support, and try to enter a closed Muslim community if he or she did not believe (as God's word teaches) that Muslims are in desperate trouble without Christ?

4. If we do come into contact with someone using inaccurate exegesis, in what manner are we commanded to help that person?

I asked a Swiss worker what he thought of the experimentation going on to help whole families "bow the knee to Jesus Christ." He gave me his version of Gamaliel: "Do not disturb; the Holy Spirit may be at work." That same Holy Spirit, speaking through the Apostle Paul, also instructed Timothy to "guard the deposit entrusted to you…" May we be wise as serpents but gentle as doves as we tackle the tough issues of contextualization and engage those who don't yet know Jesus. And may the *ekklesia* in every community be birthed and nourished until it reaches the full expression of the Body of Christ.

INTRODUCTION

WHEN *EVANGELICAL MISSIONS QUARTERLY* WAS FIRST PUBLISHED in 1964, it was intended to encourage and inspire North American evangelical Christians involved in ministry overseas. And although throughout the years we have published articles on everything from church planting to fundraising to discipleship, more than any other topic, we have received feedback on those having to do with Muslim ministry and contextualized approaches.

Putting together this collection of articles has been a tremendous privilege—and one that didn't come with more than a few bumps in the road. As I have gained knowledge of the various facets of Muslim ministry, I have also learned one valuable lesson—God's workers in Muslim ministry are a passionate bunch of people! There have been a few fleeting moments when I have lamented the lack of passion we occasionally see in other segments of the Christian community. In other moments I have excitedly prayed that God would ignite that same fervor in every sector of missionary activity in every last place on earth.

Those in Muslim ministry are an excellent example of what it can mean to have iron sharpen iron—to balance wisdom and grace with both those we are trying to minister to (those not yet followers of Christ) and those who are doing ministry in other areas of the world (fellow mission workers).

After a few steps forward and one step back more than once, we have what we feel is an extraordinary collection of best practices, guidance, and wisdom from those who have been in ministry for anywhere from five years up to six decades.

Over the past forty-six years more than one hundred articles on Muslim ministry and contextualization have appeared in *EMQ*. In this volume, we have included nearly fifty of what we perceive as the most helpful. We begin with a foreword by Greg Livingstone and the C1 to C6 Spectrum by John Travis. We conclude with an epilogue by my co-editor, Gary Corwin, and an appendix on preparing spiritually for ministry among Muslims by John Travis. In between you will find five sections:

• **Understanding Islam** gives a general and historical overview of Islam and Muslim ministry.

• **Theology** seeks to give a sampling of some of the hot theological topics related to contextualization and Muslim ministry.

• **Contextualization** takes you on a chronological journey of how Christian workers have thought about and used (or not) contextualized methods.

• **Building Relationships** discusses issues related to family, community, morality, and integrity.

• **Evangelistic Methods & Church Planting** addresses strategies for those in Muslim ministry to effectively share the gospel.

Each section includes an introduction with a short synopsis of each article. Feel free to read the book from front to back or skip around. Each chapter and article can be read on its own, although the impact of what is being said is magnified when read in tandem with other contributions.

As we were putting this volume together, I asked a good friend, Roy Oksnevad (director of Muslim Ministries at the Billy Graham Center at Wheaton College), why there seemed to be so much spiritual warfare and conflict in the area of Muslim ministry. He responded, "Whenever you are involved in ground-breaking work where the gospel has not penetrated, you will encounter severe resistance." Brilliant, I thought. But also a wonderful reminder that what those in Muslim ministry are doing is so very important for the Kingdom of God. It is a high calling!

Thank you, Gary, for your expertise and open door/email inbox when issues of insider approaches and other terminology/specifics came up. Thank you also to Gloria McDowell, for her gift as a proofreader, and to Dona Diehl, for her creativity in designing the book. Thank you also to Ken Gill, director of the Evangelism and Missions Information Service (EMIS), for his oversight in the whole process of creating this compilation.

With that I leave you to read what our authors have to say on the issue of ministry to Muslims. We pray this volume will be a valuable part of your toolbox as you reach the Muslim world for our great and high priest, Jesus.

—*Laurie Fortunak Nichols, co-editor*

October 1998

The C1 to C6 Spectrum:
A Practical Tool for Defining Six Types of "Christ-centered Communities" ("C") Found in the Muslim Context

John Travis

An explanation of the six types of groups of believers found in the Muslim world.

THE **C1-C6 SPECTRUM** compares and contrasts types of "Christ-centered communities" (groups of believers in Christ) found in the Muslim world. The six types in the spectrum are differentiated by language, culture, worship forms, degree of freedom to worship with others, and religious identity. All worship Jesus as Lord, and core elements of the gospel are the same from group to group. The spectrum attempts to address the enormous diversity which exists throughout the Muslim world in terms of ethnicity, history, traditions, language, culture, and, in some cases, theology.

This diversity means that myriad approaches are needed to successfully share the gospel and plant Christ-centered communities among the world's one billion followers of Islam. The purpose of the spectrum is to assist church planters and Muslim Background Believers to ascertain which type of Christ-centered communities may draw the most people from the target group to Christ and best fit in a given context. All of these six types are presently found in some part of the Muslim world.

C1: Traditional Church Using Outsider* Language

May be Orthodox, Catholic, or Protestant. Some predate Islam. Thousands of C1 churches are found in Muslim lands today. Many reflect Western culture. A huge cultural chasm often exists between the church and the surrounding Muslim community. Some Muslim Background Believers may be found in C1 churches. C1 believers call themselves "Christians."

C2: Traditional Church Using Insider* Language

Essentially the same as C1, except for language. Although insider language is used, religious vocabulary is probably non-Islamic (distinctively "Christian"). The cultural gap between Muslims and C2 is still large. Often, more Muslim Background Believers are found in C2 than C1. The majority of churches located in the Muslim world today are C1 or C2. C2 believers call themselves "Christians."

C3: Contextualized Christ-centered Communities Using Insider Language and Religiously Neutral Insider Cultural Forms

Religiously neutral forms may include folk music, ethnic dress, artwork, etc. Islamic elements (where present) are "filtered out" so as to use purely "cultural" forms. The aim is to reduce foreignness of the gospel and the church by contextualizing to biblically permissible cultural forms. May meet in a church building or more religiously neutral location. C3 congregations are comprised of a majority of Muslim Background Believers. C3 believers call themselves "Christians."

C4: Contextualized Christ-centered Communities Using Insider Language and Biblically Permissible Cultural and Islamic Forms

Similar to C3, however, biblically permissible Islamic forms and practices are also utilized (e.g., praying with raised hands; keeping the fast; avoiding pork, alcohol, and dogs as pets; using Islamic terms, dress, etc.). C1 and C2 forms avoided. Meetings not held in church buildings. C4 communities comprised almost entirely of Muslim Background Believers. C4 believers, although highly contextualized, are usually not seen as Muslim by the Muslim community. C4 believers identify themselves as "followers of *Isa* the Messiah" (or something similar).

C5: Christ-centered Communities of "Messianic Muslims" Who Have Accepted Jesus as Lord and Savior

C5 believers remain legally and socially within the community of Islam. Somewhat similar to the Messianic Jewish movement. Aspects of Islamic theology which are incompatible with the Bible are rejected, or reinterpreted if possible. Participation in corporate Islamic worship varies from person to person and group to group. C5 believers meet regularly with other C5 believers and share their faith with unsaved Muslims. Unsaved Muslims may see C5 believers as theologically deviant and may eventually expel them from the community of Islam. Where entire villages accept Christ, C5 may result in "Messianic mosques." C5 believers are viewed as Muslims by the Muslim community and refer to themselves as Muslims who follow *Isa* the Messiah.

C6: Small Christ-centered Communities of Secret/ Underground Believers

Similar to persecuted believers suffering under totalitarian regimes. Due to fear, isolation, or threat of extreme governmental/community legal action or retaliation (including capital punishment), C6 believers worship Christ secretly (individually or perhaps infrequently in small clusters). Many come to Christ through dreams, visions, miracles, radio broadcasts, tracts, Christian witness while abroad, or reading the Bible on their own initiative. C6 (as opposed to

C5) believers are usually silent about their faith. C6 is not ideal; God desires his people to witness and have regular fellowship (Heb. 10:25). Nonetheless, C6 believers are part of our family in Christ. Although God may call some to a life of suffering, imprisonment, or martyrdom, he may be pleased to have some worship him in secret, at least for a time. C6 believers are perceived as Muslims by the Muslim community and identify themselves as Muslims.

* "Insider" pertains to the local Muslim population; "outsider" pertains to the local non-Muslim population.

SECTION 1

Understanding Islam

IF YOU ARE READING THIS compilation, likely you well know that ministry to Muslims is not simple. Patience, clarity of thought, and a firm reliance upon the Holy Spirit for wisdom are required. Unfortunately, too many lay people and missionaries jump into the task of evangelizing Muslims without having done sufficient homework on the different cultural, social, and religious backgrounds of those same people. A deeper understanding of Islam is needed for Christians to be effective in outreach. This chapter is designed to help you better understand what Islam is and is not—and what basic ministry elements are needed in understanding ministry to Muslims.

First, **Gary Corwin** (2004) encourages us to keep ten basic truths in mind as we minister to Muslims, and **Patrick O. Cate** (1992) discusses what it will take to win Muslims to Jesus.

After the September 11, 2001, terrorist attacks on the World Trade Center in New York, fresh views of Islam were shared: **Warren Larson** (2002) shed light on *Syed Qutb* ("martyr of the Islamic revival"), key characteristics of militant Islam, and how Christians should respond; **J. Dudley Woodberry** (2002) took an in-depth look at how terrorism and the Taliban relate to Islam—and the implications for Christian ministry and Christian/Muslim relations; and **Warren Larson** (2005) reminded us that Islam is rapidly growing in the United States and Christians must learn how to respond constructively.

To better understand discipleship to Muslim Background Believers, **Nur Armagan** (2006) says that a sociological lens offers helpful perspectives. **Clive Beestand** (2004) believes that Muslim family life and idiosyncrasies make more sense through anthropological eyes.

On the personal front, **P. J. Anderson** (1984) shares seven lessons learned over the years while ministering among Muslims.

October 2004

Ten Things Worth Knowing about Islam

Gary R. Corwin

Keeping ten basic truths in mind as we minister to Muslims.

AT A TIME WHEN more talking heads are focused on Islam than ever before, the mission community may want to keep these basic truths clearly in mind.

1. Islam is not one. It is as varied in its forms and styles as Christianity. Whether looking at major formal divisions, the various schools of law/denominational traditions, degrees of mysticism, or folk religious tendencies, a remarkable similarity exists in the degree of diversity. It isn't any more possible to understand Islam's breadth by grasping the nature of Al Qaeda terror strategies than it is to comprehend the breadth of Christianity by grasping the nature of Tuesday night bingo at St. Christopher's Catholic Church. While each provides insight into some underlying assumptions, neither is adequate as a microcosm reflecting the whole.

2. Islam is not primarily about private belief, but public observance and social structure. Generally speaking, outward conformity is a much higher value than freedom of religion or thought. The more seriously Qur'anic teaching is taken in a society, the stricter the social sanctions to encourage conformity will be.

3. Islam is a political vision as much as a religious one. Muslims believe their destiny is to rule everywhere. The world is divided into two parts, *Dar es Salaam* and *Dar el Harb*, the land of peace where Islam rules, and the land of war where the infidel does. While many Muslims don't think in the more militant ways in which these terms may be understood, most would still believe that Allah will one day bring it about.

4. Radical violent Islam is neither a fringe movement, nor the choice of the majority of Muslims, but it is the logical choice of those most devoted to core beliefs. Unlike Christianity, in which those most zealously devoted to the Master's teaching are the most loving and least to be feared, those most zealously devoted to the Qur'an's teachings and the Hadith are overwhelmingly the most violent and unmerciful.

5. Islam is a civilization at least as much as it is a religion. In its Golden Age (roughly the several centuries prior to the Reformation), in fact, it was a world leader in areas like the development of mathematics, science, and architecture. It was and still is today an all-embracing philosophy and way of life, with a catalog of explicit requirements for legal, economic, and governmental relationships. This point underlies C5 contextualization principles for introducing Muslims to the gospel. The basic argument is that Muslims who receive Christ as Savior should not have to cease being Muslims (in terms of civilization and culture) in order to follow Christ. A major problem arises, however, because the lines between Islam as religion and as civilization are so blurred.

6. There is no assurance of salvation apart from martyrdom as it is understood in some Muslim contexts. No matter how hard a Muslim might work to please Allah by obeying his commands, he or she never is confident of being good enough, or of being one day received into Paradise. The free forgiveness embodied in the Christian gospel of grace, therefore, is a powerful and attractive alternative.

7. Today in many parts of the Muslim world there is a deep questioning of Islam. This is evident in newspapers, television talk shows, and opposing *fatwas* (Islamic legal decrees) issued in regard to suicide bombings, etc. Muslims are asking themselves, "Is all the violence being perpetrated in the name of Islam a true reflection of our faith?" "Can we adapt to modernity?" "Is leadership in the Muslim world working?" There is an opening in the Muslim mind to these and other subjects.

8. Islam, like Christianity, is little more than a thin veneer over animistic folk religion in many parts of the world. While scholars and teachers dwell in the realm of holy texts, countless practitioners of both Islam and Christianity are much more concerned with issues of health, prosperity and personal welfare. The promise of power to ward off evil spirits drives the daily religious life of many Muslims and Christians.

9. When Muslims hear talk of the Trinity, or that Jesus is the Son of God, they think blasphemy (God and Mary procreated Jesus in the usual way). While this is clearly a misunderstanding of the biblical story, Muslims almost universally hold this belief. This remains a large stumbling block to a proper understanding of who Christ is.

10. The latest *surahs* of the Qur'an trump all that precede them including earlier *surahs* and the Bible. Unlike biblical revelation, which is progressive and unfolding, revelation from a Qur'anic perspective is consecutive and superceding. The "law of abrogation" makes clear that what has come more recently takes precedence and is the ultimate authority, even when it directly contradicts that which has gone before (in either the Qur'an or the Bible)—hence the conflicting messages in the Qur'an, for example, on how "People of the Book" (Christians and Jews) ought to be treated.

Much more could be said, but perhaps this brief survey can serve as a reminder of both the complexity and opportunities inherent in communicating the gospel to Muslims.

July 1992

What Will It Take to Win Muslims?

Patrick O. Cate

To win Muslims to Jesus it will take prayer, the right kind of missionaries, and more commitment to Muslim evangelism among our Western mission agencies.

JUST OVER A CENTURY AGO (1890) Samuel Zwemer began his work among Muslims in the Middle East, when there were perhaps some 300 million Muslims worldwide. He labored in the cause of Muslim evangelism for more than fifty years and fully expected to see the collapse of Islam, but it did not come. After the Gulf War, other people predicted a sudden collapse. However, no such crumbling has occurred; rather, today there are almost one billion Muslims, and their religion continues to thrive. After these disappointments, what will it finally take to win Muslims? More prayer, of course, but also more of the right kind of missionaries, and more commitment to Muslim evangelism among our Western mission agencies.

Making Muslims a Priority

One of the basic reasons Muslims have not come to faith in Christ is that they have not heard of Christ, and one of the basic reasons they have not heard of Christ is that missionaries have not gone to tell them about Christ. One of the basic reasons missionaries have not gone to tell them about Christ is that the Church has not seriously prayed to the Lord of the harvest to thrust out laborers into the Muslim fields. Are Muslims, who make up one out of five people in the world, on our daily prayer lists?

Of course, some people automatically think of all the barriers to Muslim evangelism, especially the political ones, such as the inability to obtain visas for work in predominantly Muslim countries. But in countries where Muslims are a minority, one can easily get and keep a visa. You can spend one hundred percent of your time working with these Muslims. You do not have to get a "tentmaking" job that restricts your time for evangelism. Sometimes these Muslim minorities are more responsive to Christ than they are in their home countries, so we need to do some sharp thinking about reaching displaced or immigrant Muslims. Mission agencies also need to think about developing new ministries in countries where Muslims constitute the majority. Some agencies work in such countries, but are not doing anything to reach Muslims. They are reaching professing Christians, or other minorities, the "easier people."

We will never know about some doors, unless we knock, shake, or kick them a little bit. We always ought to be pushing on doors to see what will happen. Sometimes, after years of pushing, they open.

We have workers among Muslims who recently had to leave their country after twenty-three years. In their first fifteen years they did not see a single one of them come to faith in Christ. But they did not quit because they were called by God to be faithful. Between their fifteenth and twenty-third years hundreds of Muslims made decisions for Christ. Today, 4,500 people in that needy Muslim country are taking Bible correspondence courses because of their ministry. A church has been planted, comprised of Muslim converts, with indigenous leadership. What if they had quit earlier? It's going to take prayer, shaking some doors, perseverance, and trusting in God to see the harvest.

Mission agencies focusing on Muslim lands need to figure out how to capture a new generation of missionary recruits to work in countries where quick, easy responses are not forthcoming. These people *do* exist; in my visits to churches and schools I have found some who believe that God's standard is faithfulness, not immediate results. Missionary recruiters need to ask

Missionary recruiters will need to ask what it will take to enable workers to have the long-term commitment level needed to reach Muslims.

what it will take to enable workers to have the long-term commitment needed to reach Muslims. What will it take for workers to gain the attitude of leaving their bones on the mission field, if God would so permit?

One of the keys to reaching Muslims is *relationships*. It takes time for relationships to develop, and repeated visits. On the other hand, we need to be careful of only developing friendships but never sharing Christ.

We also must recognize that some people with "tentmaking" skills tend to go out with only a three- to five-year commitment. Sometimes, sadly, they are more interested in developing professionally than in using their skills to penetrate the culture and the country with the gospel. Sometimes their desire for career security and professional development can make them too timid in witnessing. "Tentmakers" need to be trained in the "how" of Muslim evangelism, in biblical and theological foundations, and in the ethics of "tentmaking."

We need to mobilize *prayer*, not only for Muslims to believe and for more workers, but also for religious freedom and human rights. Mission agencies and churches could sponsor days of prayer and fasting for the Muslim world. One of the challenges in the Muslim world is that the good is often the enemy of the best. It is so easy to spend our time doing good things. This is true any place, of course, but it seems to be intensified in the Muslim world. We can give ourselves to the mechanics of living, to our jobs, to team responsibilities, to mission paper work, and really end up not logging very many hours, either in language study during the first years, or in ministry to Muslims later on.

We need *accountability*. What level have we reached on the language proficiency checklist? How many hours a week do we study the language during our first years? After that, how many hours a week do we spend with Muslims? What is the quality of our relationships and the quality of our sharing Christ with Muslims?

There's another pitfall we must avoid: always studying Islam and never *evangelizing Muslims*. It really can be said that Islam is the most studied and least evangelized religion. The number of books on understanding Islam is phenomenal. Much has been written to help us understand the Muslim mind, but we need to be careful, lest we merely become scholars, divorcing our scholarship from the Great Commission.

On the other hand, before they go and while they are on furlough, people need to sharpen their biblical, theological, and ministry skills, and sometimes

As we grow in our understanding of Islam, we learn that it is quite pluralistic, with differing shades of religious and political beliefs.

their secular skills as well. In his book, *America, Oil, and the Islamic Mind*, Michael Youssef says, "The crisis is the gulf between our ways of thinking" (1991). If we will give ourselves to better understanding the Muslim mind, we will gain valuable help in sharing Christ with Muslims. This means not just understanding classical Islam, but also animism, because each Muslim is to some degree animistic. Animism has influenced the whole fiber of Islam.

As we grow in our understanding of Islam, we learn that it is quite pluralistic, with differing shades of religious and political beliefs. For instance, many Muslims are against Islamic fundamentalism and *sharia* law. Unfortunately, one of the reasons more Muslims do not respond to the gospel is that some missionaries have not really learned the Muslim mind. They may have read one or two books or taken a course on Islam, but that's not enough.

One worker who has spent a lifetime in the Muslim world, and who has nurtured and led more than two hundred missionaries to work among Muslims, made an interesting observation. He said that although we have many more workers than in the days of Zwemer and the other pioneers, in terms of quality, Zwemer and company beat us hands down. Today, he said, we do not have people like Temple Gairdner (1873-1928, Church Missionary Society, Cairo) or Samuel Zwemer, who combined their sharp minds with a love for people and a passion for God.

He suggested that we generally ignore some of the best sources of candidates and said we should recruit Christian students at Harvard, Yale, Princeton, the University of Chicago, the University of California at Berkeley, and so on. Some feel we should also recruit more at seminaries, because not only do we need sharp minds, we need workers who can handle some of the theological issues that separate one billion Muslims from faith in Christ. Some seminary students possess secular degrees and secular professional backgrounds. We need to encourage these people to pursue opportunities in Muslim countries.

What about *power encounter* in winning Muslims? It's surprising for many evangelicals to learn that a large percentage of Muslim converts have had a dream in which Christ appeared to them and said something like, "I am the way," or, "Follow me." This has led them to find a Christian or a Bible, where they learned more about Jesus and put their faith in him.

However, we need to caution against going into Muslim areas expecting miracles to occur right and left. Thank God for the miracles we have seen and heard of, but some workers have left the field discouraged after four or five years because they saw no miracles, could not raise anyone from the grave, and saw no one healed. They reasoned that they were not properly related to God, not properly gifted, or not called, and therefore quit. Missionaries to Muslims must believe that the gospel is the power of God unto salvation to everyone who believes (Rom. 1:16). Their faith must not rest in their ability to execute miracles and healings. Being filled with the Holy Spirit does not equal the ability to perform signs and wonders. *Christ crucified is God's power* (1 Cor. 1:22-24).

What to Do with the Historic Churches

Throughout most of the Muslim world there are historic churches not made up of Muslim converts, such as Roman Catholics, Greek Orthodox, Armenians, Assyrians, and Copts. Some come from Hindu backgrounds. It could be argued that over the last two centuries a majority of missionaries going to the Muslim world to evangelize Muslims have spent most of their time evangelizing and discipling people from these historic churches. Compared to Muslims, they are easier to reach and more responsive. But the danger is that we will spend all our time trying to revive these churches and ignore the Muslims.

On the other hand, there is a tiny minority of people in some national churches who do work at Muslim evangelism. There's much we can learn from them. We should listen to them, work with them, and have them speak in our weekly mission gatherings, monthly meetings, and annual conferences. We cannot take a know-it-all attitude; we need to come as learners.

For example, I know of one national elder who has baptized about two hundred Muslim converts. We can learn much from people like him. A worthy goal would be to find at least one promising person in the national church. Have that person teach us culture and language, while the missionary teaches Muslim evangelism, praying that the national will catch the vision for it.

Using Media to Support Priorities

We need to keep asking which media best communicate in the Muslim world and into specific countries. I lived in a middle-class (and a lower-class) neighborhood in the Muslim world and three video stores operated within two blocks of our home. Most Muslims read little, but they watch videos and television for hours. A Christian television network, broadcasting from a satellite, could penetrate Muslim walls and be received by many more Muslims once they get receiving dishes.

The *Jesus* film possibly has been the medium used by God to lead more Muslims to faith in Christ in recent years than any other media tool. It has been translated into almost every major Muslim language.

However, better-trained workers and the latest technology will be of no avail unless mission agencies and churches consider their part in reaching Muslims. Agencies and churches need to look at their budgets and personnel and ask what percentage is dedicated to reaching the one billion lost Muslims around the world. What part of their prayer life is devoted to asking God to open closed Muslim hearts and doors, and to thrust out new laborers? We need to take a hard look at our prayers, priorities, and preparation if we want to see Muslims won for Christ.

Reference

Youssef, Michael. 1991. *America, Oil & The Islamic Mind: The Real Crisis Is the Gulf Between Our Ways of Thinking.* Grand Rapids, Mich.: Zondervan.

How Islam Sees Itself

Warren Larson

A look at Syed Qutb ("martyr of the Islamic revival"), key characteristics of militant Islam, and how Christians should respond.

EVER SINCE 9/11 we have been bombarded with generalizations as to the peaceful nature of Islam: "Islam is traditionally a religion of tolerance." "Our enemy is fanaticism, not Islam." "*Jihad* does not mean holy war." "Islam calls for racial and religious harmony, not violence." It is not surprising such generalizations have confused a number of people as to another face of Islam they have witnessed—militancy. For a fuller understanding of how Islam sees itself, we will not only look at the Qur'an, but at other Islamic roots and sources. We will then consider practical suggestions as to how Christians might respond biblically to the current threat of Islamic terrorism. But first it will be helpful to see how one extremist has influenced an entire generation of Muslims.

Journey of a Militant Muslim

Syed Qutb has been called martyr, ideologue, and theoretician of Islamic fundamentalism—an indication of sufferings he endured and the way his radical thinking shaped the movement. Such terms also reveal his total faith in Islam, and how much he was loved and respected by those who witnessed his moral courage and intellectual capacity.

He was born in 1906, in the village of Qaha, in the province of Asyut, Egypt. His father was a well-to-do farmer and respected member of the community. Yet with a dark complexion, slight build and frail disposition, the boy was not at all striking or attractive. Besides, he was naturally timid and sensitive. But what he lacked in physical appearance he more than compensated for in intellect. By the time he was ten, he had already memorized the entire Muslim holy book. This thorough knowledge of the Qur'an early in life proved to be the beginning of a life totally dedicated to Islam.

At age thirteen, Qutb was sent to Cairo for schooling. There he quickly displayed a remarkable penchant for English literature and read everything within sight. By the time he graduated from *Dar al-Ulum* (House of Knowledge) he had become well acquainted with the "westernizing tendencies" of many Egyptians. As a result of his mental prowess, he was appointed inspector in the Ministry of Education, but later abandoned this prestigious post in order to write. Thus, he provided a system whereby Egyptian nationalism could be combated. He felt Nasser's bid for the Arab world was a challenge to Islam so he gave fellow Muslims in Egypt, and elsewhere, sound reasons for rejecting it.

As to literary achievement, Qutb resembles Abul Ala Mawdudi of Pakistan. He wrote a total of twenty-four books and numerous magazine articles. Several of his publications have been translated into English by the International Islamic Federation of Student Organizations in Kuwait. His books have also been popular with black Muslims in the United States and influenced Iranians to overthrow the Shah.

His major publication was an interpretive study of the Qur'an. Again, he was influenced by Mawdudi in that he held to Qur'anic "literalism." His thirty-two volume commentary is famous for homiletical content, simplicity of style, and clarity of thought. It has sold thousands of copies, and today is being used as a standard in the privacy of Muslim homes and the public arena of mosques all across the Arab world.

In 1949, Qutb went to the United States and studied educational administration for two years, but his exposure to American life turned him totally against the West. First, partially because of a swarthy complexion, he sensed deep racial prejudice. Second, he observed overwhelming support for Israel in the newspapers. For Qutb, this was a combination of personal and national rejection.

For Qutb, there was no difference
between a communist and a capitalist westerner. Both were enemies and harmful to Muslims.

Moreover, like many of his Arab contemporaries, he experienced a profound sense of displacement. He felt the British had denied the Arab the right to self-determination at the end of World War II and the United States supported and perpetuated this deplorable crime. Eventually, his bitterness grew to the point that he hated and despised everything for which the West stood.

This negative reaction included all Western methods, models, values, and styles as dangerous and harmful to Muslims and non-Muslims. So he began calling fellow Muslims to total and irrevocable rejection of Christians and Jews whom he viewed as synonymous with the West. Based on his own Qur'anic interpretation, he forbade contact with "people of the book" because he felt they led Muslims astray.

Furthermore, for Qutb there was no difference between a communist and a capitalist westerner. Both were enemies and harmful to Muslims. He concluded that communism and capitalism would surely fall for their failure to protect and provide for the good of humanity. Rooted in human origins, they were doomed, whereas the divinely-revealed Islam would triumph in the end. It is interesting that his prediction—at least in reference to the fate of communism—has already taken place.

After his brief, but unfortunate, stay in the United States, he joined the Muslim Brotherhood and continued his literary influence. Although he learned from Mawdudi, he went further into militancy than the Pakistani leader ever intended—or even dared to go. Consequently, he was arrested along with others for extremist views, and for attempting to assassinate Gamil Abd Nasser. The sentence was fifteen years of hard labor.

Qutb was released after ten years—now a victim of deep hardness and bitterness from the torture he had endured. What he once offered as advice now became rigid dogma. He spoke openly of violence for the good of the *ummah* (Muslim community) and enjoined *jihad* (struggle for Islam) against forces that resist by force. In this spirit, he wrote his most controversial book, *Maalim fi al tariq* (*Milestones*), a publication that precipitated his re-arrest in 1965. Qutb was executed in 1966 by the Egyptian government and buried in an unmarked grave. He had become "Martyr of the Islamic Revival." Obviously, Qutb does not speak for all Muslims, but he does speak for some of them. His pilgrimage from reformer to radical sheds light on the world of militant Islam and provides a context for what follows.

Discussing the Main Issues

1. The sources of Islam. Islam is more than the Qur'an, as all through history Muslims have drawn on several sources: the Qur'an, the Hadith (canonical tradition), *ijma* (Islamic community consensus), and *qiyas* (analogy). By community consensus, these four sources form the basis of the *sharia*, God's holy law and the manifestation of his will and guidance for all humankind. The *sharia* molds Muslims into "the best of peoples, evolved for mankind" (Qur'an 3:110).

At the heart of the *sharia* is first the Qur'an, God's verbally inspired, eternal, and unalterable word revealed to Muhammad and the Muslim community. Next is the Hadith, God's inspired accounts of the words and actions of Muhammad, who was the recipient of the Qur'an. As such, the Hadith serves as an indispensable commentary for Muslim understanding and interpretation of the Qur'an. It is also the path for all Muslims to follow because Muslims must obey God and their Prophet. These sources give us a self-understanding of Islam.

2. Peaceful and/or militant Islam. Peaceful Islam does in fact exist. The Qur'an says: "Let there be no compulsion in religion" (Qur'an 2:256); and, "... nearest among them in love to the believers wilt thou find those who say, 'We are Christians'" (Qur'an 5:82). Militant Muslims supplement Qur'anic peaceful verses with militant references: "Fighting is prescribed upon you ..."(Qur'an, 2:216). "Fight and slay the pagans wherever ye find them..." (Qur'an 9:5).

"Fight those who believe not in Allah nor the Last Day, nor hold that forbidden which hath been forbidden by Allah and his Apostle, nor acknowledge the religion of truth, (even if they are) of the People of the Book, until they pay the *jizya* with willing submission, and feel themselves subdued" (Qur'an 9:29). As in the above verses, Muslim theologians have appealed to their "Doctrine of Abrogation." Thus, in this case, the "Sword Verse" (Qur'an 9:5) has abrogated other peaceful verses because it is chronologically later. In *Milestones*, Qutb argues strongly for *jihad* from select Qur'anic verses (Qur'an 4:74-76; 8:38-40; 9:29-32). These passages alone, he states, suffice to justify the universal and permanent dimensions of *jihad* (1964, 53-76).

3. Pre- and post-*Hijrah* ("Flight"). Islam's official calendar dates from the Hijrah (A.D. 622), when Muhammad emigrated from his home town of Mecca to Medina. Muslims have divided the Qur'an into Meccan and Medinan *surahs* (chapters). For thirteen years prior to the *Hijrah* Muhammad spread the message of Islam among the Arabs in and around Mecca. His followers were few and mostly of low status. Throughout this period, Muhammad received messages, telling him to endure the rejection and to remember his role as only a "warner," to proclaim God's message, and to graciously reason with opponents. He was even commanded to "repel evil with that which is best" (Qur'an 23:96). After the *Hijrah*, Muhammad continued on in the prophetic role, but assumed political leadership of the first Islamic state. It is here that fighting becomes the next stage. It is here that religion and state go hand-in-hand.

4. The Islamic concept of peace. Does Islam mean peace? Muslims want us to believe that Islam is a peaceful religion, claiming that the Arabic word *Islam* means "peace." The word for peace in Arabic is *Salaam*, not *Islam*. The word *Islam* is a related word, but means "to surrender, or to make peace by laying down one's arms in submission" (military use), or "slave submission to one's master—Allah" (religious use). To claim that *Islam* means "peace" is just one more attempt to mislead the public. The Islamic "peace" can come only when all people submit to the rule of God and obey his apostle.

5. The Islamic concept of *jihad*. Muslim leaders are quick to explain that *jihad* does not mean holy war, but rather to strive in the cause of Allah by study and personal devotion. This is true if only the literal meaning of the Arabic word is considered. Muhammad's exhortation to *jihad* however is almost always in the context of fighting infidels (pagans), Jews and Christians. It is this meaning that *jihad* is given in the commentaries and classical writings of Islam. Jews, Christians, and *munaffiqin* (hypocrites) who do not convert are allowed to live, but they must pay *jizya*, a protection tax levied on "People of the Book."

Islamic sources frequently refer to fighting and holy war. In fact, nearly one-third of volume four of the nine-volume, canonized collection of Bukhari's Hadith deals with *jihad*. The Qur'an says jihad receives the highest reward and is the surest way to Paradise if the fighter dies: "Think not of those who are slain in Allah's way as dead ... they live ... in the presence of their Lord" (Qur'an, 3:169)."... To him who fighteth in the cause of Allah ... soon shall we [God] give him a reward" (Qur'an, 4:74). *Ibn Ishaq*, the oldest biographer on the Arabian Prophet, says "... [when] the Arabs knew that they could not fight the apostle ... they entered into God's religion 'in batches' as God said, coming to him from all directions" (Guillaume 1978, 628).

Let it be clearly stated, however, that it is wrong to say Muslims have always converted non-Muslims through the sword. In the U.S., for example, there are purportedly between two and three million converts to Islam, and none of them converted by the sword. In other lands Muslim merchants and Sufis have been successful Muslim missionaries. Moreover, Islamic law clearly forbids Muslims to force "People of the Book" (Christians and Jews) to become Muslims. Yet, under *dhimmi* status, with the right to practice their religion as long as they remain loyal citizens, they are considered second-class citizens.

6. The apostate and punishment. As noted, Muslims particularly in the West, say that Islam proclaims freedom of religion. They quote 2:256 in the Qur'an: "Let there be no compulsion in religion." But does this exhaust Islam's commentary on the subject? No doubt Jews and Christians can remain in the religion they were born into, but a Muslim is not free to abandon Islam

Today, in Muslim nations from Nigeria to Indonesia, many Christians are suffering persecution because of their faith.

and embrace another religion. One of Islam's most respected theologians and prolific writers in the last century, Pakistani Abul Ala Mawdudi, insists that both Qur'an and Hadith demand an apostate's execution. He quotes the Qur'an (9:11-12) and the canonized Hadith: "Any person, i.e. Muslim, who has changed his religion, kill him" (Khan n.d., 45). The Islamic scholar, Majid Khadduri, agrees that Qur'anic commentaries say a believer who turns back from his religion must be killed if he persists in disbelief (1955, 150).

7. Persecution of Christians. In the Middle Ages, Islamic governments were usually more tolerant of Jews and Christians than Christian governments were of Jews and Muslims. But today, in Muslim nations from Nigeria to Indonesia, many Christians are suffering persecution because of their faith. On Sunday, October 28, 2001, Islamic militants brutally killed sixteen Pakistani Christians and wounded six others as they sang the last hymn in a worship service. Again, on Sunday, March 19, 2002, grenades thrown into the midst of worshipers in Islamabad left five Christians dead and nearly fifty wounded. Several hours away in the city of Multan, Ayub Masih, who has been accused of insulting the Prophet Muhammad under the Blasphemy Law, languishes in solitary confinement in a four-by-six foot cell. In jail for five-and-a-half-years, the last four on death row, he may hang—although the charges were fabricated because Muslims wanted to oust Christian settlers in order to take over their land.

8. Islam is more than a religion. Whether all Muslims are aware of it or not, Islam is not a religion in the same way religion is understood in the West. Islam is much more than a religion. A leading expert on the history of Arabs and Islam was the late Lebanese-American scholar, Philip Hitti, who taught at Princeton University for nearly fifty years. One of his books has three parts: Islam as Religion, Islam as State, and Islam as Culture. Muslims are tied together as a homogenous unit regardless of geographic or racial diversity. This makes Islam a socio-cultural and religio-economic political system.

9. Islam's global agenda. Muhammad taught his followers that all religions before him, including Judaism and Christianity, were good in their time, but Islam is the final and universal religion. Where Islamic law has been instituted, no other religion is tolerated, unless it agrees to submit to Islamic rule. Today, more than forty nations have a majority population of Muslims, and Muslim leaders have spoken of their goal to spread Islam in the West until Islam becomes a dominant, global power.

Choosing Right Responses

1. Self-evaluation and repentance. Whenever we face calamity, the Bible instructs us to humble ourselves, repent of our own sins, and turn to God (2 Chron. 7:14). As horrific as the September 2001 events were, we must recall the words of our Lord: "Why do you look at the speck of sawdust in your brother's eye and pay no attention to the plank in your own eye?" (Matt. 7:3). Or, "... unless you repent, you too will perish" (Luke 13:3). America is the world's number one advertiser of a life-style allowing adultery, homosexuality, pornography, and abortion. And far too many professing Christians participate in these sins. As the Church of Christ we need to repent and cry out for God's mercy.

2. Trust in God. Christians need to trust that God is in control and will bring good out of evil in these turbulent times: "And we know that in all things God works for the good to those who love him, who have been called according to his purpose" (Rom. 8:28). After immense suffering, Joseph was able to say to his brothers: "You meant evil against me; but God meant it for good" (Gen. 50:20). It has been refreshing to see how this generation, often bent on selfishness, has banded together to sacrifice and serve. Since the arrest of Christian aid workers in Afghanistan for sharing their faith, and their subsequent miraculous release, God will surely raise up many more to pray and go to Muslims with the gospel. Christians are becoming more aware of the great physical and spiritual needs of Muslims throughout the world.

3. Engage in dialogue. In some cases, Muslim activists have been given an open platform in churches to explain Islam. If we do invite a Muslim to speak in church we should also invite a Christian who is knowledgeable in Islam to present the Christian perspective on the subject at hand. Giving Muslims an open platform to propagate their faith confuses Christians and sends the wrong message about Islam. Also, it only seems fair that Christians should in turn be invited to mosques to give the Christian view, in order to have true Muslim-Christian dialogue.

4. Anticipate greater receptivity. We should anticipate greater Muslim receptivity in the days ahead as they hear the gospel. Christians have been praying for centuries that Muslims would respond but often there has been little lasting fruit. Research study on Islamic fundamentalism and Christian conversion indicates that when Muslims see the rigidity and severity of the *sharia*, they tend to reject Islam and embrace the Prince of Peace.

5. Prepare for total commitment. There is a parallel between our present crisis and biblical records about the circumstances surrounding Queen Esther. Her people were targeted for destruction, but facing this dilemma, she sensed that God had placed her in the kingdom "for such a time as this" (Esther 4:14). In simple faith, she said, "If I perish, I perish" (Esther 4:16). As God worked out his plan then to save his people through Esther, it seems that God now wants to use the Church to avert the eternal destruction of innocent Muslims around the world. With more than a billion Muslims in our world, who awaken daily without the Scriptures, and have no assurance that their sins are forgiven, we must redouble our efforts in prayer, giving and going. Will we respond as our Lord desires for such a time as this?

References

Ali, Abdullah Yusaf. 1989. *The Meaning of the Holy Qur'an*, new ed. Beltsville, Md.: Amana Publications.

Guillaume, A. 1978. *The Life of Muhammad: A Translation of Ibn Ishaq's Sirat Rasul Allah*. Karachi, Pakistan: Oxford University Press.

Haddad, Yvonne Y. 1983. "Sayyid Qutb: Ideologue of Islamic Revival." In *Voices of Resurgent Islam*. Ed. John L. Esposito, 67-98. New York: Oxford University Press.

Khadduri, Majid. 1955. *War and Peace in the Law of Islam*. Baltimore, Md.: Johns Hopkins Press.

Khan, Muhammad Muhsin. n.d. *The Translation of the Meanings of Sahih Al-Bukhari Arabic-English*, Vols. 1-9. Beirut: Dar Al Arabia.

Larson, Warren F. 1998. *Islamic Ideology and Fundamentalism in Pakistan: Climate for Conversion to Christianity?* Lantham, N.Y.: Oxford University Press of America.

Mawdudi, Abul Ala. 1994. *The Punishment of the Apostate According to Islamic Law.* Translated and annotated by Syed Silas Husain and Ernest Hahn, n.p.

Qutb, Syed. 1964. *Milestones*. Cedar Rapids, Iowa: Unity Publishing Company.

January 2002

Muslim Missions after September 11

J. Dudley Woodberry

How terrorism and the Taliban relate to Islam—and implications for Christian ministry and Christian/Muslim relations.

MY WIFE, ROBERTA, AND I had just been evacuated from Peshawar, Pakistan—the birthplace of the Taliban and Osama bin Laden's main conduit to the world. As we waited in Thailand with other Christian aid workers among Afghans to see if we could return, we walked the beach. Dark storm clouds were clustering around a crescent moon (the symbol of Islam) as boats moved out for a night of fishing. The scene started my reflection on the gathering storm in Afghanistan and the Muslim world: How do terrorism and the Taliban relate to Islam? What grievances drive the terrorists and their admirers?

During a service on World Communion Sunday, a day after we arrived in the United States, we learned that bombs were falling on Afghanistan. As the round loaf of bread was broken, symbolizing Christ's broken body, I also thought of our broken world. As the cup was poured, commemorating his shed blood, I also thought of the blood being shed right then in Afghanistan, a land that had been our home. Each bomb landed in or near a place where we had been. Some craters were in the actual dirt where we had walked.

When we turned on our car radio, we heard a recording of Bin Laden calling on all Muslims to join a holy war against the infidel West, especially Americans. Yet Muslims had been our hosts during our years of living in Afghanistan, Pakistan, Lebanon, and Saudi Arabia, and our ministry had made us guests for shorter periods in most Muslim lands. Again questions arose: What are the implications for concerned governments, Muslim-Christian relations, and for missions? What follows are my initial and tentative answers.

How Do Terrorism and the Taliban Relate to Islam?

In the news we have been bombarded by generalizations about the peacefulness or militancy of Islam or by the equating of fundamentalists (Islamists) and militants. All fail to grasp the diversity within Islam and its roots. The Qur'an is comprised of recitations by Muhammad, believed to come from God, to meet the needs that arose on specific occasions. Some were peaceful; others were militant. Therefore, either position can be argued by selecting specific verses or illustrations from history. The peaceful interpretation held by a majority of Muslims is based on verses like 2:256 ("There is no compulsion in religion") and 5:82 ("The nearest in affection to the believers are those who say, 'We are Christians.'"). The *dhimmi* classification, applied to Jews and Christians in particular, gave them the right to practice their faith as long as they were loyal citizens and performed their obligations. In the Middle Ages Muslim governments were commonly more tolerant of Jews and Christians than Christian governments were of Jews and Muslims.

The militants, however, base their position on Qur'anic verses like 2:216 ("Fighting is prescribed for you..."); 2:190-192 ("Fight in the cause of God those who fight you and slay them...for tumult and oppression are worse than slaughter....Fight them until there is no more persecution and oppression and there prevails justice and faith in God"); 9:5 ("Fight and slay the infidels") and 49:15 ("The true believers are those who...strive with...their lives for the cause of God"). Militants like Bin Laden use the words I have highlighted in their rationale: Fighting and slaying is prescribed by God. Americans cause oppression, injustice, and are infidels (although the Qur'an is referring to polytheists); so Muslims must strive with their lives for the cause of God.

According to the canonical traditions, Muhammad taught that a martyr would have his sins forgiven, be shown his abode in Paradise, avoid purgatory, and receive the crown of honor. The "suicide bombers" thus see themselves as performing a sacred obligation for God and his community and acquiring honor and an eternal reward. Furthermore, their experiences have led them to believe that they do not have diplomatic or military power to overcome God's enemies by any other means.

Another question that arises is how the rigid faith and practice of the Taliban fits into Islam. The Taliban have their historic roots in Hanbalism, the most fundamentalist of the four schools of the Sunni branch of Islam. By "fundamentalists" I mean that they turn for guidance to the fundamentals of their faith—the Qur'an and practice (*Sunna*) of Muhammad and the earliest Muslims—and reject later adaptations. They hold that their understanding of the society of the earliest Muslims is the model for society even today, and it applies to all areas of life.

Since there are plenty of peaceful and militant examples in Islam, these fundamentalists can be peaceful or militant. The *Wahhabism* of Saudi Arabia is a modern example of this Islamism—which was militant when the families of Ibn Saud and Ibn Abd al-Wahhab were conquering most of Arabia and destroying popular saint veneration from the eighteenth century to the twentieth century. Today, however, its expression in the Saudi government is largely peaceful.

From these same roots have grown the current Islamist groups starting with the Muslim Brethren in the Arab World, some of whose leaders I met with secretly in the 1960s when they were outlawed, and I was writing my doctoral dissertation on the theology of their founder. They were pious and idealistic, but their goal was so important to them that they would commit terrorism if other means were blocked. One member greatly influenced Bin Laden in his student days in Saudi Arabia while others taught in the schools and mosques of southwestern Arabia which produced a number of the plane hijackers on September 11.

The Taliban are another such group. These movements normally arise from the interaction of a feeling of trauma, local conditions, and a millennial ideology. The trauma and local conditions in this case included the fighting between the seven major *mujahideen* groups (with their rival ethnicities and leaders), after they had driven the Soviets out of Afghanistan. The original *Taliban* (literally, "students") included many orphans who had lost their fathers in the previous fifteen years of fighting and were raised in the religious schools around Peshawar, where they learned little beyond the Qur'an and the ideology that all would be well if they got rid of external enemies and initiated a social system based upon that of the early Muslim community.

After initial success against *mujahideen* militias, they were seen as a source of law and order—and hence got Pakistani support and recruits from Pashtuns (also called Pashtuns and Pathans) in Afghanistan and Pakistan. But power corrupted many of them, and many Afghans came to resent their strict laws and punishments and the increasing number and influence of outsiders called "Arab Afghans" that they harbored.

What Grievances Drive the Terrorists and Their Admirers?

Terrorism is a response to a build-up of grievances, real or imagined. Therefore, one cannot drive out terrorism without dealing with the grievances that lead to it. The most obvious of these is the Israel-Palestine conflict because of the frequent news coverage of rock-throwing Palestinian youths, and some suicide bombs, against vastly superior Israeli firepower.

The resentment has been building for years. Arab anger started with the Zionists' encouragement of Jewish immigration into Palestine in the late 1800s under the slogan "A land without a people for a people without a land," when Palestine had been Arabized for over twelve centuries. The resentment increased after the British promised at the beginning of World War I to support Arab independence in exchange for Arab support in the war effort against their Ottoman Turkish masters. Instead they made the Psykes-Pecot agreement (to divide the Near East into European protectorates) and then the Balfour Declaration (to look with favor upon the creation of a national home for the Jewish people in Palestine that should not interfere with the rights of the local inhabitants).

The anger turned against the United States, when after World War II, President Truman not only did not honor President Roosevelt's promise to King Ibn Saud not to make any decisions concerning Palestine without consulting with the Arabs, but he and American officials twisted arms in the United Nations to offer the Jews over half of Palestine when they were still only a third of the population and owned only twelve percent of the land. In subsequent fighting the Israelis gained control of all of it and have continued, Arabs point out, to build settlements in the occupied West Bank despite UN resolutions to return the lands conquered in 1967.

I know something of Jewish desperation after the Holocaust, having worked on a rusty tramp steamer out of Haifa that had previously smuggled Jews to Palestine following World War II, but I have also seen the Palestinian refugee camps filled with people whose families had owned the land for centuries. Now they watch its occupiers on television defending it and killing other Palestinians with missiles and F-16s made in the U.S. and purchased with $3 billion in American military aid each year. Bin Laden and the Taliban's Mullah Omar ask, where are the Americans when they want justice? And Arabs and Muslims around the world agree—especially since Jerusalem is the third holiest Muslim site.

Another obvious grievance is the continued sanctions against, and occasional bombings of, Iraq ten years after the Gulf War. The reasons are obvious, but pictures and reports of civilian casualties or UN reports of the thousands of children dying from malnutrition and disease—the major victims—continue to inflame passions. For many Arabs, Saddam Hussein was another Nass-

One person's "terrorist" is another person's "freedom fighter," and many governments in the coalition against terrorism expect support for suppressing their own opposition groups.

er uniting the Arab World, to many Muslims another Saladin fighting the most recent Crusade, and to many Third World people another Robin Hood stealing from the corrupt rich to share with the poor. Sanctions against Syria, Libya, Iran, and Sudan—plus bombing of a pharmaceutical factory in Sudan without convincing proof of its military use—have fanned the flames of hatred.

A third grievance is the stage on which all the others play—the Muslims' sense of being humiliated and in danger. For over a millennium the Islamic empires were the superpowers, and the Sunni Islam of the majority did not develop a theology of suffering, for God seemed obviously to be on their side. Then, Western colonial powers divided the Muslim World between them. Today, Muslims have not only been humiliated by the Jews in Palestine, but by the Christian Serbs in Bosnia and Kosovo, by the atheistic or Christian Russians in Chechnya and sometimes by the Hindus in Kashmir. After the bomb blasts that killed twenty-four Americans in Saudi Arabia in 1995 and 1996, Bin Laden is quoted as saying, "They have raised the nation's head high and washed away a great part of the shame that has enveloped us."

The ascending of the West is seen, fourth, as affecting Muslims in a number of ways. It has corroded morality with the flow of alcoholism, drugs, materialism, sexual promiscuity, and arrogance through movies, television, and two-way travel. Modernist Muslim states have tended to continue the adoption of Western law codes rather than what is believed to be the divinely ordained Islamic laws. Economically the world is seen as controlled by Western global economic ideas based, for example, on charging interest, which is not allowed by Islam. The majority of Muslim nations are poor and under a crippling foreign debt burden; so obviously it is not seen as working for them. To sum up, Islamists are angered by the fact that they believe they have a superior culture but the West, especially Americans, have the superior power.

Last, with their superior power Americans have espoused democracy but backed Muslim regimes that Islamists feel have tried to crush their own aspirations (e.g., Iran under the Shah). For many years, Americans have built the Saudi military bases and overseen the training and equipping of both their military and national guard. (A significant number of the alleged hijackers in the September 11 tragedies came from Saudi Arabia.) All of us who lived there had daily reminders of the American presence with the planes flying out of the local air bases.

Osama bin Laden directed his sights on Americans after the Saudi government declined his offer to use Muslim veterans of the Afghan war against the Soviets for the Gulf War. Instead, Saudis brought thousands of "infidel" Americans onto the holy soil of Islam's Prophet, and a significant number stayed after the conflict. In 1998, he protested, "For more than seven years the U.S. has been occupying the lands of Islam in the holiest of its territories, Arabia, plundering its riches, overwhelming its rulers, humiliating its people, threatening its neighbors, and using its bases in the peninsula as a spearhead to fight against the neighboring Islamic people."

Implications for Concerned Governments

Since much of the anger that has led to terrorism has resulted from years of certain people feeling that the foreign policy of the U.S. and others with power has been unjust, the first area that must be addressed is *foreign policy*. Although Americans cannot police the world, there are issues like the Palestine conflict where we can help the opposing parties work out solutions, and we must strive for a maximum of justice rather than just do what is politically expedient at home. One person's "terrorist" is another person's "freedom fighter," and many governments in the coalition against terrorism expect support for suppressing their own opposition groups.

Therefore, any action will require a delicate hand—be it in Palestine/Israel, Kashmir, Chechnya, Sri Lanka, or Kurdish areas of Turkey. Also, the world community needs to build on the opportunities the new coalition brings for approachment between nations.

Next, *relief and development* in Afghanistan cannot stop at the end of the military action, as much of it did after the expulsion of the Soviets in 1989. Twenty-two years of fighting, three years of famine, and five years of Taliban rule in Kabul and much of the country have made the situation desperate. There are millions of landmines and hundreds of men and children minus arms or legs on the streets of Afghanistan and Peshawar. Much of Kabul is in ruins. And there is little food.

Third, as Americans call for revenge, we need to be aware of the *limitations of military action alone*. To kill a "terrorist" makes him a "martyr" that inspires new "terrorists" as the Israel-Palestine conflict has shown. Furthermore, a broader action, particularly if it kills civilians, just increases the militants (as the same conflict shows). Coordinated international pressure on a country harboring terrorists until they give them up proved effective with Pan AM flight 103 and the Libyans—although less effective with Iraq.

Last, although the Afghans were not able to hold together a united government on their own in the early 1990s, American and other foreign powers must *keep as low a profile as possible* in any help they give in nation building. History has shown that the one thing that unites Afghans is the presence of a foreign power on their soil.

Implications for Muslim-Christian Relations

1. The present crisis underlines the urgency of improving Muslim-Christian relations. The repeated assertion by President Bush and coalition members that the War on Terrorism is not a war against Islam has often been drowned out by the call of Bin Laden and militants for all Muslims to rise up in holy war against the "Crusade on Islam," and mutual demonization has been a common result.

Yet the crisis presents a unique opportunity to work on long-overdue issues. The coalition against terrorism has drawn together some Muslim and non-Muslim nations that have recently been on opposite sides of the table. Now we can work on some of the issues that have divided us. Recent events force attention to festering wounds like Israel/Palestine, Iraq, Kashmir, and Chechnya where religion is one of the components. It has also forced Muslims to delineate more clearly what are legitimate and illegitimate means to reach what are considered to be just goals, even as it has given many Christians their first awareness of some of the concerns Muslims have for justice.

2. Christians need to affirm strongly that we, with Muslims, reject many of the values and results of globalizing Western culture led by Americans—materialism, consumerism, alcoholism, drug use, sexual promiscuity, individualism, and arrogance. Christians' highest loyalty is to the one God, and we affirm family values and concern for the poor and marginalized, as do pious Muslims.

3. We need to avoid judging Muslims based upon news sound bites or the reductionism of focusing primarily on religion as the cause of conflicts between Muslim and Christian communities. There are many perspectives in the Muslim community, and even these are changing. Conflicts between Muslim and Christian communities in places like Indonesia and Sudan have ethnic, economic, political, as well as religious roots. Muslims in turn need to realize how out of date it is to charge the West with a "crusade" against Islamic nations when the West is in a post-Christendom period.

4. We need an attitude of empathy, repentance, forgiveness, and willingness to be forgiven even for things for which we do not feel responsible. Muslims in the West feel threatened and need our empathy, even as Christians in some Muslim lands feel threatened. Because westerners are individualistic, we often do not understand the non-Western Muslim's sense of group responsibility. Therefore, we may not feel responsible for American actions with which we disagree nor the aggression of Christendom historically; yet Eastern Muslims tend to make the connection. In a dialogue with a Muslim theological faculty in Turkey this summer (of which I was a part), there was applause when we Christians apologized for the harm caused by the Crusades.

5. We need to be involved in concrete communication and working together. One of the first things my wife did upon our return from Peshawar was to visit our Pakistani-American Muslim neighbors. Many of us Christians across the country are meeting with Muslim and civic leaders to see what we can do—one good result of the tragedies.

Implications for Missions

1. Crises can awaken us to learn. Initially we can turn to scripture to help us face the crises. When I was privileged to speak to the Christian aid workers after their expulsion from Afghanistan by the Taliban in September, we looked at passages God had given us in previous crises. After the incarceration of two visitors for giving out four Gospels of Luke in 1971, we saw in scripture how God saved Shadrach, Meshach, and Abednego, not out of the fire but in the fire when he burned their bonds, sent a divine companion, and was glorified in the nation (Dan. 3:17-30).

When the church building was torn down by the Afghan government in 1973 and the government fell the next day, we were led to Joseph's words to his brothers: "You meant evil against me, but God meant it for good" (Gen. 50:20). And we looked for the good that God was bringing in increased prayer and flexibility of ministry. We returned to that verse again in 1998 during an evacuation of Christian workers by the Taliban. This fall, with the imprisonment of expatriates and Afghans from one agency and the expulsion of expatriates with other agencies, we were led to Philippians 1:12-30, where Paul overcame the circumstances of his imprisonment through prayer and the Holy Spirit. It is when we pass through situations like those in the biblical records that God uses them to encourage and guide us.

2. We can look to scripture to see how God in Christ reaches militant fundamentalists like the Taliban. During the previous expulsion from Afghanistan, we found a parallel in Saul on his way to Damascus "breathing out threats and murder" against the Christians. The Jews, like Muslims more recently, faced their imperialists—for them the Romans. And they, like Muslims today, were being engulfed by an alien globalizing culture—for them Hellenism. The response of Pharisaism was similar to today's Islamists, a return to the law in their scripture—for them the Torah. Some became peaceful Pharisees like Nicodemus, others militant ones like Saul. It took a vision of Jesus to change him, even as it has in a significant percentage of the Muslim conversions to Christ today.

3. We can play off the domino pattern. Research at Fuller Theological Seminary's School of World Mission has shown that where Islamists have imposed *sharia* law and there are local friendly Christians, there is receptivity to the gospel, which in turn can lead to persecution of Christians. This domino pattern, first noted after the Khomeini revolution in Iran, then in Zia al-Haq's Islamization in Pakistan, is also observed elsewhere. We can expect the same disillusionment and hunger for grace under Taliban rule to be fertile ground for the seed of the gospel. Research has also demonstrated that other facets of the present crisis have been the contexts elsewhere for people turning to Christ when they see Christian love demonstrated in their midst. These contexts include political or military turmoil, natural disasters like famines, migration of refugees, and urbanization.

4. We should distinguish between Christian faith and Western culture. Where militants warn of the "Western (or American) Crusade," is the obvious need to redouble our efforts to distinguish between Christian faith and Western culture through the contextualization of word and deed and raising up of more non-Western missionaries.

5. We should establish appropriate witness. The imprisoning of Christian aid personnel by charging them with "preaching Christianity" and the expulsion of others highlights the need to study relevant scripture passages, pray through, think through, and try to reach a consensus with colleagues concerning the form of witness appropriate in the cycles of greater suppression or freedom in countries opposed to traditional missions. Attention needs to be given to long-term and short-term goals, integrity, and the leading of the Spirit in the community.

6. We can help moderate Muslims reason with extremists. The imprisoning of expatriate Christian aid workers and Afghan colleagues showed the value of being able to help moderate Muslims reason with extremists. We offered those associated with the case arguments from the earliest Muslim sources for greater religious freedom; thirty years earlier, when people were incarcerated for passing out four Gospels of Luke, we offered a Muslim lawyer a case based on the Qur'an. In 1979 in Saudi Arabia, when the government would not let us worship in one auditorium, we provided letters which early Muslim sources ascribe to Muhammad that let the Christians in Najran in Arabia retain their churches and priests.

7. God has "given to us the ministry of reconciliation." The last twelve of the twenty-two years of fighting have been between Afghan factions, showing the need for this reconciliation. The results of this gospel was demonstrated recently when I was privileged to visit the worship of new believers in a country in western Africa where two ethnic groups that had been killing each other on the streets were eating and worshipping together because they were one in Christ.

8. Other implications. As mission agencies prepare for post-September 11 ministries in the Muslim world, there are a cluster of implications:

- Continuing the trend for coalitions of mission agencies
- Increasing relief and development capabilities for the tremendous human need
- Facilitating programs for youth (including orphans), who make up a major segment of Muslim countries
- Retaining at least skeleton teams for quick mobility when places like Afghanistan reopen
- With the heightened danger and anti-American feeling, providing orientation in security measures and deploying more personnel without children at home and more non-Americans
- Developing guidelines for appropriate forms of witness, discussed in orientation and broadly agreed upon by workers
- Repeatedly updating evacuation plans for a variety of emergencies with designated tasks, accessible cash and documents, backup of computer and paper records, and adequate communication (even satellite phones) and transportation

As noted, my wife and I learned of the start of the Allied bombing of Afghanistan as we were participating in a communion service. A few days earlier I had been privileged to preach at and lead a communion service with aid workers who had just been expelled from Afghanistan. As we reflected on how God had cared for us in previous crises, we felt led to make a pile of stones as God's people did when they crossed the Jordan to commemorate God's care (Josh. 4). Each person carried a stone to the pile that will be taken back to Afghanistan when the time of destruction is over and the time to build returns.

I described how Roberta and I subsequently walked the beach in Thailand and began reflecting on the questions above as we saw storm clouds gathering around the crescent moon. By the time we returned, darkness had settled in. But lights now appeared on each fishing boat to lighten the places where they worked until the dawn came—and we knew a little better what we needed to do.

A Christian Response to Islam in America

Warren Larson

Islam is growing rapidly in the United States and Christians must learn how to respond constructively.

JOHN ESPOSITO, arguably the most influential non-Muslim American scholar on Islam, at times sounds prophetic. His book, *The Islamic Threat: Myth or Reality?* (1992), suggests Islam is a threat to the West—particularly America. His book a decade later, *Unholy War: Terror in the Name of Islam* (2002), could have been titled: "I told you so." He says a war conducted militarily, rather than diplomatically, will lead to rising anti-Americanism, global instability, and bloodshed. The root of militant Muslims' anger and agenda, he says, is American foreign policy.

Certainly, American foreign policy angers Muslims. Among the offending policy points are support for Israel, U.S. troops in Saudi Arabia, and military action in Afghanistan and Iraq. The Bush Administration's goal to root out radical Islam has enraged many Muslims.

But the U.S. is not solely to blame for Islamic extremism. Globalization, years of unhappy Muslim-Christian encounters, and "Westophobia" in the Muslim media are factors. Also at fault are conspiracy theories, such as one claiming Jews carried out the terrorist acts of 9/11, which are rampant across the Muslim world (Riddell and Cotterell 2003, 152-160). It is also true that a major reason for Muslim militancy is found deep within Islam. This is not to say that most Muslims do not want peace, but an American convert to Islam (who later turned to Christ) offers this insider perspective:

Christianity teaches us to love our enemies. With Islam it's quite the opposite. You should be just, but you should hate the enemies of Islam. And if they openly struggle against Islam, they should be eliminated (*Christianity Today* 1989, 38). Such sentiments can be traced back to the Qur'an: "Fighting is a grave offense; but graver is it in the sight of Allah to prevent access to the path of Allah" (Qur'an 2:217). One Muslim put it this way: "The world as we know it today is how others have shaped it, so we have two choices: either to accept it with submission, which means letting Islam die, or to destroy it, so that we can construct a world as Islam requires."

In *Islam Under Siege* (2003), Akbar Ahmed says that many Muslims feel they are not only under siege politically and militarily but culturally as well. Attempting to set things right, militant Muslims are using negative portrayals of non-Muslims in Islam's sacred scriptures. According to surveys by the BBC and *Q News*, the largest Muslim periodical in the U.K., Muslim radicalization is rising worldwide (Riddell and Cotterell 2003, 193-194). Groups like al-Mahijiroun in England, under the fiery preaching of Sheikh Omar Bakri Muhammad, use Western freedoms to mold the minds of fellow Muslims.

This article does not minimize dangers faced because of a growing Muslim perception that America has targeted Islam. The threat from militants is very real, but the material below builds on what Carl Ellis has been saying for years: "Islam is the greatest threat to the Church" (2000). Christians can be instruments of peace in the face of rising tensions.

Why Americans Convert

The *Time* magazine article, "Should Christians Convert Muslims?" (Van Biema 2003), suggested evangelicals are wrongheaded when they try to convert Muslims, but it failed to mention Muslim attempts—and success—in converting Christians. Below are some reasons why an estimated two million African-Americans, many of whom claim to be former Christians, have embraced Islam.

1. Decadence of Western society. They are seeking self-respect, discipline, family values, moral standards, and deliverance from drugs and alcohol. According to Islam, they can change the stereotype of the young black male on drugs, out of work, and in jail. It's a new way of life, a path not only to God, but of dignity and self-respect.

African-American women convert because in Islam they see an emphasis on modesty, chastity and economic rights. Many had been abandoned to fend for themselves and their children because of unfaithful and irresponsible men. An African-American imam (mosque leader), invited to speak in my class at Columbia International University, said, "*Jesus paid it all* is not what American blacks must hear!" Islam then becomes an alternative to corruption and immorality—symptoms of a society in its final stages of breakdown. Islam comes with family values, guidelines on relationships, clear male leadership roles, a well-ordered prayer ritual, and even a new name! While Christianity is deemed powerless to effect social change, Islam can establish laws, control moral behavior, and produce reform.

2. Failure by the Church. Converts to Islam say while Christian discrimination left them cut off and disenfranchised, now as vice-regents in Islam, they have purpose, distinction, and empowerment that even the civil rights movement did not give them. As Bruce Fields notes in Introducing *Black Theology: Three Crucial Questions for the Evangelical Church*, it is unfortunate that "because the issue of racism still exists in our society, it still exists in the Church" (2001, 53). He adds that "if the world does not see true unity among those who claim allegiance to Jesus Christ, the Church should not be surprised when the world is unimpressed with our proclamation that the Father has sent the Son" (2001, 64).

Something similar is happening to Latinos. In its article, "Islam is Luring More Latinos," *The Washington Post* (January 29, 2001) quotes a young woman who had been devoutly Catholic: "I felt a strong sense of belonging." Another says she felt a "sense of sisterhood with others who wore hijab (veil)."

3. Failure to understand Islam. Ignorance abounds about Islam. Muslims equate Islam with peace, but the word for peace in Arabic is *"salaam,"* not *"Islam." Islam* means "surrender or to make peace by laying down one's arms in submission." To claim that *jihad* means "striving in the cause of Allah by personal devotion" is not the whole truth. Muhammad's call to *jihad* was first and foremost to fight infidels (pagans): Jews and Christians. In the oldest biography on Muhammad, author Ibn Ishaq states that the Prophet conducted twenty-nine battles and planned thirty-nine others (1978, 628). And, supported by commentaries and classical writings, the Qur'an claims that *jihad* is the only sure way to paradise (Qur'an, 3:169). Ideologue Syed Qutb, motivator of militant Islam, appeals to the Qur'an when he builds his case for jihad (Qur'an 4:74-76; 8:38-40; 9:29-32). These passages alone, he states, justify the universal and permanent dimensions of *jihad* (1964, 53-76).

Americans must understand that where Islam dominates, Muslims are never free to abandon Islam.

Americans also must understand that where Islam dominates, Muslims are never free to abandon Islam. Maududi, the most influential Muslim scholar in the twentieth century, insists that both the Qur'an and traditions demand an apostate's execution. He might be faulted for quoting the Qur'an (9:11-12), as it says to fight only against those who "violate their oaths," but is on more solid footing with Bukhari's canonized tradition: "Any person, i.e., Muslim, who has changed his religion, kill him" (Al-Bukhari Vol. 9, 45).

One problem is that Islam's sacred scriptures send mixed signals on how to treat non-Muslims. While the Qur'an admonishes Muslims to ask "People of the Book" if they have questions (10:94; 21:7, 48) and condemns violence and killing (5:32), the next verse says those who war against Allah should have their hands and feet cut off (5:33). A few verses later it says Muslims should not take Jews and Christians as friends (5:51).

Notably in Islam's sacred writings, numerous references call for militants to further their deadly cause and "fight against" unbelievers (Qur'an 9:5, 29; 8:39; 4:74). Islamic traditions that predict how Jews will ultimately be exterminated are equally disturbing: "The Last Hour would not come till the Muslims fight against the Jews and the Muslims will kill them until the Jews hide themselves, and the stones and trees would speak up saying 'There is a Jew hiding behind me, come and kill him'" (Al-Muslim Book 40, No. 6985).

Where to Go from Here

1. Christians need a good dose of optimism. Stan Guthrie concurs in *Missions in the Third Millennia: 21 Key Trends for the 21st Century* that ministry to Muslims is difficult, and that nine-tenths of the worst persecution takes place in Islamic states. But he reminds us that many Muslims are embracing Christ. For example, Indonesia's Church may have grown to twenty million, far beyond official estimates.

Similarly, in *The Next Christendom: The Coming of Global Christianity*, Philip Jenkins, distinguished professor of history and religious studies at Penn State University, wonders if Islam and Christianity can peacefully co-exist (2002, 168, 179). He sees more Muslim-Christian conflict looming on the horizon (2002, 188). Although he does not consider the dangers of nominal Christianity, his work is encouraging because it provides research from the secular viewpoint of Africa, Asia and Latin America's phenomenal church growth.

Jenkins says that the total number of American Muslims is closer to four million—not eight million as claimed (2002, 105), and that Muslim immigrations to the United States will be exceeded by a larger influx of Christians from Africa, Asia and above all, Latin America (2002, 105). Mohamed Nimer, board chairman of the Council on American-Islamic Relations (CAIR), concurs in *The North American Resource Guide*. Although it is difficult to estimate both immigrant and black Muslims because of religion policies at the U.S. Census Bureau, he believes Muslims in the U.S. number closer to 4.1 million, including immigrants.

2. Christians need training on theological, evangelical, and historical levels. American Christians must be prepared for Muslim missionaries because Islam is a missionary faith: "Call men to the path of your Lord" (Qur'an 16:125) and "Witness to the nations" (Qur'an 2:143) are for Muslims what the "Great Commission" is for Christians. This is why the Muslim World League spends huge sums on missions—building mosques, sending missionaries, and printing literature. Islam has been successful in getting into American schools. The leader of Arab World and Islamic Resources and School Services in Berkeley, California, says that a decade ago the average social studies class spent little time studying Islam and the Middle East. She said, "It would have been three or four days, and now it's three or four weeks, maybe six. This is a huge change" (Collier 2002).

American Christians should know that according to the Qur'an, Muslims believe Christians worship three gods: "Say not three" (Qur'an 4:171; 5:171). Christians need skill in responding to Muslim assertions that Jesus did not die. This might include knowing Qur'anic references that suggest he did in fact die (Qur'an 5:117; 19:19; 3:55). And Christians must be able to articulate that Christians do not view Jesus as son in a physical way, as Muslims charge. Christians need to know that in the Qur'an, Jesus is sinless (Qur'an 19:19) whereas Muhammad is not (Qur'an 36:27; 40:55; 47:19; 48:2).

Furthermore, how many Americans understand that not even one of Allah's ninety-nine names say he is longing and willing to save? In Islam, God has the power but lacks the will to save lost, helpless sinners. Compare this with the Bible: God is not willing that any should perish (2 Pet. 3:9). How many would-be American converts to Islam know that in the Qur'an, God loves only the righteous (Qur'an 3:76)—not the sinful (Qur'an 4:107)? The Bible, in contrast, says he even loves his enemies (Rom. 5:10).

From the above, Muslims seem to be on a treadmill where they can never do enough to please God. During a recent Muslim-Christian dialog I attended in Columbia, South Carolina, the Muslim speaker from India stated that God draws near only when Muslims pray more than the prescribed five times a day.

Finally, many American converts to Islam believe Christianity sanctions slavery whereas Islam has always been against it. The truth is that the influence of evangelical Christians such as John Wesley and William Wilberforce, who fought slavery, helped end it. They need to know that because Muhammad kept slaves, Islamic countries like Somalia and Mauritania were among the last to abolish it.

3. Christians need to wage peace on Islam. Judaism, Christianity and Islam lay claim to the God of Abraham and believe that "peace" is one of God's names. Amazingly, all three faiths believe peace will only come through the Messiah, the Prince of Peace. Note that in the Qur'an it is Jesus (*Isa al-Masih*) who is Messiah—not Muhammad (Qur'an 3:45).

According to the Bible, the Messiah will exercise awesome power by restraining evil and judging fairly: "He will judge between the nations...They will beat their swords into plowshares" (Isa. 2:4) and "will rule them with an iron scepter" (Ps. 2:9). Micah also describes the Messiah's global reign: "... for then his greatness will reach to the ends of the earth. And he will be their peace" (Mic. 5:4b-5a).

So rather than defend Israeli policy in the Middle East, we should "pray for the peace of Jerusalem" (Ps. 122:6). God's "Road Map for Peace in the Middle East" culminates in the just reign of the Messiah who will judge all nations—including Israel. The Old Testament's last book says that when he comes, he will be like a "refiner's fire" and put the Jews on trial for their many sins (Mal. 3:2).

Yet he will also be "very angry with the nations," some of whom hate the Jews with an implacable hatred (Zech. 1:15). He will "gather all the nations" and "fight against those nations" (Zech. 14:3). His judgment will be against the entire world, including America as the world's number one advertiser of a lifestyle allowing adultery, abortion, homosexuality and pornography.

The good news is that when all else fails, people in Jerusalem will recognize their crime of crucifying the Messiah, and they will grieve and repent for their sin (Zech. 12:1-10). They had rejected him when he had wept over Jerusalem: "If you, even you, had only known...what would bring you peace" (Luke 19:42). And repentance will not only occur among the Jews: "All the nations of the earth will mourn" (Matt. 24:30). The Bible's last book reiterates that Jews will grieve and repent as "those who pierced him," but adds that "all the peoples of the earth will mourn because of him" (Rev. 1:7). This surely includes Muslims who have some understanding of Jesus but do not see him as Savior in all his glory, majesty and divinity. Remember that one in every five citizens of Israel is a Palestinian Israeli Arab.

Christians know that Jesus not only will be the bridge between people of all races and religions, but he is the bridge between humankind and God. This is the only way Muslims, Christians and Jews can have peace among themselves. When Jesus forgave sin (Mark 2:10-12; Luke 7:48) as only God can do (Isa. 43:25; Mark 2:7; Qur'an 3:135), he also said, "Go in peace" (Luke 7:48-50). It is no coincidence that at birth the Messiah was called "Jesus, because he will save his people from their sins" (Matt. 1:21). The Apostle Paul says, "We have peace with God through our Lord Jesus Christ" (Rom. 5:1). "He himself is our peace, who has...destroyed the barrier, the dividing wall of hostility" (Eph. 2:14).

Waging peace on Islam means reaching out to Muslim immigrants among us. Nearly sixty percent of American Muslims are immigrants.

We need not publicly defame Islam and demean the Prophet of Islam as some American Christian leaders have since September 11, 2001. This creates more cultural and social stumbling blocks than already exist before Muslims get to the stumbling block of the cross. Doing so defies the biblical injunction, "If it is possible, as far as it depends on you, live at peace with everyone" (Rom. 12:18), because it stirs up hatred, fosters mistrust and suspicion, and unnecessarily hurts Muslim sentiments.

And we can even be people of peace in the way we greet Muslims. Jesus commanded us to love our enemies and pray for those who persecute us. The Hebrew greeting Jesus probably used, *Shalom aleichem*, is close to the universal Arabic Muslim greeting, *Salaam aleikum* ("Peace to you"). This blesses Muslims by greeting them with warmth, goodwill and sincerity.

Finally, waging peace on Islam means reaching out to Muslim immigrants among us (nearly sixty percent of American Muslims are immigrants) and not hating them. Unfortunately since 9/11, some who look Middle Eastern have been unjustly harassed and unfairly treated. It is instructive to see that the Bible commanded the Israelites to "love those who are aliens, for you yourselves were aliens in Egypt" (Deut. 10:19). Scripture commanded them to gather the aliens in their towns so they and their children would "hear it and learn about the Lord" (Deut. 31:12-13).

In conclusion, Muslim militants have turned to hatred and violence because they believe Islam is under attack. That perception is real and spreading all over the world. Since Islam does not teach love for enemies, but rather hatred, some Muslims are tempted to fight America. The best way for Christians to respond is to look to the cross as the bridge to reconciliation. The battle will not be won by wrapping ourselves in the flag of patriotism. Nor will missiles bring victory. Esposito is right on that point. Most Muslims are true seekers after God as indicated by their prayer several times a day that God would lead them in a straight path (Qur'an 1:6). Christians must reach out to Muslims with the gospel of peace.

References

Ahmed, Akbar S. 2003. *Islam Under Siege: Living Dangerously in a Post-Honor World.* Cambridge, Mass.: Blackwell Publishing Ltd.

Ali, Abdullah Yusaf. 1989. *The Meaning of the Holy Qur'an.* new ed. Beltsville, Md.: Amana Publications.

Collier, Ellen Mansoor. 2002. "Taking the Mystery Out of the Middle East." *Saudi Aramco World,* January/February.

Ellis, Carl. 2000. "Answering Islam's questions." *Christianity Today,* April, 7.

Esposito, John L. 1992. *The Islamic Threat: Myth or Reality?* New York: Oxford University Press.

_____. 2002. *Unholy War: Terror in the Name of Islam.* New York: Oxford University Press.

Fields, Bruce L. 2001. *Introducing Black Theology: Crucial Questions for the Evangelical Church.* Grand Rapids, Mich.: Baker Books.

Guillaume, A. 1978. *The Life of Muhammad: A Translation of Ibn Ishaq's Sirat Rasul Allah.* Karachi, Pakistan: Oxford University Press.

Guthrie, Stan. 2001. *Missions in the Third Millennia: 21 Key Trends for the 21st Century.* London: Paternoster Press.

Ishaq, Ibn. 1978. *The Life of Muhammad: A Translation of Ibn Ishaq's Sirat Rasul Allah.* Translated by Alfred Guillaume. Oxford: Oxford University Press.

Jenkins, Philip. 2002. *The Next Christendom: The Coming of Global Christianity.* New York: Oxford University Press.

Johnson, Steve. 1989. "Rushdie Furor Highlights the Nature of Islamic Faith." *Christianity Today,* April, 38.

Mawdudi, Abul Ala. 1994. *The Punishment of the Apostate According to Islamic Law.* Translated and annotated by Syed Silas Husain and Ernest Hahn. Toronto, Ontario: FFM.

Nimer, Mohamed. 2002. *The North American Muslim Resource Guide: Muslim Community Life in the United States and Canada.* New York: Routledge.

Qutb, Syed. 1964. *Milestones.* Cedar Rapids, Iowa: Unity Publishing Company.

Riddell, Peter G., and Peter Cotterell. 2003. *Islam in Context: Past, Present and Future.* Grand Rapids, Mich.: Baker Books.

Van Biema, David. 2003. "Should Christians Convert Muslims?" *Time,* June 30.

October 2006

Conversion and Apostasy: A Sociological Perspective

Nur Armagan

A sociological lens offers helpful perspectives in discipling Muslim Background Believers.

WE HAVE LOOKED AT LENGTH into how to be a better witness to the Islamic world. We have explored and experimented how to contextualize our message and congregations so that the gospel message can be heard through the thick curtain of prejudice, misconception, and hatred. For most of us, the explorations and experiments end at the moment of conversion. Yet conversion is only the beginning of a life with Christ, and for a Muslim who becomes a Christian, the real challenge begins after the conversion.

It would be safe to say that quite a few converts from Islam give up their new faith within the first two years of their initial decision. Given the reality of life conditions of Christians living in Islamic countries, we cannot fully understand what that "giving up" refers to. In most cases, it is simply a decision to leave the local church and sever relationships with other Christians. Only a small segment of those who leave cite doctrinal issues or have rational reasons for leaving the church. Some return to Islam with greater zeal; some to a quiet life which includes holding their religious convictions to themselves.

This article attempts to analyze the human reality of conversion and apostasy in order to draw application points for healthy discipleship strategies that move beyond initial evangelism. We will look at the case study of a local church in Turkey with the understanding that the situation the church finds itself in is similar to those of other minority churches located in Islamic settings. Although various sociological perspectives are used in the process, this is not a purely academic sociological exercise. Sociological ideas are only used to the level that they can help answer our theological and missiological questions. In the preface of his book on apologetics, sociologist Peter Berger humbly notes,

> If some professional theologians should read [my book], they will undoubtedly find various errors and misinterpretations in the discussion of religious thinkers and doctrines. That is a risk that must be taken by a lay person who ventures into a field in which he [or she] is not academically accredited. Evidently, I think that the risk is worth taking. (2004, vii)

The same applies to this article; if some professional sociologists should read it, they will undoubtedly realize its amateur nature. However, the risk is worth taking.

The Church's Relation to Society

According to the *CIA World Factbook*, 99.8% of Turkey's sixty-eight million people are Sunni Muslim and 0.2% are "other," mostly Christians and Jews (2000). Of this latter group, approximately 2,500 are evangelical Christians. The country's republican parliamentary democracy guarantees religious freedom; however, this official stance is shadowed by the strong Islamic worldview and nationalism of local authorities and society. Even though Turkey is a secular state, Turkish identity is strongly identified with being a Muslim. This creates tension for individual Christians and for the Church as a whole. We will look at two of these tensions: *anomy* and *alienation* from the wider society.

Anomy

Most of the members of Umut Protestant Church* are converts from Islam. Being a Muslim means following a strict code of law provided by Islam which covers every aspect of life. Therefore, when a Muslim becomes a Christian, he or she faces a real life version of Friedrich Nietzsche's "re-evaluation of all values" or a break from the "taken for granted *nomos*" (the orderly world operating according to understandable laws) which the person had been operating under. Most of the guidelines, from what to wear to what to eat, are replaced with a confusing "freedom in Christ."

The new convert, devoid of any religious rituals and regulations, often feels lost and seeks to find practices like quiet times to cope with that feeling. Instead of serving as flexible personal prayer and reflection time, most converts see this time as replacing their early morning Islamic prayers. For Muslims, missing even one prayer demands penance and church members often feel guilty and in need of God's forgiveness when they miss early morning devotions.

This anomic state is much more complicated than simply not knowing how to operate under a new system. Conversion from Islam equals a breakaway from society. Berger emphasizes that the "society is the guardian of order and meaning not only objectively, in its institutional structures, but subjectively as well, in its structuring of individual consciousness. It is for this reason that radical separation from the social world, or anomy, constitutes such a powerful threat to the individual" (1973, 31).

This powerful threat is increased by the communal mindset of the Middle East. By leaving Islam, the convert loses his or her identity in relation to his or her local community and the world of Islam (*dar al-Islam*) and is seen as a part of *dar al-harb* (the world of war, or the infidels). Thus, church members continually live in a confusing and emotionally draining state. Additionally, a strong sense of shame is often present due to the social pressure that labels them as enemies and betrayers of their nation.

Alienation from Society

One leader of Umut Protestant Church (who is also a local evangelist) notes that a new believer who is still connected with the church two years after conversion is likely to stay with the faith; only after the fifth year has the believer deeply internalized his or her faith and Christian identity, and will likely remain a Christian. This leader's observation has been proven to be true time and time again. This should not come as a surprise to any outsider. The transitioning process from the Islamic *nomos* to a Christian one and the development of social networks with Christians occurs primarily within the first two years. As the convert experiences a break in relation from his or her society, both the person's identity and his or her connection to the church and other Christians grows significantly.

According to Christian Smith, "The human drives for meaning and belonging are satisfied primarily by locating human selves within social groups that sustain distinctive, morally orienting collective identities" (1998, 90). Thus, the church serves as "a shield against terror" (Berger 1973, 31). The local church provides an identity and the social support the convert needs to be able to operate and live as a Christian. Only those who have been able to develop strong relationships with other church members are able to continue their new-found faith. Throughout this process of belonging and establishment of a new *nomos*, the convert grows stronger in understanding his or her faith.

The local church provides an identity and the social support the convert needs to be able to operate and live as a Christian.

Umut Protestant Church, like any other persecuted church, has a strong collective identity which owes its source to the distinction it finds from the dominant Islamic culture (Smith 1998, 91). This constant distinction results in a strong defense to the challenge of Islam and society. The high cost of being a Christian pushes the new convert to have reasons to believe and in return to deeply internalize his or her faith. By the fifth year, the convert is well secured in understanding and being able to defend his or her faith. The person also enjoys the strong ties he or she has developed with the church.

Islam serves as the negative reference group through which the church understands itself in relation to what it is not (Smith 1998, 105). However, the same strengthening effect has a darker side. For most members of the church, it results both in a strong opposition to or reaction against Islam and in understanding Christianity only to the degree that it is different from Islam. Thus the convert, who fasted for thirty days as a Muslim, ceases to fast as a Christian and reacts to any spiritual discipline.

This anti-Islamic attitude, together with the presence of Western missionaries in Christian circles, gives birth to a modification and adaptation of Western practices and perspectives. As the sub-cultural identity of the church is formed, its cultural alienation from the larger society seems complete. The outsider observes the change in the practices, dress, habits and language of the convert, which reinforces the instinct that to be Christian is to be a foreigner. When the theological emphasis on personal spiritual life and the lack of teaching on the wider concerns of the gospel message are mixed with the secondary status ascribed to the church by society, the church becomes alienated as a small social enclave. This fuels the suspicions of the society and leads to further persecution.

How Rational Is the Choice to Convert?

Rodney Stark and Roger Finke argue that "people attempt to make rational choices, which substantially expands the principle of microeconomics that people attempt to maximize gain. As used in economics, maximization usually involves capital and the attempt to acquire the most while expending the least" (2000, 118).

In sociological terms, there are two forms of capital a person would seek to increase or sustain in converting to another religion: social and religious. Social capital consists of interpersonal attachments (2000, 118) and plays the major role in the decision-making process. Stark and Finke propose that these attachments, which are valuable to the individual, lead the person to conform to the beliefs of those to whom he or she is attached: "Conversion is seldom about seeking or embracing an ideology; it is about bringing one's religious behavior into alignment with that of one's friends and family members" (2000, 117).

This makes sense for a person who lives in a country where there is religious freedom and where those close to the person have a belief that society finds plausible. Thus, the young adult who grows up in a church eventually becomes Christian since he or she does not want to risk his or her attachments by failing to conform (2000, 119).

For congregants of Umut Protestant Church, being a member means a significant loss in social capital. The social networks the church provides can never replace what the member will lose since there are less than two hundred Christians in a city with 4.5 million people. Being a Christian will mean a lifelong struggle in finding jobs, securing housing and making friends.

Religious capital accumulated by the convert who grew up Muslim will also be lost upon conversion. According to Stark and Finke, "In making religious choices, people will attempt to save as much of their religious capital as they can and to expend as little investment in new capital as possible" (2000, 121). Thus, should the decision to be a Christian and a member of the church be evaluated through the rational choice theory, it would prove to be irrational. On this point the theory argues that there must be some sort of "reward" which compensates for the loss. As argued above, there is little satisfying social reward for the member. This creates the anticipation of an otherworldly reward which can be observed in continuing emphasis on trusting God's providence and salvation. However, even this falls short of the strong eschatological emphasis of cults or sects.

Rational choice theory is still helpful in understanding the high rate of drop-outs, and the high level of commitment of those who stay. The convert eventually realizes the irrational nature of his or her decision to be a member and makes a conscious decision to stay or leave. This serves as the natural separation process between genuine believers and profit-seeking individuals. Since the churches in Turkey have a history of being the target of Islamic press which regularly accuses them of converting Muslims by offering money and visas for Western countries, the churches continually attract those who seek personal gain. It does not take long for the profit-seeker to realize that the "reward" offered by being a member does not match the "cost." The person will then leave.

The positive outcome of this self-questioning process for those with genuine faith largely depends on the social support the member receives from the church and on personal confidence in the truth of the Christian faith. Most of the conversion stories include dreams, visitations, or other mystical experi-

Umut Protestant Church has a strong theology of the cross and its reality for today's world. The members are under no illusion and are continually reminded of the difficulties that come with being Christian.

ences. These provide emotional support and legitimization for the member's deeply rooted fear of committing a mistake by being a Christian and denying Islam, thus being doomed to eternal punishment.

Additionally, the pastor's strong charisma and convictions make him "the significant other" for the members and a continuous source of legitimization. Umut Protestant Church has a strong theology of the cross and its reality for today's world. The members are under no illusion and are continually reminded of the difficulties which come with being Christian. Those who choose to stay demonstrate a much stronger personal faith, since the high level of sacrifice demanded to be a member is equal to an increased investment of social and religious capital. This results in an increase of the personal value of the person's religious belief. The fear, shame and loneliness that come from being a Christian in such a setting never leave the church member, yet the price the person pays for his or her faith brings him or her to a resolution similar to that of a marriage vow, for better or for worse.

What Can Be Done?

There are three application points that surface from this article: (1) a relevant theology, (2) the conscious integration of new believers, and (3) a holistic discipleship strategy. Perhaps nowhere else does the urgent need for the development of a relevant theology surface as much as it does in a sociological look at the conversion process. There will always be an inevitable breakaway from the society for the Islamic convert; however, a local theology can provide the necessary tools for the convert to understand his or her new faith in continuation of his or her cultural identity.

Such a theology will not only lessen the personal effects of anomy on the convert, but it will also strengthen society's perception of the Church. A relevant theology can only play an effective role within the local church that takes conscious steps to provide close emotional and relational support to the new convert, especially during the first two years following conversion. Integration efforts must include the family of the convert, even if they remain Muslim. The family will play a significant role and winning their trust will lessen much of the personal tensions the convert will face.

However, a relevant theology and strong relationships are only the foundation for a long-term walk with Christ. A holistic discipleship program will strengthen the difficult journey that awaits the convert. This program is different from a baptismal class or a Bible study, although it includes both. It is a close mentorship relationship that provides a role model, emotional support, and teachings on relevant subjects. Only these three safety nets—relevant theology, integration, and discipleship—will allow the convert the strength needed to carry out his or her faith by the grace and work of the Holy Spirit.

* pseudonym

References

Berger, Peter. 1973. *The Social Reality of Religion*. Harmondsworth, U.K.: Penguin Books.
_____. 2004. *Questions of Faith*. Oxford: Blackwell Publishing.
CIA World Factbook. 2000. Accessed May 16, 2006 from www.cia.gov/cia/publications/factbook/geos/tu.html
Smith, Christian. 1998. *American Evangelicalism: Embattled and Thriving*. Chicago, Ill.: University of Chicago Press.
Stark, Rodney and Roger Finke. 2000. *Acts of Faith; Explaining the Human Side of Religion*. Berkeley, Calif.: University of California Press.

Islam's Patriarchal Clan System

Clive Beestand

Muslim family life and idiosyncrasies make more sense through anthropological eyes.

MY HUSBAND RAN AWAY with my children."
"No, lady, I'm sorry, but he didn't take your children. He took his children. They never were your children. They were his! You just didn't understand the system you were getting into when you married him."

Even now amid her pain, few can explain to this distraught wife and mother exactly what she encountered. Even Western journalists who sympathetically recount stories like hers usually don't understand why it happened, either. From her point of view, what her husband did was reprehensible. But from his and his government's point of view, what he did was perfectly logical, normal, and correct.

The pain she feels is only one of several consequences of marrying into a patriarchal clan system, which will affect every aspect of her life. And like a native language speaker who understands and speaks fluently his mother tongue but can't explain its grammar, her friends or enemies in this system probably won't be able to explain it logically. They just understand it, take it for granted and operate naturally within it. But when she tests with them the theories of the anthropologists explained below, they will nod their heads and say, "Why, of course!"

I am greatly indebted to a college anthropology course in which the professor defined and described a patriarchal clan system. Unfortunately, it is almost never explained in popular articles, probably because the writers themselves do not really understand the "why" of what they are describing. The anthropologist and sociologist's observations explain what's behind it.

First, a definition from *Webster's New World Dictionary*: "Patriarchy: A form of social organization in which the father or oldest male is recognized as the head of the family or tribe, descent and kinship being traced through the male line" (note that matriarchal clan systems, where the lineage is traced through the mother's family, although rarer, also exist in some societies.)

In the West we think of the parents of the nuclear family as being "joint heirs" and co-parents of the children. A man and woman leave their respective families and become a new unit.

You are probably saying, "Well, of course."

That's precisely the point: it's different in a patriarchal or matriarchal clan system.

In a patriarchal clan system, the wife NEVER joins the husband's clan. Even in marriage she always remains a member of her clan. She doesn't take her husband's name. And if something goes wrong in the marriage, she returns to her family clan where she is still a member.

The patriarchal clan system has many ramifications:

1. *Relatives—grandparents, aunts, uncles, cousins—on the father's side are much more important than those on the mother's side.* They even have different names (*Ami* versus *Khali* and *Amati* versus *Khalati*). In the Arabic language, the father's cousin, *Ben/Bent Ami*, is much more important than *Ben/Bent Khali*, the mother's cousin. Uncle *Ami*, the father's brother, is much more important than Uncle *Khali*, the mother's brother. Sometimes I forget this, although I know the system. Recently I was talking with a dear friend and referred to her mother's relatives as "your family." She corrected me: "They are not my family. They are my mother's family."

2. *Children born to the marriage are a net gain to the father's clan.*

3. *While it is true that the clan system predates Islam, the children born to a Muslim father and a Western mother are a net gain for Islam, since they belong to his family.*

4. The reverse is also true. *Children born to a "Christian" (read "Western" or "heathen") father and a Muslim mother belong to the father's clan—not the mother's.* This is regarded as a net loss for Islam.

5. This is why in all the Islamic countries with which I am familiar, *Muslim families may readily permit their men to marry foreign wives, but will vigorously oppose their women marrying foreign men.* At one time I lived and taught in a capital city of a progressive modern Islamic state where numerous nationals, even government ministers, were married to foreign women. This seemed to be almost "in style," and did not seem to be resented.

In an intermediate-level English class, I tested the proposition that the reverse would not be accepted. I asked class members if it were acceptable for the country's men to marry foreign women. They had no problem with that. But when I asked whether the country's women could marry foreign men, the teacher was taken aback by their hostile reactions. Everyone in the class was strongly negative.

"No!"

"Why?"

"Because it means a loss for Islam!"

The class was composed of both men and women who disagreed about many things. But in this they agreed. This same country receives many foreign tourists. Many local young men enjoyed wooing and seducing visiting foreign females who often seemed to bask in all the unaccustomed attention. The rub was that if the visiting foreign men ever were to try the same policy with the local young women, they would be quickly picked up and dealt with by the local police. The privileges extended were not reciprocal.

6. *A major role of the new wife is to provide heirs, especially males, for the hus-*

band. Thus the birth of a child early in the marriage is expected. And after a certain time, if this does not happen, the wife should not be surprised if the husband begins looking for a wife who can produce the required child, preferably a male. This is true not only for kings, but for commoners as well.

7. *A woman has little value in society until she produces a son.* She is often identified by her relationship to him. For example, "Um Abdul" is the mother of Abdul.

8. *If she doesn't produce children, she can be divorced in favor of a new woman who can.* Recently in our town, a woman with a loving relationship with her husband went to the hospital to give birth to her first child. But something went wrong in the delivery. The baby died, and the mother had to have a hysterectomy to save her life, ending prospects for future children. Three days later, as she was leaving the hospital sad, sick, and torn, her mother-in-law met her at the hospital door. "I'm sorry. We love you. But my son has to have a son. So he is divorcing you!"

"What? But I love my husband. How can that be? Where am I going to go?" the distraught wife said. She had no living relatives in her clan.

"I'm sorry, but that's the way it is." They also stuck her with the hospital bill. Two weeks later the would-be happy mother who failed to fulfill her expected duty committed suicide.

9. *In marital struggles, her clan members should be available to intervene, or failing all, if there is a divorce, to receive her back.* Beware of the implications, if you, a foreigner, help arrange a marriage. You may have ongoing responsibilities that you weren't aware of.

10. *Other important elements relate to the importance of a son's role.* Here I am less clear on the reasons. These important facts may be related more to Islam than to the patriarchal clan system.

- All children, both boys and girls, belong to the father's clan.
- Boys are more important than girls, and often spoiled, while girls usually learn to work and carry responsibility. While society may be changing, it remains male-dominated.
- Men are expected to control their wives.
- Brothers boss their sisters. Women cannot leave the country without the consent of a man in her family. Sometimes, however, this male domination can spring from the positive ideal of wanting to protect their women folk.
- To be a divorced woman is very shameful.
- Additionally, a divorcee has no man to protect her or give her importance. She cannot leave the country or get a family card or identification card. She is "manless," hence has no one to be responsible for her—unless she has a son, which is curious, because even though the son belongs to her ex-husband's clan, simply having him gives her some honor and importance and, eventually, protection. But without a son, she is a nobody.
- Often the mother will spoil the boy to gain his love and affection in hopes that later he will come to her defense. What the mother can never obtain le-

gally in the clan system, placing the son on her side of the solid line that separates him from her, she attempts to do on the emotional level.

• The authorities usually are not as concerned when a woman is touched by or responds to Christianity, or another foreign idea, as when a man does. It is expected that sooner or later her father, brother, uncle, or husband will bring her into line.

• Islamic law (*sharia*) carefully delineates the major inheritance to the male heirs.

• Adoption, when it is allowed—and this has not always been the case—is much easier when adopting a girl than a boy. A boy jeopardizes the family inheritance. I observed that in a local home for abandoned children, adoptions are much more needed for girls than for boys.

Conclusion

I have tested my conclusions about the Islamic patriarchal clan system in discussions with my Arab friends. Invariably, their response has been, "Why, of course!"

But what to them is so obvious, although indefinable, often is much less so to well-meaning Western women, who, in the name of equality, open-mindedness, non-prejudice, independence, nonconformity, or whatever, decide to marry a Muslim. Whatever the reason, they should know in advance that they are marrying into a non-reciprocal system.

If things go wrong in the marriage to Prince Charming, wives can complain all they want, but the laws are based upon this system. No matter the intensity of their emotions, the strength of their arguments, or the depth of their feelings of injustice, there will be no legal comprehension of their pleas. Their protests will fall upon deaf ears. That's just the way it is. The system is the system. They will not change it.

Note: While writing this article, I showed it to a colleague who volunteered that she had seen numerous foreign wives married to Muslims, but who had not yet converted to Islam. Instinctively, these women felt that they were not totally accepted by the husband's family because they were not Muslims. Insecure in their position, and afraid of what would happen if something happened to their husband, several of them were considering converting to Islam, so in the event of the death or divorce of the husband, they would not be cut off from their children by the husband's family.

I believe that to choose one's faith, because one happens to believe it is true, is a valid choice. But to choose one's faith out of fear is not.

October 1984

The Lessons of 27 Years' Gleaning among Muslims

P. J. Anderson

The author shares seven lessons learned over the years while ministering among Muslims. These include faithfulness, patience, acceptance, and discipline.

THE *AMERICAN COLLEGE DICTIONARY* defines "to glean" as "to gather slowly and laboriously in bits." Old Testament Mosaic Law set regulations for the corners of the field at harvest time to be left for the needy. The grain was not inferior or useless; it was more difficult to harvest. It was not assigned to inept or duller workers, but to those with a real need.

"My meat is to do my Father's will" (John 4:34), said the Lord of the harvest, the Lord Jesus Christ. So in his train must follow those called by his Spirit to labor among Muslim millions. A prerequisite for such laborers is that they have a need to see Muslims find Christ. May the Lord of the harvest send forth such "needy" laborers to his work of gleaning his harvest among Muslims. Here are seven lessons I have learned in my twenty-seven years of gleaning. I trust they will be used to further the gospel ministry to Muslims.

1. The common Muslim concept of God is that Allah must be appeased by good works in atonement for sin. Therefore, the love of God is foreign. Muslims often resort to revenge and retaliation. They try to get something from every relationship, either material gain or prestige. They have no awareness of a love that is not self-seeking. Therefore, gleaners must have the love of an open heart and hand. They must not draw back in hurt, anger, fear, disappointment, or resentment. They must be willing to be vilified, spat upon, publicly threatened, dishonored, and ridiculed. In the midst of the shouting and swearing, they must respond with a quiet yet firm demonstration of God's love.

God must do his deep work in the laborer's life. To be lied to and about, deceived, and morally smeared by one you have toiled over in prayer and Bible study for hours, or perhaps years, requires God's response of love. Muslims may seek your material aid and then scoff at it as too little and too late. To remain steadfast, patiently helping in spite of rebuke, requires God's love.

"And seek great things for yourself? Seek them not," Jeremiah told Baruch (Jer. 45:5). God's love flowing through a laborer devoid of self-seeking makes a greater impact on Muslims than many other so-called evangelistic tools.

2. Gleaners among Muslims should not try to prove who is wrong or

who has the better view of God. They should avoid trying to impress them with their great knowledge of the Qur'an. Such tactics not only are useless, they are counterproductive. A Muslim so pressed will very quickly rally others to the defense of Islamic teachings as a point of honor. Politicians use this technique frequently. They whip up religious fervor to a high pitch by making claims and counterclaims for and against Islam.

3. Faithfulness in life situations, not only in true doctrinal teachings, makes a telling impact on Muslims. It is relatively easy to be accurate, true, and eloquent in proclaiming the word of God. But that same word also compels us to be absolutely honest, truthful, kind-hearted, and loving. That's not so easy. Muslims love to probe our Christian character. Gleefully, they observe the eloquent preacher screaming as he runs down the street after boys who have stolen fruit from his trees or borrowed a child's toy. One of their favorite village sports is to pound loudly on the missionary's door and then hide just to see his or her anger. Because anger generally is condemned above other sins by Muslims, it's great fun to antagonize or set up Christians. They may deliberately give wrong change or overcharge.

A gleaner who smiles, laughs at his own errors, and radiates God's love is far more effective than a cold, eloquent, grammatically accurate speaker.

Paul teaches us to "walk circumspect" (Eph. 5:15) with good reason. Abstaining "from all appearance of evil" (1 Thess. 5:22), particularly in moral aspects or situations, requires a wide knowledge of the local culture. Muslim leaders will capitalize on our failures.

4. Acceptance is a vital path to reaching Muslims. We cannot afford to joke about their appearance, clothes, intelligence, or manners of speech. Neither should their personal mannerisms of hygiene, motions of hands or feet, clicking of the tongue, spitting, throat clearing, and repeating various phrases be a distraction for very long. Learning their language is essential. It should be learned to the very best of one's ability. However, a gleaner who smiles, laughs at his own errors, and radiates God's love is far more effective than a cold, eloquent, grammatically accurate speaker.

The acceptance of new converts is just as vital as acceptance of inquirers. The New Testament makes it clear that labor is needed to "disciple," "bring to maturity," "present perfect," and "discipline." Growing up spiritually includes stumbling, stubbornness, falling, misspeaking, lack of comprehension, and failure to obey revealed truth instantly.

Because evil is harder to unlearn than to learn, spiritual growth takes time and requires patient teaching and understanding. In our human families, a young child who fails repeatedly is not "put out," or told "never return here again," or "black listed" with neighbors, relatives, or friends. We ought not to treat the person that way who has turned from darkness to light and then has stumbled. We must "grow up" young believers with a God-like acceptance of them with all their blemishes. Neither sincere Nathaniels nor instant super St. Pauls are what God ordains all inquirers or young believers to be (John 1:47; Acts 9:17-22).

5. Patience (long-suffering) is a fruit of the Holy Spirit that must flourish in the lives of those who seek the lost (Gal. 5:22). We may encounter repeated occasions of faithlessness, dishonoring, or planned disrespect. This may be how backslidden believers or inquirers test to determine what we are thinking or saying about them. Like the farmer who waits for the harvest (James 5:7), missionaries must water, prune, and give tender care. To continue the analogy, they must also fend off the "insects" and the "rodents." They do this during the time between the effective hearing of the gospel and the believing faith in the Lord Jesus Christ.

Blocking time for visiting, teaching, and reaching out is excellent, but it must be done within the cultural frame, not at your convenience.

"Insects" may be actual haunting doubts, misconceptions from former teachings, cultural taboos, or fearful threats. "Rodents" may be those of family or community who deliberately set out to destroy budding interest or faith. Sometimes actual physical protection may be required. In the former case, it takes many hours of prayer for and with the inquirer or believer. At the same time, quiet, low-keyed teaching by the hour is necessary to overcome fear, doubt, and misconceptions.

6. Discipline applies to both the missionary and inquirers or believers. We must carefully plan our time if we are to do what the Bible says about "buying up every opportunity" (Gal. 6:10) and "redeeming the time because the days are evil" (Eph. 5:16). The discipline of study and preparation is essential. Knowing your topic is critical in Muslim cultures where memorization of large volumes of material is the usual way of teaching. Off the cuff, off the top of the head, or out of the sermon barrel lessons are not enough to attract even passing interest.

Blocking off time for visiting, teaching, and reaching out is excellent, but it must be done within the cultural frame, not at your convenience. For example, late afternoon or evening is a poor time to visit Muslim women, because the men of the house are home. Interruptions can be somewhat avoided by planning. But counseling emergencies, like medical ones, cannot wait. Your availability to the people must be known. Your willingness to be available will soon be known as the criterion of your service.

Discipline of the inquirers, or believers, must be just, consistent, fair, equal, and, above all, biblical. Favoritism—"This is my spiritual son," "my convert"— must be stamped out forever. Competition between workers over converts, whether in numbers or supposed spiritual achievement, is a cancer of the devil's own origin and delight.

7. Cultural adaptation must be done within a biblical framework. What difference will it make in eternity if your trained senses in music or art are jarred by scales, notes, or rhythm (or lack thereof), or color, or form clashes? Separation of the men and women by a screen or curtain during a worship service is not unbiblical. It fits the culture of many lands.

Baptism is an open testimony after conversion, in front of witnesses. We must be sensitive about how we do it. A mixed male-female or Christian-Muslim audience is not required by scripture. I recommend parental permission for those under age, and the husband's or father's permission for all women. I agree with the requirement set by a recently organized church of Muslim converts that one year of Christian living precede application for baptism. It is not a scriptural requirement that baptism be performed by an ordained male. In many lands a male touching the woman convert is culturally unacceptable.

However, incorporation of Muslim holidays, or their Christianization, is not an acceptable adaptation to me. Celebrations and traditions that are biblical, not Western, must be established. Forms of worship, songs, types and positions of prayer, teaching, and outreach methods must be compatible first with the Bible and then with the culture.

Those are some of the lessons I have learned from gleaning the harvest during twenty-seven years of labor in a remote corner of God's harvest field. Today, in that corner a small group of baptized believers is meeting as an organized church and functioning through its committee, despite the fact that as yet there is no resident pastor. This group is a witness of light in the darkness of Islam.

Section 2

Theology

AN IMPORTANT PART of understanding Islam and ministering to Muslims is having a solid theological foundation—certainly a firm grasp of Christian theology, and to varying degrees, a good handle on Muslim theology. Some Christian terms, phrases, and euphemisms are not directly translatable and require a great deal of care when sharing the gospel with Muslims. It is tragic to think of the number of times missionaries with good intentions have directly stated, "Jesus is the Son of God!" without knowing how that phrase is received by someone from an Islamic background. In this chapter, we touch upon a few issues related to theology and Muslim evangelism.

To get us started **Scott Woods** (2003) shares that interacting biblically and critically with practitioners is essential as we look to God for church-planting movements among Muslims. Next, **Gerald Wiens** (2005) reminds Western missionaries that a new, contextualized interpretation of the events in Jesus' life is needed. Lastly, **David Teague** (2008) asks, "How do missionaries in Muslim churches speak of the divinity of Christ without appearing to contradict their belief in monotheism?"

April 2003

A Biblical Look at C5 Muslim Evangelism

Scott Woods

Interacting biblically and critically with practitioners is essential as we look to God for church-planting movements among Muslims.

WITH THE DAWN OF THE NEW MILLENNIUM, missionaries from all over the globe have set their sights on the sons of Ishmael. Islam is Christianity's only serious competitor as the fastest-growing religion in the world and has drawn the attention of savvy cross-cultural missionaries. This article is written with a desire to further the dialogue in missiological circles between C4 and C5 practitioners (see page 22). In no way do I want to disparage anyone's motivation in using a model for ministry. Many saints are laboring hard to find the key that will unlock the harvest among the sons of Ishmael.

However, Paul encouraged the leaders of the church in Corinth to be wise builders. What we build will be tested with fire (1 Cor. 3:13). Interacting biblically and critically with other practitioners is essential as we look to the Lord of the harvest for church-planting movements among the sons of Ishmael. It is with this desire that I invite you to revisit the C5 model and relevant biblical passages.

How far is too far in contextualization? The word means to take the unchanging truth and make it understandable in a given context. We do it all the time in life. Children are told Bible stories in a way that allows them to understand the truth from within their context as little children. The goal in contextualization is not to make the gospel as Islamic as possible. Rather, it is to communicate the unchanging truth to an Islamic audience so that it makes sense to them. How far can we go in accommodating Islam? This is a theological as well as a poignantly practical question for us missionaries to Muslims.

Today, in missiological circles, I see a different trend on the horizon. It is motivated by several factors. In the past, many missionaries were woefully ethnocentric, approaching host cultures as if they were totally lacking in positive characteristics. This has generated a sensitivity to look for things from Muslim cultures that can be redeemed to provide a launching pad for the gospel. The other motivation is the desire to see more Muslims reached. Greg Livingstone's thesis in *Planting Churches in Muslim Cities* is correct. God wants to reach Muslims, but, by and large, they are not being reached.

Therefore, we must examine our methods for church planting among Muslims. Being both culturally sensitive and more fruitful in the Muslim milieu are God-given desires to which the Body of Christ globally would say "Amen." In an effort to pursue these desires, many missionaries are flocking to the "cutting edge" of missiology by becoming a Muslim to win Muslims (or training Christians to become Muslims to win Muslims). C5 has been embraced by many with the hope of seeing successful people movements to Christ. Too often this has been adopted without looking critically at the Bible.

A brief overview of some of the C4 and C5 similarities and differences are necessary before we proceed. C4 and C5ers are persuaded that we can use the forms Muslims use while giving them new meaning. Dudley Woodberry wrote an excellent article, "Contextualization among Muslims: Reusing Common Pillars," delineating the redemptive forms in Islam for MBB (Muslim Background Believer) congregations. Both C4 and C5 would subscribe to vocabulary, diets, clothing, and culture that is Muslim friendly. Neither model would support extraction of Muslim converts and placing them in churches that are culturally foreign.

One of the major differences between C4 and C5 is identity. In C4, believers call themselves followers of Isa, whereas in C5 they say they are Muslims and may or may not say they are followers of *Isa Al Masih*. In practice, C5ers are encouraged to continue going to the mosque.

Almost all C4 practitioners would say that a transition time of coming out of the mosque is best. Better still if the converts are the ones determining the timing of their exodus based upon the Holy Spirit's conviction and not as a result of the missionary's impetus. C5 MBBs are encouraged to stay in the mosque and use it as a platform for reaching other Muslims. So C5 groups perform the *shalat* (while praying to *Isa*), recite the *shahada* (with a variation of the confession), fast during Ramadan, give the *zakat* (offering) to the poor, and theoretically go on the *Haj* (although I know of no C5 believer who has ever done this). C5 embraces Islam and the mosque by trying to carve out a niche within Islam for a community of MBBs. C4 embraces the local culture and forms of Islam while distinguishing itself from Islam as followers of *Isa Al Masih*.

A Look at Some of the Biblical Passages

One of the main passages used to support a C5 strategy for church planting among Muslims is 1 Corinthians 7:20. "Each one should remain in the situation which he was in when God called him." The theory goes that if a person was a Muslim, he or she should remain a Muslim after coming to Christ.

The context in 1 Corinthians 7 is addressing the issues of marriage and singleness, believers married to unbelievers, circumcision and uncircumcision, and finally slaves and free. The passage has nothing to do with dictating that people from a false religion should remain in their false religion so as not to upset the apple cart. C5 proponents could be accused of isogesis (reading their desired interpretation into the text) here. This passage makes provision for believers remaining in their familial and social status where they were prior to knowing Christ, but it is not encouraging believers to continue in their former religion. There is a difference between a Muslim's religion and his or her cultural familial milieu.

Too often, those desiring to respect the family and social community end up defending the religion and theology that are contra-biblical. Culture should be embraced only to the extent that it does not cause syncretism. The mosque and Islam, although a portion of the fabric of society, do not make up the entire picture in terms of the target people. We must not use this passage to say people should remain as they always have without any exceptions. What is important is obeying God's commands.

First Corinthians 9:19-22 has often been cited as support for a contextualized ministry. This is indeed correct as Paul engaged the people in a way that was relevant to each group, depending upon their contexts:

> Though I am free and belong to no man, I make myself a slave to everyone, to win as many as possible. To the Jews I became like a Jew, to win the Jews. To those under the law I became like one under the law (though I myself am not under the law), so as to win those under the law. To those not having the law I became like one not having the law (though I am not free from God's law but am under Christ's law), so as to win those not having the law. To the weak I became weak, to win the weak. I have become all things to all men so that by all possible means I might save some.

The goal was to win more people to Christ by varying methods to fit each group. This is precisely what C5 proponents are arguing for. The tension arises in what Paul means when he says he becomes like a Jew to win the Jews. Ethnically, he already was a Jew. Does he become a Jew without any qualification? It says he became "like a Jew." Does he embrace their system of beliefs? Is he still waiting for the Jewish Messiah to appear like the rest of the Jews? Do the rest of the Jews know where he stands in relation to his faith in the risen Lord Jesus? What one finds in his becoming like a Jew is that he took on the Jewish traditions and culture as much as possible, consistently maintaining a vibrant faith in Jesus and allowing people to see that at work in his life. This was all done so that as many Jews as possible would come to Jesus.

The problem with using this passage to support a C5 ministry strategy is that there is a vast difference between being culturally relevant and theologically accommodating. He becomes like a Jew, but he is not embracing all of Judaism. He looks like a Jew culturally and within the traditions as much as possible, but holds firmly to the truth and the other Jews know that he does. This is a critical distinction that C5 does not follow; the people know what Paul believes. Very few Muslims at the mosque or elsewhere know what a C5 person believes.

Also cited in support of C5 strategy is 2 Kings 5:18-19. Naaman asks for pardon when his master goes into the temple of Rimmon and he himself bows down to the idol. We would expect the prophet to say, "No, you must not compromise your faith." But instead Elisha says, "Go in peace." Therefore, C5ers believe that we have a scriptural precedence for continuing on in a false religion even after new birth.

My contention is that this line of reasoning is an argument from silence and therefore is weak. What about the balance of the entire Old Testament where wrath and destruction consistently came upon God's people because of their idolatry and "committing the harlot" with other nations and their false gods? This one verse is hardly sufficient to build a theology of incorporating Islam and the mosque in the believing community's faith. Is it not more likely that Elisha's response is allowing Naaman time for a transition out of that environment with the Spirit's guidance?

Perhaps, one of the most clear passages dealing with the dangers of syncretism and the believing community can be found in 2 Corinthians 6:14–7:1:

> Do not be yoked together with unbelievers. For what do righteousness and wickedness have in common? Or what fellowship can light have with darkness? What harmony is there between Christ and Belial? What does a believer have in common with an unbeliever? What agreement is there between the temple of God and idols? For we are the temple of the living God. As God has said: "I will live with them and walk among them, and I will be their God, and they will be my people. Therefore, come out from them and be separate," says the Lord. "Touch no unclean thing, and I will receive you. I will be a Father to you, and you will be my sons and daughters," says the Lord Almighty. Since we have these promises, dear friends, let us purify ourselves from everything that contaminates body and spirit, perfecting holiness out of reverence for God.

This passage is often misquoted when dealing with a believer wanting to marry an unbeliever. The context is about believers from pagan backgrounds continuing to worship in their former context. This is exactly what C5 proponents want us to embrace concerning the mosque as a strategy for reaching Muslims. Interesting to note, we do not know why the new Gentile believers continued to go to the temple. They may have been afraid of their community, perhaps some still had faith in the idols there, or maybe they wanted to reach their pagan worshipping friends in the temple.

Regardless of the reason for their existence in that community, God's command to them is extremely clear, "Get out!" Paul gives five rhetorical questions at the beginning of this passage—all of which are to be answered resoundingly in the negative. Separation from the worshipping unbelievers is God's command.

Before my C5 brethren rebut this passage because it is not germane, let's have a closer look. Perhaps some would think that this passage only relates to idol worshippers. These were pagan temples. Therefore, we should expect the Triune God to command believers to come out from idol worship. Islam worships Allah—the One and Only God—having similarities with our God. Most missionaries are practical: "If it works, then use it."

But a heavy dose of caution needs to be administered to those who assume that the Allah of Islam is the same as the Triune God of the Bible. I am not talking about using the term *Allah*—both Christians and Muslims use it. But the person of Allah is very different. Ali Imran 3:54 has a description of the Islamic Allah, "And the unbelievers plotted and deceived, and Allah too deceived, and the best deceiver is Allah." This is the god of Islam from their book. The Arabic word translated "deceived" is *makara* and has both a positive and negative meaning, here being the latter. John 8:44 says the devil is the "father of lies." Here we have the case of someone portraying himself to be God but really is a devil "parading as an angel of light."

Giving examples of MBB scholars that have studied the Qur'an and then come to this same conclusion may not pacify the C5ers who have MBBs who say their understanding of Allah is now complete with *Isa*. I do not agree that the god of Islam and our Triune God are the same person, just less understood by our Islamic friends—neither do most theologians. It would take this article too far afield, however, to prove here that the god of Islam and the Triune God are not one and the same.

Another reason I believe the 2 Corinthians 6 passage is germane to the Muslim convert's case is that we often wrongly assume that Islam is practiced in its orthodox form. Most of its adherents practice Folk Islam and have a myriad of *jinn*, spirits, and powers that they are trying to master, even though orthodox Islam teaches otherwise. Is this not exactly what was going on in the pagan context of 2 Corinthians? Should we be encouraging believers in *Isa Al Masih* to hold onto a structure that permits and at times promotes appeasement of the spirits when the scriptures tell us clearly to come out?

C5 Practice

Paul is sometimes portrayed as having used C5 strategy in entering the synagogue and evangelizing. This is a far cry from what happens in most C5 contexts. Paul came as the Pharisee of Pharisees to preach Jesus the Messiah to the synagogue members. Most C5ers come into the mosque and line up in the *shalat* line. They are perceived as Muslims. They have no distinguishing mark that says they are followers of *Isa*. Even if they pray to *Isa*, the perception is that they are Muslims. Paul was clearly received (at times) within the Jewish setting, but acknowledged as a follower of the risen Messiah. Is this the same with our C5 MBBs?

The assumption that since Judaism and Islam both contain some truth—therefore we can compare these two faiths as a foil for ministry and use what Paul did—is a poor one. It is true that Islam contains some truth. However, the bulk of Muslim faith and practice is incompatible with the scriptures. In the first century people flocked to Judaism to know truth because that was where God had revealed himself. Today, to introduce people to God we do not point people toward Islam because Muslims do not have special revelation about God without error.

The Creed also is fraught with problems for the C5 believer. "There is no God but God and Muhammad is his prophet." The *shahada* cannot be confessed by a believer without compromising his faith. Muhammad is definitely not God's prophet. I am not proscribing this as an evangelistic introduction. But the truth remains, if a person goes into a mosque, people assume he or she is a Muslim and will recite this Creed. Even if he or she prays in his or her heart to Jesus, the community will perceive him or her as a card-carrying Muslim. Is this not compromise? Deceit?

To change the *shahada* and use a creed like, "There is no God but God and *Isa Al Masih* is His Savior" is excellent. Many C4 models are using something similar to this in their house church meetings. But changing the *shahada* (like some C5ers have proposed) in the mosque is not likely unless the whole village converts. This is not the experience of most of us laboring in the trenches among Muslims and therefore should not be made the norm.

Again, the form and creed can be used effectively, but do we have to embrace the mosque and Islam to do that? Doesn't this lead new converts into confusion? I know it does because we have a young man who is praying to Isa as well as reciting the *shahada*, asking both to show him the truth. We are not encouraging him to continue on in his old Islamic roots, but because of his habit and desire to cover all the bases, he does. How much more so if we encouraged him to continue going to the mosque and doing his *shalat* there?

Personhood of *Isa Al Masih*

My final concern related to C5 is who the person of *Isa* is for a new MBB. Is he Savior only or Lord? What difference is there from the perspective of a twenty-first-century Muslim and a first-century Jew as it relates to answering the question, "Who is Jesus?" His lordship is the same stumbling block for both. First-century believers responded with the creed "Jesus is Lord." C5 is blurring the lines of who he is.

The 1998 report from the most advanced C5 work in the world claimed only fifty-five percent of the C5 convert leaders ascribe God as being Father, Son, and Holy Spirit. Where does that leave the other forty-five percent of those leaders and the rest of the followers? Is this a need for discipleship, as many C5 proponents are arguing for? Some C5 MBBs, who later are confronted with the fact that *Isa*, who is Savior, is also Lord, find it hard to swallow. Couple that with the incentive to keep them in the mosque, and there is added confusion. Missionaries may be able to train theologically astute students for the first generation, but things for each subsequent generation get more cloudy. Is the movement getting more orthodox or more syncretistic? If the foundation is not good, the building will crumble. Already the case being propped up for praise as the latest and greatest thing for missions toward Muslims is fraught with many troubling signs.

Conclusion

C5 as a strategy embraces the mosque for doing evangelism as well as church planting. The mosque is pregnant with theology that says, "Jesus was not crucified, the Bible has been corrupted, Muhammad is Allah's prophet, and salvation is by merit and not by grace." Is this where new believers will find sanctification and edification? Most C5 proponents advocate a separate meeting for believers for these aspects. But will real spiritual growth take place? Is there deception in continuing to stay in the mosque and parade around as a Muslim surrendered to God through *Isa Al Masih*?

A clearer line needs to be highlighted by missionaries working among Muslims delineating the difference between culture and religion. We have from Revelation 7 and elsewhere the promise of every tribe, tongue, and nation present in heaven worshipping Jesus. The promise is not extended to every religion. Religion and culture are not one and the same. Embracing the people without their mosque and religion seems to be the wiser and safer way of speaking the truth in love.

How does C5 deal with the 2 Corinthians 6 passage? The clear command is to be separate. Even though pagans are the specific context there, would Paul change his message to the adherents of Islam? Does this clear passage dealing with the dangers of syncretism just evaporate from our thinking in reaching the Sons of Ishmael? Regardless of how good our intentions are, we must obey the scriptures. C5 clearly crosses the line here and warrants concerns of syncretism. God is indeed God and will sovereignly act as he chooses, even surprising us at times. However, as his people, we must do all we can to build his Church with integrity and truth. Because our work will one day be tested by fire, my plea is that we will go back to the scriptures and clearly understand what they are saying about his Church.

References

Livingstone, Greg. 1993. *Planting Churches in Muslim Cities: A Team Approach.* Grand Rapids, Mich.: Baker Book House.

Travis, John. 1998. "Must All Muslims Leave Islam to 'Follow Jesus?'" *Evangelical Missions Quarterly* 34(4): 411-415.

Woodberry, J. Dudley. 1996. "Contextualization among Muslims: Reusing Common Pillars." *International Journal of Frontier Missions* 13: 171-186.

A Muslim Theology of Jesus' Virgin Birth and His Death

Gerald Wiens

A missionary among Muslims reminds Western missionaries that a new, contextualized interpretation of the events in Jesus' life is needed.

DURING A WEEKLY EVANGELISTIC BIBLE STUDY with college-aged Muslims in Central Asia, I led the group through the seven signs in John's gospel, attempting to draw out the implications of Jesus' miracles. Each week, I would go over the miracle passage to make sure everyone understood the basic plot. I then concluded by emphasizing the contemporary relevance that illustrated some aspect of the Christian gospel. I questioned my approach when they agreed with everything I said about Jesus without changing to a Christ-centered lifestyle. I was making the miracles of Jesus relevant from a Western perspective, to someone who desires to add another element of personal happiness to their life (the water to wine represents lasting joy offered by Jesus, the feeding of five thousand signifies the permanent satisfaction from Jesus, etc.).

The "add Jesus to your life to make it better" evangelistic approach was not relevant for a person who had already accepted Jesus as miraculously conceived in Mary, commissioned by God as a miracle-performing prophet, ascended to heaven and the one who will return to judge the world in the final day. The theological significance of each miracle story as I understood it was actually too insignificant for my Muslim friends. After several weeks, I knew that I had to consider a new, Muslim interpretation of the events in Jesus' life.

Theology is the significant and relevant meaning of historical facts. Events are merely happenings unless they are interpreted for significance. For example, handing my wife flowers is an event; that I love her is the significance and meaning of that event. Western theology has interpreted the facts of Jesus' life to make them meaningful for Christians who have a Western worldview.

Over the centuries, Christian theologians have unknowingly limited themselves to a narrow meaning of Jesus' life that fails to address the worldview of others. Therefore, missionaries in the Muslim world must contextually reinterpret the events of Jesus' life to draw out the significance of those events most relevant for a Muslim. In this article, I examine how two historical events (Jesus' virgin birth and his death) have been interpreted by two groups (the apostolic church and the modern, Western church) to address their cultural needs. I then propose how missionaries may relevantly interpret those same historical events for a Muslim audience.

The Virgin Birth of Jesus

Matthew 1:18-25 and Luke 1:34-35 both record that Jesus was miraculously conceived through the Spirit in Mary without any form of intercourse. Matthew and Luke primarily record the fact of Messiah's coming, only secondarily discussing the nature and significance of the miracle. What is the theological significance (meaning) of Jesus' birth (event)? Why is it important that Jesus was miraculously conceived?

Matthew was the first to theologically interpret Jesus' miraculous birth for a particular purpose. Writing to a group of Jewish Christians who were seeking to establish the validity of their new faith for non-Christian Jews, Matthew teaches that the virgin birth of Jesus is meaningful for his audience because it is a sign of God's salvific presence. Just as God originally gave a sign to Ahaz to show that he was present ("Immanuel" in Isaiah 7:14) to deliver Ahaz from foreign invasion, God has given a similar (even greater) sign to show that he is present in the person of Jesus to deliver his people again (Matt. 1:22-23; 28:20).

For the earliest Jewish audience, Jesus' birth was significant because it was a divine sign that God is repeating a work of salvation for his people, similar to his salvific work seven centuries earlier. Matthew used a recurring pattern

Because the empirical, mechanistic

worldview of the West demands scientific proof for every claim, Western Christians typically comb their Bibles looking for apologetic evidence to verify the truth claims about Jesus.

of God's activity in salvation history—a unique birth means God is at work to save—for his theological purposes. God's deliverance of Ahaz is not personally significant for westerners who do not view Ahaz as one of "us," so comparing God's work in Jesus to God's mighty salvation for Ahaz downplays rather than magnifies God's redemptive work signified by the virgin birth. Therefore, the Western church emphasizes a different aspect of the virgin birth.

Because the empirical, mechanistic worldview of the West demands scientific proof for every claim, Western Christians typically comb their Bibles looking for apologetic evidence to verify the truth claims about Jesus. Prophecy is especially attractive to us, since we can calculate the odds of all the prophecies being fulfilled in one person.

We assert, "There is a one in a gazillion chance of a person fulfilling all these prophecies, and Jesus fulfilled all of them, therefore Jesus must be the Son of God!" Since such mathematical evidence from prophecy seduces the scientific mind, the virgin conception is significant to modern westerners because it demonstrates that Jesus is the fulfillment of a specific prediction given seven hundred years before his birth. But such numerical analysis may not be as significant for non-Western Muslims.

The virgin conception is significant for Muslims because it shows Jesus is a unique prophet—unlike any other of God's messengers, including Muhammad. Adam is our first father, and thus he is the father of all the prophets. Adam was made from the ground which is impure and dirty. Jesus came from heaven (Matt. 1:18). He is pure, clean and without sin. Jesus was not born on earth, but left his home in heaven to come to this world. Jesus is not a descendant of Adam like other prophets, but comes from God himself (Marsh 1975, 46).

Although a westerner may question such an explanation of inherited sin, one must not be preoccupied by the constraints of Western theology. Muslims are usually impacted by the unique origins of Jesus' virgin birth. Jesus is not merely another of Allah's many prophets, but a unique messenger by virtue of his unique birth. Jesus' virgin conception and unique birth are relevant for Muslims because they teach the unique nature of Jesus' prophetic ministry, not because they are like God's work seven hundred years prior for Ahaz or a miraculous fulfillment of prophecy.

The Death of Jesus

In the ancient world, thousands of people, Jesus being one of them, were crucified. The fact of Jesus' death was hardly unique to Jesus himself, but the significance and meaning of his death is unparalleled. Christianity claims that Christ died for us. What is the significance of Jesus' death? How did the early Church interpret it? How does the modern, Western Church apply Jesus' death to its needs? How is Jesus' death significant to modern Muslims? Again, how is that historical event relevant?

The early, apostolic Church understood Jesus' death to be relevant in a variety of ways. When Paul was struggling with Judaizers who required Gentiles to adopt Jewish ordinances, the death of Jesus was significant because it allowed non-Jews to become part of God's people without obeying the Jewish law (Eph. 3:11-13; Gal. 2:21; 3:13-14).

But in a Greco-Roman context, Paul explains Jesus' death as the display of God's wisdom in order to silence the prideful philosophers in Corinth (1 Cor. 1:18-25). For Matthew, the death of Jesus marks the climax of Israel's rejection of the Messiah (Matt. 27:25). According to Mark, the death of Jesus is the ultimate display of his faithful service as the Son of God (Mark 15:39), an example for the suffering community of disciples to whom Mark wrote. For John, Jesus' death is not a testimony of humility, but the moment of Jesus' exaltation. In the book of Hebrews, Jesus' death is significant because it renders the Old Testament sacrificial system invalid and useless. James never mentions Jesus' death. While atonement of sins is the central theological interpretation of

Jesus' death in the early church, the way each New Testament author interprets Jesus' death to make the historical event significant for his community directs contemporary theologies in new ways to meet new needs.

In modern, Western theology, Jesus' death is interpreted existentially —it brings personal benefits to individuals. Since a westerner views himself as an autonomous person with a separate identity, the death of Jesus is interpreted through these lenses. For example, Jesus' death is significant because it offers the introspective, psychologically-oriented westerner freedom from guilt.

This is a carryover from Augustine's and Luther's understanding of Jesus' death. The "penal substitutionary atonement" which emphasizes the appeasement of God's wrath on our behalf over our individual sins dominates Western theology because it offers psychological assurance (Green and Baker 2000, 142-152). Also, for the individual in this world who hopes to discover personal identity and purpose, Jesus' death is the means by which he or she can be identified as God's child and thereby find a purpose for life. Moreover, Jesus' death is a demonstration of God's love (i.e., Four Spiritual Laws), offering security to the group-less individual seeker. For westerners who tend to value personal satisfaction and interests over those of the group, Jesus' death

Offering identity and purpose to a Muslim who already possesses an identity as a member of the family group is like bathing a fish.

purchased for you and me the true joy that we seek (Hiebert 1985, 122-26). Undergirding all such applications of Jesus' death is the Western Church's praiseworthy desire to make Jesus' death relevant for one particular worldview.

Unfortunately, this is the only understanding of Jesus' death westerners know. Therefore, it becomes the orthodox, universal, monolithic theology exported to the Muslim world.

The formation of a Muslim theology of Jesus' death must re-examine the individualistic orientation behind westerners' understandings of Jesus' death and consider Islamic doctrine about Jesus. Since most Muslims live in a group-oriented culture, existential interpretations of Jesus' death carry little significance. Offering identity and purpose to a Muslim who already possesses an identity as a member of the family group is like bathing a fish. Group-oriented people do not feel guilt for failing to maintain an absolute standard, but shame for disrupting or dishonoring their community.

Therefore, since Jesus experienced isolation and rejection (Matt. 26:31, 69-75), his death is significant for Muslims because it paid for feelings of shame and social alienation in the group. Jesus' death restores humanity to God not simply by paying the punishment demanded by absolute justice, but also by dispelling the shame, abandonment and disgrace that results when humans fail to remain faithful. For westerners, Jesus' death is an example of someone who laid aside personal desires to follow God's will. For Muslims, Jesus is an example of someone who remained faithful to his God-given mission to the point of death, despite social rejection.

The fact that most Muslims already accept Jesus as a great prophet should not be forgotten when illustrating the significance of Jesus' death. Jesus' death becomes meaningful to a Muslim when it demonstrates Jesus' uniqueness. Death is the great equalizer of humanity that affects everyone, regardless of age, status, race or position before God. Anyone, including God's prophets, can lose his or her life anywhere, any way and anytime; only God himself knows and determines the details surrounding the death of humans.

Even though the prophets had a unique relationship with God, their death was still determined and known only by God. But Jesus is unlike any prophet before or after him; in Matthew 20:17-19, Jesus knew where (in Jerusalem), how (beating and crucifixion from Gentiles) and when (during the Passover) his death would occur. Matthew 20:28 shows Jesus even knew the purpose of his death—it was a ransom for other people. Nobody's death, not even another prophet's, has ever been a ransom to God for many other people. Not only does Jesus understand the events surrounding his death, he also controls them (John 10:18). Jesus had unique knowledge of his fate. Therefore, Jesus' death is theologically significant to a Muslim because it demonstrates the incomparable uniqueness of his life compared to other people, including other prophets.

Conclusion

After conducting several studies emphasizing the uniqueness of Jesus in contrast to other prophets, several of my friends recognized their need to respond to Jesus' uniqueness by trusting solely in him. God allowed me to construct a theology for Muslims that confronted critical areas of their worldview and addressed their genuine human problems, rather than a theology that simply regurgitated Western ideas. Such a re-interpretation of Jesus' life for the Muslim bore much fruit.

In this article I have illustrated that Jesus' virgin birth and death can be significant for various reasons to different people. Cultural needs do not determine theology, but they do determine the questions which theology is expected to answer. The process of theological contextualization does not imply creating relevance for Jesus' death, but purposefully seeking and emphasizing the theological aspects in scripture most relevant to our audience. Missionaries to Muslims must not settle for the imposition of Western theologies, but strive to construct a biblically-grounded theology of Jesus' life that answers the questions of the Muslim worldview.

While we have shown here how to develop a Muslim theology for Jesus' birth and death; there still lies the possibilities of developing a Muslim theol-

ogy for other events in Jesus' life—miracles, teaching, call of discipleship, resurrection, ascension, future judgment and so on—not to mention other major
events throughout the Bible (creation, fall, exodus, exile, etc.). It is my desire
that this examination of a Muslim orientation to Jesus' virgin birth and death
inspires readers to apply the same method of (1) investigating the apostles'
contextualization of an event for a specific purpose, (2) realizing how cultural
conditions of the West have shaped modern theology, and (3) asking how biblical events can be interpreted to relevantly address the questions of the Muslim world. May the nations know a relevant Jesus!

References

Green, Joel B. and Mark D. Baker. 2000. *Recovering the Scandal of the Cross: The Atonement in New Testament and Contemporary Contexts.* Downers Grove, Ill.: InterVarsity Press.

Hiebert, Paul G. 1985. *Anthropological Insights for Missionaries.* Grand Rapids, Mich.:
Baker Books.

Marsh, C.R. 1975. *Share Your Faith with a Muslim.* Chicago: Moody Press.

October 2008

Christological Monotheism and Muslim Evangelism

David Teague

How do missionaries in Muslim churches speak of the divinity of Christ without appearing to contradict their belief in monotheism?

AN IMPORTANT QUESTION within recent New Testament scholarship has been: "If the first Christians were strict monotheists, how did they come to worship Christ as divine?" In other words, how did they deal with the seeming contradiction? This relates to another important question for Christians who live in Muslim cultures today: How do we speak of the divinity of Christ without appearing to contradict our belief in monotheism? The early Church began under the strict monotheism of first century Palestinian Judaism. Many Christians today live under the strict monotheism of Islam. Can an analogy be drawn across the centuries to teach us how to communicate Christ's divinity to Muslims?

Strict Monotheism

Most Christians do not know what life is like in a strictly monotheistic culture. We are not first century Jewish villagers who daily recite the *Shema*: "Hear, O Israel: The Lord our God, the Lord is one" (Mark 12:28-31; Deut. 6:4). Most of us are not awakened at four a.m. in Amman, Jordan, to the sound of the *muezzin* calling out, "There is no God but Allah." Most do not hear Muslim television preachers wail about the heresy of *shirk*, the association of anything material or human with Allah (Qur'an 4:48). "Nothing, nothing," Muslims say, "can be associated with God lest it diminish the holy transcendence of God."

Today, the Church outside of the Middle East is largely ignorant of all this difficulty. Christians freely say, "Jesus is God," but they have no idea how this sounds to a strict monotheist. Once, in my theological role in the Middle East, my Arab colleagues cautioned me not to blithely say, "Jesus is God." I was dumbfounded, but they explained, "It's carelessness. To Muslim ears, when you talk like that, all they hear is the heresy of *shirk*. Besides, it's sloppy thinking." Quoting Athanasius, the early church father, they continued: "The Son is God in all things, except that he is not the Father."

In other words, they carefully preserved the distinction between the Son and God the Father in heaven while I blurred it. They felt the distinction was essential in explaining who Christ is within Muslim contexts. The Son is divine, but the Father—God in heaven—is still infinite, eternal, and beyond human conception.

They encouraged me to use indirect language in how I spoke of Christ's divinity. The New Testament never has the direct equivalency statement, "Jesus is God." We do have some close statements, as in Thomas' confession, but never a simple, clear declaration. Instead, we find a series of indirect statements: Hebrews 1:3—the Son "is the radiance of God's glory" and "the exact representation of his being"; Colossians 1:15—"the image of the invisible God"; Philippians 2:6—"who, being in the very form of God"; and 1 Corinthians 8:6—"through whom all things came and through whom we live." Then there is the use of the title Lord with a divine charge (cf. Rom. 10:9).

This hesitation to use direct equivalency statements seems due to the difficulty of speaking of the divinity of Christ in first century Palestinian monotheism. The indirect language indicates divinity, but in a way that respects the position of God the Father in heaven.

Christological Monotheism

Some Western scholars have now become aware of the difficulty of speaking of Christ's divinity within a strictly monotheistic culture. In his commentary on Philippians, Ralph Martin first cites a number of Paul's circumlocutions concerning Christ's divinity and then concludes: "Why this restraint in vocabulary on the part of an apostle so obviously committed to the lordship of Jesus Christ? Perhaps it was due to the influence of Jewish monotheism on Paul, the former Pharisee (2004, lxiii; cf. 1 Cor. 8:5–6).

Richard Bauckham is another scholar who recognizes the difficulty (Bauckham, 1999). He affirms that the New Testament writers assert the divinity of Christ, not by making bold equivalency statements, but by including Jesus in the unique identity of Yahweh. He and other scholars use the phrase Christological monotheism to describe how the first Christians included Christ in this unique identity of Yahweh.

This unique identity developed within the Hebrew's covenant relationship with Yahweh. As the centuries passed, the Hebrews experienced Yahweh guiding them, defending them, and instructing and chastising them. They developed a covenantal knowledge of Yahweh. When the first disciples encountered Jesus, they confessed that their experience was consistent with their prior covenantal knowledge of Yahweh. They witnessed Jesus' sovereignty over all things. He calmed the storm, cast out demons, forgave sin, healed the sick, and raised the dead. His death was an atonement for the sins of the world. He ascended to heaven as the judge of the world. They prayed in Jesus' name and miracles happened.

They included Jesus in the unique identity of Yahweh because of what they had experienced. This did not create a philosophical problem with their monotheism because they were not thinking about God philosophically; they were experiencing God covenantally. Their encounter with Christ was consistent with what they already knew about Yahweh, so they chose the language of Christological monotheism to describe Christ's divinity.

This is why the New Testament quotes Psalm 110 some twenty-two times to identify the Messiah with the sovereignty of God. This is also why Paul composes a "messianic *Shema*" in 1 Corinthians 8:6 by weaving the name of Christ into the traditional Jewish *Shema*. And this is why the New Testament speaks of Christ as involved in the creation of all things (John 1:1-3; Col. 1:15-17).

Perhaps most importantly, the New Testament authors confessed that Christ was the fulfillment of the story of God. Isaiah 40-55 promised that there would be a final, eschatological victory of God in the world and that it would happen through the atoning death of a servant (Isa. 53:10). Bauckham argues convincingly that three major NT scriptures about Christ's divine identity (Phil. 2:6-11, Revelation, and John) look to Isaiah 40-55 as their source (1999, 45-69). In short, Bauckham argues that the first Christians confessed Christ to be divine without contradiction with their monotheism because their experience of Christ was consistent with their prior convenantal knowledge of Yahweh.

What Is Useful?

Christological monotheism raises two important questions as we seek to communicate Christ's divinity within Muslim contexts: (1) Are we making a proper analogy? and (2) If we are, what can be learned? Christological monotheism describes how the first Christians included Christ in the unique identity of Yahweh.

At first glance, this seems to offer a striking analogy to Christians living in Muslim cultures. Both situations concern how to communicate the divinity of Christ within a culture dominated by a strict monotheism. But there is an important difference: The monotheism of Islam is not the monotheism of the Bible. Islam focuses on the transcendence of God. The Bible, on the other hand, also describes God's immanence.

In the Bible, we read of theophanies, such as the Lord God walking in the cool of the day in Eden. God communicates through the prophets and acts within the covenant. Salvation is described as peace with God. Messianic prophecies speak of Immanuel, God with us. The earliest Christians felt that God wanted to know and to be known: "That which was from the beginning, which we have heard, which we have seen with our eyes, which we have looked at and our hands have touched—this we proclaim concerning the word of life" (1 John 1:1).

Muslims do not share this same understanding of the immanence of God. For this reason, their concept of monotheism differs from the covenantal monotheism of the Hebrews, causing the analogy between first century Judaism and Muslim cultures to be imperfect.

We also have to acknowledge that Islam developed independently from the Bible. Indeed, the words "Allah" and "Yahweh" do not share the same cultural and contextual associations. In the Bible, Yahweh constantly acts for the redemption of the world through a covenant people, a depiction not shared in the same way in the Qur'an. However, despite the lack of a perfect analogy, Christological monotheism can still be helpful for communicating Christ's divinity within Muslim cultures. It is useful when we teach it as part of the biblical metanarrative.

Although Muslims lack a covenantal knowledge of Yahweh, they can still learn it. The biblical metanarrative is the story of God—the self-revelation of God to the world through a chosen people. Muslims need to comprehend this before they can understand how it is completed in Christ. Metanarrative approaches, such as chronological Bible storying, provide the proper interpretive framework for communicating the divinity of Christ to Muslim cultures. In that framework, Christological monotheism does have value.

It also has value when we seek to explain the meaning of the cross. Muslims do not understand how God would allow his holy prophet to suffer the shameful death of crucifixion. Christological monotheism explains how. It re-

The biblical metanarrative is the story of God—the self-revelation of God to the world through a chosen people. Muslims need to comprehend this before they can understand how it is completed in Christ.

minds us that Jesus is not just a part of the story of God—he is intrinsic to it. He completes it. There is something within his death that we need to grasp in order to know God.

Understood apart from the biblical metanarrative, Christ's crucifixion does seem utterly shameful. But within the context of the story of God, it is the fullest revelation of the identity of God, as foretold in Isaiah 40-55. We cannot know what God is really like apart from the atoning death of the Messiah. Concerning this, Bauckham makes a crucial point:

> While the Fathers successfully appropriated, in their own way in Nicene theology, the New Testament's inclusion of Jesus in the identity of God, they were less successful in appropriating this corollary, the revelation of the divine identity in Jesus' human life and passion. To see justice done to this aspect of New Testament Christology we have to turn to the kind of theology of the cross which Martin Luther adumbrated and which has come into its own in the twentieth century. (1999, viii-ix)

In other words, our task is not simply to communicate words about the deity of Christ. We are also to live out a sacrificial witness. In the cross, we find redemption, but we also learn how to live a life of redemptive sacrifice for the sake of others. Both our teaching and our passionate service are needed to help our Muslim friends to know who Christ really is.

Aiding us in this endeavor will be the Holy Spirit. It is no slight matter that many Muslims are now experiencing God through dreams, visions, and miracles. Since Muslims do not understand the biblical metanarrative, they lack the conceptual framework to understand the divinity of Christ. It takes time to teach the biblical metanarrative. Our merciful God seems to be helping many Muslims "catch up" by sending them experiences to open them to the divine nature of Christ. To fully understand these experiences, however, inquirers will need to become grounded in the biblical metanarrative and in Christological monotheism.

Conclusion

Christological monotheism can be used to teach the divinity of Christ in Muslim cultures, but it should be taught as part of the biblical metanarrative. Within that context, the incarnation is no longer shirk; instead, it is the fulfillment of the story of Yahweh. The crucifixion is no longer shameful; rather, it provides us a glimpse into the true heart of God.

References

Bauckham, Richard. 1999. *God Crucified: Monotheism and Christology in the New Testament*. Grand Rapids, Mich.: William B. Eerdmans Publishing Co.

Martin, Ralph and Gerald F. Hawthorne. 2004. *Word Biblical Commentary, Volume 43: Philippians* (Revised Edition). Nashville, Tenn.: Thomas Nelson Publishers.

Section 3

Contextualization

PERHAPS TO NO OTHER RELIGIOUS/CULTURAL BLOCK has the issue of contextualization been so hotly debated. The views on how much to contextualize words and actions vary as much as the settings where and peoples to whom practitioners are serving. A certain balance of truth and love is needed when discerning what methods to use when witnessing to Muslims—and to know when you have gone too far. We have kept this chapter in chronological order to give you a clear view of the progression of the discussion over the years.

In 1982, **Richard Heldenbrand** discussed the idea that we cannot abandon both absolute truth and an objective revelation in order to be free to interpret scripture as we please.

Five years after that **Don Eenigenburg** wrote that an alternative to Islamicized contextualization is to enable believers to practice their faith meaningfully and relevantly, yet without demonstrating allegiance to Islam.

Several of the 1998 issues of *EMQ* cut deep to the heart of contextualization. **Jay Smith** said that instead of running from a healthy exchange with our Muslim friends, we must begin finding answers. **Phil Parshall** warned that C5 missionaries are on very shaky theological and missiological ground. **John Travis** wrote that if the single greatest hindrance to seeing Muslims come to faith concerns cultural and religious identity, much of our missiological energy should be devoted to seeking a path whereby Muslims can remain Muslims, yet live as true followers of the Lord Jesus. **Dean S. Gilliland** shared why one group of Muslim Background Believers must be taken very seriously.

In 2004, **Joshua Massey** wrote that judging C5 ministry from Greco-Roman Gentile categories of orthodoxy, distance, or church-centered can lead to misunderstandings. That same year, **Phil Parshall** said that those in Muslim ministry must move toward dialogue regarding seven major issues. In 2008, **Gary Corwin** shared seven beliefs which may open up paths to unity among those who minister to Muslims. A year later, **Herbert Hoefer** said that if followers of Christ want Muslims to feel comfortable in Christian worship services, then they need to consider at least seven issues. That same year, **Erik Hyatt** shared his research and interview data of Muslim ministry practitioners and missiologists to formulate "Questions and Biblical Guidelines" for ministering to Muslims.

In 2010, **Carlos Diaz** discussed three new perspectives among Latino missionaries to Muslims.

July 1982

Missions to Muslims: Cutting the Nerve?

Richard Heldenbrand

We cannot abandon both absolute truth and an objective revelation in order to be free to interpret scripture as we please.

IF REVIVAL MOVEMENTS HAVE OFTEN LED THE WAY to missionary advance, philosophical and theological speculation have too frequently cut the nerve of biblical evangelism and contributed to missionary retrenchment. Today, such speculation, coupled with the disciplines of anthropology and sociology, has markedly influenced certain innovative missiologists—in particular, their views about missions to Muslims.

In recent years, at least two evangelicals, Charles Kraft and Phil Parshall, have published their versions of what has been called the "Christian-Qur'an Hermeneutic." This has been one of the most significant attempts at theological contextualization. Samuel P. Schlorff discussed it in a 1980 article in *EMQ*. However, with the recent publication of Phil Parshall's book, *New Paths in Muslim Evangelism* (1980), further analysis seems required.

Parshall frankly states his purpose: "I am writing a book which deals with the subject of possible adaptations of Islamic forms of Christianity"(1980, 257). He reassures his readers, "This book is dedicated to the formulation of a contextualized Christianity that in no way disturbs basic biblical truth" (1980, 196). This is subject for question, since he equates "Islamic forms" with the "Five Pillars" of Islam: the creed, ritual prayers, the fast month of Ramadan, almsgiving, and pilgrimage (1980, 58).

On the basis of his missionary experience, Parshall favors the keeping of the fast month. He asks, "Should missionaries and converts keep the fast in the prescribed Muslim manner?" His response: "There can be no dogmatic answer. I do feel Muslims would appreciate such a gesture of identification. However, the Christian position on fasting should be made clear" (1980, 210).

In much the same way, he commends the observance of the Muslim Sheep Feast, *Qurbani Id*, quoting Erich Bethman, "If converts emphasize the elements of remembrance, might they not be allowed to continue to observe *Qurbani Id* much as traditional Christians celebrate the Lord's Supper?" (1980, 146). Not only so, but he would bypass the term "Christian": "The word Christian is avoided because of negative connotations. Presently, 'Followers of *Isa* (Jesus)' is being used in Bangladesh" (1980, 26).

The question is whether forms which, Parshall concedes, are deeply imbedded in the very innermost being of every "Muslim," can be retained with Christian integrity, or whether the Christian understanding of things is lost in practices which, far from being even syncretistic, remain essentially Islamic.

I asked a new convert from Islam what he thought about Christians who keep Ramadan and the Sheep Feast. He replied that since Islam includes teachings about Moses and *Isa*, in his opinion such people are essentially Muslim and not distinctively Christian. Both his and my own observations over many years force me to consider very naïve indeed the assumption that making clear "the Christian position on fasting" or attempting to associate the Islamic sheep sacrifice with the death of Christ alters in any measurable way the real meaning of these Muslim practices for the people who engage in them.

Let us suppose that Christians in Islamic lands were to adopt the Sheep Feast as practiced by Muslims and to teach that it was in memory of Christ's death. What would this accomplish? In point of fact, the sheep, at least to all

While Jesus Christ is a stumbling-stone
because he became a curse for us, *Isa* is not a stumbling-stone, for he never became a curse because he never died.

Muslims, would still be sacrificed in memory of Abraham's offering of Ishmael, a complete twisting of the biblical facts of the case. More serious, the Lord's Supper concept of believers as a people set apart by God from idolatrous feasts and sacrifices would be lost. Most serious by far, the once-for-all nature of the death of Christ would be compromised, for the Sheep Feast involves an annual sacrifice. In suggesting that missions to Muslims utilize the Sheep Feast, Parshall proposes something that would be fully as great a problem as the Roman Catholic mass.

Little better can be said for the substitution of *Isa* for Jesus. Far from the Qur'anic *Isa* calling up only positive mental images, it has negative historical connotations. More to the point, the *Isa* of the Qur'an has different attributes from the Jesus of the Bible. The *Sidna Isa* of current Muslim theology never died. He was a prophet superseded by Muhammad. Because man, according to Islam, must stand on his own merits, *Isa* is not only not the savior of the world, he is not a savior at all. While Jesus Christ is a stumbling-stone because he became a curse for us, *Isa* is not a stumbling-stone, for he never became a curse because he never died. In the interests of both candor and cross-cultural communication, I would advocate the transliteration of the Hebrew word *YASHOUA*, meaning "salvation." When in any language we call Jesus *Savior*, we call him by his name.

Such, in brief, is the outward shape of Parshall's "new paths" for influencing and winning Muslims. But what of the inner rationale behind such proposals? Charles Kraft has spelled out some of the presuppositions. He distinguishes between the form of theological terms and their real meaning. At a 1974 conference he emphasized "the sonship analogy in speaking of Christ" (68). For him, the term "Son of God" is analogical rather than definitive. In this Parshall follows him: "The words *Father, Son,* and *begotten* must be viewed as figurative and metaphysical. Arabs utilize such figures of speech as *ibn al'sabil,* which literally means 'the son of the road.' All Arabs know that a road has no son and that the real meaning is 'traveler'" (1980, 143). Thus he places "Son of God" on the same level as an Arab figure of speech, quite forgetting that the Arab figure is human whereas Christ's eternal Sonship is a truth divinely revealed.

Again, Kraft laments "the extremely high value that we put on the necessity of knowledge to faith." Whereas "God requires faith alone, we, due to our peculiar cultural conditioning, often cannot even conceive of true faith without a rather

One gains the impression in Kraft's writings, especially, that in his eagerness to find common ground with Muslims, he has clearly overstepped the biblical boundaries.

detailed, often philosophic, knowledge of an elaborate doctrinal scheme." He feels that it is wrong to hold the potential convert from Islam "'accountable for a type of knowledge that (1) may be true, (2) may be appropriate for us, but (3) is not necessary and often very misleading for him" (1974, 69-70). Parshall approvingly quotes Kraft as saying, "Christian-ness lies primarily in the functions served and the meanings conveyed by the cultural forms employed, rather than in the forms themselves" (1980, 56). But what if the forms themselves are supra-cultural, as suggested by Paul's words to Timothy: "Hold fast the form of sound words?"

One gains the impression in Kraft's writings, especially, that in his eagerness to find common ground with Muslims, he has clearly overstepped the biblical boundaries. When he speaks of the faith which God accepts as having been originally "a behavior"(1974, 69-71); when he suggests that a man can be saved independently of any conscious faith in Jesus Christ, that "he simply has to pledge in faith as much of himself as he can to as much of God as he understands, even the Muslim Allah" (1974, 71); when he assigns our contemporary Christian stress on individual guilt to Western acculturation—in each of these matters he has crossed over onto Islamic turf.

Nor is Parshall on much safer territory when he presses his thesis that "the transforming of the worldviews and allegiances of Muslims should be carried out as a process which involves minimal dislocation" (1980, 90-91). With respect to sin, he proposes a Muslim-Christian synthesis:

Guilt is a normal reaction of a Western Christian to sin....By contrast, the Muslim focuses on the penalty for sin. He does not usually experience sin as guilt but rather as shame and embarrassment...the ideal would seem to be a merger of the vertical and the horizontal—of guilt before God along with the shame and embarrassment one feels in relation to other human beings. (1980, 77)

I contend that this accommodation effectively negates the Holy Spirit's conviction of sin, all of it, as first and last against God.

In summary, what shall be said of this well-meaning but sub-biblical approach to the Muslim world? It is evident that anthropology and sociology, rather than theology, are the determining disciplines. Kraft states quite frankly, "The issues that we deal with, even the so-called religious issues, are primarily cultural, and only secondarily religious" (1974, 65). How can we exchange revelational absolutes for cultural relativities? We cannot abandon both absolute truth and an objective revelation in order to be free to interpret scripture as we please.

This faulty method of Bible interpretation is seen in Kraft's call for Christianity and Islam to discover "communality" in the imposing figure of Abraham. He finds backing for a common theology centered in "the faith of Abraham" in Romans 4, Galatians 3, and Hebrews 11. It would seem, however, that he is more interested in finding a basis for communication with Muslims than in sticking with biblical facts.

What about the fact that Abraham, contrary to Islamic teaching, was not a Muslim and that the son whom he would have offered was not Ishmael, but Isaac? Does not Kraft validate the non-historical elements of Islam in order to promote Christian-Muslim synthesis?

I would press hard for a faith relationship with God and for a faith renewal movement starting within Islam as a culture based on the faith of Abraham (or Ibrahim), pointing to the Qur'an, Old Testament, and New Testament as the source of our information concerning this faith... (1974, 76)

Kraft apparently follows existential relativism, as for example in this statement regarding the nature of faith and the one who believes:

What is necessary to faith, apparently, is some feeling of need or inadequacy that stimulates a person to turn in faith to God. Similarly, he doesn't have to be convinced of the death of Christ; he simply has to pledge allegiance and faith to the God who worked out the details to make it possible for his faith response to take the place of a righteous requirement. He may not, in fact, be able to believe in the death of Christ especially if he knowingly places his faith in God through Christ, for within his frame of reference, if Christ died, God was defeated by men, and this of course is unthinkable. (1974, 70-71)

Here there is no recognition of a biblical frame of reference, only of various human frames, each of which is to be honored more than the scriptures themselves. It is one thing to be sensitive to human feelings, but quite another to avoid an open declaration of God's revealed mind and will.

It is that the gospel might be faithfully proclaimed and Muslims truly won to Christ that numbers of us object to certain of the Parshall and Kraft proposals. By way of contrast, I would propose the following affirmative guidelines for the evangelizing of Muslims: (1) evangelism should be defined in terms of a message delivered, not an effect produced on the hearers; (2) Christ must, from the start, be presented for who he is, God's eternal Son and the object of our faith; (3) the divine command to repent of sin must be proclaimed; (4) Christ Jesus, the living Savior and reigning Lord, must be set forth as he himself is, not simply as an historic figure of significance or an effective communicator; (5) his saving work on the cross must be central in the presentation, since it is central in the message we have been charged to deliver as his ambassadors; and (6) we must exhort Muslims as sinners to accept Christ as their Savior and Lord, recognizing that they are lost without him, rather than presenting him as a subject for critical and comparative study.

References

Kraft, Charles. 1974. Conference on Media in Islamic Culture Report. Marseilles.

Parshall, Phil. 1980. *New Paths in Muslim Evangelism*. Grand Rapids, Mich.: Baker Books.

July 1997

The Pros and Cons of Islamicized Contextualization

Don Eenigenburg

An alternative to Islamicized contextualization is to enable believers to practice their faith meaningfully and relevantly, yet without demonstrating allegiance to Islam.

CHURCH PLANTING WITHIN MUSLIM SOCIETIES presents a major challenge for Christian missions. As the year 2000 approaches, mission agencies are scrambling for strategies suitable for reaching Islam with the gospel. In the last few decades, the popularity of contextualization has spurred on the search for new ways of expressing the gospel in forming new believing communities. Contextualization seeks to express the Christian faith in a way which is both true to scripture and relevant to the cultural context of the recipients.

Recently, some missionaries to Muslims have suggested a different kind of contextualization. In this new approach, missionaries encourage believers from a Muslim background to remain within the Muslim community. Believers maintain their Muslim identity and learn to practice their faith using Islamic forms and terminology. They meet in congregations culturally distinct from existing Christian congregations in the area. We will call this approach "Islamicized contextualization."

Maintaining a Muslim Identity

David Teeter works with Muslim university students through a "Friendship Center" in the Bethlehem area. He writes about a "Muslim followers of Jesus" model he and his colleagues have employed. In this model, Muslims coming to Christ do not convert to Christianity. They remain with their families trying to maintain their support despite their "heretical" beliefs about Jesus (1990, 306-307).

Some missionaries, attempting to identify with their hosts, have called themselves Muslims. Pointing to the example of Paul, who "became a Jew to the Jews," they assert that to the Muslims they must become Muslims. One team in the Middle East has a policy of not allowing missionaries to identify themselves as Christians. Some team members identify themselves as Muslims with immediate or later qualification.

Remaining within the Community

This enables believers to remain part of the Muslim community and display loyalty by their normal participation in Muslim communal life. John Wilder served for twenty years in the non-Arab Muslim world. He tells of a group of believers from a Muslim background who called themselves "Jesus-ists." They remained separate from local Christians. Other Muslims considered them one of many Sufi or dervish mystical orders. Wilder maintains that a movement to Christ might begin from inside the Muslim community. He states that although a "Christian Muslim" sect would offend some Muslims, most might see the group as just one of many sects under the Islamic umbrella (1977, 310-311).

Advocates of Islamicized contextualization criticize Christian attempts to make Muslims leave their community. They compare Christians with the Judaizers of the first century who wanted to circumcise (proselytize) Gentiles before they could become part of the church. Paul condemned the Judaizers for placing unnecessary burdens on Gentiles coming to faith.

Islamic Forms of Worship

In Islamicized contextualization, believers from a Muslim background practice Islamic forms of worship. Advocates say nearly all Islamic forms are redeemable. Some even maintain that believers should replace distinctly Christian forms (e.g., baptism) with culturally equivalent forms.

Rafique Uddin, a believer from a Muslim background and an evangelist, relates an experience in training people to work with Muslims. Throughout the training period they prayed five times daily using the Islamic form of prayer (*salat*). When they returned to their villages after the training, they continued the Islamic prayers. Some of them even went to the mosques to pray. He says these trainees are aware that prayer and fasting are not obligatory for them. However, they have now become regular expressions of praise to God (1989. 271-272). Contextualization rightly acknowledges the need to select forms relevant to the new believer. What distinguishes Islamicized contextualization is that Islamic identity, community, and forms are to show that the believer is still Muslim in essence. This claim requires redefining what it means to be Muslim (or Christian for that matter).

Rationale

The rationale behind Islamicized contextualization boils down to historical, cultural, and evangelistic reasons.

1. Historical reasons. Proponents point out the historic failure of Christians to attract Muslims to faith in Christ. Previous approaches have been ineffective, they say, because they have not taken seriously historical barriers between the two faiths.

John Anderson presented a paper at the 1976 conference on "The World of Islam Today" in England. He reviewed the historical barriers between the Christian and Muslim communities. The Church in Arabia at the time of Muhammad was divided into Greek Orthodox, Nestorian, and Monophysite sects. These divisions gave Muhammad a distorted picture of Christianity. Later, the medieval Church created additional barriers by supporting the Crusaders' attempts to conquer Islam by sword. In the 1800s, missionaries infuriated Muslims by relying upon controversy to attack Islam. More recently, Muslims have observed in the Western Church an almost uncritical support for the State of Israel. Modern missions have largely bypassed the Muslim world to reach more accessible fields. Those who have focused on Muslims have often appeared subversive, unmoved by the impoverished, and insensitive to the culture of Islam (1977, 2).

Anderson acknowledged other factors limiting the effectiveness of Muslim evangelism. Yet, he said, these factors often cover the blame that rests squarely with the Church.

2. Cultural reasons. Islamicized contextualization identifies cultural differences between Muslims and Christians as a major barrier to conversion. Frederick and Margaret Stock speak from their experience in Pakistan. They say we often assume that the primary barriers to winning Muslims are theological barriers. In reality, many Muslims are theologically convinced of Christiani-

Islamicized contextualization identifies cultural differences between Muslims and Christians as a major barrier to conversion.

ty. However, they cannot get over the social and cultural hurdles (Conn 1979, 100). Muslims often have a low view of Christian morality. Christian dietary, hygienic, and dress habits are offensive to most Muslims.

3. Evangelistic reasons. Who is better able to reach family and friends with the gospel than the convert him or herself? If he or she leaves the community, or becomes a traitor (Christian), how can he or she influence his or her family and friends? Near the turn of the century, missionaries baptized D. A. Chowdhury, a convert from Islam, in the Bengal province of India. That same day, they sent him off to Calcutta (five hundred miles from home). Chowdhury claims it took ten years to rebuild the trust of his Muslim friends. He observes, "This uprooting of converts from their natural environment has been a serious hindrance to the propagation of Christianity amongst Bengali Muslims" (1939, 345).

Believers who remain within the Muslim community are arguably better able to reach family and friends for Christ. If believers continue to leave the community, hopes for a mass movement to Christ diminish.

Presuppositions

To determine the validity of this approach, we need to evaluate its presuppositions.

1. The fault of traditional approaches. Proponents quickly point out the failure of traditional approaches. They say these have largely ignored the tremendous historical and cultural barriers between the two communities. However, blaming traditional approaches for the lack of results ignores significant hindrances to the gospel. Satan has blinded the eyes of Muslims toward the gospel. Muslim leaders do not want to relinquish their control over their people. This assessment also ignores significant advances for the gospel in areas like Indonesia, India, and Iran.

Perhaps the major reason more Muslims have not responded to the gospel is that the Church has largely neglected Muslim evangelism altogether. Greg Livingstone recounts how much effort missionaries expended in China, Japan, India, Korea, and Colombia before Christianity began to take root. Until the Church exerts the prayers and efforts in Muslim lands that it has exerted in other "difficult" lands, it cannot expect a significant harvest.

I believe that remaining fully part of the Muslim community may not be the best way for new believers to win the community. One pastor who has bap-

If believers try to appear as part of the Muslim community, they will appear deceptive. Muslims would have more respect for someone who acknowledges he is a Christian and stands up for his beliefs.

tized many Muslims has said that Muslims respect courage. If believers try to appear as part of the Muslim community, they will appear deceptive. Muslims would have more respect for someone who acknowledges he is a Christian and stands up for his beliefs.

2. Islam's compatibility with the gospel. Islam's presumed ability to accommodate the gospel is critical to Islamicized contextualization approaches. Some proponents argue that Islam is primarily a cultural rather than a religious entity. Anglican Canon Isaac Taylor read a paper at the Wolverhampton Church Congress (1887) in which he stated that Islam stands halfway between Judaism and Christianity.

The goal of Islamicized contextualization is to transform Islam rather than to replace it (Vander Werff 1977, 332). John Anderson claims that Islam entails much "that appeals to the conscience of good men" (1977, 5). However, Phil Parshall, in his book, *Beyond the Mosque,* sees sociology and theology as inseparable components in Islam. He lists four characteristics of Islam, making a Jesus sect within Islam impossible:

a. The unacceptable exaltation of the prophet Muhammad

b. The centrality of the mosque to religious expression within Islam

c. The denial by Muslims of the Christian view of biblical authority, as well as their rejection of our belief in the deity and atonement of Christ

d. The desire of both Muslims and Christians to have an exclusive *ummah* (or community) (1985, 194)

Temple Gairdner has said, "Islam and Christianity are incompatible; they are different in ethos, in aim, in scope, in sympathy" (Vander Werff 1977, 219). When missionaries ask a believer to retain his or her Muslim identity, they are asking the person to identify with more than a sociopolitical entity. They are asking him or her to identify with a religious system whose theology is incompatible with the gospel.

3. Acceptance by the Muslim community. Another presupposition is that if believers from a Muslim background remain within the Muslim community, the community may come to accept them. Beyond that, the community may even allow a movement for Christ to develop within Islam (Livingstone 1993, 179). Livingstone says that he is "empathetic of those Muslim followers of Jesus who seek to stay within the mosques as salt and light." However, he agrees with Parshall's conclusion that the nature of Islam has not allowed an Islamic sect of believers in *Isa* (Jesus) to arise within Islam (1993, 179).

Muslims are not likely to permit a "Jesus sect" to take root within their community. It is more likely that Muslim reaction to being duped will result in an even greater backlash than if conversion followed normal lines. Missionaries cannot remove the offense of the cross.

An Alternative Approach

An alternative to Islamicized contextualization is to enable believers to practice their faith meaningfully and relevantly, yet without demonstrating allegiance to Islam. Individuals still become part of a homogeneous group of believers from a Muslim background.

They develop their own meetings, religious terminology, and worship forms. The believer would not try to prove that he or she is still Muslim. If the government officially allows the believer to change his or her religion from Muslim to Christian, he or she would be free to do so. More likely, the government will not allow the person to change his or her religion. In that event, the believer's identity card would obviously continue to say "Muslim."

The group of believers would have many issues to work through. These might include: prayer, music, terminology, giving, fasting, baptism, evangelism, meeting location, training, birth rites, marriage rites, death rites, holidays, celebrations, etc.

Paul Hiebert recommends a four-step process, which will help the group develop forms that are both culturally relevant and true to scripture: (1) study the local culture—believers should uncritically gather information regarding the traditional beliefs and customs associated with the given form; (2) study scripture related to the question at hand; (3) critically evaluate past customs in light of the relevant scriptures; and (4) arrange the chosen practices into a ritual that expresses the biblical meaning behind the form (1987, 109-110).

As the group works through each of these areas, members will pool their insight into culture and develop ownership of the results. This process alleviates the concern by national leaders that contextualization is another Western innovation being imposed on the churches of the East.

Keeping the matter of approaches in perspective is important. Faithful servants have labored in Muslim lands for centuries. In some locations, they have seen excellent results using traditional approaches. This does not mean that the approach is unimportant. Those seeking to reach Muslims should use the most effective approach possible. They should also avail themselves of the best resources and obtain the best possible training. Yet, reaching Muslims goes beyond the matter of approach. Samuel Zwemer's sentiment was this: "What is needed is not simply new methods, but new men, and this happens only as men encounter Jesus Christ" (Vander Werff 1977, 260).

References

Anderson, John, D.C. 1977. "Our Approach to Islam: Christian or Cultic?" *Muslim World Pulse* 6(1): 2.

Chowdhury, D. A. 1939. "The Bengal Church and the Convert." *The Moslem World* 29. Hartford, Conn.: Hartford Seminary Foundation.

Conn, Harvie M. 1979. "The Muslim Convert and His Culture." In *The Gospel and Islam*. Monrovia, Calif.: MARC.

Hiebert, Paul G. 1987. "Critical Contextualization." *International Bulletin of Missionary Research* 11(3): 109-110.

Livingstone, Greg. 1993. *Planting Churches in Muslim Cities*. Grand Rapids, Mich.: Baker Books.

Parshall, Phil. 1985. *Beyond the Mosque*. Grand Rapids, Mich.: Baker Books.

Teeter, David. 1990. "Dynamic Equivalent Conversion for Tentative Muslim Believers." *Missiology* 18(3): 306-307.

Uddin, Rafique. 1989. "Contextualized Worship and Witness." In *Muslims and Christians on the Emmaus Road*. Ed. J. Dudley Woodberry, 271-271. Monrovia, Calif.: MARC.

Vander Werff, Lyle L. 1977. *Christian Mission to Muslims: The Record*. Pasadena, Calif.: William Carey Library.

Wilder, John. 1977. "Some Reflections on Possibilities for People Movements among Muslims." *Missiology* 5(3): 310-311.

January 1998

Courage in Our Convictions:
The Case for Debate in Islamic Outreach

Jay Smith

Instead of running from a healthy exchange with our Muslim friends, we must take on their challenge and begin finding answers.

MANY HAVE QUESTIONED THE METHOD that I and others are using in England to evangelize Muslims. They say it is wrong, perhaps even dangerous. They tell us that standing on a ladder at Speaker's Corner in Hyde Park challenging Islam openly, or taking on invitations to oppose Muslim apologists in highly publicized, public debates on the authority of the Qur'an is much too confrontational. What's more, they say it is detrimental to the gospel because it "does not honor God or call people to faith in Jesus Christ."

These people fear that these methods set one side against the other rather than engineer substantive communication. They say each is trying to publicly humiliate the other, which leads to building even higher the walls of difference between the two communities. A more likely avenue, they say, is dialogue—defined as an exercise in which two opposing parties come together and discuss their differences in an atmosphere of cordiality and mutual understanding, with the hope that a consensus would then come about.

There are probably many who agree with this premise. That is inevitable, because what I and others like me are doing is not widely practiced, is controversial, and is not entirely thought out. So how should I answer the accusations?

A Redefinition of Dialogue

It might be helpful first to examine what we mean by dialogue. In the Book of Acts, the Apostle Paul used the word "dialogue" a number of times, and exemplified it in his own methodology. He first went to the Jews, and entered the synagogues, where he engaged in *dialego*, which is translated "to think different things, ponder, and then dispute" (May 1990).

Paul's premise for dialoguing was not simply to learn from others, and from there to compromise his beliefs in order to evolve another set of beliefs. He knew this would bring about syncretism—a condition plaguing the worldwide Church today. He used dialogue as a two-way flow of ideas. It was not limited to the pursuit of clear communication, as many modern missiologists define it. Rather, he sought to prove what he said (Acts 17:3). He marshaled arguments to support his case, provided evidence, and therefore engaged in argument.

By argument I do not mean belligerent, rude, or aggressive behavior. Arguments can and do come about whenever there is a difference of opinion. Aggressive behavior enters in when one party runs out of good ideas. When arguments are weak, shouting gets louder. We must make sure our arguments are not weak. As Paul said, "What I am saying is true and reasonable" (Acts 26:25). Paul's intention was not for his hearers to be converted, but to be persuaded (Acts 17:4). His job was to persuade them of the truth of the gospel. What they did with that truth was then their own responsibility.

Should we use this definition of dialogue in our work in London? Our primary intent is and always has been to defend the gospel, and to preach Christ crucified, while standing firm against those who choose to castigate these beliefs. That doesn't mean the truth will not humiliate. But the perceived humiliation evidenced by Muslims today has little to do with my tactics and everything to do with the content of my material. If what we say is true, it does not dishonor God when we speak it even if it may humiliate the people to whom it is directed.

Our primary intent is and always has been to defend the gospel, and to preach Christ crucified, while standing firm against those who choose to castigate these beliefs.

Christ himself publicly humiliated his adversaries and discredited elements of their faith. In Matthew 23:13-33 he called the Pharisees "hypocrites, blind guides, snakes and a brood of vipers!" Would we not say that he also humiliated the money changers in Luke 19:45? It was because of these actions that the leaders of the Jews sought to kill him (Luke 19:47).Why, then, are we being castigated for doing likewise?

The Old Paradigm

I have studied in four seminaries, and was taught by individuals who created their missiology while on the field as missionaries. They did so within the hostile environment of the Muslim world. In the Islamic world you cannot criticize the Qur'an or the prophet or you would find yourself on the next plane home. Missionaries return home with the same missiological principles and strategies that were formed in this hostile environment. Consequently, these principles have permeated the missiological teaching in our seminaries and churches today, and have influenced all of us.

Yet, England and the U.S. are not hostile environments. There is no longer a need to protect ourselves or our ministry from civil or religious authorities. The criteria needed for communicating the gospel in the Muslim world are not relevant for England or for the West. In fact, the limits we place upon ourselves—to not be critical or confrontational—are not practiced by our Muslim friends. It is rare that a Muslim, while in dialogue with a Christian, fails to remind us that our Bible is not only corrupt, but that our Lord is nothing more than a man. We do not castigate him or her for speaking his or her mind, because we live in an environment where the freedom of speech is cherished and practiced. Then why do we choose to censor ourselves? Is this not a double standard? The freedoms we allow our Muslim friends we refuse for ourselves.

Consequently, we are fighting the battle with one hand tied behind our backs. I believe we need to rethink our missiology, which will in turn change our methodology, to reflect this new environment.

Propositional Truth

Many believe the only credible way to do evangelism among Muslims is by a "witness to Christ (in us) and by showing how that witness changes everything." Few would quarrel that we must be a witness to Christ in us. But is that all we are to do? Muslims say it is a corrupt witness, authenticated by an even more corrupted scripture. They compare the witness of "Christians" in the West with those in Islam.

One of the primary reasons people in the U.S. give for converting to Islam is because of the witness of other Muslims. The vast majority of those in the U.S. who have converted to Islam came from Christian circles. There are many Muslims who use friendship evangelism far more effectively than we do.

The battle is much greater then simply outperforming our neighbors in kindness. The battle has to do with truth. It has to do with whether the Creator communicated his revelation to his creation, and whether we can know and recognize the difference between the communicated truth and that which is counterfeit.

Some say that a person won by an argument is at the mercy of a better argument. Similar claims can be made for the alternatives. A person won by an experience is at the mercy of a better experience. Or a person won by charity is at the mercy of a better charity. This is how cults grow. The danger of looking for experience to validate one's faith (or being dependent upon signs and wonders) is that a vacuum is created in the area of persuasion. How do we know the evangelist or healer is speaking the truth? Miracles are required to give him or her validity. The deeds become the argument. One quickly gets disillusioned if the deeds do not match the promises.

Most evangelism training is centered on how to win people to Christ. But before people give their lives to Christ, they want to know whether Christianity is true. They want to know whether it can be held up to objective verification.

We need to show that our faith does not rest solely on personal experience. It is credible because it is backed by propositional truth. It is based on criteria which can be understood (i.e., historical verification). Rendle Short tells us, "We are not concerned to argue that natural science, archaeology or any other branch of learning proves the facts of the Christian religion, but rather that they do not necessarily disprove them" (Short 1954).

I strongly disagree with those who say the Muslim world has seen far too little of a loving witness among Christians in the West (providing the Muslims have the correct definition of what a Christian is—versus simply anyone living in the West, which I believe is all they really see and know). Ask Muslims what their impression is of Bible-believing Christians and you will find few who would criticize us for the way we act. What they say is that we have no credibility for the way we act because the authority for what we believe has been invalidated by the truth of Islam. That is the bad news.

The good news is that we do have evidence for what we believe. That is where our apologetics come in. We also have evidence to dispute their contention that the Qur'an invalidates the revelation which preceded it since it is the purest and final revelation from God. New historical evidence points to many impurities in the Qur'an. It brings into question whether the Qur'an was writ-

We have evidence to dispute their contention that the Qur'an invalidates the revelation that preceded it since it is the purest and final revelation from God.

ten or even existed at the time of Muhammad. News like this must be communicated. In fact, I consider it unloving not to do so.

This brings up the question of how we define a loving witness, as exemplified by Christ and the apostles. We may need to redefine what "loving" means. I love my sons. Because I love them, I discipline them when they step out of line. To do otherwise would not be loving. We often correct friends and loved ones when we feel they are incorrect. To do otherwise would not be friendly. Why, then, is it not acceptable to do the same with our Muslim friends, particularly when to keep quiet will have eternal repercussions?

The Muslim Agenda

We need to take a closer look and ask, "To whom are we communicating the gospel?" It is they, not we, who have taken on the more confrontational, polemical agenda. Look at the literature on their book tables. Go to Muslim meetings on campus and listen to their speakers. Peruse the Muslim web pages on the Internet. There are over two hundred Muslim websites which challenge Christianity. Yet we have only seven to counter them. These Muslims are not seeking to "dialogue" with us—as defined by current missiological thinking. I would be surprised if they ever intended to follow the rules we set, because it ill reflects their own cultural forms for communicating ideas. Instead, they have chosen a tack which better reflects who they are.

And who are they? The vast majority are not from the Middle East, but from Asia. More specifically they are from the Indian subcontinent (Pakistan, India, and Bangladesh), which, along with Indonesia, now makes up almost half the Muslim world—over 500 million Muslims. They have taken on the polemical agenda, because it fits their own historical environment, as minorities among a much greater Hindu majority.

From this background, they have come up with the following three agendas: (1) the West is in decline (morally, socially, economically, spiritually); (2) Christianity is at fault, because of a corrupted scripture; and (3) Islam must and will replace it, as the final and more complete revelation.

I was born and raised in India. I had Muslim roommates and classmates. More recently, I have been to numerous Muslim student meetings on campus. I have also attended Friday sermons at a number of mosques in India, France, Senegal, the U.S., and England. The overarching impression I get is that the method Muslims use the world over to communicate their beliefs is drastically different from what we use in our European, Western settings. I rarely find a Muslim who is not ready to actively and vociferously defend his or her faith. When it comes to aggressive evangelism, they put us to shame. When we fail to do the same they assume we have little to say, and even less to impart to them. I find that sad.

The Early Church

Ironically, this proactive and confrontational method is what Jesus and his disciples used. Defense or *apologia* against an accuser is mentioned five times in the New Testament (Acts 22:1; Acts 25:16; 1 Cor. 9:3; 2 Cor. 7:11; and 2 Tim. 4:16). Twice we are asked to defend the gospel (Phil. 1:7, 16; and 1 Pet. 3:15). A strong defense of our beliefs is not foreign to New Testament teaching.

Jesus, a Jew from the Mediterranean world, was in an environment similar to that which gave birth to Islam. Jesus confronted the Pharisees. He called them hypocrites, blind fools, whitewashed tombs, as well as snakes and vipers (Matt. 23:13-33). He was equally confrontational with the money-changers at the temple (Luke 19:45). He did not seek to discuss their position in an atmosphere of mutual understanding. Rather, he stormed in and upturned their tables.

Paul, for his part, went to the synagogues and marketplaces to reason with those who were there (Acts 17:17). He went to the synagogues and announced that this Jesus, whom they had crucified, was the promised Messiah for whom they had been waiting. Paul was thrown out of the synagogues. But that didn't stop him. He continued preaching in the market squares. From there he was thrown into prison. That didn't shut him up. Paul continued on even in jail, preaching and singing to the people responsible for keeping him there. Uppermost in his mind was the need to persuade people of the truth of the gospel. He sought to, "demolish arguments and every pretension that sets itself up against the knowledge of God, and take captive every thought to make it obedient to Christ" (2 Cor. 10:5). If that isn't proactive and forthright I don't know what is.

Paul not only went to the Jews on their home ground, the synagogues, and reasoned with them using their scriptures (Acts 17:1-2), but he went outside his community to the Greeks in their territory as well. He reasoned with them from within their traditions (v. 17). In Ephesus, a pagan city, he began by "arguing persuasively" at the synagogue for three months (Acts 19:8). When he was forced to leave, he went to the lecture hall of Tyrannus, a secular institution, where he continued his discussions with both Jews and Greeks for two years (Acts 19:9-10). In Rome from morning until evening for two years he boldly "tried to convince" those who came to him about Jesus" (Acts 28:23-31).

Just as those who gave us the gospel
engaged leaders and thinkers from the surrounding world, we must do likewise in our own environment.

When Paul went to the people, he didn't go with religious platitudes. Instead, he learned to speak to them on their level. While in Athens he learned about the Greeks' beliefs. He studied the objects of their worship (Acts 17:22-23). He knew their philosophies, both Epicurean (remote God) and Stoic (pantheistic). He even quoted their writers, Epimenedes of Crete and the poet Aratus (v. 28). After understanding them on their level, he demonstrated the inadequacy of their ideas (v. 29).

Some say Paul's method in Athens was unsuccessful, and so he chose a more spiritual strategy in Corinth. Yet we find that some of the Gentiles in Athens were converted. Two are listed by Luke: Dionysius (a member of the Areopagus—possibly the same Dionysius whom Eusebius later records as the first bishop of Athens—and the woman named Damaris (Acts 17:34).

Other apostles went outside their community and used dialogue to reach those outside the Christian community. When confronted by members of the Synagogue of the Freedmen, the Jews of Cyrene, Alexandria, Cilicia, and Asia, Stephen did not return to his own. Instead, he held his ground and returned their arguments, so much so that "they could not stand up against his wisdom" (Acts 6:9-10). They finally reverted to executing him (Acts 7:57-8:1). Philip was equally comfortable in dialogue with the Ethiopian (Acts 8:26-40).

Jesus also involved himself in dialogue with outsiders. Consider his encounter with the rich young ruler (Matt. 19:16), his confrontation with the Pharisees and Herodians (Mark 12:13); the dispute with his Pharisee host at a dinner party (Luke 7:36-50); his contact with Nicodemus (John 3); and his meeting with the Samaritan woman (John 4).

Just as those who gave us the gospel engaged the leaders and thinkers from the surrounding world, we must do likewise in our own environment, be it London, the U.S., or wherever the Lord chooses to put us. The atmosphere has changed little since the first century, and has perhaps become increasingly vociferous.

What has been our response to the newly aggressive evangelistic stance taken by Islam? Here in England there are few Christians standing up to defend themselves against these attacks. Whether it is through fear, ignorance, a misguided missiological position, or simple lethargy, the church has refused to defend its beliefs. I find my job increasingly an isolated and lonely affair (2 Tim. 4:16-18). This is sad and debilitating, because I strongly believe it is giving Muslims the wrong message.

A New Paradigm

We need to ask ourselves what Muslims are hearing from us. When we fail to stand up for the authority of our scriptures, when we refrain from speaking about the lordship or divine nature of Jesus Christ, or are reluctant to define, let alone defend, the Trinity, and when we continually apologize for what we believe to be true, the message Muslims hear is that we not only misunderstand our beliefs, but we are unsure whether they are accurate. How can we convince them of the truth of the gospel when we look and talk as if we are doubtful ourselves?

Take the example of the Muslim imam, Maulvi Sahib. He is forthright, dynamic, stalwart, and triumphant in his conviction that the Qur'an is the final word of God, and that Islam is the faith for today. Those who listen to him are convicted as much by his presentation as by what he says. This has been brought home to us as we watch our television screens and wonder at the mass hysteria evidenced at many of the Friday rallies across the Muslim world. The closest parallel we have are our evangelistic crusades. Yet, the very vehicle which works so well for those coming to Christ in our own communities, we refuse to use with Muslims for fear of hurting their sensibilities. Attempting to be "Christ-like," we come across as elusive, docile, subdued, and timid.

We think we are communicating the gospel as Christ had intended, yet we fail to look at his example, an example the Muslims emulate better than we do. Meanwhile the Muslims raise up leaders in their communities who look at the model of dialogue as not an exercise for mutual understanding but as an excuse to score points and "win the day."

Have any of us wondered why so few Muslims convert to Christianity, when we know that we speak for truth? Why is it that we are so convinced of the gospel, yet the vast majority of Muslims with whom we speak walk away believing our message is wrong? Could it be our methodology is wrong? Furthermore, is it not curious that those who do come through are not the opinion-makers or leaders within their community? Certainly, one can blame the small numbers of converts on social factors. But could it not also be that our paradigm is inadequate? Could it be that we need to get away from our own ethnocentric European and American way of communicating the gospel, which reflects more our own sensibilities, and take a look at how they do it? I think we must.

Let's be honest. The battle is engaged, and for too long we have been losing it big time. Yet we have been given one of the key weapons with which to fight the battle—historically corroborated evidence which not only authenticates our scriptures but eradicates the authority for the Qur'an. I feel this will bring about a real disillusionment within Islam in the West, as it strikes at the very foundation of all they believe. We welcome criticism of our scriptures, which is proper, as it keeps open the door for a real exchange of ideas and dialogue. We castigate those who seek to do the same with the Qur'an.

We have raised a generation of students ill-equipped to define what they believe, and even less equipped to defend it in public. We expend energy creating a plethora of worn-out excuses as to why we must not hurt the sensibilities of our Muslims friends. At the same time we send our youth to take on the challenge of Islam on the campuses. They are given few rebuttals and even fewer models to emulate.

Instead of running from a healthy exchange with our Muslim friends, we must take on their challenge and begin finding answers. Let us go to those who dispute us and respond to their claims resolutely, showing them that we do have answers to their questions. But let us do it with a conviction born out of honest debate. This will help strengthen the Church, because it forces us to go back to our apologetics and find answers which we know exist. Like Peter, we must be "prepared to give an answer to everyone who asks (us) to give the reason for the hope that (we) have" (1 Pet. 3:15).

Inevitably, our convictions will engender a response in kind, particularly where it involves refuting what Islam believes. We must be prepared to not only defend against their attacks, but take the same questions to them. Those who have gone before us were prepared to die for what they believed. History tells us that all of the disciples bar one gave their lives for the gospel. Are we likewise prepared? I think it is only right that we take the challenge before us and follow their example. Then maybe we will see not just ones and twos coming to the Lord, but entire families, communities, and nations. That is my prayer. I would like to believe it is yours as well.

References

May, Peter. 1990. *Dialogue in Evangelism*. Bramcote, Nottingham: Grove Books Ltd.

Short, Rendle. 1954. *Modern Discovery and the Bible*, 4th ed. Downers Grove, Ill.: InterVarsity Press.

October 1998

Danger! New Directions in Contextualization

Phil Parshall

C5 missionaries are on very shaky theological and missiological ground.

RECENTLY, I WAS SPEAKING TO A GROUP of young people who are highly motivated about Muslim evangelism. They excitedly told me of a missionary who had shared a "new" modus operandi for winning the Sons of Ishamael to Christ. This strategy centers on the Christian evangelist declaring himself to be a Muslim. He then participates in the *salat* or official Islamic prayers within the mosque. The missionary illustrated the concept by mentioning two Asian Christians who have recently undergone legal procedures to officially become Muslims. This was done to become a Muslim to Muslims in order to win Muslims to Christ.

Actually taking on a Muslim identity and praying in the mosque is not a new strategy. But legally becoming a Muslim moves the missionary enterprise into uncharted territory. I address this issue with a sense of deep concern.

C1 to C6

John Travis, a long-term missionary among Muslims in Asia, has put us in his debt by formulating a simple categorization for stages of contextualization within Islamic outreach. He defines his six Cs as "Christ-centered Communities" (see page 22).

Some years ago, a well-known professor of Islam alluded to my belief that Muslim converts could and should remain in the mosque following conversion. Quickly I corrected him, stating that I have never held that position, either in my speaking or writing. My book, *Beyond the Mosque*, deals extensively with the issue of why, when, and how a convert must disassociate him or herself from the mosque (although not from Muslim community per se).

I do, however, make room for a transitional period wherein the new believer, while maturing in his adopted faith, slowly pulls back from mosque attendance. Too sudden of a departure may spark intense antagonism and subsequent alienation. See 2 Kings 5 for an interesting insight on how Elisha responded to the new convert, Naaman, who brought up the subject of his ongoing presence in the heathen temple of Rimmon.

I submit that C1 starts at low contextualization and works up incrementally to C4 at the high end. All within this sector is legitimate, provided it is constantly cross-referenced and subordinated to biblical truth. C5 can be placed anywhere along the syncretism spectrum, depending upon how each issue is presented to and understood by the Muslim community. Personally, I can only put conversion (or reconversion) to official Islam as high syncretism… regardless of motivation.

When, in 1975, our team of missionaries commenced a C4 strategy in an Asian Muslim country, we faced considerable opposition. One long-term Christian worker in an Islamic land told me basically, "You are on a dangerous slide. Next you will be denying the cross." Well, twenty-three years later, we are still at C4 and still preaching the cross. And the Lord has greatly honored our efforts in that country.

But now I am the one to protest the "slide," not by our team, but by others who are ministering in various parts of the Muslim world. This slide is incremental and can be insidiously deceptive, especially when led by people of highest motivation. Now it seems to me we need to bring these issues before our theologians, missiologists, and administrators. Let us critique them before we suddenly find that we have arrived at a point which is indisputably sub-Christian.

A Case Study

We do have help. In a very limited and remote geographical area in Asia, a C5 experiment has been ongoing since 1983. This ministry provides us with a pretty solid baseline for evaluation, even though it has experienced significant personnel changes over the years. Twenty-five national couples went to Islampur* to do development ministry. One of the team's goals was to see a C5 type of outreach evolve. In 1995, seventy-two key people of influence within this movement were interviewed. Researchers suggested that these nationals were representative of possibly 4,500 Muslim converts, as they came from sixty-eight congregations in sixty-six villages. Researchers also stated that the entire believing community might actually have forty-five thousand converts.

Below are the responses of these key people. One has to hypothesize about how the lay people would respond to the same queries.

The Good News
- 76 percent meet once a week in Christian worship.
- 16 percent meet more than once a week in worship.
- 66 percent read or listen to the Gospels daily.
- 21 percent read or listen to the Gospels once a week.
- None do so to the Qur'an. (It is in Arabic and not understood.)
- 55 percent say God is Father, Son, and Holy Spirit.
- 97 percent say Jesus is the only Savior.
- 93 percent say, "Allah loves and forgives because Jesus gave His life for me."
- 100 percent say, "People can be saved from evil spirits by faith in Jesus."

- 100 percent pray to Jesus for forgiveness of sin.
- 97 percent say they are not saved because of Muhammad's prayers.
- 100 percent feel peace and close to God when reading the New Testament.

The Downside
- 50 percent go to the traditional mosque on Friday.
- 31 percent go to the mosque more than once a day. They do standard Arabic prayers which affirm Muhammad as a prophet of God.
- 96 percent say there are four heavenly books—Torah, Zabur, *Injil*, and Qur'an (This is standard Muslim belief—Law, Prophets, Gospels, and Qur'an).
- 66 percent say the Qur'an is the greatest of the four books.
- 45 percent do not affirm God as Father, Son, and Holy Spirit.
- 45 percent feel peace or close to Allah when listening to the reading of the Qur'an.

What Do We Have Here?

Contextualization or syncretism? A few points to emphasize: these are leaders; the work has been ongoing for fifteen years; the believers have had access to the New Testament; there have been short-term Bible schools for leadership; and mosque attendance has been encouraged by the "outside" Bible teachers. Is this a model to follow or avoid? Certainly there is an openness and potential here that is expansive and exciting. But whereas a C5 advocate is happy to keep it all within an Islamic religious environment, I am not.

The Mosque

The mosque is pregnant with Islamic theology. There, Muhammad is affirmed as a prophet of God and the divinity of Christ is consistently denied. Uniquely Muslim prayers (*salat*) are ritually performed as in no other religion. These prayers are as sacramental to Muslims as is partaking of the Lord's Supper for Christians. How would we feel if a Muslim attended (or even joined) our evangelical church and partook of communion…all with a view to becoming an "insider"? This accomplished, he or she then begins to promote Islam and actually win our parishioners over to his or her religious persuasion.

Even C4 is open to a Muslim charge of deceit. But I disagree and see it as a proper level of indigenization. We have not become a "fifth column" within the mosque, seeking to undermine its precepts and practices. C5, to me, seems to do just that and open us to the charge of unethical and sub-Christian activity. In my former country of ministry, our team had an agreement that none of us would go into a mosque and engage in the Islamic prayers. One of our group, however, wanted to secretly "experiment" with saying the *salat*. One Friday he traveled to a remote village and became friendly with the Muslims there. Harry* expressed his desire to learn how to perform the rituals and forms of the prayers.

The Muslim leaders were quite excited to see that a foreigner wanted to learn about Islam. They gave Harry the necessary instruction. At 1 p.m., our missionary was found in the front row of the mosque going through all the bowing and prostrations of the *salat*. No matter that he was silently praying to Jesus. No one knew. After worship, the Muslim villagers all came up to Harry and congratulated him on becoming a Muslim. Embarrassed, Harry explained that he was a follower of *Isa* (Jesus) and that he just wanted to learn about Islam. Immediately, upon hearing these words, the crowd became very angry.

Harry was accused of destroying the sanctity of the mosque. Someone yelled that he should be killed. A riot was about to break out. The local imam sought to pacify the crowd by admitting that he had mistakenly taught the foreigner how to do the prayers. He asked forgiveness from his fellow Muslims. It was then decided that Harry should leave that village immediately and never return.

Another experience relates to Bob,* a very intelligent, productive, and spir-

I am not maligning the motivation of godly missionaries who are practicing and promoting C5 as an appropriate strategy to win Muslims to Christ. But, yes, I am apprehensive.

itually-oriented missionary to Muslims. We met together at a conference and exchanged letters and at least one cassette tape over several years. My great concern was that he openly and dogmatically affirmed Muhammad as a prophet of God. To me, Bob had crossed the line into syncretism. Perhaps his motives were pure, but this progression of identification with Muslims had gone much too far. Today, Bob is out of the ministry and is divorced from his wife.

Guidelines

In 1979, I wrote the following guidelines to help us avoid syncretism while engaged in Muslim evangelism. Nineteen years later, I reaffirm (and reemphasize) these principles.

1. We must be acquainted with biblical teaching on the subject of syncretism. New Testament passages on the uniqueness of Christ should be carefully observed.

2. Islam as a religion and culture must be studied in depth.

3. An open approach is desired. Careful experimentation in contextualization need not lead to syncretism as long as one is aware of all the dangers.

4. Contextualization needs constant monitoring and analysis. What are the people really thinking? What does the contextualized communication con-

vey? What do specific forms trigger in the mind of the new convert? Is there progress in the grasp of biblical truth? Are the people becoming demonstrably more spiritual?

5. Cross-cultural communicators must beware of presenting a gospel which has been syncretized with Western culture. The accretions to Christianity that have built up over the centuries as a result of the West's being the hub of Christianity should be avoided as far as possible.

Conclusion

No, I am not maligning the motivation of godly missionaries who are practicing and promoting C5 as an appropriate strategy to win Muslims to Christ. Several of these Christian workers are my friends. They long to see a breakthrough in Muslim evangelism. Their personal integrity is unquestioned.

But, yes, I am apprehensive. Where does all this lead us? In that earlier mentioned conference, one young Muslim convert came up to me and said he had followed the lead of the missionary speaker. He went in the local mosque and told the imam that he is a Muslim and wanted to learn more of Islam. His secret goal was to build a relationship with the imam. I asked Abdul* how he felt about what he did. With a look of pain and sadness, he replied that he felt very badly about it and would not do it again. Before C5 people broadly propagate this strategy to young, impressionable minds who are excited about the "new" and "untried," I urge them to more fully consider both the Islamic charge of deception as well as the long-term consequences of their actions. I am convinced that C5 missionaries are on very shaky theological and missiological ground.

Let's bring the subject out in the open and dialogue together.

* pseudonym

October 1998

Must All Muslims Leave Islam to Follow Jesus?

John Travis

If the single greatest hindrance to seeing Muslims come to faith concerns cultural and religious identity, much of our missiological energy should be devoted to seeking a path whereby Muslims can remain Muslims, yet live as true followers of the Lord Jesus.

(**Editor's note:** *This article is a response to "Danger! New Directions in Contextualization" by Phil Parshall in the October 1998 issue of* EMQ. *See page 111.*)

FOR THE PAST DECADE MY FAMILY AND I have lived in a close-knit Muslim neighborhood in Asia. My daughter, who loves our neighbors dearly, asked one day, "Daddy, can a Muslim go to heaven?" I responded with an Acts 15:11-type "yes": If a Muslim has accepted *Isa* (Jesus) the Messiah as Savior and Lord, he or she is saved, just as we are. We affirmed that people are saved by faith in Christ, not by religious affiliation. Muslim followers of Christ (i.e., "C5 believers") are our brothers and sisters in the Lord, even though they do not "change religions."

Can a Muslim truly accept Jesus as Savior and Lord, thereby rejecting some elements of normal Islamic theology, and yet (for the sake of the lost) remain in his or her family and religious community? Due to the extreme importance Islam places on community, its nearly universal disdain for those who have become "traitors" by joining Christianity, and our desire to see precious Muslims come to Christ, finding the answer to this question is essential. I agree with Dr. Parshall—it is time for missiologists, theologians, and others, especially those who work face-to-face with Muslims, to seriously seek God's will over this C5 issue.

The Islampur Case Study

The "good news" is certainly very good! These statistics indicate that there may be as many as forty-five thousand C5 believers where, of those interviewed, ninety-seven percent believe Jesus is the only Savior, one hundred percent pray to Jesus to forgive sins, seventy-six percent attend Christ-centered worship once a week, sixty-six percent read or listen to the Gospels daily, and a full fifty-five percent understand the Trinity well enough to affirm God is Father, Son, and Holy Spirit! How many American pastors would be delighted to find these same statistics true of their own congregation?

Looking at the downside statistics, we should not be surprised that forty-five percent feel close to God when hearing the Qur'an read. Since they don't understand Arabic, it must be the familiar melodious chanting that touches their hearts. (Some C4 and C5 believers where I work sing a beautiful worship song which sounds a great deal like Muslim chanting.) It is also not surprising that fifty percent continue to worship in the mosque in addition to attending weekly C5 gatherings. This practice is reminiscent of the early Jewish followers of Christ meeting both in the temple and in homes (with the old community and the new). One village C5 group I know prays at the mosque at noon on Friday, then meets afterwards in a home Bible study and prayer led by Achmad*, a C4 pastor and former Muslim teacher.

In this case, these believers actually find mosque gatherings shallow and lifeless, and, for a time, stopped attending. Their absence greatly threatened the mosque leader and he tried to stamp out their Friday afternoon meetings. Achmad suggested they go back to the mosque, meaningless as it was for them. The imam's face was saved and the new believers have continued to meet for over a year. New Muslim inquirers (even two Islamic teachers) have attended.

Concerning the high regard for the Qur'an among Islampur believers, an

Unsaved Muslims are more likely to attend Bible reading sessions when they also contain some Arabic Qur'anic reading.

apologetic response concerning the Qur'an must be developed whereby the truth in it can be affirmed (especially for purposes of a bridge for witness), yet it is not put on equal (or superior!) status to the *Injil*. Fortunately, until such an apologetic is developed, the Islampur believers are regularly reading the *Injil* rather than the Qur'an. Returning to the case of my friend Achmad, he holds evening "Holy Book reading sessions" in his home. He opens by reading a Qur'anic passage in a respectful manner, then proceeds to the heart of the evening reading from the Torah, Zabur, and *Injil* (the Bible).

Unsaved Muslims are more likely to attend Bible reading sessions when they also contain some Arabic Qur'anic reading. Achmad is careful to read Qur'anic passages which do not conflict with the Bible.

Three final points concerning the Islampur study: First, *these C5 Christ-centered communities are less than fifteen years old and consist entirely of new believers from a highly resistant people group.* They are very much *in process*, and their struggles are not unlike what many first-century congregations faced. We must hope that the same Holy Spirit whom Paul so relied upon to guide and purify those first groups of believers is active as well in these new Islampur groups.

Second, *to attain a more accurate perspective, we need to assess the quality of the new believers' lives in Christ and not just their theology.* Is the fruit of the Spirit evident and do they now show a deeper love for others? Scripture is clear that by qualities such as these we will recognize true followers of Christ (Matt. 7:20, John 13:35). Last, *were it not for the C5 approach used in this church-planting ministry, would there be these many thousands of new believers to analyze in the first place?*

C5 Missionaries (Christians Becoming Muslims to Reach Muslims)

This perhaps is Dr. Parshall's greatest concern, and overall I agree. Christians becoming Muslims to reach Muslims (i.e., C5 missionaries) is a step beyond simply urging new believers to remain in the religious community of their birth (i.e., C5 believers) for the sake of their unsaved family and friends. In our current situation I have counseled my own Christian background coworkers, especially the expatriates, to take on a C4 expression of faith, and not enter Islam to reach Muslims.

Yet I could imagine that in some instances God may call uniquely gifted, well-prepared individuals, whose ministries are firmly backed by prayer, to C5 outreach and religious identity. These C5 missionaries would be Muslims in the literal Arabic sense of the word (i.e. "one submitted to God") and their theology would, of course, differ from standard Muslim theology at a number of key points. They would have to be ready for persecution, and it would be best if these believers were of Muslim background.

If, over time, they made their beliefs clear, and the surrounding Muslim community chose to allow them to stay, should we not praise God for the opportunity they have to share the good news in a place few would dare to tread? It would appear that neither Abdul, the Muslim convert, nor Harry, the Western missionary, was neither called to nor prepared for this kind of work.

Regarding how Muslims would "feel" about such an approach, I think the question is a bit irrelevant. The majority of Muslims that I have talked to object to any activity they perceive as an attempt to attract Muslims to Christianity. However, the C5 approach, which communicates the message of salvation in Christ without the intent to persuade Muslims to "change their religion," might in fact be the one most appreciated by the Muslims.

By separating the gospel from the myriad legal, social, and cultural issues implied in changing religious camps, a more straightforward, less encumbered message can be shared and (we hope) embraced. On the question of how Christians would feel if Muslims entered a church with the purpose of winning converts to Islam, I personally would not be fearful. Indeed, for a variety of reasons, non-Christians often grace the doors of churches, and many in the process come to Christ!

Reinterpreting Muhammad and the Qur'an

Can individuals be a part of the community of Islam and not affirm standard Muslim theology? Yes, so long as they remain silent about their unorthodox beliefs. Indeed, there are millions of "cultural Muslims" who have divergent beliefs or know nothing about Islam, yet who, because of birth and the fact they have not formally left the fold, are seen as a part of the community of Islam. However, the goal of C5 believers (unlike C6 believers) is not to remain silent about their faith, but rather to be a witness for Christ. As they share, eventually the issue of the prophethood of Muhammad and the inerrancy of the Qur'an will arise. A follower of Jesus cannot affirm all that is commonly taught about the Qur'an and Muhammad.

Certain aspects of the role of Muhammad and the Qur'an must be reinterpreted. This will perhaps be the most challenging task of C5: to not do so will, in time, cause these believers to move toward C4 (contextualized, yet not Muslim) or C6 (underground/silent believers). Reinterpretation goes far beyond the scope of this brief article and would require the input of Muslim leaders who have put their faith in Christ.

A tremendous starting point toward reinterpretation is found in Fouad Elias Accad's excellent book, *Building Bridges* (1997). As an Arab scholar and pastor, he suggests ways that Muhammad, the Qur'an, and Qur'anic verses which seem to deny the crucifixion can be reinterpreted (1997, 34-46; 138-141). He cites, as well, examples of Muslims who have successfully remained in the community of Islam after accepting Christ, some referring to themselves as "Muslims who are truly surrendered to God through the sacrifice of Messiah Isa" (1997, 35).

Guidelines for Avoiding Syncretism in C5 Movements

The idea of Muslim followers of Jesus or messianic mosques has been suggested by a number of key missiologists (see Winter and Frazier 1981; Kraft 1979; Conn 1979; Woodberry 1989). We do need guidelines, however, so that a C5 expression of faith does not slip into a harmful syncretism. Those working with new believers should emphasize at least the following in the discipleship process.

1. Jesus is Lord and Savior: there is no salvation outside of him.

2. New believers are baptized, meet regularly with other believers (this may need to be done with great discretion), and take communion.

3. New believers study the *Injil* (and Torah plus Zabur if available).

4. New believers renounce and are delivered from occultism and harmful folk Islamic practices (i.e. shamanism, prayers to saints, use of charms, curses, incantations, etc.).

5. Muslim practices and traditions (e.g., fasting, alms, circumcision, attending the mosque, wearing the head covering, refraining from pork and alcohol, etc.) are done as expressions of love for God and/or respect for neighbors, rather than as acts necessary to receive forgiveness of sins.

6. The Qur'an, Muhammad, and traditional Muslim theology are exam-

ined, judged, and reinterpreted (where necessary) in light of biblical truth. Biblically acceptable Muslim beliefs and practices are maintained, others are modified, some must be rejected.

7. New believers show evidence of the new birth and growth in grace (e.g., the fruit of the Spirit, increased love, etc.) and a desire to reach the lost (e.g., verbal witness and intercession).

We must bear in mind that C5 believers, at some point, may be expelled from the community of Islam. C5 may only be transitional, as Dr. Parshall suggests. Yet, would it not be much better for Muslim followers of Jesus to share the good news over months or years with fellow Muslims who may eventually expel them, than for those new believers to leave their families and community by their own choice, being seen as traitors by those whom they leave?

Conclusion

If perhaps the single greatest hindrance to seeing Muslims come to faith in Christ is not a theological one (i.e., accepting Jesus as Lord), but rather one of culture and religious identity (i.e., having to leave the community of Islam), it seems that for the sake of God's kingdom, much of our missiological energy would be devoted to seeking a path whereby Muslims can remain Muslims, yet live as true followers of the Lord Jesus.

The issues involved in such an approach are thorny and complex and require consideration from a number of different disciplines (e.g., church history, Islamics, theology, missiology). A consultation comprised primarily of people involved in sharing Christ with Muslims, which would grapple with the implications of C5, would be beneficial. Any type of ministry undertaken in the Muslim world involves great risk. But for the sake of millions of souls bound for a Christ-less eternity, and for the sake of God, the risks, efforts, and tensions are worth the price.

* a pseudonym

References

Accad, Fouad Elias. 1997. *Building Bridges: Christianity and Islam*. Colorado Springs, Colo.: Navpress.

Conn, Harvey. 1979. "The Muslim Convert and His Culture." In *The Gospel and Islam*. Ed. Don McCurry. Monrovia, Calif.: MARC, 61-77.

Kraft, Charles H. 1979. "Dynamic Equivalence Churches in Muslim Society." In *The Gospel and Islam*. Ed. Don McCurry. Monrovia, Calif.: MARC, 78-92.

Winter, Ralph and David Frazier. 1981. "World Missions Survey." In *Perspectives on the World Christian Movement*. Eds. Steve Hawthorne and Ralph Winter. Pasadena, Calif.: William Carey Library, 198-201.

Woodberry, J. Dudley. 1989. "Contextualization among Muslims: Reusing Common Pillars." In *The Word Among Us*. Ed. Dean S. Gilliland. Dallas: Word Publishing, 282-312.

Context Is Critical in Islampur Case

Dean S. Gilliland

The Islampur believers who have turned to follow Jesus must be taken very seriously. Even though they call themselves Muslims, they are not like other Muslims.

(**Editor's note**: *This article is in response to "Danger! New Directions in Contextualization," by Phil Parshall in the October 1998 issue of* EMQ. *See page 111.*)

I HAVE THE REPORT OF THE **"ISLAMPUR"** PROJECT before me. My role was research director. The project was not limited to "Islampur." It was designed to compare and test various models for evangelizing Muslims. The particular report Phil Parshall refers to did not endorse or condemn, but provided three cases for whatever light they might shed on approaches to Muslims in various communities. As far as I know, the use and distribution of the results were left to the discretion of the foundation that provided funds for the project.

Apart from the justified concerns raised in the article, I sense a tone of defensiveness in some of the things Parshall has written. Since the late 1970s Parshall has led the way with his books on sensitive thinking about contextualization among Muslims. His writing obviously has raised controversy for some. He has helped us see how cultural innovations can become tools for evangelism among Muslims. Now, in response to a very carefully planned piece of research, he seems to be saying, "Listen, please. I meant this, but not that." He recalls how an older Christian worker had warned him about being on a "dangerous slide." Now, Parshall feels he is the one who must protest the "slide."

If "Islampur" believers have taken the idea of messianic Islam to an unacceptable extreme, Parshall wants us to know that neither he nor his team took them there. As one intimately involved in the research project, I would say that, whatever the outcome, perhaps ten to twenty years from now, it is not Parshall's burden to worry about guilt or blame. We don't know everything at this point. Conversion in any mission situation is a process. In this particular one the factors of process could not be more critical.

Since the article has revealed the "Islampur" case, more needs to be said in fairness to the research. The researcher himself concluded the data presentation with careful words:

Whether in fact a person can be an authentic follower of Jesus and still remain within the fold of Islam raises strong opinions and emotions on many sides....It is, of course, possible that those who endorse radical contextualization of the gospel within Islam are wrong.

He also wrote, however, that after looking at the entire report, "It does seem that there has been a real work of God among the (name withheld) Muslims." Little is known from Parshall's article about the internal problems caused by leaders who took these followers of Jesus in two directions, causing, finally, a near abandonment of the teaching that should have been continuing.

In the background are many painful factors which added to the burden of these simple people who say they believe in and follow Jesus. At one point, the names of key believers in the movement were turned over to the government. Despite internal and external problems, these clusters of followers were able to testify honestly and without coaching to what Jesus, the Bible, the power of the gospel, and other Jesus-people mean to them.

I must emphasize the critical issue of the context. While the context and contextualization are what this case is all about, too often conclusions about what is right or wrong are generalized without attention to a particular case. A practicable and fitting approach in one place will probably not be appropriate

While the context and contextualization
are what this case is all about, too often conclusions about what is right or wrong are generalized without attention to a particular case.

somewhere else. For example, the case behind Parshall's example does not fit the research's second case, which was done in Nigeria.

Some forty-five million Muslims live in Nigeria. The big difference with "Islampur" is that Nigeria also has forty-five to fifty million people who call themselves Christians. There is no way that Muslims who convert to Jesus Christ in Nigeria would ever call themselves Muslims.

In fact, it was a rather well-known esoteric model of evangelizing Muslims in northern Nigeria that attracted the research in the first place. The ministry was not integrated with the churches and was supposedly producing believers who were suffering intensely for their faith. Evangelical churches had come to disown the movement because of the secrecy and clandestine style of the leaders. The movement has now collapsed, even though it had received a lot of publicity and support outside of Nigeria.

Therefore, the Nigeria situation is totally different than the one in "Islampur." In Nigeria, the churches are almost apostolic in their boldness before and among Muslims. Form contextualization (except in the far north) is seen as a kind of imitation of the Muslim way and therefore is looked upon as neither necessary nor desirable. Christian-Muslim confrontation saturates the life of Nigerian people—socially, politically, and religiously.

The Parshall article discusses the appropriateness of an approach in a particular Asian context. The size and strength comparison between Muslims and Christians in "Islampur" is like the elephant to the fly, as it were. Obviously, this little flock that has turned to follow Jesus—with members who pray to Jesus for forgiveness, who believe that Jesus died for them, and who say he is the only Savior—has to be taken very seriously. Even though they call themselves Muslims, they are not like other Muslims.

The words of Jesus are poignant and sobering: "I have other sheep that are not of this fold; I must bring them also, and they will heed my voice. So there will be one flock, one shepherd" (John 10:16). I have mentioned the need for the passage of time because, like any other movement, this one is in process. In the meantime, we should never forget that the Holy Spirit does not abandon his Word or his people. While conversations are well-intended, God goes on doing his work through his Holy Spirit, to bless and honor truth and to remove his blessing from error.

I recall discussions I had with African pastors about the implications of the Apostle Paul baptizing the Philippian jailer and his family immediately, coming as they did straight out of "paganism." It was an emotional and a highly charged situation, with no church except, perhaps, some women of Lydia's household who had also been baptized quickly and privately. Then, after a confrontation with the police, Paul left them for Thessalonica (Acts 16). How much hope would there seem to have been for isolated converts in a place like Phillipi? Still, the church developed there.

I am not saying the situation in "Islampur" is the same as in Philippi, but the Holy Spirit is still at work in poorly informed, sometimes misguided believers. Beyond any human comprehension, the Spirit faithfully guides those who seek the truth. The Good Shepherd said, "I know my own and my own know me" (John 10:14). The Church has always been a mystery (Eph. 3:3, 9), but it is God's Church, and in the end God will make the judgment.

July 2004

Misunderstanding C5:
His Ways Are Not Our Orthodoxy

Joshua Massey

Judging C5 ministry from Greco-Roman Gentile categories of orthodoxy, distance, or church-centered can lead to many misunderstandings.

IMAGINE FOR A MOMENT that your best friend has been given the responsibility of writing your biography. Will he or she be able to properly describe your love life, with all its nuances, unspoken thoughts and feelings? Is there anyone who could accurately put your private story into words on paper? The heart is infinitely complex, as is any love relationship. How much more difficult is it to describe the fullness of a love relationship between humanity and God? Add to this complexity an even greater hurdle: the lover and the readers of his story are rooted in two radically different cultures. Such is the challenge of describing a C5 Muslim follower of Jesus (the lover) to most Christians (the readers) today.

Even the most sincere followers of Christ can easily misunderstand C5 when judging it from: (1) Greco-Roman Gentile categories of orthodoxy, instead of a Jewish understanding of Christ's mandate; (2) a distance, rather than in light of personal relationships with C5 Muslim believers; and (3) church-centered rather than Christ-centered missiology.

Greco-Roman Categories vs. Jewish Understanding of Christ's Mandate

It is difficult to overestimate the powerful influence of Greco-Roman thought on Gentile Christianity today. As Andrew Walls observes,

> Jewish identity has always been concerned either with what a person is and what he does rather than what he believes. But when the Christian faith [i.e., Jewish Messianism] began to penetrate the Hellenistic Roman world, it encountered a total system of thought [with] a certain inbuilt arrogance, a feature it has never quite lost….Basically, it maintained that there is one desirable pattern of life, a single "civilization" in effect, one model of society, one body of law, one universe of ideas. Accordingly, there are in essence two types of humanity: people who share that pattern and those ideas, and people who do not. (1996, 18)

Christian penetration of this total Greek system of thought put its traditions of codification and organization to work for the service of the gospel, ultimately resulting in "orthodoxy" (Walls 1990, 19). Conformity to codified doctrine determined by the ecumenical Councils of Nicaea (325) and Chalcedon (451) became supremely important—no matter how foreign or strange such doctrine would have sounded to Christ's Jewish apostles.

Could it be that many of us today are so constrained by our own Greco-Roman theological constructs that we are quick to filter every expression of cross-cultural love for God through an elaborate grid of doctrinal codifications to determine whether or not they are "orthodox"?

When one empirical study of a large C5 movement reported that more than half of the Muslim believers interviewed said God is "Father, Son, and Holy Spirit," concern was expressed about those who said otherwise, especially because (1) the movement was more than fifteen years old, (2) many respondents were leaders, and (3) they had access to the New Testament (Parshall 1998, 406). Understanding God as triune was surely common among Gentile Christians in the fourth century, but only after, in Walls' terms, the gospel had penetrated and permeated a rather arrogant Greek system of thought culminating in the development of Chalcedonian "orthodoxy."

Given the severe penalties over the centuries for those who did not conform to the elaborate and highly nuanced language of doctrinal fidelity (Moffet 1998, 174), it is surprising to learn that church history provides little evidence to suggest this understanding of God was widespread or common in earliest Christianity. The fact that not one biblical writer felt it necessary to extrapolate that God "is" Father, Son, and Holy Spirit should cause us to pause in the above-mentioned evaluation of the C5 movement. Are we evaluating movements of Christ followers by asking questions the apostles never asked and using criteria the apostles never used?

As the gospel permeated Greco-Roman society in the third and fourth century, Gentile church fathers, enmeshed in the world of neo-Platonism, began to ask questions early Jewish Christians never asked. They found answers in the scriptures that the apostles likely never saw, because their questions were so radically different (see Walls 1991, 53). Walls illustrates the dynamic role of worldview when the "Jesus Act" is seen in the human auditorium of life:

> Everyone in the packed auditorium can see the stage, but no one sees the whole of it. People seated in one place cannot see the entrances left....Seated somewhere else, the view is obstructed by a pillar, or an overhanging balcony. As a result, though everyone sees the same play and hears the same words, they have different views of the conjunction of word and action, according to their seat in the theatre. (1996, 43)

What each person sees in the Jesus Act is clearly governed by where we are sitting. People view the part of the stage most open to them from their seat in the auditorium. As the C5 interview results illustrate, the orthodoxy we take for granted based upon what we think is the "plain meaning" of the text from our theater seats is not as obvious to them from their seats. Perhaps the more amazing fact of that study is that more than half of those interviewed did affirm "Allah" as "Father, Son, and Holy Spirit."

Judging at a Distance vs. Personally from Relationships

As for confidence in our theological conclusions as meticulous students of scripture, we must humbly admit that, according to Jesus, honoring popular interpretations of scripture can sometimes be the root of our inability to see clearly: "You search the scriptures, because you think that in them you have eternal life; and it is they that bear witness to me; yet you refuse to come to me" (John 5:39-40).

While we must test all things by scripture, Jesus' statement here suggests that intensive study of scripture itself will not guarantee a correct perception of its meaning or intended application. Without the Holy Spirit's quickening, scripture can be a series of endless parables about which we can be "ever hearing but never understanding; ever seeing but never perceiving." Christians of all persuasions may sincerely believe they have seen and understood, but it is "the hour of our visitation" which truly tests us. The ways of God, unlike doctrine, cannot be put into a tidy, codified box.

In a forthcoming essay on insider movements, John Travis, architect of the C-Spectrum (1998), rightly states that our theology of mission to Muslims "can only properly be developed through a dynamic interaction of actual min-

An important point missed by C5 critics
is that first and foremost, C5 is not a strategy to reach Muslims—it is a reality effected by the Holy Spirit among numerous Muslim peoples.

istry experience, the specific leading of the Spirit, and the study of the Word of God." This can be clearly seen when Peter, Paul, and James offer case studies and experiential evidence—together with theological explanation—from their own ministries in the Jerusalem Council meeting. There, the early Church decided that Gentiles did not need to be circumcised in order to experience salvation in Christ (Acts 15).

An important point often missed by C5 critics is that first and foremost, C5 is not a strategy to reach Muslims—it is a reality effected by the Holy Spirit among numerous Muslim peoples. In other words, Muslims meet Christ as Savior and Lord and are transformed as they study the Bible and strive to obey all Christ's commands.

However, unlike C4 Muslim Background Believers (MBBs), C5 Christ followers don't see their Muslim identity as part of their background. Walls speaks of "Greek" as a cultural, not an ethnic, term, and so too "Muslim" is a cultural term. Ironically, the Muslim culture enjoyed by most C5 believers is far more "Jewish" than the "Christian culture" in most Gentile churches today. Therefore, this culture is much more similar to the piety and liturgy Jesus and his apostles observed than that of Gentile Christians today (Acts 21:20, Woodberry 1996, Massey 2004, Neusner 2000). C5 Messianic Muslims do not want to turn their back on their culture or their nation (Walls 1996, 52).

Just as in New Testament times many Gentile Christians were ready to submit to circumcision in order to achieve full status as God's people, many Muslims have been willing to convert to "Christianity"—especially those who were only nominally Muslim or disillusioned with Islam. We will discuss below the dynamic freedom of Muslims to do this. Nonetheless, a growing number of Muslim followers of Jesus have chosen not to follow the way of the Jewish proselyte. They want to follow Jesus as Muslims.

When you personally meet some of these believers, their Christ-centeredness is unmistakable. Like Peter who saw the Holy Spirit poured out on Gentiles, we are forced to reevaluate our Christianizing tendencies, even as Peter and James were forced to reevaluate their Judaizing tendencies. Reading empirical case studies on paper might help, but that is no substitute for actual ministry experience with C5 Muslim believers.

It is terribly easy to misunderstand what God is doing among C5 movements of Christ-centered Muslims if we attempt to evaluate them from a distance, based solely upon the feeble attempts of witnesses to describe (orally or in writing) a C5 Muslim believer's love relationship with Jesus. Rather, we must get to know some C5 Muslim believers ourselves, hear directly from them how they have handled the challenges of following Christ as Muslims, and see their passion to draw their fellow Muslims to the throne of Christ.

Christ-centered vs. Church-centered

Although the C-Spectrum was originally developed to describe six kinds of Christ-centered communities found in the Muslim world today, C5 nomenclature was quickly adopted by those whose theology of mission is more Christ-centered than church-centered. They were more focused on encouraging Christ-centered "insider movements" of Muslims within Islam than merely contextualizing Western Christianity.

They were more convinced that Jesus wants his disciples to plant the leaven of God's rule and reign directly within Muslim communities, letting it rise through society to permeate the very Islamic institutions that guide the faith of Muslim peoples.

Advocates of C5 insider movements are equally concerned about the dangers of syncretism and lazy tolerance, but they are also more concerned about true Christ-centeredness than with conformity to Gentile Christian traditions and doctrinal codifications developed centuries after the apostolic era. Unlike many Jewish missionaries of his day, Jesus did not ask Samaritans or Gentiles to convert to Judaism. Jesus did not call people to religion, but to himself. What mattered most was faith in him, worshiping God in spirit and truth, submitting to Christ's rule and reign as God's only anointed King. Christ-centeredness has less to do with religion, and everything to do with Jesus.

We tend to assume that if people come to Christ, they will also be "with us." Aren't we his disciples and representatives? However, we must never forget that the Kingdom of God is not about us.

A Christocentric view asserts that the fullness of divine revelation and the finality of humanity's redemption ultimately centers upon Christ. And because Muslim peoples are sitting in different seats in the human auditorium to view the Jesus Act, they may not see all that our Western church fathers saw, or add all that we added to the Palestinian Jewish original. But as they obey Jesus' commands and follow him as Lord, they will see him incarnate within their own society as Christ is introduced into areas of thinking and brought to bear upon ideas that we can scarcely glimpse (see John 14:21).

The "Christian" Direction of C4

C4 advocates appear to accept the fact that the Kingdom of God is not about "Christianity," since they generally avoid the term "Christian" because its meaning has been irreparably damaged in Muslim lands. However, despite all its contextual friendliness, C4 attitudes toward Muslim identity reveal underlying beliefs about the direction Muslims should go: "out" of Islam, although not necessarily "into" Christianity. Theoretically, this works nicely and gives Muslims permission to withdraw from all "biblically impermissible" Islamic forms (or at least from forms the missionary cannot permit). Sociologically, however, things aren't so nice or neat.

When a C4 MBB shares his or her faith, Muslims may ask, "Are you Christian?"

"Oh no!" he or she replies, "I am a follower of the True Path" [or something else creative].

"Oh," the Muslim responds, "you're a Muslim!"

"Well, uh, not actually," he or she replies and masterfully crafts some acceptable identity for his or her context—or does he or she? Actually, it can be extremely difficult to establish the necessary trust in relationship if one waffles on such basic questions about religious identity. Like most Christians, Muslims do not have a religious category for Christ followers who are neither Christian nor Muslim. You must be one or the other.

Furthermore, many C4 MBBs spend years going back and forth between Christian and Muslim communities like a sociological chameleon, trying to maintain acceptance in two different worlds. C4 identity (being neither Christian nor Muslim) is a very difficult position for MBBs to maintain. The more they behave like Gentile Christians, the more they will be trusted by C1–3 believers but distrusted by Muslims. Unfortunately, the more they retain their Muslim culture (e.g., diet, dress, beard, language, liturgy, etc.), the more suspect they tend to be in Christian communities.

Theoretically, C4 MBBs should not have to enter C1–3 communities at all. Practically, however, their paths tend to cross more often than C4 advocates would prefer, and so begins the process of Christianization which inevitably pulls Muslims "out" of their community and "into" some form of Christianity.

C5 Muslims, by contrast, don't have to bother with such religio-cultural gymnastics. They know they are Muslims, and they know they have been transformed by the Spirit of God. Like the Hellenistic-Roman world, the Muslim world represents a total system of thought which must be penetrated with the gospel of the kingdom, rising through Muslim society like leaven. C5 advocates believe that after thorough study of the Bible, Muslim believers are best equipped to make judgments about what is biblically permissible or not.

Rather than cloud their judgment with centuries of Gentile interpretations of scripture through a Greco-Roman filter, cultural outsiders (pro-C5 missionaries) keep pointing C5 Muslim leaders back to prayer and the Bible for answers, confident that the Holy Spirit will "guide them into all truth" (John 16:13). This does not imply that C5 advocates never point Muslims to specific scriptures for study, for the New Testament surely provides precedent for such directive discipleship. Nonetheless, efforts to promote true indigeneity are not just limited to various forms of worship, liturgy, sacramental rites, literature, art, and architecture. Instead, their understanding of scripture itself is also a prime candidate for indigeneity as C5 advocates encourage Muslim believers to view the Jesus Act from their seat in the human auditorium.

Rethinking Islam

C5 Muslim believers are, of course, rethinking and redefining Islam according to the authority of the Bible. Some are even calling their Muslim countrymen "back to the Qur'an," since most unbiblical Islamic beliefs are more rooted in Islamic traditions (*hadith*) or in poorly interpreted verses of the Qur'an. Once Muslims see that Qur'anic verses alluding to corruption in the Bible were rightly and only leveled against entrepreneurial Jews selling thrice-targumated phylacteries (Sura 2:79), they can better understand why the Qur'an commands all Muslims to believe the Bible, and many other verses proving the Bible could never have been corrupted (5:47, 10:94, 4:136). Although scholars of textual criticism may beg to differ (Ehrman 1993), the Qur'an itself is proving to be a powerful apologetic in the hands of Muslim believers for restoring Muslim confidence in the inerrancy of scripture.

Rethinking Islam in the light of scripture is no simple task, but our role as outsiders is not to do their thinking for them—i.e., if we really want to promote indigeneity by discipling their nation (and not just a few individuals within their nation). The fact is, as outsiders, we are scarcely qualified to rethink Islam since most of us were never reared to "think" Muslim in the first place. Our role is to keep pointing them to Jesus and the scriptures, and to resist the temptation to filter their reality through our own tradition. Walls notes:

This is likely to mean the appearance of new themes and priorities undreamt of by ourselves or by earlier Christian ages; for it is the mark of Christian faith that it must bring Christ to the big issues which are closest to men's hearts; and it does so through the structures by which people perceive and recognize their world; and these are not the same for all. (1996, 24)

For example, when C5 Muslims were translating Mark's Gospel into their language, they were perplexed at how to handle the parenthetical statement in Mark 7:19, "Thus he declared all foods clean." Clashing with their own worldview about dietary cleanliness, which agrees with the Torah and Jesus' own dietary practice, they wondered if this was a later insertion by Gentile scribes, what Bart Ehrman calls "an orthodox corruption of the scripture" (1993).

Did Jesus abrogate the Law? Is there any evidence that his Jewish disciples began eating non-kosher foods after this teaching? The most difficult thing for them to imagine, of course, was: How could Jesus have declared swine flesh clean? No one pointed out to them that the context of hand washings in Mark 7 indicates that Jesus wasn't declaring *treif* foods kosher, but rather that kosher foods weren't ritually defiled if touched by ritually unclean hands (Stern 1991, 160).

Nonetheless, they found another way to deal with that verse. After much prayer and thought, they decided not to omit the phrase but to translate it di-

Perhaps the greatest challenge for those of us separated by language, history, and culture is to recognize each other in Christ.

rectly. When the foreign translation consultant (committed to an insider model of letting them call the shots) asked how they arrived at this conclusion, they said, "It was simple: pork is not food for us. Do you eat fried scorpions, beetles, and locusts when you visit Thailand? No, because that is not food for you, just as pork is not food for us." Does God's declaration that reptiles are clean in Acts 10 mean we should all eat snakes and lizards to demonstrate our freedom in Christ?

In the study quoted above, nearly half of those interviewed did not describe God as Father, Son, and Holy Spirit. However, these same Muslim believers do not hesitate to baptize new followers of Jesus "in the name of the Father, Son, and the Holy Spirit," just as Jesus commanded. Perhaps fifteen years of baptizing in this way was the defining factor that led them to conclude that this threefold formula does describe God. If so, they seem to be well ahead of our Greco-Roman church fathers, given the length of time it took them to draw such conclusions.

Perhaps the greatest challenge for those of us separated by language, history, and culture is to recognize each other in Christ. Herein may lie the greatest difficulty for critics of C5. Those of us who whole-heartedly endorse C5 do so because, like Peter and James mentioned above, our theology has been informed by an unexpected field experience, personally knowing C5 Muslims who deeply love the Lord Jesus and desire to spread this saving knowledge to fellow Muslims. Critics don't have such relationships, and so base their objections on various biblical points of reference without having seen "the Holy Spirit poured out upon them."

Case studies can be helpful (Jameson and Scalevich 2000; Travis and Workman 2000; Dutch 2000), but they are ultimately not an effective substitute for such personal relationships, even as many Judaizers remained unconvinced after the testimonies of Paul, Barnabas, Peter, and James (Acts 15:1-29, 21:18-26). Furthermore, after seeing how some have abusively used and even published confidential case studies of C5 work, many are understandably hesitant to distribute such reports widely.

If our own history is any indication, this Messianic Muslim movement won't be tidy. The Christological controversies of the fourth century were so heated that scholars are quick to acknowledge that their so-called "settlement" involved "personal feuds between bishops and theologians, conflicts between traditionalism and unrestrained speculation, and the politics of Roman emperors who needed a united church to preserve a united empire" (Rusch 1980:17).

We must therefore give Muslim followers of Christ the same freedom enjoyed by our Greek fathers to work out their own theology of how Christ-centeredness will transform their worldview. It may be as different from ours as the fourth century Gentile Christian translation was from the Palestinian Jewish original. So let us not oppose them or be suspicious of their Christ-centeredness, "for whoever is not against us is for us" (Mark 9:40). Rather, let us embrace them with open arms "until we all attain to the unity of the faith and of the knowledge of the Son of God, to mature manhood, to the measure of the stature of the fullness of Christ" (Eph. 4:13).

Finally, let us guard against the kind of dogmatic judgmentalism that fueled the agendas of Judaizers, who couldn't see beyond God's work in their own religio-cultural history. Although convinced their arguments were solidly biblical, Ebionite Jewish Christians ultimately missed an amazing era in redemptive history as God's kingdom broke forth among Gentiles. Let us not similarly miss what God is doing among Muslim followers of Christ today.

References

Dutch, Bernard. 2000. "Should Muslims Become 'Christians'?" *International Journal of Frontier Missions* 17(1): 15-24.

Ehrman, Bart D. 1993. *The Orthodox Corruption of Scripture: The Effect of Early Christological Controversies on the Text of the New Testament.* New York: Oxford University Press.

Jameson, Richard and Nick Scalevich. 2000. "First-Century Jews and Twentieth-Century Muslims." *International Journal of Frontier Missions* 17(1): 33-39.

Massey, Joshua. 2000. "The Amazing Diversity of God in Drawing Muslims to Christ." *International Journal of Frontier Missions* 17(1):5-14.

_____. 2004. "Living Like Jesus, A Torah-Observant Jew: Delighting in God's Law for Incarnational Witness to Muslims, Part 1." *International Journal of Frontier Missions* 21(1): 33-39.

Moffet, Samuel Hugh. 1998. *A History of Christianity in Asia: Beginnings to 1500.* Maryknoll: Orbis Books.

Neusner, Jacob. 2000. *Judaism and Islam in Practice: A Sourcebook.* London: Routledge.

Parshall, Phil. 1998. "Danger! New Directions in Contextualization." *Evangelical Missions Quarterly* 34(4): 404-410.

Rusch, William G. 1980. *The Trinitarian Controversy.* Philadelphia: Fortress Press.

Stern, David H. 1991. *Messianic Jewish Manifesto.* Clarksville, Md.: Jewish New Testament Publications, Inc.

Travis, John. 1998. "The C1 to C6 Spectrum: A Practical Tool for Defining Six Types of 'Christ Centered Communities' ('C') Found in the Muslim Context." *Evangelical Missions Quarterly* 34(4): 407-408.

Travis, John and Andrew Workman. 2000. "Messianic Muslim Followers of Isa: A Closer Look at C5 Believers and Congregations." *International Journal of Frontier Missions* 17(1): 53-59.

Travis, John and Anna Travis. 2005. "Appropriate Christianity for Muslims." In *Appropriate Christianity.* Ed. Charles Kraft. Pasadena, Calif.: William Carey Library.

Walls, Andrew F. 1996. *The Missionary Movement in Christian History: Studies in the Transmission of Faith.* Maryknoll, N.Y.: Orbis Books.

Woodberry, J. Dudley. 1996. "Contextualization among Muslims: Reusing Common Pillars." *International Journal of Frontier Missions* 13(4): 171-186.

Lifting the Fatwa

Phil Parshall

Moving toward dialogue on seven major areas that serve as flashpoints among those in ministry to Muslims.

I WAS SOMEWHAT SHOCKED TO READ the following statement by a respected Christian leader who is involved in a controversial approach to Muslim evangelism: "I am praying Phil will lift his Fatwa against our ministry among the followers of Ishmael." The October 1998 *EMQ* kicked off public debate on how far contextualization has gone, is going, and will probably continue to go. My lead article expressed concern that a legitimate strategy could tumble into syncretism if great care is not exercised.

And so, where are we now—six years down the road? It is appropriate, I think, to say that the flashpoints center around seven major areas: (1) usage of the C1 to C6 spectrum as conceptualized by John Travis; (2) usage of certain scriptures to validate one's position; (3) encouraging the Muslim Background Believer (MBB) to continue calling himself or herself a "Muslim" without qualifier; (4) the MBB remaining in the mosque permanently as a strategy to win Muslims to Christ; (5) explicitly or implicitly affirming the Islamic creed *shahada*, "There is no God but Allah and Muhammad is His Prophet"; (6) insertion of *Isa-al-Masih* (Jesus the Messiah) for "Son of God" in Bible translations; and (7) delineating an appropriate response toward those who disagree with one's position on some or all of the above.

The purpose of this article is to briefly explore these seven areas. Unfortunately, space restrictions will inevitably bring the critique that I have dealt superficially with some or all of these issues. But, at minimum, these thoughts should move us more toward a dialogue rather than the in-house monologue that currently is pervasive among concerned churches, mission boards, missionaries, and MBBs.

1. Usage of the C1 to C6 Continuum

All of us are indebted to Travis for his abbreviating an evangelistic strategy. It is much more convenient to say, "I practice C4," rather than give a lengthy, but accurate, description that loses the audience. But unfortunately, a heavy fog has resulted, producing more confusion than clarity. Numerous times I have heard people who profess to be C5 vehemently deny that they believe in some important strategy point that another self-declared C5er holds. Let me illustrate. Some of us naively thought that comprehensive contextualized

Muslim evangelism outreach originated in the mid-1970s in a certain South Asian country.

Enter Sadrach (Partonadi 1988). This Indonesian man was born in 1835 and died in 1928 at age ninety-three. Until he was thirty-two, Sadrach was a devout Muslim. Following his conversion, he worked tirelessly to create a church. At the time of his death, there were 7,500 MBBs on the island of Java who related to his work. Some characteristics of his contextualized ministry were:

- Leaders were called *imams.*
- Festivals similar to that of Islam were observed.
- They collected *zakat* (offerings).
- Church buildings were called mosques. No crosses were displayed.
- They used a drum to call people to worship as did the Muslims.
- Cows were prayed over at the time of their slaughter in Islamic fashion.
- The following creed was recited in their churches: "I believe that God is one. There is no God but God. Jesus Christ is the Spirit of God, whose power is over everything. There is no God but God. Jesus Christ is the Spirit of God." This was chanted in a *dhikr* (recitation) style with intense emotion, which was purported to lead to some sort of mystical union between God and devotee.
- Believers called themselves "Christians." They did not affirm Muhammad in any manner, but rather spoke very openly of the superiority of Jesus over Muhammad.

So, do we have C1, C2, C3, C4, C5, or an amalgam of all five? Without seeking to annihilate the Cs, I only press the need for clarity when using such an identification of strategy.

2. Hermeneutical Integrity or Carelessness?

The answer depends somewhat upon where you have come from and where you want to go. Contextualists have always relied heavily on 1 Corinthians 9:19-22. In the present controversy, "becoming a Muslim in order to win Muslims" has a very different meaning to the C4 and C5 camps. Each insists that their own exegesis of these verses is proof positive of their position's validity.

But the new hermeneutic on the block swirls around 1 Corinthians 7. In the passage, "Each one should remain in the situation which he was in when God called him" (vs. 20), certain contextualists see an exhortation for MBBs to remain maximally Muslim. Scott Woods, an experienced missionary among Muslims in Indonesia, comments:

The context in 1 Corinthians 7 is addressing the issues of marriage and singleness; believers married to unbelievers; circumcision and uncircumcision; and finally slaves and free. This passage has nothing to do with dictating that people from a false religion should remain in their false religion so as not to upset the apple cart. C5 proponents could be accused of isogesis here....This passage makes provision for believers remaining in their familial and social status where they were prior to knowing Christ, but it is not giving an allowance for believers to continue in their former religion. (2003, 190)

As each strategist carves out his or her theological apologetic, it is important to grapple with biblical teaching and implication. Admittedly, church history has proven repeatedly through the centuries that the one absolute certainty in this process is that God-fearing, true believers will frequently differ with one another in their conclusions!

Some say, "Just give the Bible to the MBB and let him or her come to his or her own conclusion." But we must remember the scriptural mandate to teach new believers.

3. Identity Issues

Does the MBB continue to bear the name 'Muslim" without any qualifier? Ramsay Harris,* a long-term missionary among Arabs, told me:

> Most of those I have led to Christ do NOT identify themselves as Muslims anymore, but some do. I do not push them either way....For most people the word "Muslim" means "an adherent of the religion of Muhammad"....But there is one principle which must be universal: one must always identify oneself with the person of Jesus Christ (Matt. 10:33 and 1 Pet. 4:16).

Harris' latter point highlights the controversy. "I am a Muslim follower of *Isa-al-Masih*" is much more readily accepted by certain missionaries than just the designation "Muslim." The word "Muslim" is defined as one who is submitted to God. In practice, however, every Muslim worldwide thinks of this term as referring to those who adhere to Islam's theological tenants. At this point the charge of deceit kicks in.

Are we purposefully misleading? Is integrity at stake? The answer for some is, "Definitely not." They say one must look at "Muslim" in its broadest cultural and societal context like with the word "Christian." How many people who call themselves Christians are really practitioners of the faith? Are they then deceivers or just going with the flow of society?

The rebuttal will say, "Yes, but these people are not seeking to use the term as a strategy to win others to their faith." And so, the arguments and counter-arguments go on and on.

4. Should the MBB Remain in the Mosque?

The pro camp points to early Christians continuing to worship in the synagogue. Woods writes:

> Paul came...to preach Jesus…to the synagogue members. Most C5ers come into the mosque and line up in the *shalat* line. They are perceived as Muslims. They have no distinguishing mark that says they are followers of *Isa*. Even if they pray to *Isa*, the perception is that they are Muslims. Paul was clearly received (at times) within the Jewish setting but acknowledged as a follower of the risen Messiah. Is this the same with our C5 MBBs? (2003, 193-194)

All of us would probably agree that there is validity in MBBs remaining in the mosque for a brief time following conversion. Otherwise there would be a serious societal dislocation. The disagreement is over whether they should remain permanently within the context of false religious teaching. The pro-mosque position emphasizes that the MBBs will give discrete testimony of their faith to the Muslims in the mosque.

Therefore, it would be up to the imams to excommunicate the MBB. He or she is free to stay as long as they will have him. Harris believes MBBs could continue to pray in the mosque with these conditions: (1) it does not violate the MBB's own conscience, (2) it is not done for purposes of deceit or denial of Christ, and (3) the MBB does not speak in prayer words which the MBB does not believe (for me, personally, this includes the *shahada*). Harris goes on to say, "All of the MBBs I have led to Christ simply find the mosque BORING and depressing after they have come to know the spiritual riches of Jesus Christ."

5. Recitation of the Islamic Creed

This issue flows from one's identification as a Muslim and continued mosque attendance. The creed is a central foundation upon which all of Islam rests. It not only affirms the oneness of Allah, but also the centrality of Mu-hammad as a prophet or messenger of God. It is impossible to be a true Mus-lim without affirming this creed.

Brian Armstrong,* who served many years in the Middle East, was an early theoretician and practitioner of the C5 movement. He told me this concern-ing the creed:

I believe that an MBB can repeat the creed with conviction and integrity, without compromising or syncretizing his faith in Jesus....the recognition of Muhammad would be in his prophetic mission as a messenger proclaiming one god and submission to his will in the context of idolatrous seventh century Arabia, or, in the pagan pre-Islamic setting of any given people who have subsequently accepted Islam. Although Muham-mad's mission was chronologically A.D., we should not allow this to cloud the fact that the spiritual milieu to which he spoke was substantially B.C....In a Jesus movement in Islam, Muhammad would be understood as an Old Testament-style messenger. For those Christians who may stumble at certain aspects of Muhammad's lifestyle, I urge them to study more objectively the lives of the Old Testament prophets where both holy war, in a form more violent than Islam calls for (genocide in the book of Joshua), and polygamy were quite common."

Okay, but if one affirms the "prophet" of the creed, doesn't it follow that one must therefore believe his prophecy? And that prophecy, being the Qur'an, presents us with a major problem. It is not my place here to exegete the vary-ing views of Qur'anic teaching, but my conclusion is that I cannot affirm the Qur'an as the word of God. In my opinion, articulating the creed automatical-ly defines me theologically. However I may reinterpret the words, onlooking Muslims would accept me as one of theirs, in every sense of the word.

6. "Son of God" Becomes *Isa-al-Masih*

The words "Son of God" have always been repugnant to Muslims. They can only understand this term in a biological framework. For God to have offspring is pure blasphemy. Understood—but how can we overcome this error of understanding among our Muslim friends? Some current contextualists have opted for radical surgery followed by a linguistic transplant: just remove "Son of God" and insert *Isa-al-Masih*. This new translation is being promoted in a number of languages throughout the Islamic world. Early feedback from Muslims and MBBs is positive. The offense of the word "son" is gone. Jesus as Messiah is retained and highlighted. The meaning of "Messiah" can then be explained.

This approach's defense is that certain NT passages place Son of God and Messiah together, thus proving the term's interchangeability (see Luke 4:41; Matt. 16:16; and Matt. 26:63-64).

Rick Brown is an international translation consultant. He shares these insights:

The fact is, although Jews had different concepts for the awaited Messiah, they used most titles interchangeably, and both "Christ" and "Son of God" were fairly equivalent. But because these were favored by nationalistic zealots, Jesus generally avoided them both, preferring the inclusivist heavenly savior title, "the Son of Man," or the shortened form, "the Son," and sometimes "the Lord." (2000, 48)

In a personal letter I asked Rick his view about replacing "Son of God" with *Isa-al-Masih* in Bible passages where they do not appear together. He responded:

Although the title "Son of God" evokes the same concept as *Masih*, it also evokes the concept of God, and this will be lost if one says only *Isa-al-Masih*. So I would suggest, "the *Masih* whom God has sent"....In general, for our audience, it is best to put "Son of God" in the footnote or introduction.

I leave it to linguistic experts to grapple with this, the newest contextual controversy to come down the pike.

7. How Do We Respond?

Adherents to some or all of the C5 position are growing. The country where C5 was birthed now lays claim to tens of thousands of MBBs of the C5 variety. Thousands of C4 MBBs are found there as well.

Scores of missionaries and several evangelical mission boards are practicing and promoting C5 in a significant number of Muslim countries. I personally have known many of these missionaries, some for twenty years. There is no doubt that they are sincere, and long with all their hearts to see Muslims come to Christ. In one instance, a highly respected evangelical Islamist checked out a large C5 movement and declared it to be a wonderful work of God. Armstrong comments:

Those who will be involved in encouraging a movement for Jesus in Islam cannot be heresy-hunters or suspicious types, always ready to pounce on every manifestation of Christ that does not immediately stack up to what they have been used to before. They cannot be the kind of people that can only see "black and white," for the world they will be laboring in will be full of shades of gray.

He continues, "If we are so unfortunate to be the mission that plants a heresy, are those that adhere to it any worse off than before?" It is his view that such a "heresy" could be a future stepping-stone for those Muslims to come to full-blown faith in Christ. I struggle to form a personal position on such an important issue.

The Lord has been speaking to me as I have been seeking to process the macro picture. Scripturally, I have been meditating on these verses:

• Romans 14:10: "Why do you judge your brother? Why do you look down on your brother?"
• Romans 14:13: "Let us stop passing judgment on one another."
• Romans 15:7: "Accept one another as Christ accepted you."
• Romans 15:2: "Each of us should build up our neighbor."

I am quite aware of other New Testament scriptures that call theological aberrants "dogs," call down a curse on them, and designate them as anti-Christs. In church history we find the same theme in the Inquisition. Even the Reformers had heavy words for those who dared disagree with their interpretation of scripture. And so, where do we end up? Consider the Fatwa (which was never decreed!) lifted. I do not want to end my life (now sixty-five years into it) known as a heresy-hunter. Yes, I will continue (with greater sensitivity, I trust) to voice my concerns. But if I am to err toward imbalance, I want it to be on the side of love, affirmation, and lifting up my colleagues as better than myself. Even at this late stage in life, I am not prepared to profess personal infallibility. As for who is right or wrong, and to what degree, let us lean heavily on the ultimate Judge of our hearts' intents.

*pseudonym

References
Brown, Rick. 2000. "The 'Son of God'—Understanding the Messianic Titles of Jesus." *International Journal of Frontier Missions* 17(1): 39-52.

Partonadi, Sutarman Soedeman. 1988. *Sadrach's Community and Its Contextual Roots.* Amsterdam: Rodopi.

Woods, Scott. 2003. "A Biblical Look at C5 Muslim Evangelism." *Evangelical Missions Quarterly* 39(2): 188-195.

Issues of Identity in a Muslim Context: Common Ground?

Gary Corwin

Seven beliefs which may open up paths to unity among those who minister to Muslims.

FOR THE LAST DECADE THERE HAS BEEN AN ONGOING DEBATE in mission circles on appropriate limits to contextualization among various socio-religious groups—Muslim peoples in particular. Our comments will speak to those Muslim contexts where in the last two years the focus of the debate has become more vigorous and public.

The crux of the issue has to do with the identity of new believers. On the one hand, if belief means anything, it seems obvious that followers of Jesus Christ are Christians and not Muslims. On the other hand, it seems perfectly logical that those born in a Muslim land and following the social dictates of their Muslim community are not "Christian" ("one who walks in the degenerate and depraved ways of the West"), whatever they may believe about Jesus Christ. Hence the confusion and debate about identity.

As I have engaged publicly in this debate recently, it has struck me that there are certain things on which most followers of Christ should be able to agree. Furthermore, some of these things may open up paths that lead to greater understanding and unity. Here are seven:

1. All believers must answer to the Lord for their own decisions regarding what is biblically permissible in their own personal conduct. It is not the role of a follower of Christ to judge issues of conscience for his or her fellow servants (Rom. 14:4). This would seem particularly so where issues of life, death and persecution are involved.

2. At the same time, new believers are by no means the only party cross-cultural workers and local believers must have in view. With regard to contextualization, it is the opinions of non-believing Muslims that matter most in determining whether an act is viewed as having either appropriate respect for one's community or having disgraceful deception.

3. The acceptability of followers of Jesus Christ engaging in some Muslim practices will vary greatly depending on the local context. The greater the distance from Mecca, the more "wiggle room" there will be for reinterpreting certain practices without charges of defilement or deception being leveled.

**4. While all Christians agree that "biblically permissible" is the stan-

**dard by which all actions must be assessed, there is significant differ-
ence of opinion concerning what meets that standard.** It is that high and
peculiar standard, however, and not personal comfort levels, that must be normative.

**5. Both self-identity and community-assigned identity are at the
center of the current debate, and while inter-related, both must be
addressed on their own terms.** Individual believers are obviously in the
driver's seat when it comes to self-identity—they determine how they will describe themselves. This is not the case with their community-assigned identity
which will be determined more than anything else by the theological sophis-
tication of the community and its history of interaction with both Islamic and
biblical teaching. An unsophisticated community, for example, might define
a "good Muslim" simply as anyone who does not eat pork or drink alcohol.
Conforming to that definition would certainly seem a biblically permissible
accommodation of "becoming all things to all men." Likewise, being known
as a "Muslim" in that context would offer few risks to the testimony of a true
believer in Christ as long as there was clarity that confidence of salvation did
not rest on following those proscriptions.

6. Defining terms is essential. In some contexts, it may be possible and
desirable to be considered a "Muslim" in the eyes of a community. The chief
obstacle to be overcome is to make clear that one is not a Muslim in terms of
faith commitment (as that has been historically and theologically defined),
because too much is denied about Christ and the authority of the Bible. Where
being a Muslim is understood as (1) affirming that Muhammad is the "seal of
the prophets" (the final authoritative word), (2) affirming the "law of abrogation" (asserting that the most recent prophecy supersedes what came before),
or (3) assuming the corruption of our current Bible, it is hard to imagine how
one could affirm all that without also denying Jesus Christ.

**7. In situations where behavior is indeed biblically permissible, there
is no need of transition.** For many believers in Christ within Muslim communities, however, there are behaviors which are not biblically permissible
that will continue for a time. Both the conversion process and sanctification
take time, and evangelistic opportunity is fertile in such a period. The transition that will come, however, may take several forms: (1) believers will win
over enough hearts (through respect for their character, life and love) to become an accepted part of the community even though they have ceased to be
believing Muslims, (2) believers will be thrown out or killed, or (3) the community itself will transition to Christ. What will actually happen depends at
least as much on the nature of Muslim belief in the community as it does on
what the new believer does and how he or she lives. Ultimately, of course, it all
depends on what the Spirit of God does in the hearts of people. Perhaps that
is also true in the hearts of debaters.

Muslim-friendly Christian Worship

Herbert Hoefer

If followers of Christ want Muslims to feel comfortable in Christian worship services, then they need to consider at least seven issues.

WE KNOW WELL HOW MANY MISCONCEPTIONS THERE ARE among Muslims about Christian teachings. In fact, many of them come from misconceptions in the Qur'an itself (i.e., the sonship of the Second Person of the Trinity; the nature of the Trinity; Jesus' crucifixion, resurrection, and return). In order to address these misconceptions effectively, it is important that our public witness be clear and sensitive in these areas. The most frequent public statement of the Christian faith comes in public worship. Below are several areas in which Christians might adjust their worship practices to ensure a clear witness in Muslim contexts. If we want Muslims to feel comfortable in our Christian worship services, whether in Muslim countries or in Muslim contexts elsewhere, what issues do we need to consider?

Worshiping Jesus

The first area came to my awareness during a visit to our Concordia University–Portland, Oregon, campus by a group of Muslim academics in October 2004. Our university is on the regular itinerary of a State Department-sponsored program which takes Muslim educators around to visit a variety of college campuses. We are on the itinerary because Muslims often wonder how a conservative Christian university can responsibly teach about other religions in a respectful and positive manner. Our discussions were scheduled at the conclusion of our chapel, and the venue was in the fellowship hall of the church where daily chapel is held. The visitors arrived while the worship was going on and were invited to sit and observe.

The itinerary leader was a bit apologetic that this Christian worship was presented to them. However, the Muslim academics (from Saudi Arabia) expressed their delight and surprise at what they heard. They discussed that they could have worshiped with the same words they heard, for it so happened that the songs they heard only referred to God and not to Jesus.

This experience caused me to reflect on the Muslim misconception about Christian worship. They think we worship a human being. They understand that all throughout history humankind has had the tendency to turn the prophet of God into a divine being after his death; therefore, people commit the unforgivable sin of worshiping someone other than God himself.

Subsequently, I've reflected and researched our scriptures on this topic. I've asked the question, "Is it proper to worship Jesus?" We understand that the Second Person of the Trinity became a man named Jesus. However, is it still Jesus who is now on the right hand of the Father? As I've searched the New Testament, I find the instance of Paul's vision on the Damascus Road where the Second Person identifies himself: "I am Jesus whom you are persecuting" (Acts 9:5). Prayers and worship are addressed to the Lord (and to the Lamb in Revelation). We are called to pray in Jesus' name, but are we called to use that name as our object of worship and prayer?

The one possible reference in Paul's epistles to worship a heavenly Jesus is the early church hymn in Philippians 2:5-11. In this passage, the direction is to "confess that Jesus Christ is Lord." The Second Person's incarnated name is honored, but his resurrected and exalted proper title is "Lord." Even if prayers and worship might justifiably be addressed to the name of Jesus, I would urge that such a practice is unhelpful as a Christian witness in a Muslim context. We have strong biblical authority for using the most common term "Lord" when addressing the Resurrected One. That term would not feed Muslim misconceptions as the name Jesus does.

Affirming God's Oneness

A second area in which there are serious misconceptions is the Muslim understanding that Christians are polytheists. Muslims think we violate the oneness of God by worshiping three deities. During that same visit, for example, the academics expressed shock that Christians believe God is one God. I tried to explain that there is a great mystery in the oneness of God, for we understand that oneness to be expressed as three Persons.

How can we address this common misconception in our public worship? I propose we reconsider how our classical creeds are expressed. This matter was brought to my attention at a conference of missionaries that my Lutheran Church-Missouri Synod Board for Missions held in July 2005. One of the participants, Rev. Carlton Riemer, urged that the conference members petition our church body's worship commission, as they were in the process of producing a new hymnal. Rev. Riemer's proposal was that the grammatical phrasing of the creeds makes the oneness of God clear. The conference affirmed his proposal and petitioned (unsuccessfully) that the creeds begin with grammatical phrasing that makes clear our belief in the oneness of God. The usual way the creeds are written out joins the belief in God with the First Person:

I believe in God, the Father Almighty, maker of heaven and earth, And in Jesus Christ... (Apostles' Creed)
I believe in one God, the Father Almighty... (Nicene Creed)

The suggestion was that the witness to our affirmation of the oneness of God would be much clearer in our public worship if the creeds were written out in this manner:

> *I believe in God, The Father Almighty … (Apostles' Creed)*
> *I believe in one God, The Father Almighty… (Nicene Creed)*

Especially in public worship in Muslim contexts, this clear grammatical presentation of the witness of the creeds might be considered.

Revising the Creeds

The ancient creeds were written to address the heresies of their day. Might we revise the creeds in Muslim contexts to address their misconceptions? Picking up on the above discussion about Muslims' typical misconception that we violate the oneness of God, might we add more emphasis to that part of the creeds? Might we bring in biblical adjectives on the nature of God, expressed in a manner similar to the way Muslims do in their recitations? We might then add something like this to our creedal statement in public worship:

> *I believe in one God, all-knowing, all-loving, and all-saving, The Father Almighty…*

With the Qur'anic rejection of Jesus' crucifixion and resurrection, it is very helpful in our public witness that the second article of the creed references Pontius Pilate ("crucified under Pontius Pilate"). It grounds these crucial events of the faith in verifiable history. This historical grounding makes the testimony and the basis of our witness clear and open to scrutiny.

However, in the third article, we have a problem. The reference to the "Christian… Church" can cause misunderstandings, as can the term *catholic*. Missionaries and Christians in the Muslim world are very aware that these two terms are negatively loaded. The Christian communities in those lands are typically isolated and despised, and the Church is associated in Muslim experience with all the negative connotations of the Crusades, colonialism, and Western military/political aggressiveness and decadent morality. Rather than raise up all those negative connotations, might this statement in the creeds be revised?

The point of this statement in the creeds is that present worshipers are part of the long history of God's people all over the world. We might clearly express this conviction (without feeding Muslim misconceptions) by stating our belief something like this:

> *I believe in the Holy Spirit, The holy, universal fellowship of believers… (Apostles' Creed)*
> *And I believe in one holy, universal fellowship and apostolic witness… (Nicene Creed)*

In addition, such a clear affirmation would relate meaningfully to the Muslim concept of *umma*. It would testify clearly that Christians also have an *umma*—a transnational fellowship of faith and support.

Using Epistle Readings

A fourth area in which we might reconsider our practices of public worship is in the use of lessons from the epistles. Muslims have great respect for Jesus and accept him as the Christ, the Messiah. They believe he taught Islam, but that his teachings were corrupted and perverted by subsequent followers. Therefore, the Gospels have much greater authority for Muslims than the epistles. One will often hear knowledgeable Muslims particularly degrade Paul. They deride Christianity as "Paulianity." They attribute the subsequent loss of Jesus' Islamic teaching to the influence of Paul. Of course, we affirm the inspiration of the whole Bible, including the letters of Paul.

However, in a Muslim context, it may not be judicious to present them as our authority. Indeed, even Paul would understand his writings only to be a witness to Jesus Christ, and that should continue to be the clear focus of our public worship. Therefore, might we forego the reading of lessons from the epistles and focus wholly on the Gospels? Might we especially make the words and actions of Jesus the basis for our public preaching? Muslims would be much more attentive and receptive.

Using "Son of God"

Another instance of serious misunderstanding among Muslims is in referring to Jesus as the "Son of God." Muslims understand from the Qur'an that we think Jesus was the product of a physical relationship between God and Mary, and frequently God states to Muhammad that God does not have a son. Of course, that is not the Christian understanding of the term. However, when we use the term, this is what Muslims think we mean, for it is what the Qur'an says we mean. Whenever we use the term "Son of God," Muslims immediately think blasphemy. Rick Brown even characterizes the term as a taboo so that, for a pious Muslim, even to hear the term will provoke God's fierce, eternal wrath (2007, 424-426).

We need to explain to Muslims that the term is a biblical metaphor that is used of individuals and even of Israel. It is not a biological description, but a theological affirmation using a human metaphor. The Second Person of the Trinity participates in the same nature as the Father, just as a son does. We need to make that explanation, but public worship typically is not the proper venue for that discussion. It would be best simply to avoid the term in our preaching and guide our people also to avoid it in their witnessing.

Offensive Welcoming

At Christian worship, we tend to take our welcoming of each other, and especially guests, very seriously. With Muslim guests, however, our enthusiastic welcoming can be very offensive. Most Christians are aware that they should not shake hands, much less hug, between genders among Muslims. Even touching someone of the same sex may be too intimate, especially in a crowd. Men and women should not even make eye contact. Some churches practice the "passing of the peace," and most have some ritual of welcoming in their worship time. It is best simply to give a nod of acknowledgement, unless the Muslim guest offers his or her hand first. One must even be cautious with using the traditional *salaam alaikum* greeting, as many conservative Muslims understand this term to be used exclusively between fellow Muslims.

Related to these considerations is where a Muslim guest can comfortably sit. In mosques, women are happy to have a totally separate place of prayer, even out of sight of the imam who is addressing the crowd and leading the prayers. For a Muslim-friendly atmosphere, a congregation might train their people to sit with men on one side and women on the other. Couples and families who want to sit together might be instructed to sit at the front.

Using Wine, Images, and Music

Finally, there are some issues that can be very sensitive to discuss in our Christian circles. These have to do with theological and traditional matters that are very close to the heritage of some denominations. While some will be a big issue for one denomination, others will not.

1. The use of wine in the Lord's Supper. The use of wine in our celebration of the Lord's Supper is very important in liturgical denominations, but is very problematic for Muslims. Christians typically have a bad reputation for drinking alcohol, which is forbidden in Islam. Besides foregoing the consumption of alcohol in our personal lives, might we also forego it in our public worship? Many Protestant denominations already prefer the use of grape juice. It would be prudent for liturgical churches in Muslim contexts to do the same.

2. The use of images and statues in worship sanctuaries. In liturgical denominations, crucifixes and statues of saints and pictures or stained glass windows of biblical events and figures are often integral to the worship atmosphere. However, the presence of such images can be very upsetting to Muslim visitors. When I was with a group of Muslims in Nagpur, India, in 2007, one of the Muslim leaders brought up the "idolatry" practiced by Christians. She assumed Christians were worshiping the images she saw in churches, just as Hindus do. Fortunately, the group leader had enough insight to explain that these statues have a different function for Christians than they do for Hindus in their temples. Christians understand that these images are just reminders of spiritual realities and historic examples; yet most Muslims will process these images in terms of the way the Qur'an speaks of them.

3. The use of enthusiastic music in worship. This third issue is more problematic for non-liturgical denominations. Once when I was conducting a series of Sunday morning classes at a church in Portland, I had a Muslim come for one of the sessions. He brought his two sons for the event. As they entered the church, a worship service had started in the sanctuary; there was a band and people were clapping and waving their hands in the air. The two boys were curious about what was going on and walked to the sanctuary door to observe. Their father said, "Please go and see what they are doing. They call that worship!" Muslim worship is prescribed in detail and is very solemn, reserved, and dignified. They find our enthusiastic, seemingly chaotic, worship quite confusing and strange. If we want Muslims to feel comfortable in our worship contexts, should we have music at all? If so, what kind of music should it be?

In all of these matters, the process of discussing the reasons for the changes would become a great opportunity for educating and training Christians as we try to witness effectively to our Muslim neighbors.

Reference

Brown, Rick. 2007. "Why Muslims Are Repelled by the Term 'Son of God.'" *Evangelical Missions Quarterly* 43(4):422-429.

Christian Witness in Muslim Settings

Erik Hyatt

Hyatt researched and interviewed many practitioners and missiologists to formulate "Questions and Biblical Guidelines" for ministering to Muslims.

WHAT DO I SAY TO THIS DEAR CO-WORKER who is using the Qur'an so much in his attempts to share the gospel that the local Muslims believe he (and the rest of us, by implication) is interested in becoming a Muslim?" This problem was posed to me, the mission pastor, by one of our local missionaries. This missionary had joined a group of other local missionaries to start an English as a Second Language (ESL) ministry among the hundreds of Muslim immigrants in our neighborhood. It was opening some significant doors in building relationships with these Muslim neighbors. They started meeting in the recreation room of the apartment complex across the street from our church, Bethlehem Baptist Church in Minneapolis, Minnesota. The apartment manager eventually decided to close the recreation room to this kind of gathering, so they agreed to meet at our church across the street—something they would never have agreed to do a few years ago.

But a new challenge arose during the week of Easter 2003. One of the local missionaries made a presentation to explain to the Muslim students what the Easter holiday was all about. This particular missionary had recently received some training in reaching Muslims on the basis of the common ground Christians and Muslims share in matters of faith. This training taught him how to use portions of the Qur'an in an attempt to build a bridge to biblical truth.

The Muslim students came away from the missionary's Easter message excited. In small group discussion afterward, one missionary asked his group, "What did you like about that message?" He was not prepared for the answer he received. One of the Muslim participants said, "We are happy to hear that the teacher is so close to becoming a Muslim!" They were impressed that he had such knowledge, respect, and interest in the Qur'an. It seemed to boost their confidence in the power of their holy book and in their Muslim faith. This was not the message the missionaries were hoping to communicate.

So the missionary from our church finally came to me asking, "What is our church's position on gospel contextualization among Muslims? Are the pastors and elders comfortable with this kind of a presentation of the gospel at our church?" This launched me into a study of the contextualization debate, particularly among Muslims, for the next several years. I investigated the local "insider" training, interviewed Muslim Background Believers (MBBs) and veteran missionaries in Muslim fields, and read numerous books and articles on the subject. I read with great interest arguments from Joshua Massey, Phil Parshall, Gary Corwin, Ralph Winter, Rick Love, Timothy Tennett, and many more—examining all the biblical texts I could find in relation to their arguments.

This informal research motivated me to write a position paper for our church leaders. Entitled "A Statement of Boundaries for Gospel Contextualization among Muslims," I gave the paper to some veteran missionaries working among Muslims and some MBBs for feedback. I received both glowing affirmations and notes of alarming concern. Those who were concerned felt the paper oversimplified the issue and made it too "black and white." I agreed.

So after thinking, praying, and having long discussions with trusted missionaries and ministry colleagues, we came up with the idea of turning the previous "Statement of Boundaries" into "Questions and Biblical Considerations." We now ask all of our missionary candidates seeking to reach Muslims for Christ to answer these questions and to offer biblical rationale for their answers. We find this allows the missionary candidates to think through the issues before accepting (uncritically) a packaged "training" on Muslim evangelism with claims of amazing results.

We realize that every context for ministry among Muslims is different; therefore, we want to avoid a "one-size-fits-all" approach.

So far, those who have answered these questions have found them to be helpful in formulating their own thoughts on these issues. It has given us an opportunity to enter a dialogue with our missionaries about the issues, rather than simply laying down a law. We realize that every context for ministry among Muslims is different; therefore, we want to avoid a "one-size-fits-all" approach. At the same time, we want to be careful that we are not unwittingly affirming Islam or diminishing the true nature and work of Jesus Christ.

We have also sent these questions to our missionaries who are working among Muslims in other parts of the world. One of our supported missionaries in Central Asia gave copies of the document to some of his co-workers. Most of the responses he relayed back to me were very positive. He reported that one missionary said, "I have been out here for several years now and must admit that I have never been asked to articulate answers to such questions."

In the end, the various evangelistic approaches being promoted to reach Muslims in our neighborhood has forced us to articulate questions and biblical considerations that we may never have felt the need to do otherwise. It is my hope and prayer that this will be a means of helping our sent-ones to think, act, and speak among Muslims in such a way that Jesus Christ is clearly exalted, embraced, or rejected as "the only name under heaven given among men by which we must be saved" (Acts 4:12).

Questions and Biblical Guidelines for Bethlehem's Cross-cultural Missionaries Who Seek to Minister among Muslim Peoples

"I have become all things to all people that by all means I might save some. I do it all for the sake of the gospel, that I may share with them in its blessings." (1 Cor. 9:22-23)

"But we have renounced disgraceful, underhanded ways. We refuse to practice cunning or to tamper with God's word, but by the open statement of the truth we would commend ourselves to everyone's conscience in the sight of God." (2 Cor. 4:2)

It brings us great joy to see God raising up laborers from our midst to enter into his harvest among the millions of unreached Muslims throughout the world. As we interact with other missionaries and agencies at work among Muslims, we are encouraged by the praise-worthy progress of the gospel through many creative and culturally-relevant means. At the same time, we also recognize the potential for dangerous misunderstandings to occur as a result of certain contextualization strategies. Therefore, we believe that it is of strategic importance for our missionaries to articulate the biblical values that guide their missiological practices, particularly as they relate to gospel contextualization among Muslims.

We believe the Bible both governs and fuels missiological practice. Our strategies, therefore, must stem from a biblical/theological understanding rather than pragmatic considerations. Our ultimate aim in contextualization is to spread a passion for the supremacy of God, through the exaltation of Jesus Christ, for the joy and deliverance of all peoples in bondage to Christ-denying religions—particularly the millions in bondage to Islam. We long to see members of our body establish missiological strategies that fly the banner of this glorious aim.

General Theological Presuppositions Regarding Culture and Contextualization

We believe that some level of contextualization is necessary for the gospel to be effectively proclaimed and understood across ethno-linguistic cultural barriers (e.g., Jesus' use of parables in the Gospels; Paul's use of redemptive analogies and indigenous pagan poets in Acts 17:28-29 and Titus 1:12-13). We believe that the ultimate goal in utilizing contextualization ought to be the exaltation of Christ to the glory of God (as revealed in the Bible) for the transformation of peoples from all former Christ-denying practices and into the image of Christ (Rom. 12:2; Eph. 4:12-15, 20-24; Col. 3:9-10). We believe that God created all languages on earth (Gen. 11:1-10) and that he is gathering worshipers from every tribe, people, and language to exalt the risen Christ through their mother tongues (Acts 1:8; 2:1-5; Rev. 5:9; 7:9).

And while language and culture are intimately linked, we believe that the gospel aims to transform culture, rather than to simply redeem culture. As regenerate men and women seek to bring their lives into conformance with Christ, social behaviors, local customs, and religious practices radically change (Col. 2:18-23; Acts 19:18-20). Everything once done in ignorance is now to be made obedient to the will of God (1 Pet. 1:13-18; Rom. 12:1-2). Some cultural practices must be abandoned as they are examined in light of the scriptures—especially those practices that are identified with a local Christ-denying religious system (Acts 15:28-29; 19:17-20).

Other cultural practices may be identified as biblically-permissible and be reoriented to clearly magnify the greatness of God so that all things are done to the glory of God in Christ (1 Cor. 10:28-31).

The following questions are aimed at helping our missionaries consider how to most faithfully and clearly communicate the gospel in their respective contexts. The biblical considerations that follow are what we consider to be the key texts and issues that should help inform your answers.

As a cross-cultural minister of the gospel joyfully called to make disciples of Jesus Christ (Matt. 28:18-20) among a particular people (particularly Muslim people groups):

1. How will you help a new believer express his or her identity in Christ within his or her community?

Biblical guidelines to consider: The person who trusts in Christ is a new creation (2 Cor. 5:17-18). He or she is one whom God has miraculously rescued out of the darkness of idolatry and rebellion and into his own family (1 Pet. 2:9) that the person might be to the praise of his glory in Christ (Eph.1:12). The new believer's personal identification with Christ is a declaration of this change of allegiance (1 Thess. 1:9; cf. 1 Kings 18:21). Ethnic, social, economic, gender, and class distinctions are no longer that which primarily defines a new believer's identity (Gal. 3:28-29, 6:15). Rather, for the one who is in Christ, his or her identity is organically tied to Jesus himself and those elect for whom he died (2 Cor. 6:14). Thus, the new believer's identity is not to be understood in purely individualistic terms, nor simply hidden within former religious community terms, for he or she is part of the Body of Christ (1 Cor. 12:13-27).

Sub-questions to consider:

• What aspects of the culture and former religion should be considered "darkness" from which new believers in Christ should repent and walk in "newness of life"?

• When does the missiological goal of "staying within one's community," as new believers in Christ, violate Christ's warnings in Matthew 10:32-39 of loving family more than him?

2. In your ministry context, what aspects of the local culture may be retained and which aspects must be rejected?

Biblical guidelines to consider: While "culture" is a morally neutral term, there are positive potentials and intrinsic vulnerabilities in every culture. In a culture that is intimately tied to a religious system, discerning what is to be retained and what is to be rejected is crucial for the clear communication of the gospel—both in the lives of new believers and through their lives to the larger community. The New Birth, allegiance to Christ alone, identification with the local and global expression of Christ's Church, and the implications of persecution and suffering are realities that will have a deep impact on this question (Acts 19:17-20). Our emphasis must be the clear communication of the gospel and a clean conscience. We must encourage that which cultivates faith and removes confusion (2 Cor. 4:2; Heb. 12:1-2). We must also be careful not to advocate liberties or adherence to former religious practices that would violate the consciences of new believers and miscommunicate/confuse the gospel message within their communities (Rom. 14; 1 Cor. 8:1-13).

Sub-question to consider:

• What terminology (or terms of identity) of the surrounding culture is so closely tied to the predominant non-Christian religion that, if the new believer were to continue using them, would cause the non-Christian community to believe that the so-called "new believer" is still an adherent to the non-Christian religion?

3. As a minister of the gospel, how will you communicate your identity in Christ to those whom you seek to minister among?

Biblical guidelines to consider: While there is no biblical mandate to call oneself a "Christian," our aim is to communicate in a way that honestly and clearly identifies us with the Christ of the Bible (2 Cor. 4:5-6). Language is important (Ps. 19:14; Matt. 16:15-18; 2 Cor. 2:17). We must reject any community-dominant religious terminology that would bring reproach upon Christ or leave our identity with the God/Christ of the Bible in question (Dan. 3; 2 Cor. 4:2)

4. How will you communicate the identity of Jesus in the language and culture of the context in which you minister?

Biblical guidelines to consider: The identity of Jesus is at the center of the gospel (Matt. 16:13-18; Acts 4:12). The gospel writers go to great lengths to show the significance of Jesus' unique and historically significant titles. Jesus, in fulfillment of prophecy, is the Messiah, the one-of-a-kind Son of God (a title for the Savior, Jesus, is used thirty-seven times in the New Testament),[1] and the divine Son of Man (a title for the Savior, Jesus, is used forty-three times in the NT, twenty-nine times in Matthew's Gospel alone). Jesus is the one by whom, and for whom, all things were created (Col. 1:13-20). The resurrected Christ taught his disciples that only through an understanding of the Old Testament will the deep significance of his death, resurrection, and global proclamation be seen as the apex of all of redemptive history (Luke 24:44-49). From the beginning of the Church age, the apostles' task was to communicate these deep realities in different cultures and contexts—even when the concepts themselves were highly offensive (or ridiculous) to their hearers (1 Cor. 1:18-31).

5. What will cross-bearing look like for new believers in your context? And in what ways are the new believers to be "salt and light" in their communities? Are new believers truly ready to suffer for Christ? How will you prepare them?

Biblical guidelines to consider: While there are many places in the world where visible persecution on account of Christ does not occur, the Bible anticipates suffering as part of every believer's experience (Phil. 1:27-28; 1 Pet. 4:12-19). The Apostle Paul experienced great persecution as a missionary and reminded fellow believers that anyone who desired to live for Christ would also be persecuted (2 Tim. 3:12). Jesus taught that his followers would experience suffering and persecution on account of him, sometimes coming from their own friends and family (Matt. 10:16-33). When persecution occurs, there must be prayerful discernment whether to stay and endure persecution or to flee from it (Matt. 10:23; Luke 21:21; Acts 9:24-25). The all-surpassing pleasure to be found in Christ is what enables and drives radical self-denial in the life of the believer (Luke 9:23-26).

Sub-questions to consider:
• When does "salt lose its saltiness" in your host community?
• How is the light of Christ shining, or hidden under a bushel, in your host community (Mark 9:42-49)?
• How are God's "chosen ones" proclaiming the excellencies of him who called them out of darkness and into his marvelous light (1 Pet. 2:9)?

6. How will you present the gospel in such a way that Jesus is the stumbling block (not cultural practices, leadership style, dress, customs, habits)?

Biblical guidelines to consider: Paul strove to communicate the gospel clearly and compellingly both in his speech and his lifestyle. When his financial support was an obstacle, he made tents to support himself (1 Thess. 2:5-9). His aim was to orient his life in such a way that the only stumbling block to faith was the message of Jesus crucified (1 Cor. 1:18-31). He rejected the notion of avoiding persecution by adhering to former religious practices (Gal. 6:12-14). Paul's evangelism was grounded in the reality that, although Paul planted and Apollos watered, it was only God who could give the growth (1 Cor. 3:6-7). Because of this precious reality, there was no impetus for Paul to impress people with flawless oratory or esoteric knowledge (1 Cor. 1:17, 2:1-5).

7. How will you proclaim the gospel with gentleness, respect, and with all boldness in your host context (especially in highly-restricted

areas)?

Biblical guidelines to consider: The Apostle Peter wrote that in a hostile environment we should communicate the gospel with gentleness and respect (I Pet. 3:15-16). Yet when Peter was dragged before local leadership, beaten, and told not to preach the name of Jesus, he declared, "We cannot but tell all that we have seen and heard." This was followed by fervent prayer with the Body of Christ for greater boldness as the word of God was fulfilled (Acts 4:29-30). As ministers of the gospel, we are being sent out as sheep in the midst of wolves (Luke 10:3). Jesus exhorted us to be "wise as serpents and innocent as doves" (Matt. 10:16) in our gospel ministry. When we are dragged before religious authorities and secular governors we will have opportunity, in the midst of persecution and physical suffering, to communicate his supremacy. Our confidence is to be in the Father's promise to give us words to speak by his Spirit (Matt. 10:19-20).

8. What role will the predominant holy books of the people (like the Qur'an) have in your ministry? How will you demonstrate the supreme and exclusive authority of the Bible among people who revere other so-called sacred texts as the supreme authority?

Biblical guidelines to consider: While the New Testament indicates that there is a place for using brief quotes from local religious or cultural literature as a pointer to Christ (Acts 17:23, 28; Tit. 1:12), the apostles were exceedingly careful to show that God's word alone is the ultimate and authoritative truth (2 Tim. 3:16-17). The on-going comparative study of the Bible with any other religious book is unheard of in the NT and runs the risk of subtly affirming the other religious book as equally authoritative to the Bible. We must be careful in our discipleship to distinguish the supreme authority of the Bible above every other holy book, striving to understand the uniqueness of the word of Christ and its purpose in redemptive history (John 17:17; 2 Pet. 1:16-21; Rom. 10:17).

Sub-questions to consider:

• Will using extensive quotes or studying local holy books (like the Qur'an) in an attempt to point to the supremacy of Christ serve to undermine or confirm one's faith in its divine inspiration?

• If the local holy book is regarded as divinely inspired (even in part) by the missionary, how does he or she explain the canonicity and ultimate authority of the Bible?[2]

9. How will you instruct the new believer in Christ regarding his or her involvement in former institutions of worship (like the mosque)?

Biblical guidelines to consider: The new believer's understanding of his or her identity in Christ and the implications of being a new creation (2 Cor. 5:17) and a member of Christ's body (1 Cor. 12:7, 27) will impact his or her view of former institutions of worship (Eph.19:18-20, 26-27). There are significant redemptive historical differences between the interaction of early church believers with the Jewish temples and synagogues and the believer's interactions with other religious institutions (mosques, temples, shrines, etc.). Jesus himself declared, "Salvation is from the Jews" (John 4:22). And it is clear that the gospel Jesus and the apostles preached, which has the power to save all who believe, is solely from the Hebrew scriptures (Luke 24:44-49; Rom. 1:16). Therefore, we must be careful not to assume that any religion or religious writings which bear similarities to Judaism (like Islam) are essentially equated with Judaism. Salvation is not from any other people or religion, nor do any other religious writings have the power to save. New believers who are truly repentant and growing in the grace and knowledge of our Lord Jesus Christ will eventually and inevitably feel compelled to sever all connections with their former Christ-denying religion and way of life (Acts 19:18-20; 2 Cor. 5:17). Therefore, we should be careful not to violate the teachings of our Lord Jesus, or the consciences of new believers, by instructing them to remain cultural/religious "insiders" (Matt. 10:21-25; Luke 9:59-62).

Sub-questions to consider:

• For Muslim fields, will saying the *shahada* (explicitly or implicitly by being in a mosque at prayer times) be understood by the local community as your adherence to Islam?

• What other Muslim phrases or practices could give the false impression to the community that you are a Muslim?

Endnotes

1. The confession that Jesus is the Christ, the Son of the living God, first ventured by Peter at Caesarea Philippi (Matt. 16:16), is the heart of the Christian faith. It is this confession that makes one a Christian, and all Christian theology is thinking, in light of this confession, about the meaning of this confession. The first major theological decision of the Church resulting from such believing thought was the affirmation of the essential deity of Jesus as the Son of God. As such, he was declared to be of one essence with the Father and the Spirit (the dogma of the Trinity promulgated at Nicaea, A.D. 325).

2. A 1995 survey of national C5 MBBs, representing sixty-eight congregations from sixty-six villages, revealed that ninety-six percent still believed that the Qur'an was divinely inspired; sixty-six percent said that the Qur'an was greater than the Bible; and forty-five percent felt peace or close to Allah when listening to the reading of the Qur'an (Parshall 2003, 70).

Reference

Parshall, Phil. 2003. *Muslim Evangelism: A Contemporary Approach to Contextualization.* Waynesboro, Ga.: Gabriel Publishers.

January 2009

Insider Approach to Muslim Ministry: A Latino Perspective

Carlos Diaz

Latino missionaries hold new perspectives related to relationships with Muslim neighbors, methods of communicating and developing church-planting movements, and a unique viewpoint of possible problems.

TEACHING IN THE HUMID WARMTH OF A TROPICAL CLIMATE in the Brazilian hill country of the Minas Gerais province, north of Brazil's largest and capital city, Sao Paulo, I saw the expressions on my students' faces register uncertainty and objection to what I was presenting.

I was a visiting professor teaching a course on "Islam and Approaches to Muslim Ministry" to over seventy students at an evangelical training institute near Belo Horizonte. The students came from various backgrounds and ministry experiences. Some had been working among Muslims in Brazil and elsewhere; others were in the process of training and raising support to enter into full-time mission work among Muslims. A few were working on degrees but already had vast experience in cross-cultural work, having spent lengthy periods working with the indigenous cultures in the jungles of Brazil or the deserts of Argentina.

Hands shot up and, typical to the Latin culture, questions and conversations sprang up among the students. The objections and arguments began when I introduced my presentation on approaches to church planting using the model of the levels of contextualization, C1-C5, as described by John Travis (1998, 407-408. See page 22.).

The problem was not the model: the levels were clear. These students understood the problems with creating churches that reflected the missionary's own culture and forsook the local customs (a C1 or C2 model). They had personally experienced the consequences of this culture clash in their own country and were anxious to avoid such problems in their own approach to church planting. No, what they were so strongly reacting to was the discussion of the insider movement, an approach to Muslim ministry advocating and practicing a C5 approach to such a degree as to encourage a convert to remain a practicing Muslim.

Concerns regarding the insider approach to church planting are not limited to a small group of Latinos in one location in the world. For years, I have been involved in the Latino missionary movement, teaching and training hundreds of Latino student courses on Muslim ministry and participating with Latinos, mission leaders, and active missionaries in a number of conferences concerning approaches to Muslim ministry. I have seen and heard the concerns of many.

The insider movement has been, in general, developed and practiced by North Americans and Europeans, while Christian laborers from Majority World nations who question such practices have been overlooked. It is imperative that the concerns and questions of those in Majority World countries be heard, and their views be taken into consideration. This is especially important in the face of the changes we are seeing, with the main missionary force now built in Majority World nations, including Latin American countries.

Thousands of Latino missionaries are serving in foreign missions today. A number of church-planting teams once exclusively made up of North Americans and Europeans now have at least one or two Latino members. When I first went to South Asia twenty years ago, I was the only Latino missionary in the country. Today there are twenty. These Latinos will not only have to learn to work with other missionaries, but will be fully involved in the development of their team's strategy and approach to church planting. However, the impact of Majority World workers will not only be felt locally in small church-planting teams around the world. As more enter missions from Majority World countries, Majority World workers will have an increasing role in research and strategy in fruitful practices in Muslim ministry.

While my views and the views shared by many Latino missionaries and church leaders may not reflect the opinions of all Latinos, I hope that, in raising a number of questions and concerns regarding the insider movement in Muslim ministry, I will shed some light on the different views in this debate. I also hope to remind readers that the debate is not limited to Western workers and that the opinions of others, especially those already working on these fields, should be taken into consideration.

Positive Aspects of the Insider Movement

Before we look at some of the concerns of Latino workers, I would first like to reflect upon some of the positive developments we see in more contextual approaches. These contributions have challenged our thinking and practices, and have caused us to re-evaluate our approach in seeking lasting fruit.

First, the insider movement has helped us all in the enhanced awareness and appreciation of the Muslim person and his or her culture. Islam is not simply a religion filled with prescribed regulations and practices, but the religious expression of many millions of Muslims around the world. It is a culture that is expressed in different shapes and colors in individual nations. The insider movement has also shown a great willingness to examine each culture from within rather than from without.

The practitioner is viewing the world through the eyes of Islam and its different cultures. There is concern and sensitivity for the individual's beliefs and culture. In particular, this means showing understanding of the problems of those who become disconnected to families and society because of their new faith. It also means caring for those relationships so Muslim Background Believers (MBBs) can remain with loved ones in the hope that they can communicate God's salvation to their lost family and friends. The day I left the Catholic Church my family did not really see it as an abandonment of our faith but of our family and culture.

Second, the insider movement has called us to become better students and practitioners—something the Latino missionary movement is at the very early stages of developing. We have been motivated to learn and study the heart languages of the people we are reaching, and create understandable translations of the Bible and training materials for those in these cultures. It has also caused us to become more insightful students of Islam, not only in its basic principles, popular beliefs, and practices, but its history and current trends. In addition, it has encouraged study of past and present writers from Muslim cultures, allowing us to enter into levels of communication and debate with Muslims on a

While the debate of the insider movement continues, much research, questioning, and information has resulted, helping us to reflect upon our own practices.

more equal basis. While the debate of the insider movement continues, much research, questioning, and information has resulted, helping us to reflect upon our own practices.

Last, the insider movement has taught us to hold to good practices within each culture to express devotion, worship, and communication with God. The good practices once ignored can be sanctified for the worship and glory of the true God. This has helped smooth the transition of each new believer into the new faith without forcing him or her into worship that is offensive and foreign to those in his or her community. For many years, Latino churches were confined by a Western style of worship and the use of Western musical instruments. Early missionaries, knowing that many of the local instruments were used for pagan, indigenous, religious practices, would not allow new converts to use them. Even today in various seminaries and Bible colleges established by Western missionaries in South and Central America, only Western instruments are used and taught.

Today, younger Christian Latino leaders are introducing local musical instruments and style of music in their churches. Worship and praise have taken on a wonderful and exciting form. In my own Cuban community,

Latino Caribbean style of music has been introduced by various new Christian performers, allowing us to worship God within our culture and opening the message of the gospel to those outside the church.

These are but a few observations that we, those who have been on the receiving end of evangelism and church planting, have been able to make. We have been fortunate that, while reflecting upon our own history, we have been able to make changes that have led to more contextualized forms of ministry and worship in our churches and in outreach to our communities. These forms have allowed us to express our own culture while not forsaking biblical doctrine or norms.

Concerns with the Insider Movement

Some of the concerns raised by Latinos with regard to the insider movement are based upon their reflections of their own Christian history. Early missionaries, coming mainly from Catholic churches in Europe, brought teaching from the scriptures, church traditions, and a message of a Savior to the indigenous people of the land. However, in the early years of the development of the Church, Catholic priests allowed indigenous beliefs to co-mingle with the teachings of the Church. Today, in many areas of Latin America, Catholicism is a mixture of Bible teaching and local beliefs and practices. Much of the biblical doctrine has been compromised, and the true nature of Christianity has lost its power.

With this in mind, the insider movement raises many concerns. *First, if MBBs remain insiders—continuing belief in either Islamic orthodoxy or popular folk Islam—will not the mistake of early Catholic missionaries in Latin America be made in the development of the Church in Muslim lands?* One of the beliefs that has dominated those in the Catholic Church in Latin America has been the adoration of the person of Mary, the mother of Jesus. Mary is highly esteemed, and great devotion is given to her. Beautiful statues are decorated with robes of satin and crowns of gold. While the Roman Catholic Church recognizes Mary as a "Holy Queen," "Mother of God," and "Mother of all believers," to many Catholics in Latin America she is revered as a member of the divine triune Godhead and a mediator between God and humanity.

Folkloric traditions tell us that divine powers have been given to her; she is credited with miraculous appearances and healings. The introduction of another person into the Godhead has taken away much of the greatness and worship that Christ alone deserves. Many have been led astray from the truth and salvation in Christ.

As we reflect upon the problem of attaching equality of any person to Christ as is seen in the Latin American Catholic worship of Mary, the question that must be asked is this: are those Muslim-background followers of *Isa Masih* (Jesus Christ) in the insider movement in danger of perpetuating the importance of Muhammad, giving him greater importance than he deserves? Most Muslims discourage the worship of Muhammad, and teach his prophethood, attributing only a few miracles to him, such as the introduction of the Qur'an and his journey to heaven. Yet there remain those in Islam who follow traditional practices, popular Islamic beliefs, or Sufi teachings that lift Muhammad, to greater heights, crediting him with miracles of healing and even raising the dead. By remaining in traditional beliefs and practices concerning Muhammad, is it not easily conceivable that Muslim-background followers of *Isa* might fall into the trap of giving worship and reverence to someone other than Christ?

Second, we must look at the problem of contextualization leading to syncretism. This combining of past unbiblical beliefs and practices with new faith in *Isa* may result in continual bondage to the spirit world, as well as a lack of biblical truth, thereby stunting new believers' growth in Christ and eventually leading new believers away from the truth itself.

As a former Catholic growing up in a Cuban home, I can look back and see that many of the religious traditions practiced in my home were far from biblical. Most Cuban Catholics practice, in one form or another, a mixture of

Even today, it is common to see glasses filled with water and a bowl of fruit sitting next to a picture of a dead relative.

Christian teaching and a folk religion called *Santeria*. These pagan beliefs and practices were introduced into the newfound colonies by early African slaves.

After the Africans were converted to Christianity, they continued in these beliefs and practices, learning to combine them with their new faith. These practices slowly penetrated the Cuban society and through the years became commonplace for many Cuban Catholics. Even today, it is common to see glasses filled with water and a bowl of fruit sitting next to a picture of a dead relative in Cuban homes.

I have observed similar practices in the Dominican Republic and Brazil, other countries that had great numbers of African slaves. But this view of the spirit world goes beyond the appeasement of dead relatives. Similar practices are necessary for other aspects of daily life, such as protection from enemies and physical healing. Rituals are performed with the help of a mediator or *shaman* who knows how to incite powers from the spirit world.

When I was a teenager, I developed a bad case of shingles. My mother quickly called a local Cuban spiritualist who came to our home and began to chant names of popular spirit deities and spells. The spiritist then applied a silver spoon to my back in the area affected by the shingles and said that I would be cured.

Such beliefs and practices are not uncommon. Those in ministry in Latin America often find themselves confronting such beliefs in new believers and opposing dark forces. Can the beliefs and practices that have found such a strong place in Latin American Christianity possibly be compared to those practiced by followers of *Isa* who remain steeped in their own popular beliefs while embracing their new faith in Christ?

Much of the Muslim world is clouded with popular beliefs outside the basic orthodox teaching of Islam. According to Rick Love, "Folk Muslims confess Allah but worship spirits and are more concerned with magic than with Muhammad" (2003, 2). While some orthodox Muslim teachers discourage people from following such practices, more than three-fourths of Muslims adhere to some form of belief or practice pertaining to popular beliefs (2003, 2). Examples of popular Islam are amulets on animals and children to protect them from evil, and shrines to saints believed to have held special powers (*Barakat*) or performed various miracles. These shrines are constantly visited by Muslim worshipers.

While living in Central Asia, I often saw amulets holding Qur'anic verses around the necks of sick children or sewn on their clothing. Parents would visit

The insider movement promotes Muslims who are believers in Jesus Christ. They remain in the mosque and in the spiritual community of the mosque.

the local shrines or mosques for healing before coming to a medical clinic. On Thursdays, women would go to local shrines where a Muslim saint was buried. Those who were troubled by evil spirits would seek a religious person, whether it be a *mullah*, Muslim priest, or Sufi, to conduct a special reading of verses from the Qur'an and blow in their ears in hopes of removing the troubling spirit.

The insider movement promotes Muslims who are believers in Jesus Christ. They remain in the mosque and in the spiritual community of the mosque. Is it not possible that these people will hold on to the same belief system they once had and, while choosing to follow *Isa*, find ways of blending popular Islamic beliefs with Christ's teaching? This has become quite evident in Latin America—those who believe in Christ but have held onto a worldview opposed to biblical teaching.

The syncretism has continued to such an extent that the worlds are not easily separated. Not only has this led many astray, but it continues to cause them to be held in the bondage from which Christ has freed them. This is a serious problem that we must prevent from happening to those in the Muslim world who are seeking truth and grace in *Isa*.

There are many other doctrinal and cultural issues concerning the insider movement that have been raised by Latino field workers. They have pointed out many possible pitfalls and have cautioned against the dangers of such a radical contextualization approach. However, one main issue remains: *the insider movement is an almost exclusively Western approach to Muslim ministry*. Many of the courses given on the Insider Approach to Muslim ministry are held in the United States by Western organizations and, as mentioned in the beginning of this article, many of the writings and debates are from North American missiologists. The issue expands to this: Are Western missionaries to Muslims promoting this approach as the one and only correct method?

While the Latino Church is greatly indebted to European and North American Christian missionaries because of their sacrifice in bringing us the truth of the whole gospel, planting communities of believers, and establishing Christian institutions to train pastors and Christian leaders, many of the approaches to evangelism, church development, and education were modeled after Western practices and methods. Although the Latino Church has matured, especially in the expansion of Christian missionary efforts, Western Christian leaders continue to expect Latino churches to follow Western styles of leadership, church governance and finance, approaches to evangelism, and methods of training and education.

While many of these have been successful in Latin America, we are seeing that as Latinos take greater responsibility in Christian leadership in their countries, as well as in the world, they bring different styles and methods more suited to their culture and not totally compatible to Western models. This demonstrates the importance of being sensitive to the needs of those on the receiving end of ministry. Those with experience and power need to be cautious and sensitive to the ideas and desires of those seeking guidance.

My wife and I, and the teams with whom we worked, were blessed to have had the opportunity to see many Muslims come to Christ. Several communities of MBBs were established in two major cities in South Asia. For the most part, our approach to evangelism was a contextualized level of C4.

We lived in a Muslim community and dressed like our Muslim neighbors. When sharing concepts of God and his kingdom, we used Islamic vocabulary and terms. Prayers and some religious practices we emulated from our surrounding culture. When we began to see fruit, we encouraged the new followers to study the scriptures, pray, and remain in their families and communities. The person of Muhammad and the authority of the Qur'an were not issues to many of them as they themselves had come to the conclusion that Muhammad was a false prophet and the Qur'an was not the word of God.

However, more difficult questions began to arise from the new believers, such as: should they go to the mosque, do the *Namaz*, pray Muslim prayers, and fast during Ramadan. We felt it was not our place to tell them what they should do. Instead, we encouraged them to seek answers by prayer, reading their Bibles, and fasting. In our ministry, we discovered that over ninety-five percent of the MBBs felt they should not continue in their former Islamic practices. While we showed concern about such a decision, we supported them. Today, we are excited as they continue to grow in the knowledge of the scripture, walk in faith, and develop indigenous forms and symbols of worship and their unique way of interpreting scripture.

Conclusion

The mission fields of the world are no longer two-dimensional (the culture of the land and that of those who have come to make disciples of Christ). Today, mission fields have become multi-dimensional. The Great Commission is being heard and obeyed by those from countries that were, not long ago, unreached fields. As these fields continue to send out workers, the discussion of approaches to Muslim ministry and expression of field experience needs to be open to all who are involved. While the new Latino missionary movement has a great deal to learn, its Christian history and its recent evangelical church movement have a lot to offer in the development of approaches to Muslim work. Latino missionaries hold new perspectives related to relationships with our Muslim neighbors, methods of communicating and developing church-planting movements, and a unique viewpoint of possible problems.

Above all, we need to offer loving concern to all people, especially those now in the family of Christ. We cannot let the zeal of having them come into the Kingdom of God prevent us from the striving for truth. As Paul writes in Colossians 2:2, "...attaining to all the wealth that comes from the full assurance of understanding, resulting in a true knowledge of God's mystery, that is, Christ himself." We seek after those approaches that will not keep them in bondage, but will set them free in Christ.

The obvious challenge that lies ahead of us is bringing together all those from various nations and cultures, including MBBs, who work among Muslims, and patiently learning to discuss the pros and cons of approaches to Muslim ministries, not holding any one nationality as superior or wiser than another, but humbly debating and considering these issues in light of the wisdom of God.

References

Love, Rick. 2003. *Muslims, Magic and the Kingdom of God.* Pasadena, Calif.: William Carey Library.

Travis, John. 1998. "The C1 to C6 Spectrum." *Evangelical Missions Quarterly* 34(4): 407-408.

Section 4

Building Relationships

THE GOSPEL CANNOT BE FULLY SHARED without words; however, those in Muslim ministry understand that the gospel shared in Islamic contexts frequently, if not always, includes friendship and relationship building. Many Muslims are drawn to Jesus by interacting with solid Christians for a period of time—days, months, sometimes years. But how do we befriend Muslims? What is important about Islamic culture, society, and community? How do we go about building relationships with Muslims while simultaneously remembering our primary call to make Jesus known to those who don't know him? This chapter addresses these questions.

Phil Parshall (1982) writes that those in the missionary community should sensitize themselves to the locally relevant issues and then prayerfully map out a program of involvement. **Bruce Bradshaw** (1988) suggests three avenues Christians can use to demonstrate their spiritual integrity in Muslim cultures. **Sue Eenigenburg** (2001) discusses the issue of women and Muslims, sharing that, although operating in three very different worlds, the Muslim woman, the Muslim woman who trusts Christ, and the missionary woman to Muslims all share basic human responses to their situations. **Merlin W. Inniger** (1979) says that unless Christian witnesses and evangelists take heed to the "hunger of the heart" and the felt needs of Muslims, only the few Muslims who are able to read and understand doctrinal issues will be reached.

In relation to following religious laws and rituals, **John Speers** (1991) believes Christians should keep the Muslim fast because it may be the best time to make new friends or to develop deeper levels of spiritual relationships. Similarly, **Bradford Greer** (2002) writes that if Paul could comfortably live under the law for personal and missiological reasons, surely missionaries should be able to as well, especially in those contexts where rituals are integral to the people's lives. Six years later, Greer writes that by identifying themselves as people who love and follow the *sharia* of God, missionaries ministering to Muslims can better communicate the Christian faith and disciple those who seek to follow Jesus.

Finally, **H. M. Dard** (1984) reflects upon the Christian mission to Muslims after having endured the grief and pain of seeing a 10-year-old Muslim boy killed.

January 1982

Muslim Misconceptions about "Missionary"

Phil Parshall

We, in the missionary community, should sensitize ourselves to the locally relevant issues and then prayerfully map out a program of involvement that will align us to that which allows the gospel to flow through us in the most productive manner.

RECENTLY, MY **16**-YEAR-OLD DAUGHTER, Lindy, was walking down a street of Manila with my wife. As they passed a store that specialized in custom designed T-shirts, Lindy blurted out, "I would like a shirt with 'Missionary Kid and Proud of It' stenciled on it." Fortunately, my daughter has positive feelings about being associated with the word "missionary." Most missionaries wouldn't care to advertise their high calling in Christ through the pop medium of printed T-shirts. Yet, I'm sure we are comfortable and even proud to be members of the select fraternity of people called *missionaries*. To us and to our Western Church supporters this time-worn word communicates spiritual commitment, willingness to sacrifice, and a deep love for a world of lost people.

Unfortunately, however, perceptions can be radically altered as they traverse time and space across geographical, cultural, linguistic, and religious barriers. The process of reinterpretation can often be so subtle as to substantially alter communication, without the involved parties even realizing it. This is what happened among missionaries living in the old-style compounds of India.

In India the missionaries were called dore. The word is used for rich farmers and small-time kings. These petty rulers bought large pieces of land, put up compound walls, built bungalows, and had servants. They also erected separate bungalows for their second and third wives. When the missionaries came they bought large pieces of land, put up compound walls, built bungalows and had servants. They, too, erected separate bungalows, but for the missionary ladies stationed on the same compound. Missionary wives were called dorasani. The term is used not for the wife of a dore, for she should be kept in isolation away from the public eye, but for his mistress whom he often took with him in his cart or car. The problem here is one of cross-cultural misunderstanding.

The missionary thought of himself as a "missionary," not realizing that there is no such thing in the traditional Indian society. In order to relate to him the people had to find him a role within their own set of roles, and they did so. Unfortunately, the missionaries were not aware of how the people perceived them. (Hiebert 1976, 63)

My own research has led to a startling conclusion. The missionary is often perceived by the Muslim community as nothing more than an efficient secular administrator. He or she is a person who has great resources available and is able effectively to stimulate and oversee progress to successful completion.

This was personally brought home to me in a powerful, painful manner a few years ago. At the time, I was renting office space from a highly-placed Muslim government official. We had many talks together on a great variety of subjects. One day he piercingly looked at me and said, "Mr. Parshall, are you a man of God like my friend Mr. Lakin?" That question caught me off guard. Mr. Lakin, a missionary colleague, looks, acts, and talks like one of God's special saints. Regaining my composure, I sought to assure the official of my theological orthodoxy. After a few moments of reflection, he quietly said, "But Mr. Parshall, you are more like an American diplomat."

We were as ships passing in the night. I was being perceived as informed, articulate, and dynamic. My desire was to be perceived as godly and humble. That encounter led me to do the following study on the distinctives of how Muslim priests and Christian missionaries are perceived in society.

A. "Image" as Perceived by Muslims
MUSLIM PRIEST (IMAM)
1. Passive disposition
2. Subjective in outlook
3. People-oriented
4. Financially poor
5. Would not attend drama, watch television, or go to movies
6. Would not eat in expensive restaurants
7. Would not eat pork
8. Wife would wear a veil and would appear only in culturally modest clothes.
9. Man's clothes depict him as religious person
10. Wears a beard
11. Cares very much about his image in society

CHRISTIAN MISSIONARY
1. A driver, a doer
2. Objective in orientation to life
3. Task-oriented
4. Possessor of a car, camera, tape recorder, etc. Regarded as extremely rich
5. Would attend drama, watch television, or go to movies
6. Would eat in expensive restaurants
7. Would eat pork
8. Missionary wives have not always dressed in culturally appropriate, modest clothes; thus, their identification with the "sinful" actresses as seen in Western movies and television imports
9. Clothes depict him or her as a secular person
10. Infrequently has a beard

11. Does not care very much about his or her image in society. Easily passes off this concern with the statement, "I will never be able to be a person of another culture."

B. "Ministry" as Perceived by Muslims
MUSLIM PRIEST (IMAM)
1. Mosque is focus of life
2. Prays openly five times a day
3. Fasts for one month during daylight hours
4. Constant use of religious vocabulary
5. Not a giver of relief and financial aid; is a recipient of local money only
6. Has no employees
7. Puts little value on non-Qur'anic education
8. Memorizes vast parts of the Qur'an in Arabic
9. Involves himself in a healing ministry by pouring consecrated water on a sick person, putting charms on the diseased, chanting the Qur'an, and saying prayers

CHRISTIAN MISSIONARY
1. Goes to church one hour on Sunday
2. Little public prayer
3. Seldom, if ever, fasts
4. Little use of religious vocabulary
5. Is a dispenser of foreign funds—for relief, jobs, training institutions, hospitals, etc.
6. Has employees with accompanying status
7. Great value on formal, secular education and degrees
8. Memorizes very little of the Bible—in any language
9. Gives a mild prayer for the sick with little faith or conviction; people go to the missionary for medicine, not prayer; emphasis is on the scientific, not the spiritual.

So much for the objective data. In one Muslim country a team of missionaries analyzed these empirical observations and then hammered out the following *modus operandi* in the hope that the barriers created by diverse presuppositional filters would be neutralized or at least minimized. This methodological approach is utilized while they are in residence among their target people.

• Missionaries wear the pants and shirts that are worn by Muslim priests. The men have beards. The wives wear the conservative dress of local women.

• Rented houses are simple and conducive to physical and emotional health

• Eating pork is avoided

• A greater sensitivity is directed toward individuals and away from programs

- Religious vocabulary, at times in the Arabic language, is frequently utilized
- A higher profile of religious form and ritual is practiced
- No institutions are operated, but missionaries are glad to give counsel to Christian development organizations that are working among the needy of the country.
- There is a meaningful involvement of prayer with the sick and suffering.

These and other adaptations have caused Muslim contacts to veer away from the normal flow of interaction with the foreigner on such subjects as politics, geography, and economics. They now are prepared to discuss the weighty matters of sin, salvation and eternal life. Missionaries are being perceived as "People of the Book" who are keenly motivated to dialogue the great issues of life. "Perception" has made a dramatic shift that puts the missionary on a religious track and away from the "secular administrator" image that has been so counter-productive to his God-given task.

Incarnation into local rhythms of life in a foreign context is never easy for the western missionary. We enjoy life on our terms. Mixing with the foreign community with its pattern of familiarity gives us a sense of security and continuity of self-identity.

Then, of course, there is the whole question of our children to consider. How far can we go in making legitimate incarnational demands on those who are not full partners in the decision-making processes? Also, what about our emotional capabilities to adjust to the rigors of a third world life style?

Dogmatic assertions are not called for. Rather, we in the missionary community should sensitize ourselves to the locally relevant issues and then prayerfully map out a program of involvement that will align us as close as possible (and practical) to that which allows the gospel to flow through us in the most productive manner. It would seem to me that is the extent of what our Lord requires and expects from each of his children.

Reference
Hiebert, Paul. 1976. "Social Structures and Church Growth." In *Crucial Dimensions in World Evangelization*. Ed. Arthur F. Glasser. Pasadena, Calif.: William Carey Library.

Integrity and Respect Are Keys to Muslim Witness

Bruce Bradshaw

Three avenues Christians can use to demonstrate their spiritual integrity in Muslim cultures.

I BECAME A CHRISTIAN WHILE LIVING IN EASTERN EUROPE," a student once confessed to me.

"How did that happen?" I asked him.

"I stopped praying. I ate pork and drank wine," he said.

"You did not become a Christian," I told him. "You stopped being a Muslim."

"There's no difference," he retorted. "When a man falls from Islam he becomes a Christian."

In the ensuing discussion we sorted out the most serious challenge for Christians seeking to penetrate Islam with the gospel of Jesus Christ: how to demonstrate the spiritual validity of Christianity. To do so, we must develop relationships with Muslims that are based on integrity and respect. Muslims do not accept the faith of people for whom they have no respect, or from whom they receive no respect.

The different approaches to spirituality in Islam and Christianity seriously impede relationships. Whereas Islamic spirituality is expressed externally and publicly, Christian spiritual disciplines are more private and internal. Christians are told to pray where only God can see them; Muslims are comfortable praying in airplanes and on street corners. Christians emphasize pure hearts and minds in their worship; Muslims wash their hands and feet to prepare for worship. Christians let their fasting be known only to God; Muslims corporately fast during daylight hours during Ramadan.

Since they can't distinguish between internal spiritual development and spiritual neglect, Muslims think Christianity has no spiritual validity. In some Islamic societies, Muslim apostates, like my student, are thought to be Christians.

In light of these differences and misunderstandings, Christians find it hard to demonstrate their spiritual integrity. We cannot impose our Western ideas of Christian faithfulness on Islamic culture. Rather, we must find ways to express our Christian integrity within Islamic culture.

For example, some Christians have thought about setting aside a special period for fasting. Others have considered how to make their prayers more public. The possibility of Islamicizing Christian worship has been debated. Let me suggest some other avenues in Islamic culture that lend themselves to the expression of Christian spiritual discipline: (1) giving to the poor, (2) showing hospitality, and (3) honoring Abraham for his faithfulness.

Giving to All Who Ask

On an examination I once asked my Muslim students whether giving money to beggars is an "exchange." Surprisingly, most of them answered yes. I explained that an exchange connotes reciprocity. Giving to beggars is not reciprocal. They protested that giving to beggars brings Allah's blessing in exchange. That's why they give. They were satisfied when I concluded that beggars are "brokers of blessing."

I went on to explain that as a Christian I give because God has given to me, not to get a blessing, but because I have received one. Muslims can't understand this motivation of Christian giving.

However, beggars trouble Christians. Our culture tends to think of beggars as irresponsible and that giving them money only enforces their irresponsibility and keeps them from gainful employment. Therefore, because we want to be good stewards and a help to society, generally we don't give to beggars. Instead, we donate to charities that try to reclaim beggars.

In our culture, this is fairly sound reasoning. But it doesn't work to try to impose our logic on Muslims. Most beggars in their culture aren't touched by charitable institutions. Begging is their livelihood. Giving to people through an institution is foreign to Muslims. Giving to beggars, one of the five pillars of Islam and a spiritual obligation for every Muslim, is personal. So, even though we may give to institutions, we are thought to be neglecting a spiritual obligation, especially in light of our relative wealth.

Beggars in Islamic societies challenge Christians to pay closer attention to what Jesus said: "Give to everyone who asks you" (Luke 6: 30). They are part of the fabric of society. They do not carry the stigma we assign them in Western culture. They give us opportunities to share, with our Muslim friends, our motivation for deeds of love and charity.

Showing Hospitality

After a meal of freshly killed chicken, our Muslim host introduced us to his family. His son, having been severely malnourished, suffered from diarrhea. My wife made an oral rehydration solution for him while I reflected on the value of hospitality. A popular proverb says: "The daughters of the inhospitable man will never marry"—not because of who they are, but because no one wants to marry into a dishonorable family.

Hospitality is the primary way Muslims establish, express, and defend their honor and esteem. A man will sacrifice his only animal or go into debt to entertain a guest. The financial cost is incidental to his sense of honor. Our host did not hesitate to serve us a high protein meal, even though his son suffered protein deficiency. He had to bolster his honor.

Somehow, the strong biblical emphasis on hospitality has never gripped so-called Christian, Western culture. Our neglect of hospitality is a major roadblock to reaching Muslims with the gospel. Not only do we ignore a major theme of both Islam and Christianity, we also lose the chance to share the Christian motive for being hospitable, a motive that Muslims can appreciate—namely, that we express honor to God by sharing our blessings with other people.

Our hospitality is not meant to bring honor to ourselves. Rather, we want to be gracious to other people because God has been gracious to us. As a Christian duty, hospitality is included with caring for our families, worshiping, praying, reading our Bibles, and so on.

Honoring Abraham

When you try to build friendships with Muslims, invariably you are invited to religious and cultural celebrations. One of them, El-Adha, more than other Islamic celebrations, gives Christians a chance to share their hope in Jesus Christ.

This celebration consists of the sacrifice of an unblemished lamb or goat

The important issue to communicate
to Muslims is our belief that the animal sacrifices of the Mosaic Law, upon which the Islamic sacrificial system is based, were never able to cleanse from sin.

to acknowledge God's mercy in providing Abraham, their spiritual ancestor, with a sacrificial lamb in lieu of his son. The sacrifice serves as a propitiation for sin, an acknowledgement of God's mercy, and a commemoration of Abraham's faithfulness.

Our Christian esteem for Abraham as our spiritual ancestor gives us significant credibility with Muslims on the day of Idd El-Adha. With full integrity, we can share the Islamic reverence for Abraham's faithfulness. Of course, we differ over which son Abraham was to sacrifice—Muslims believing it was Ishmael and Christians believing it was Isaac—but in the light of what Abraham means to us, this difference is not critical.

The important issue to communicate to Muslims is our belief that the animal sacrifices of the Mosaic Law, upon which the Islamic sacrificial system is based, were unable to cleanse from sin. They were periodic reminders of the need for an ultimate sacrifice that could cleanse from sin. The ultimate sacrifice was Jesus Christ.

My last celebration of Idd El-Adha, coming on Sunday, challenged my commitment to show the spiritual integrity of my faith. I had to choose between church and the celebration. Since it comes only once a year, and because I valued the relationship with the person who invited me, I chose the celebration.

Shortly after starting a two-hour journey through the desert to the village where the celebration was held, I was convicted that I had made the wrong choice. I chose not to worship so I could go to an event where worship was highly valued.

I recalled an incident during President Carter's visit to Saudi Arabia in 1978. As preparations for his arrival were being made at Riyadh airport, the call to prayer went up. All the band members dropped to their knees right on the tarmac for their prayers. The scene made a bizarre picture in U.S. newspapers, with men and trombones prostrate together, but it didn't strike the Saudis as odd. It was time for prayer, so they prayed.

I pondered my dilemma. After driving forty-five minutes, I stopped the car and reminded my passenger that this was my day of worship. I told him that God was calling me to return to my church. He agreed that obeying God's call was the right thing to do, even though it meant being three hours late for the celebration.

Of course, when the guest of honor shows up three hours late, some explanation must be given. My host told his family what had happened and they listened intently. Everyone was satisfied that responding to God's call was the supreme value of our lives.

As we ate our meal of goat meat, bananas, and rice from a common platter, we talked about Abraham's faith and my faith in Jesus Christ. Afterwards, I met the village religious leaders. We discussed our faith and developed greater respect for each other. We agreed that in worshipping the same God and in honoring the same spiritual ancestor (Abraham) we were closer to each other than past and present hostilities might lead us to think.

However, we are separated by our Christian belief in the significance of the life, death, and resurrection of Jesus Christ in reconciling us to God. Muslims cling to Abraham's temporal sacrifice, while Christians enjoy the eternal benefits of Christ's sacrifice.

Bridging the gap is the greatest missionary challenge of the Church. It's a challenge that requires us to penetrate Muslim culture, to gain their respect, and to give a reason for the hope that is in us.

October 2001

Women Muslims, Converts, Missionaries: Dealing with Fear

Sue Eenigenburg

Although operating in three very different worlds, the Muslim woman, the Muslim woman who trusts Christ, and the mission- ary woman to Muslims all share the basic human responses to their situations.

WHEN WE FIRST MOVED TO THE MIDDLE EAST, I was excited but nervous as I met my neighbor. She looked so different from me. She was veiled, wearing a long loose coat and gloves. Her native language was different as well. I knew that her worldview was different from mine. She was as foreign to me as I am sure I was to her. Yet, as we talked we discovered that we also had much in common. We loved our families and wanted what was best for them. We wor- ried when our kids were sick. We liked to laugh and shop. We both loved God and were happy with our own religious beliefs.

These initial perceived similarities and differences have been refined by a doz- en years of ministry experience in the Middle East. Although operating in three very different worlds, the Muslim woman, the Muslim woman who trusts Christ, and the missionary woman to Muslims all share in the basic human respons- es to their situations. Let's take a look at these three women and focus on what their concerns are and what their main, natural response is to these concerns.

Muslim Women

From the time a Muslim girl is born, she realizes that she is at a disadvan- tage because she is not a boy. In some countries, this excludes her from educa- tional opportunities. It decreases her value to her family and forces her into a role where it is assumed she needs constant supervision. She cannot be trust- ed without the family's supervision to keep morally pure. She grows up with pressure to marry as soon as possible and she must marry someone approved by her family. They have either chosen him for her or approved of her choice.

Once married, she worries about how to fulfill her duties to her husband. She should have a baby within that first year of marriage, preferably a boy. If she doesn't, she could be divorced. She must do all she can to keep her hus- band happy so he feels no need for another wife. While her husband goes to the coffeehouse to relax with friends, or works two jobs to support his fami- ly, she is at home taking care of the kids and supervising their homework for most of the evening. Even if she has a full-time job, she still does all of the housework. She must try to please her in-laws. This is even more important when her mother-in-law lives in the same home. Expectations of her are high, and the pressure is on for her to conform to the ideal of the traditional Muslim woman in a modern world.

How can she pursue education, modern or Western trends, and social equality, and yet maintain her Islamic and traditional values? She is concerned with political, religious, scientific, and social concerns—how do these fit together and how do they affect her and her family? How should she raise her children? What can a person do in the face of political corruption? Is Western technology more important than her religious convictions and Muslim traditions? Are they compatible? The Muslim woman must deal with these tensions.

She hears that her country is poor because it has forsaken Islam, so she dresses in Islamic garb and reaffirms her Muslim faith and heritage. She longs to walk closely with God and obey him. Yet her religion doesn't allow her to

I met a woman who gave a report on how to protect oneself from evil spirits in the bathroom. She said to repeat a verse of the Qur'an when entering the bathroom and then repeat several verses when leaving.

touch the Qur'an or pray during her monthly cycle and she cannot pray with men in the mosque.

She is plagued by fears that exist throughout all economic levels of society for the Muslim woman. She is afraid of curses from jealous neighbors. The evil eye is a serious threat to her well-being. To protect her son, she may dress him like a little girl because the evil spirits are less interested in girls than boys. She and her children wear charms to ward off the evil eye. She is afraid of evil spirits.

At one home Qur'anic study I attended with upper-middle-class, college-educated women, I met a woman who gave a report on how to protect oneself from evil spirits in the bathroom. She said to repeat a verse of the Qur'an when entering the bathroom and then repeat several verses when leaving.

What does the future hold for her? She has others read her coffee grounds to try to find out. She uses numerous means to gain her desires, whether praying to dead saints, eating or drinking Qur'anic inscriptions on paper, or paying money to a sheik to pray for her. She must try hard to win the favor of the God she fears. What do others think of her? She must guard her reputation fiercely. If the slightest rumor of immorality reaches her family, she may be killed for tainting her family's honor. She is afraid of death. In her religion, she finds no peace or security regarding where she will spend eternity. Although she tries hard to pray and obey God, he may decide she still cannot enter paradise. She has no way of escape from this fear that entraps her and holds her captive in its tireless grip.

Converts

When a Muslim woman becomes a believer in Jesus Christ, she deals with many of these and other issues. If she is married, she has an unbelieving husband to deal with. If he disapproves of her faith, it is his right and obligation to divorce her and take the children away from her. Her family may not want her back. If she is single, how will she handle it when her family burns her Bible and any other religious materials? How will she cope with possible death threats if she doesn't forget this Christian faith? Whom should she marry? What will she do when her parents try to force her to marry a strong Muslim man so she will come back to Islam?

One young Muslim woman who came to know Christ kept refusing the

A Muslim Background Believer doesn't want to marry an unbeliever, but her family— her entire society—would never approve of her marriage to a Christian.

Muslim men her parents brought home. Her parents got more and more upset with her. They assumed that if she married a strong Muslim man, she would forget her new faith. Their pressure on her to marry kept increasing. Finally, her mother wanted to take her to the sheik so that he could talk some sense into her and force her to marry.

As this young woman met with our cell group, she wondered what to do. Should she go or not go? Should she run away? As we met and prayed together, we encouraged her to go with her mother. Meanwhile, we fasted and prayed for her. Her mother took her to the sheik. He told them, "Your daughter, as well as everyone else, has a 'double' (*qarina*) in the spirit world. This double is jealous of all the men you are bringing to the house and is causing your daughter to refuse them all. Back off and leave her alone for a while. Then her spirit double will be appeased and eventually she will marry!" She came back to our cell church confident that God had delivered her and would continue to take care of her in spite of her family's threats.

A Muslim Background Believer doesn't want to marry an unbeliever, but her family—her entire society—would never approve of her marriage to a Christian. Even if she does meet another believer from a Muslim background, and they get married, it will be challenging to maintain a Christian home. When the children are born, they will have *Muslim* written on their identity cards as their religion. The children must participate in Muslim religious classes at their school. If the children share their true faith at school, the whole family will face bitter opposition.

These are some of the situations the believing woman from a Muslim background encounters. Even though Jesus has delivered her from fear, she can easily slide back into fear. She is afraid she may lose her job if her faith is exposed. She may lose her family or even her own life when others learn of her faith. She cannot worship freely in churches for fear of spies reporting her to the authorities. Even in cell churches, people have informed on others to the secret police. Fear can entrap her and hold her back from trusting God to take care of her.

If she depends upon herself and her own strength and attends to the words of others more than the word of God, then fear becomes a ruthless tyrant. It is as she walks by faith, deepens her relationship with Christ, and is encouraged by other believers that she knows true freedom. Freedom from fear is a minute-by-minute walk of faith, not a once-in-a-lifetime occurrence.

Missionaries

The missionary woman who goes to work with Muslim women also encounters difficulties that can lead to fear. She deals with the stress of culture shock. She must learn a new language as well as the rules and taboos of another culture. Things that she would do at home—smiling and chatting with a man behind her in the grocery line, or looking in the eyes of the men she passes in the street, or simply answering a question from a taxi driver—are all considered in her host country as come-ons and invitations to a sexual relationship. She not only goes through culture shock, but she watches as her husband and children deal with it as well. She may deal with guilt as she knows her children are suffering because of her calling and wonders if it is really worth it. She and her husband must re-evaluate their roles in this new culture.

Decisions are made on how to educate their children. She must keep up with her family and their needs as well as keeping up with her housework, correspondence, and ministry, in spite of the homesickness that threatens to overwhelm her. The missionary woman must balance her time and keep up with her different tasks without the support of extended family and the familiarity of dealing with issues in her native language.

The missionary woman also faces fear. She can be afraid to go out on the street because of harassment by men. She can be pinched, fondled, followed, and propositioned by strangers. Men assume she will be open to their advances just like the women they see in foreign films. A simple taxi ride can become a ride of terror as she pushes probing hands away. She is afraid for her children as they go through their adjustments.

National children laugh at their Western looks and lunches—how can they eat peanut butter and banana sandwiches? Will their negative experiences scar them emotionally for life? Will the amoebic dysentery cause long-term damage to her children's intestines? As she struggles in ministry, she wonders if she will ever learn the language well enough. Will she ever lead someone to Christ? She is afraid of failing in ministry, in the eyes of both her family and the nationals.

She is also afraid of exposure in creative access countries. If the authorities find out that she and her husband are church planting among Muslims, the authorities could arrest her or her husband, or they could get kicked out of the country with no time to adequately prepare. What if her husband is kicked out or imprisoned? How could she handle all that would need to be done on her own? How would this affect her family? What would her neighbors say or think about her?

Overcoming Fears

These three types of women—the Muslim who hasn't been set free, the Muslim Background Believer who is new in her faith, and the missionary woman who is expected to be more mature in her faith—although different in many ways, all struggle with fear.

Fear is the opposite of faith. For many years, I assumed that doubt was the opposite of faith. It is not. Fear is. When I have faith in God—in who he is and all he can do—I cannot be defeated by fear. I need not be afraid. It is when I take my eyes off of him and look at my circumstances, my own strengths and weaknesses, or the power of others that I become afraid.

The Muslim woman can be released from fear by placing her trust in the Lord Jesus Christ. She need not fear death, her future, or evil spirits as she comes to know the God who loves her and delivers her from death into life. The Muslim woman who comes to faith in Christ no longer needs to be held captive by the sinewy tentacles of fear. Through her growing trust in the Trustworthy One, she can walk by faith as she looks to him.

One young believer, experiencing persecution at her work place, was terrified of what might happen to her. As she focused on her circumstances and the people around her, as she tried to figure out how she was going to take care of herself, her eyes were no longer on Jesus and his ability to keep her. Fear once again tried to ensnare her in its grasp. She met with two other believers who talked with her about Jesus' character. As they encouraged her to trust him and reminded her of his faithfulness in the past, she grew in her faith. Fear lost its power over her. She returned to work; faith overcoming her fears. The circumstances were no different, but she was!

Before the missionary woman goes to the field, she must demonstrate faith. In spite of her fears or concerns of what may happen, her faith remains strong. She knows God has called her. She sees God provide for her as people give and pray so she can go. Preparing herself through Bible study, reading books on Islam, and attending classes on Muslim evangelism gives her confidence.

She is sent by a church that supports her and honors her for her commitment to serve the Lord.

She then arrives in a country that probably does not want her and dishonors her because of her religion and gender. Communicating in a new language is difficult and her self-image plummets as she becomes aware that little children know more of it than she does. All the evangelism methods she studied don't seem to be enough to convince her friends of the truth.

Could it be that her confidence has been in herself more than in God? Has her self-esteem been based more on what others have thought of her than God's perception of her? Has her faith been strong only because life was easier in her home country where she was surrounded by people who encouraged her and responded to her ministry? Where does she turn for help? As she hangs on, trusting God becomes all she has to see her through.

The Word of God becomes her lifeline and prayer becomes a necessity to survive. She must choose between faith and despair. As her walk with God deepens, she faces her weaknesses and sinfulness. She confesses the shallow-

The Muslim woman can be released from fear by placing her trust in the Lord Jesus Christ. She need not fear death, her future, or evil spirits as she comes to know the God who loves her.

ness of her faith and realizes her need to really know God. She begins to depend less on herself and her own abilities and more on the God who has called her. By faith, she looks to God to use her. In time, she may begin to see some fruit. She is encouraged.

Then the police send for her husband to come for an "interview." She doesn't know where he is, how long he will be gone, whether he will come back or be sent out of the country. Fear comes knocking on her door. Fear wants to take over, wants to send her packing. Faith in God in the face of fear is what keeps her strong, even when she is surrounded by events that could lead to despair. Faith in God gives courage to continue on. Though fear seems ever present, it is not allowed to flourish because she has come to know God, who he is and how he works, and she trusts him.

It is only by faith that fear is conquered. We must turn our eyes on the Fearless One. He experienced death and conquered it. He fought the enemy and vanquished him. He is the sovereign Lord. He delivers Muslim women from darkness to light. He protects his believers in any and all situations. He sustains his workers in the fields. Faith, it truly is the victory.

Getting to Know Their Heart Hunger Is Key to Reaching Muslims

Merlin W. Inniger

Unless Christian witnesses and evangelists take heed to the deeply felt needs of the Muslim masses, only the few who are able to read and understand doctrinal issues will be reached.

BY AND LARGE, THE RELIGION OF ISLAM has been presented to Western readers in its theologically orthodox aspect. Anyone who has read a fair amount of material on Islam is familiar with the confession, "There is no god but Allah, and Muhammad is his prophet." It is also widely known that the religious practice of Muslims is based upon the "five pillars," viz., recitation of the creed, prayers, fasting, alms, and the pilgrimage to Mecca. Orthodox Muslim beliefs about Christ and denials of the Trinity are likewise common knowledge of Christians who have even a superficial interest in Islamic studies.

What is not so well known is that the practice of Islam among the common people differs widely from the "ideal" Islam that is preached in many mosques and explained in books. My own observation and experience is limited largely to Pakistan, where I have served since 1954, but the reality and existence throughout the Muslim world of a "popular Islam" as distinct from the "ideal Islam" was observed and explained more than forty years ago by Dr. Samuel Zwemer, particularly in his *Studies in Popular Islam* (1939). Recently, a paper written for the North American Conference on Muslim Evangelization has also called attention to this phenomenon (Musk 1978).

Missionary outreach that has been dominated by Western personnel and funds has tended to present the gospel in an intellectual way, more as a set of propositions which must be rationally accepted rather than as the power and grace of the person of Christ who meets daily, felt needs. This whole tendency and thrust is evident in literature produced and distributed, correspondence courses offered, and in preaching and teaching as well. Not that the propositions are unimportant, or the teaching of Christian doctrine unnecessary. I am personally committed to such teaching, and to the production and distribution of literature. But the danger is that we minister only to the head, rather than to the heart and the emotions.

Unless Christian witnesses and evangelists take heed to the "hunger of the heart" and the deeply felt needs of the masses, only the few who are able to read and understand doctrinal issues will be reached.

Some Features of Pakistani "Popular Islam"

Millions of the common people of Pakistan wear somewhere on their bodies a charm or amulet (*ta'wiz*) which is supposed to ward off evil and bring good luck. The *ta'wiz* consists of a Qur'anic formula, written by someone thought to have spiritual authority, enclosed in a small metal case and suspended by a black thread. In the same way, the Holy Qur'an itself is believed to have the capacity to bless, to bring happiness, to ward off evil. Not that one needs to read and understand the text, but the very presence of the Holy Book is enough to bring such blessing. The Book, for this reason, is highly reverenced, kept away from "unclean" places or things, and placed above other objects in the room.

Some years ago a village woman in Pakistan asked me for a copy of the *Injil* (Gospel, New Testament). Knowing she was totally illiterate, I asked her why she wanted it. Her answer was that she would place it under her pillow each night, and thus she and her children would be safe from the "evil eye," and become prosperous. At that time, I tried to dissuade her from such an idea. But I now see that a better response would have been to give her the book, let her use it for the time being according to her simple faith, then encourage her to have a neighbor read it to her, or learn to read it herself through the adult literacy method.

The *pir* (spiritual guide or holy man) also occupies a very important place in the common man's religion throughout Pakistan. There are countless numbers of these "holy men" who receive great reverence as well as gifts in cash or kind from their followers. Many *pirs* belong to one of the four Sufi (mystic) orders, and thus constitute a hierarchy of sorts. Those who occupy high positions in this hierarchy wield tremendous power and play an influential role in public affairs. Besides these, there are many self-appointed *pirs* who practice locally without being officially a part of one of the four orders. A *pir's* power and authority may pass on to one of his *murids* (disciples) who may also be a son or near relative.

A *pir's darbar* or court, when open, is usually filled with crowds of his followers who have come for his counsel, intercession, or special blessing. A *ta'wiz* which is written by an influential *pir* is considered especially effective in warding off evil and bringing blessing. Muslim wives who have not been successful in providing sons for their husbands will be found in abundance in the court of a *pir*, asking for his intercession and blessing in what is to them the most important thing in life. Many others will be there, seeking favors, or just to absorb the sanctity and charisma resident in one so favored of Allah.

In such a system, so deep-rooted among Muslims of South Asia, there are without doubt many unworthy men who thrive on the primitive faith and devotion of their followers. But there are others as well who possess the kind of authority and charisma which, according to their light and understanding, meets the needs of multitudes of the common people. Although there is no authority for this practice in the Qur'an, the veneration of *pirs* in Islamic society throughout Pakistan and India surely reveals a deep spiritual hunger and a residue of primitive faith that predates Islam.

How may a faithful Christian witness be given to Muslims whose lives are so closely bound to and influenced by the *pir's* authority? One can readily agree that, at least in the initial stages, literature will not be very effective, and presentation of bare Christian theology will not penetrate this veil of superstition and tradition in the hearts of multitudes.

Should there be "Christian *pirs*" who can exercise a spiritual ministry among searching souls and needy people, and who can ultimately point such people to the only true Mediator between God and man? (cf. 1 Tim. 2:5.) We can expect there will be a response if we begin on the level where they are.

Recently, in Pakistan, a young soldier whom I met while traveling told me all about his *pir*. He related to me how this *pir* had at one time regained his speech after being unable to utter a sound for fifteen years, and since then had exercised great power in fulfilling the needs of his followers. After listening to his enthusiastic testimony, I asked, "Would you like to hear about my *pir*?" I've seldom had a more intent listener as I told him of one who invited all who were weary and heavy-laden to come, who healed the sick and blessed little

The aura and influence of the "holy man" goes on after he is dead and buried. This explains the existence of hundreds of shrines throughout Pakistan.

children, and finally laid down his life for his followers, yet arose the third day and lives on. When we finally parted, the soldier assured me he wanted to learn more. We need to talk in idiom people can understand.

The aura and influence of the "holy man" goes on after he is dead and buried. This explains the existence of hundreds of shrines throughout Pakistan where yearly *melas* (festivals) draw multitudes who seek the fulfillment of needs and, above all, peace of heart.

At Pakpattan, in the Punjab, devotees flock to worship at the shrine of Baba Farid, a well-known thirteenth century saint, and to seek his intercession. Singers, instrumentalists, and drum beaters heighten the emotion of the scene, and *derveshes* dance themselves into *wajid* (ecstasy). Here is found the *Bahishti Darwaza* (Door to Paradise), and believers wait in long lines to pass through this door, for anyone who does so during the festival is promised a sure entrance to Heaven. Here one meets not only the poor and illiterate, but intellectuals, government officials, and wealthy landlords also. National leaders recognize the great influence of this festival, which is usually inaugurated by some important official.

At Bhit Shah, located thirty miles north of Hyderabad, Sind, the shrine of Shad Abdul Latif, a great poet and philosopher, is similarly venerated by the Sindhi people. In the Punjab's great cultural center, Lahore, the shrine of that city's patron saint, Data Ganj Bakhsh, dominates the religious life of more than a million Punjabis.

Reaching Out for Reality

Many more examples could be cited, but the above should be sufficient to indicate that the Muslims of South Asia reach out for more than orthodox Islam can supply. The journeys to the shrines, the desire for intercession, the offerings given to the *pir* all reflect personal, felt needs of human beings.

There are the physical needs, the request for healing, the desire to have a son; there are the outstretched hands seeking blessing, charisma, or grace from one close to Allah. But deeper than all of these is the need for peace of heart, that spiritual rest which was once promised by Jesus in a very definite, uncomplicated way.

Do Christians, national Christians and missionaries alike, recognize these needs? To be honest, we have not recognized them as we ought. What are some things that would bring us closer to the masses, and make us more available to them?

1. *We need to depend more upon prayer, less on material means.* Privately and publicly (public prayer is no shame or stumbling block to Muslims), we need to be far more a praying people.

2. *We need more illumination of the Spirit.* Knowing our Bibles is not enough. We need to demonstrate that we are led by the Spirit, and that we discern needs and reach out to meet them. We need to look to God for more actual demonstration in "signs and wonders."

3. *Our preaching needs more spirit and zeal*—yes, more emotion, if you will! Zeal "with knowledge," to be sure, but truth and knowledge must be on fire.

4. *Finally, is the Western Church, which still sends out missionaries, willing to pay the price to reach the masses of South Asia with the love of Jesus?* Materialism and other values that Western Christians have embraced are rejected by many easterners. Faith, hope, and love must have a revival in our churches soon, or the opportunity to reach many for Christ will be lost.

References

Musk, Bill. 1978. "Popular Islam: The Hunger of the Heart." In *The Gospel and Islam: A 1978 Compendium*. Ed. Don McCurry. Monrovia, Calif.: MARC.

Zwemer, Samuel. 1939. *Studies in Popular Islam*. London: The Sheldon Press.

Ramadan: Should Missionaries Keep the Muslim Fast?

John Speers

The author believes Christians should keep the Muslim fast because it may be the best time to make new friends or develop deeper levels of spiritual relationships.

THE SHIFT FROM A FRUITFUL MINISTRY among nominal Catholics our first term to Muslim evangelism our second term had not been easy. Our transfer to a poor, urban Muslim community had coincided with Ramadan, the month of fasting. Strict prohibition applies to food, drink, cigarettes, and lovemaking during the fourteen daylight hours throughout the 30-day period.

The nights had been noisy as people feasted, while the days found those same people more religiously minded than normal and very suspicious at our arrival. It had not been a good time for us. We decided Ramadan was perhaps the best time to go away for a vacation. A year later, with nothing to show for our efforts at making some inroads into this resistant community, Ramadan came around again. Perhaps with some desperation, and certainly with some apprehension, we decided that I would try to keep the fast, while my wife, Brenda, would support and encourage me.

Compromise or Contextualization?

When my missionary friends and some of our supporters heard about it, a lot of questions popped up. Generally, evangelicals are indifferent—if not hostile—toward missionaries who observe Ramadan. The team leader of one Muslim ministry told me that only four of his twenty members were keeping the fast. That ratio is probably a fair representation of missionaries' attitudes. To keep Ramadan or not has serious theological repercussions. Does participation equal compromise?

Two conclusions freed me to keep the fast. First was the realization that equally devoted missionaries differ. A number of missionaries in evangelical agencies advocate a contextual approach to the fast. They withstand their critics with scriptural evidence, chiefly Paul's argument in 1 Corinthians 9:22: "To the weak I became weak, that I might win the weak. I have become all things to all men, that I might by all means save some."

Who would not keep the fast, if it were known that by so doing some people would come to faith in Christ? To me, emanating from Paul's argument is my second reason for keeping the fast: "...that by all means I might save some." How can we know if identification with Muslims at this level will produce fruit, unless we try?

Benefits

It would be gratifying to say that some have been saved as a direct result of my contextualized Ramadan fast. Regardless, the following benefits—perhaps neither conclusive nor spectacular—have convinced me of the potential of continuing to observe the fast.

1. Interpretation of presence. After looking at several potential homes to rent in our Muslim community, we stopped for a Coke at a local eatery. Soon, a curious crowd gathered and the inevitable question arose, "Who are you and why do you want to move into our community?" We cringed as we sought an inoffensive yet ethical response.

"Missionary" is an acceptable title in many parts of the world. It is well understood and interpreted by the people in a way that gives both respect and an open door for telling the gospel. Among Muslims, however, many missionaries continue to seek a different term to explain their presence. Linguist, teacher, student,

Without any point of reference, Muslims often stereotype missionaries first as Americans and then as Christians. Both are derogatory terms.

and language learner, among others, have been tried and often found lacking.

Without any point of reference, Muslims often stereotype missionaries first as Americans and then as Christians. Both are derogatory terms. They see missionaries through the lens of American mass media and conclude that we represent the antithesis to their own values. The missionary begins lower than "square one" in establishing a viable witness.

Ramadan offers the chance for a very different interpretation of the strange visitors. Because Ramadan is the essence of Muslim piety, anyone who observes it is recognized as a devoted seeker of God. In some languages, a special word is used to mark those who have completed the entire thirty days without fault. I have found that as a direct result of my participation in Ramadan, I am being seen much differently by our community. This is most noticeable in people's introductions: "This is John, a follower of the Prophet Jesus. He doesn't eat pork and he kept the whole fast." Spiritual conversations born of mutual respect, rather than the customary debate, repeatedly follow this introduction.

2. Initiation of friendships. In some Islamic nations shopkeepers report sales increases of up to fifty percent during Ramadan. The days of fasting are offset by evenings of feasting. Food, fellowship, and Qur'anic readings are the order of the night. The bond of the Islamic community grows deeper at Ramadan, as rich and poor alike share in the fast and the feast. It is not surprising, then, that many missionaries find it difficult to maintain or initiate new friendships during this time. When the total focus for thirty days is piety and fellowship within the community, the Muslims easily forget their Christian friends. Missionaries are especially frustrated.

Participation in the fast offers a different perspective. Near the end of our first week, we ventured into the unknown and invited a family to break the fast in our home at sunset. The meal was so positive that Brenda's supporting role became primary. During the next three weeks we entertained another fifty people, many previously unknown to us, and sent food to an additional one hundred. Their response was remarkable.

Actually, Ramadan may be the best time to initiate new friendships, or to cultivate old ones to deeper spiritual levels. The natural tendency toward feasting offers ample opportunities for initiating new relationships. The prevailing

Without an appropriate understanding
of our presence in the community, it is hard to start friendships. Without friendships, it is hard to learn language and culture.

spirit of piety opens the door for discussions about spiritual matters.

3. Instruction in culture. Without an appropriate understanding of our presence in their community, it is hard to start friendships. Without friendships, it is hard to learn language and culture. By participating in the fast we entered into the heart of both language and culture. We learned more about social structures, the Muslim faith, and felt needs during those thirty days than in the previous eight months.

4. Identification. From the outset, we have sought an incarnational ministry. Our location, home, and lifestyle (including going without a car) have been part of our identification with the people. But we are still considered to be the wealthiest residents.

The fast gave us the chance for a truer assimilation into their society. I shared in their thirst, hunger, and the feast. I identified with them at the core of their lives. For the first time I felt more on the inside of their society than on the outside.

5. Intercession. Christians are instructed to fast in secret. Ramadan is a public display of perceived righteousness. It wasn't easy to find the balance. Before beginning the fast, I decided that Ramadan would simply be a method of identification, an experiment in empathy. However, Brenda and I agreed to cover the entire month in prayer. As the fast progressed, two things happened. More time for prayer, weakness, and a focus on the Lord deepened our intercessory burden. Our new friendships and freshly acquired knowledge of the culture in turn fueled our intercession.

6. Inspiration to persevere. Building deeper friendships is a slow process in the Muslim community. Our results are so negligible for so long that our supporters at home don't understand what we are doing. Discouragement sets in. However, we found that Ramadan gave us our first ministry encouragement in more than a year. Not only budding friendships, but the community's new respect for our spirituality brightened our outlook and gave us new outlets for ministry. We were inspired to press on, both in our mundane daily tasks, and also in creative experiments to find other bridges to our Muslim friends.

Conclusion

Gaining benefits from keeping the fast does not come without risks. Misunderstandings arise, not just among fellow missionaries, but also among Muslims. Some of the latter thought I had converted. I had to make long explanations. However, not once did I get a negative response from a Muslim for keeping Ramadan.

Ramadan regresses fourteen days each year on the Gregorian calendar. The next ten years will be the easiest in a physical sense to keep the fast in the Muslim world, as it progressively falls in the cooler season with shorter days.

I suggest that an experimental approach, coupled with sensitive education of our supporters, mission colleagues, and Muslim friends can clear the way to a profitable Ramadan experience. Can we continue to neglect the Ramadan fast with such potential benefits?

October 2002

Free to Live under the Law: A Model for Islamic Witness

Bradford Greer

If Paul could comfortably live under the law for personal and missiological reasons, surely missionaries should be able to also, especially in those contexts where rituals are integral to the people's lives.

I MEANT WELL. My heart was filled with love for my Muslim friends and I wanted them to know how liberating salvation in Christ was. The more acquainted I became with my friends' religion, the more I realized how bound they were to the plethora of futile rituals. Their rituals appeared to have a numbing effect on their spiritual condition. By performing rituals they mistakenly thought that God would weigh those good deeds against the sins they committed. They figured that by following their religious practices they could work their way into heaven.

I wanted my friends to know the freedom from empty rituals that followers of Jesus have. So when the opportunity arose to discuss my faith, I shared how I was free from the law. Jesus had earned salvation for me; therefore, I no longer had to try to earn salvation by my works. Salvation is received by faith in what the Messiah had done. All who followed Jesus were no longer expected to perform empty religious rituals, but were the recipients of the mighty grace of God.

As I spoke, I saw that they listened intently. On my way home I was elated at the anointing I experienced while speaking. I felt that God had finally opened the door for me to share and my friends had heard what I had said. I was certain my words had made a permanent impression on their minds.

The next time I was together with my friends they gave me a cool reception. They had no interest in talking with me about religion. I wondered what the reason was for their response. I thought that maybe our talk together had brought too much conviction on them and they had to retreat into the safety of their religion for a while.

After a few days I discovered the reason for the ongoing coolness in our relationship. The discussion had indeed made a profound impression on my friends, but the impact was not what I had anticipated. I discovered that my friends had no respect for my religion and they questioned my character. When I had said that I was free from the law I unknowingly used a term that had been redefined in their minds. When I was speaking about freedom from vain ritual, they thought that I was speaking about freedom from morality. They understood my words to mean what they had been taught, that Christians believe that they have permission to get drunk and commit adultery.

Taking a Second Look at Freedom from the Law

This narrative is a consolidation of a number of incidents that occurred during my initial years on the field. Through my experiences, I discovered that my understanding of "freedom from the law" did not translate well into my host, Muslim culture. "Freedom from the law" was a culturally loaded phrase. I used it while not understanding the implications it held for Muslims. Each time I had used it I was setting off "red flags" for my friends who could not understand what I meant.

As I realized how difficult it was to communicate about the freedom that we Christians have in Christ, I sought for an alternative. I am not sure that the alternative I have found is valid. It is for this reason I am writing this article. I hope to stimulate discussion in the mission circles as to how to effectively communicate the truths of the gospel to Muslim communities. Second, I hope to spare others from being misinterpreted as I have been.

This is not a misunderstanding that is limited to the area in which I have worked for seventeen years. My wife and I have seen how widespread this perception is in the Muslim world. Just recently, my wife was visiting with a group of Muslim women in a major city in the U.S. One of them, the only one who grew up and was educated in the U.S., exclaimed that Christians think it is permissible to commit adultery. How did that woman, a Muslim from birth, raised in the U.S., get such a preposterous idea? It appears that this perception is endemic in the Muslim *ummah* (community). We only reinforce it when we declare our freedom in Christ.

What is an alternative to such a declaration? First, gospel communicators must ask themselves what they mean by this terminology. What did Paul really mean when he said that believers were no longer "under the law" (Gal. 4:21)? Does freedom from the law mean that Christians are no longer bound by the moral restrictions of the law? Second, Western evangelicals are fundamentally anti-ritual. Many missionaries I know are strongly opposed to religious rituals. Initially I was too; however, I have softened in my stance over the years. Is it right for us to be opposed to religious rituals?

These are important questions. The way we answer them will have great impact on how we communicate our faith in a Muslim context, a context immersed in law and ritual. Do the scriptures give us insight in how to proceed? Is the declaration of our freedom the only declaration we have as followers of Jesus?

An Alternative Missiological Paradigm

Interestingly, the apostle who gave us the theological paradigm of "freedom from the law" also gave us an alternative missiological paradigm useful for rigorous legalistic contexts in which we can incarnate the gospel message. Even

though Paul declared the Gentiles were no longer under the law as we read in
the Book of Acts, Paul continued to live as if he was. Therefore, I propose that
"living under the law" is a more viable Pauline missiological model for incar-
nating the gospel message in an Islamic contest than "living free from the law."
A demonstration of this model is provided in the pericope of Acts 24:10-16,
where Paul makes his defense before the governor, Felix:

> When the governor had nodded for him to speak, Paul responded: "Knowing that
> for many years you have been a judge to this nation, I cheerfully make my defense, since
> you can take note of the fact that no more than twelve days ago I went up to Jerusalem
> to worship. Neither in the temple, nor in the synagogues, nor in the city itself did they
> find me carrying on a discussion with anyone or causing a riot. Nor can they prove to
> you the charges of which they now accuse me. But this I admit to you, that according
> to the Way which they call a sect I do serve the God of our fathers, believing everything
> that is in accordance with the law and that is written in the Prophets; having a hope in
> God, which these men cherish themselves, that there shall certainly be a resurrection of
> both the righteous and the wicked. In view of this, I also do my best to maintain always
> a blameless conscience both before God and before men..."

The context of this pericope centers around Paul's trip to Jerusalem to present the financial gift he had collected from the Gentile congregations in Southern Europe and Asia at the end of his third missionary journey (Acts 21:15-17).
In Paul's mind this was a good opportunity to offer a love offering from the primarily Gentile churches who desired to show their love and solidarity with the
Jewish churches in Judea. After arriving in Jerusalem and being given a warm reception by the church, the elders asked Paul to publicly show the Jewish community that he was not against the law. They asked Paul to purify himself along
with some men who were under a vow and cover their expenses, so that Paul
could publicly show that he walked "orderly, keeping the law" (Acts 21:23-24).

While nearing the completion of the seven-day ritual, some Jews from Asia
stirred up the crowd against Paul and he was arrested. As the narrative proceeds Paul must defend himself before the governor, Felix. In Paul's defense
before Felix, Luke gives us a portrait of Paul's self-identity and his missiological methodology. Both offer solid biblical justification for viewing "living under the law" as a viable missiological paradigm.

Paul begins his defense with the rhetorical device, *captatio benevolentia*:
"Knowing that for many years you have been a judge to this nation, I cheerfully make my defense..." Paul refers to the longevity of Felix's term as governor, which was from 52-60 A.D., longer than any other since Pontius Pilate
(Fitzmyer 1998, 735). Paul says nothing about the character of Felix's rule, although his admission of cheerfully making his defense is meant to appeal to
the positive sensibilities of the governor.

Paul does not spend much time flattering Felix. He gets right into his defense. He denies the charge by Tertullus that he was forging a conspiracy (Acts
24:5-8). Paul points out that he was only a very short time in Jerusalem and
this fact was easily verifiable. Paul says: "...you can take note of the fact that no

more than twelve days ago I went up to Jerusalem to worship" (Acts 24:11). Since he was there only a short time it was inconceivable that he was maliciously intent on causing any disturbance. Paul declares that his purpose in going to Jerusalem was to worship God.

A key word in this verse is "worship." By his own words Paul validates the use of ritualistic forms of worship which he considered no longer necessary. He did not simply sponsor these Jewish believers; he was in the temple with these men, participating with them in fulfilling their purification rites and in worship. Evidently, Paul was not troubled by the use of these rituals. He experienced no internal conflict in paying for the men to have their heads shaved to be purified. In fact, Paul himself did a similar thing after he had left Corinth (Acts 18:18). Also, Paul defined his performance of these rituals as "worship," an unusually strong word.

Paul's personal behavior and methodology appear to conflict with his theology. Paul dogmatically states that believers are no longer under the law, and no one should resubmit to it (Gal. 4:21-5:1). Although Paul theologically had

Although Paul theologically had an aversion to people seeking to be accepted by God on the basis of the law (Gal. 5:4), he had no aversion to living under the law.

an aversion to people seeking to be accepted by God on the basis of law (Gal. 5:4), he had no aversion to living under the law. He was free to conform his lifestyle to the law to win those under the law (1 Cor. 9:19-23). He also appears to have used rituals of the law when he personally felt a need or was in times of duress.

Paul is shown using the rituals of the Nazirite vow to psychologically support himself as he went through a very dangerous time in Corinth (Acts 18:18; 2 Cor. 1: 8-10). Barnabas and he tore their clothes in Lystra when the people were trying to sacrifice animals to them, misperceiving that they were Zeus and Hermes. Tearing clothes was a Jewish form of grief and repentance, a form that apparently was not understood by their Gentile audience. It took a considerable amount of effort for them to stop the people from making the sacrifices (Acts 14:8-18).

From this biographical data Paul is shown to be fundamentally Jewish in disposition. He could live free from the law when he was with Gentiles, but he also couldn't deny who he intrinsically was. He is seen freely living under the law, using his Jewish rituals in meaningful ways to support his faith. Due to his methodological flexibility and Jewish heritage he was able to positively respond to the Jerusalem elders and go to the Temple to worship. It was while he was worshipping God with traditional rituals that he was arrested.

Denying any wrongdoing to Felix, Paul interestingly admits to part of the charges against him. He confesses that he is a member of the Way (Greek: *hodos*), which the Jewish leaders pejoratively called a sect (Greek: *haireses*). However, Paul draws an important distinction here. By differentiating the Way from the term "sect," Paul implies that the Way is normative and binding for all the people of Israel (Barrett 1994, 1104).

No information is given in Acts on how the term developed among the Christian community but according to Isaiah 40:3 and 43:16-19, the Way of the Lord can "refer to God's provision of deliverance from enslavement or exile" (Freedman 2000, 1371). This eschatological freedom from exile, referred to in Isaiah, is one of Luke's defining characteristics of the self-understanding of the Jewish Messianic community.

At the transfiguration, Moses and Elijah speak of the "exodus" Jesus was "to bring to fulfillment at Jerusalem" (Luke 9:30-31). Peter in his first speeches in Acts quoted a prophecy from Amos, an eschatological passage, and spoke of its fulfillment. Paul develops the theme of Israel's eschatological deliverance through a promise-fulfillment motif in his sermon at Pisidian Antioch (Acts

In the Muslim context the central issues presented are their misunderstanding of what Christians mean by freedom, the centrality of morality in the Christian faith, and the function of ritual in believers' lives.

13:16-41). Paul concludes that sermon with a message of hope and liberation:"...and by him every one that believes is freed from everything from which you could not be freed by the law of Moses" (Acts 13:39). According to N.T. Wright it was on the basis of this eschatological deliverance of Israel that Paul engaged in his ministry to the Gentiles (Wright 1997, 37).

Such an eschatological understanding seems to make sense out of Paul's next four statements in Acts 24. Paul says that he: (1) serves the God of his ancestors; (2) believes everything in the Law and Prophets; (3) has the same hope in God that the Jewish leaders do, which is the resurrection of the righteous and the wicked; and (4) seeks to always keep a clear conscience before God and humankind.

These four declarations substantiate that Paul understood himself to be fundamentally a Jew, a Pharisee, and a disciple of Jesus. By saying he serves the

God of his ancestors and that he believes everything in the Law and Prophets, Paul is declaring his continuity with the faith his ancestors had.

He is not a member of a sect; his faith is an expression of true Judaism (Wright 1997, 39). By declaring he has the same hope that the Jewish leaders have, he was declaring that he was a Pharisee—he believed in the resurrection of the righteous. However, Paul goes on to add an extra element that (according to Josephus) the Pharisees did not believe in—the resurrection of the wicked (Haenchen 1971, 655).

Since this continuity with Judaism existed in his faith, and although being Jewish and performing Jewish rituals did not justify Paul before God, being a follower of Jesus did not compel him to deny who he was and discontinue practicing the law.

Freeing from Rituals—or Doing Harm?

Understanding Paul's self-identity and his flexible methodology is important as Western missionaries seek to minister to people who live under legalistic religious systems. In the Muslim context the central issues presented are their misunderstanding of what Christians mean by freedom, the centrality of morality in the Christian faith and the function of ritual in believers' lives.

All too often, missionaries seek to free their friends from rituals that have brought meaning and stability into their fairly unstable lives. Paul theologically established the way Gentiles could live free from such forms and be assured that God would accept them in the same way as he accepted the Jewish people, by their faith.

As we have seen, even though Paul articulated the way of freedom for the Gentiles, he still utilized his religious-cultural forms for worship and prayer. Becoming a Christian for Paul did not mean that he was no longer to practice the rituals of his Jewish faith. He used those rituals for personal reasons because he was a Jew and they were meaningful for him, and he used them as a missiological strategy to reach out to other Jews.

Paul's freedom to "live under the law" provides those missionaries who are theologically uncomfortable with legalistic rituals with the liberty to expand the parameters of their thinking in developing ways to more adequately contextualize their message. If Paul could comfortably live under the law for personal and missiological reasons, surely missionaries should be able to also, especially in those contexts where rituals are integral to the people's lives. In addition to that, missionaries need to seriously consider the implications of removing rituals. The rituals that appear to an outsider to function oppressively may actually provide a community with a framework of stability at the social and psychological levels. Their removal may have harmful repercussions.

I must say that I personally will never feel comfortable creating or establishing rituals that are meant to enhance another person's faith. I think that believers can themselves individually and corporately determine what rituals are meaningful for them. However, I am now more ready to encourage the development of such rituals than I was seventeen years ago.

How are we to cope with the antinomian charge against us? How can we contextualize our message in our specific Islamic contexts to counter it? I did find something in the culture I could use. Conservative Muslims have a strong allegiance to their *sharia* (Islamic Law). Their antinomian perception of Christians, that we are free from the healthy restrictions of law, is a gross misunderstanding of the Christian faith.

From what I see in the New Testament there is plenty of *sharia* or law. Jesus proclaimed the law in the Sermon on the Mount; Paul did as well in Romans 12-15, Galatians 5-6, Ephesians 4-6, and Colossians 3-4. These passages highlight the role of law as a standard for morality in the Christian life. My understanding is that, no matter how Christians perceive Jesus' teachings on the law, whether they are seen as deeper or fuller explanations of the Mosaic Law, or whether they are presentations of a new law, almost all believers agree that Christians are expected to live in accordance with their moral standards, empowered to do so by the Holy Spirit. The covenant promised by God in Jeremiah 31:33 and Ezekiel 36:25-27, that God would write his law on the hearts of his people, was fulfilled in Christ's death, resurrection and Pentecost. Therefore, as a Christian, I am not free from living up to these standards. I may fall short in specific instances, but the Spirit is working to conform my overall lifestyle to these standards (Rom. 8:12-14).

Living under God's *Sharia*

When communicating the good news, I tell my Muslim friends that followers of Jesus are people who "live under God's *sharia*," redefining the concept of *sharia* by focusing on moral excellence. Such an approach seems to challenge my friends' misconceptions with a new image. I stress Romans chapters six and eight, demonstrating that under the "Law of the Spirit of Life" a Christian is empowered to fulfill the righteous requirement(s) of the law (Rom. 8:2, 4). Christian freedom is freedom from the tyranny and dominion of sin (Rom. 6:6-7); it is not an antinomian freedom (Rom. 6:1-2).

The Muslim community in my area seems to have a concept that, while not equivalent to the sinful nature, seems to function well as a substitute. It is an Arabic term: *nafs*. It is because of the internal conflict between the good and bad *nafs* that a person cannot live as she or he would like. So in my communication I declare that the Messiah is one who has set me free from the dominion of the bad *nafs*. Followers of the Messiah have been set free to obey the law of God, not set free from it.

Does this sound like I am advocating sinless perfection? I don't think so. It is simply the vocalization of truths that Paul wrote under inspiration, but which some of us American evangelicals are at times reluctant to verbalize. "Living under the law" seems to be a biblically viable, missiological paradigm that contradicts the antinomian stereotype of Christians and can inspire a Muslim to learn more about the gospel. By presenting an admirable image different from the one expected, missionaries can soften the hardened resistance to the gospel and open "closed" Islamic communities to the gospel.

References

Barrett, C. K. 1994. *A Critical and Exegetical Commentary on the Acts of the Apostles*, Vol. 1. Edinburgh, Scotland: T&T Clark.

Fitzmyer, Joseph A. 1998. *The Acts of the Apostles: The Anchor Bible*. New York: Doubleday.

Freedman, David Noel, ed. 1975. *Acts, the Expanding Church*. Chicago: Moody Press.

Haenchen, Ernst. 1971. *The Acts of the Apostles, A Commentary*. Philadelphia, Pa.: The Westminster Press.

Wright, N.T. 1997. *What Saint Paul Really Said*. Grand Rapids, Mich.: William B. Eerdmans Publishing Co.

The *Sharia* of God: A Contextual Bridge for Islamic Contexts

Bradford Greer

By *identifying themselves as people who love and follow the* sharia *of God, missionaries ministering to Muslims can better communicate the Christian faith and disciple those who seek to follow Jesus.*

IS THE *SHARIA* (HOLY LAW) OF GOD a useful bridge in contextually communicating our faith with our Muslim background friends? Justification for using *sharia* as a bridge exists linguistically because the Arabic Bible uses the word *sharia* for God's law (Ps. 119:1, 97). In the dominant language of the area I work, *sharia* is the word one uses to refer to God's law (e.g., *sharia* is used for the word "law" each time the word occurs in Romans 8:2-4, 1 Corinthians 9:20-21, and Galatians 3).

Therefore, can followers of Jesus present themselves as those who love and follow the *sharia* of God? I have asked co-workers (from both Muslim backgrounds and non-Muslim backgrounds) in my geographical region. Workers from non-Muslim backgrounds objected to using *sharia* as a bridge; workers from Muslim backgrounds accepted the idea. Below is an explanation of (1) why non-Muslim background workers object to using this as a bridge, (2) why the approach is theologically viable, and (3) why this approach is advantageous in communicating our faith and in discipling those who seek to follow Jesus.

Legalism

The objections workers have expressed relate in one way or another to the adverse effects of legalism. Jesus died to bring us freedom from the law and all the ways in which law oppresses people. One worker felt we should protect the *sharia* victims and everyone fed up with the implications of *sharia* in their lives. Another said that to use *sharia* as a bridge would put people again under law and inadvertently result in unanticipated forms of bondage. The Western Church spent centuries breaking free from legalism, so why should we even consider afflicting that upon someone else?

The Western Church has unquestionably had a long-standing tradition of falling into legalistic traps (e.g., it was evil to have sex in marriage [except to procreate], to go to the cinema, to play cards, or to wear make-up). We seem to have had a penchant for making up rules to validate our holiness. Has our historic inability to deliver ourselves from legalism caused us to overcompensate? Let me ask, what do we mean when we say we are free from the law?

Freedom from What Law?

Paul states, "Now before faith came, we were imprisoned and guarded under the law until faith would be revealed. Therefore, the law was our disciplinarian until Christ came, so that we might be justified by faith" (Gal. 3:23-24). What was Paul talking about here? Was he concerned with legalism? The issue was not our concept of legalism; rather, the issue was whether a person had to "become a Jew in order to belong to the people of God" (Wright 1991, 173; see also Flemming 2005, 135). Acts 15:1-2 tells us that some Jews had come from Jerusalem and insisted that the Gentiles needed to be circumcised in order to be saved (become members of the family of God). Paul responded to this problem by writing to the Galatians (Witherington 1998, 328).

In Paul's mind, what enabled people to be saved was their reception of the gift of the Spirit, not by becoming Jews (Gal. 3:2). It is the Spirit who changes the heart of the believer and empowers that person to bear the fruit of the Spirit, fruit which manifests itself in changed, relationally-oriented behaviors (Gal. 5:16-26).

Paul affirms this elsewhere; however, he describes it by using the term "law": "For the law of the Spirit of life has set you free in Christ Jesus from the law of sin and death" (Rom. 8:2). He asserts that in Christ a different law governs us, the Law of the Spirit of life. He adds that the righteous requirement of the law will be fulfilled in us as we obediently live under the power and guidance of the Holy Spirit (Rom. 8:4; see Witherington and Hyatt 2004, 214-215).

In 1 Corinthians 9 Paul makes a series of seemingly contradictory statements about law as he describes his approach to contextualizing his life and message:

> To the Jews, I became as a Jew, in order to win Jews. To those under the law I became as one under the law (though I myself am not under the law), so that I might win those under the law. To those outside the law I became as one outside the law (though I am not free from God's law but am under Christ's law) so that I might win those outside the law. (9:20-21)

How can Paul be "not under the law" and "outside the law," yet never "free from God's law" and always "under Christ's law"? The question remains a conundrum if we insist on using the same meaning for *law* each time Paul uses the term.

However, Paul's statement makes sense if we discern the subtle differences among the Mosaic Law, God's Law, and the Law of the Spirit of life. It appears that Paul viewed the Mosaic Law as a particular expression of God's Law for the Israelite people. This law did not achieve its desired objectives due to the people's inclination to disobey (Deut. 31:26-29). This helps to explain Paul's statement: "What the law [Mosaic Law] could not do, weakened as it was by the flesh…" (Rom. 8:3). Later in Israel's history God responded to the continued failing of the Israelites by promising to write his law upon people's hearts and to give them his Spirit so that they could obey his law (Ezek. 36:25-27; Jer. 31:31-33). Since God had promised to write the law on his people's hearts and enable them to obey it, God had no intention of getting rid of his law.[1] In addition, while God had intended that the Gentiles would one day obey his law[2] (see Wright 2006, 454-500), he never expected them to become Jews (Wright 2006, 516-519). Thus, in some respects God's Law can be seen as distinct from the Mosaic Law.

Jesus' summary of the Mosaic Law, that is, to love God and one's neighbor (Matt. 22:34-40), along with Paul's assertion that the one who loves fulfills the law (Rom. 13:8), sheds further light on this distinction between God's Law and the Mosaic Law. Although the Mosaic Law contained particular injunctions for the Jewish people, there was also a relational dimension embedded within it that was universal in its applicability.[3]

It is from this relational dimension of the Mosaic Law (i.e., Job's defense of his innocence in Job 31 and Isaiah's definition of true fasting in Isaiah 58:3-14) that Paul was never free. This relational dimension of the Mosaic Law is what Paul refers to as God's Law. In addition, it is due to the gift of the Spirit that we are enabled to live according to God's Law. This merging of the relational dimension of the Mosaic Law with the gift of the Spirit is what Paul calls the Law of the Spirit of life.

A Heavy Burden?

Is obedience to God's Law a heavy burden? Practically, we do not think so because we expect our children to obey it. We teach our children not to cheat, steal, or lie. If they do, we discipline them. We also expect the people around us to abide by this law because we have formed our civil societies around it. However, when we begin to think theologically about the law, something strange happens to us. We automatically shift gears and think about legalism, heavy burdens, and our need to be free from the law. Yet none of us think we have the freedom to cheat on our spouses, lie to our customers, or kill the people who offend us. Since this is the case, does this not indicate that we are reacting to a peculiar theological preconditioning rather than to the Law of God?

Grace Permeates the Law

Perhaps our perception of the Mosaic Law as graceless negatively impairs our ability to think wholesomely about the law. Yet this is a jaundiced view of the Mosaic Law because grace was embedded within it (Wright 1991, 145). If an Israelite had broken a command, there was a complete system of atonement and restoration to fellowship with God.

We also tend to think about the law in terms of "works-righteousness." This is something we want to avoid at all costs. However, the Mosaic Law was never given to be a means of producing salvation by works. Christopher Wright points out that salvation and the presence of God were free gifts to the Israelites. The people had been slaves in Egypt. They had been set free, not because they had obeyed the Mosaic Law, but because God was rich in mercy. It was only after God had delivered them that he brought them to Mt. Sinai and gave them his law (Wright 2006, 370). The law was given so that the Israelites would know how to live as God's covenant people within the land God was about to give them (Wright 2004, 25).

Likewise, our obedience of the Law of God brings us neither salvation nor the presence of God. Salvation comes only through faith. God includes in this salvation acceptance, forgiveness, and cleansing from our sins (Rom. 5:1; Eph. 1:7; 1 John 1:9), and a changed and empowered heart by giving us his promised Holy Spirit[4] (John 3:5; Rom. 2:29, 8:9; Titus 2:11-14). The Spirit enables us to live according to the law (i.e., Matt. 5-7; Rom. 12:9-21; Eph. 4:17-5:21).[5] Our adherence to the Law of God results in good works which demonstrate to those around us that God is with us (Matt. 5:16).

Another objection may stem from Romans 7 and our ongoing struggle with sin. However, in the mercy of God, we no longer walk with a medieval mindset, perceiving our Christian experience as "a glass half empty," laden with guilt and preoccupied with our shortcomings. The contemporary Christian experience is one of "a glass half full," where we celebrate Christ in us and our ongoing transformation. We are cognizant of our faults; however, we are also aware that our lives and behaviors are changing for the better. Living by the Law of God is not legalism; it is true spirituality, a grateful and Spirit-empowered response to the mercy of God in our lives.

Conclusion

Exporting our theological preoccupation with being free from the law creates unnecessary problems. Many Muslims already view Christians as lawless. We reinforce this perception whenever we talk about our freedom from the law. Emphasizing our freedom also impairs discipleship because we present a faith that appears substance-less to our Muslim background friends. Many do not intuitively know how to take our cognitive-oriented faith and apply it to their daily lives. However, we counter these problems when we introduce our friends to a faith that expresses itself by having a love for and a desire to obey the *sharia* of God (does this sound like Psalm 119?), a *sharia* that focuses our attention on how to treat God and our neighbor.

Let us introduce our friends to a living faith that is a response to Jesus' gracious outpouring of his life on our behalf, filled with the presence and power of God through the promised Holy Spirit. We might find that in doing so our faith becomes much more intelligible—even to ourselves.

Endnotes

1. It was no accident that the Spirit descended on Pentecost because Pentecost was "the anniversary of the giving of the law at Mount Sinai" (Longnecker 1995, 65; also Turner 2004, 111).

2. In the poetry of Isaiah 2:2-4, the law (*Torah*) is juxtaposed with the word (*logos* in the Septuagint). The *Torah* goes out from Zion; the *logos* goes out from Jerusalem. David Pao has shown how Luke traces the journey of the *logos* as it travels out from Jerusalem (2000, 147-180). The early Church chose to capitalize on the term *logos* rather than *To-*

rah as it contextualized within its context. Due to the parallelism in Isaiah 2:3, it is possible for us to choose to capitalize on *Torah* instead of *logos*.

3. Christopher Wright concurs that the Mosaic Law has a dimension that is universal in its applicability. He refers to this universality as the ethical dimension of the Law. This explains the title of his book, *Old Testament Ethics for the People of God*.

4. The Western Church traditionally has not known how to relate to the Holy Spirit. It has tended to reduce the work of the Spirit in our lives to an impersonal power, i.e., grace (see McGrath 1998, 3). Reflecting this tradition, Wright virtually ignores the role of the Spirit in his book, *The Mission of God*.

5. We should not reduce God's Law to a set of rules. Even the Mosaic Law was more than that (Wright 2004, 26). The Law of God has rules governing behavior; but, it is also filled with the story of God's actions in history so that we can know God and have complete confidence in him.

References

Flemming, Dean. 2005. *Contextualization in the New Testament: Patterns for Theology and Mission*. Downers Grove, Ill.: InterVarsity Press.

Longnecker, Richard N. 1995. *Acts in The Expositor's Bible Commentary with the New International Version series*. Eds. F. E. Gaebelein, J. D. Douglas, and R. P. Polcyn. Grand Rapids, Mich.: Zondervan.

McGrath, Alister E. 1998. *Justitia Dei: A History of the Christian Doctrine of Justification*. 2nd ed. Cambridge: Cambridge University Press.

Pao, David W. 2000. *Acts and the Isaianic New Exodus*. Grand Rapids, Mich.: Baker Academic.

Turner, Max. 2004. "The Spirit and Salvation in Luke-Acts." In *The Holy Spirit and Christian Origins: Essays in Honor of James D. G. Dunn*. Eds. G. N. Stanton, B. W. Longnecker, and S. C. Barton, 103-117. Grand Rapids, Mich.: William B. Eerdmans Publishing Co.

Witherington III, Ben. 1998. *The Paul Quest: The Renewed Search for the Jew of Tarsus*. Downers Grove, Ill.: InterVarsity Press.

Witherington III, Ben, and Darlene Hyatt. 2004. *Paul's Letter to the Romans: A Socio-Rhetorical Commentary*. Grand Rapids, Mich.: William B. Eerdmans Publishing Co.

Wright, Christopher J. H. 2004. *Old Testament Ethics for the People of God*. Downers Grove, Ill.: InterVarsity Press.

————. 2006. *The Mission of God: Unlocking the Bible's Grand Narrative*. Downers Grove, Ill.: InterVarsity Press.

Wright, Nicholas Thomas. 1991. *The Climax of the Covenant: Christ and the Law in Pauline Theology*. Minneapolis, Minn.: Fortress Press.

April 1984

Reflections at a Muslim Grave

H. M. Dard

After enduring the grief and pain of seeing a 10-year-old Muslim boy killed, the author reflects on the Christian mission to Muslims.

A FEW MINUTES AGO my wife and I returned from standing at the grave of the 10-year-old son of our Muslim neighbors. This keen, alert boy, full of life and questions, was suddenly taken from this life twelve days ago when his school bus skidded into a wall. We stood with his mother, her sister, and her 14-year-old son as they wept and offered the customary prayers at the graveside. We grieved with them.

Ahmad had often been in our home, and his exploring mind left no stone unturned. He questioned everything in sight and offered his own opinion on many matters. Just a few weeks before, when I was away from home overnight, his mother had sent her two sons over to talk with my wife for an hour. Ahmad wanted an explanation of the plaque hanging on our wall. It reads, "Joy is the most infallible sign of the presence of God." He struggled through the words, but they didn't make sense to him. In response to my wife's saying that a person is supremely happy if he or she knows God is with him or her, he responded, "If I knew God were with me, I would be afraid!"

As we took the weeping mother to the hospital and looked on as life ebbed from young Ahmad…as I walked with a large company of men the one mile to a rugged hillside cemetery…as I stood on the fringe of the crowd in an open field during funeral prayers, while the imam called out four times, "Allah *Akbar*" (God is great)…as I sat with the men during their long talks about the last events in the life of Ahmad and during their many prayers for his eternal welfare…as my wife spent hours every day sharing the grief of the mother and family, helping to entertain an endless stream of sympathizers from miles away and acting as "auntie" and "*nani*" to all the visiting nieces and nephews who needed diversion outside the home, I wondered, I wondered and inwardly wept, how does Christ enter the Muslim world?

How does his eternal message of grace and justice penetrate this maze of tradition, custom, and religion to meet men and women as they are, where they are? Why have I and my generation been so unsuccessful in seeing Muslims brought into life and hope? How long do we have to continue to stand at the graves of bright 10-year-olds and at the gravesides of their aged grandfathers? (Ahmad's died six months earlier and we shared that grief.)

How long do we have to stand and listen to the stoic cry of "God is great" and watch men and women in silent grief lower loved ones into a grave, while an empty void possesses heart and mind?

During this time of hurting and reflection I picked up the July 1982 *Evangelical Missions Quarterly*, and eagerly read the debates about how to declare Christ and develop a believing community in the Muslim world. Is proclamation alone the great necessity, or do we need development projects? I read the articles with intense interest because, having lived in this Muslim country for most of the past twenty-seven years, I have wrestled with these issues and have tried to live next to the people.

But as I stood at the grave this morning and quietly said to the grieving mother, "We share this grief with you," it made contextualization, proclamation, community development, health care, and so on seem like the morning mist in the cool valley below slowly dissipating under the warming sun. Is Christ going to penetrate the Muslim world through strategies cooked up in classrooms? Will the statistics about hundreds of "hidden people" in the Muslim world make our hearts bleed? Will our books on methodology precipitate some great new movement to Christ?

How long do we have to stand and listen to the stoic cry of "God is great" and watch men and women in silent grief lower loved ones into a grave, while an empty void possesses heart and mind?

Do we come as insiders and share the grief of Muslims, or do we preach as outsiders? Will our Friday "Christian" prayers and ablutions genuinely merge us into one with them? The Apostle Paul wept and said, "I could wish myself cut off from Christ for the sake of…"

The first appearance of the "Angel of the Lord" in recorded history is understood by many scholars to be a pre-incarnate appearance of our Lord Jesus Christ. He drew near to a woman who had been treated as less than the scum of the earth. Hagar had become pregnant through two persons' intense, but misdirected, desire to help God fulfill his promise to them.

Having used her to achieve their own purposes, they thrust her out into the harsh, foreboding, lifeless Sinai Peninsula. There, blinded by tears of agony, heartache, and hopelessness, she struggled through the burning heat and biting sand, hoping to regain her roots in Egypt. With Hagar in this desperate state, the pre-incarnate God-Man drew near to share her grief and give her a most remarkable promise for her unborn son (Gen. 16: 7-14).

I believe that this pre-incarnate Christ will again draw near to the vast off-spring of Hagar and Ishmael through his "reincarnation" (I use the term carefully and those with hearts to hear will understand) in men and women who become insiders and grief-sharers. He will do it through those who preach—and with their preaching weep; through those who heal and develop—and with their good deeds also grieve; through those who sit on the floor and worship—and with it feel what others really feel; and through those who retain their foreign ways and language—but learn to embrace others as one of their own.

Bevan Jones, in his classic, *People of the Mosque*, observes that we (missions) have offered Muslims hospitals and schools (and now he could add development projects), but have failed to give them what they want more than anything else—our genuine friendship, and with that, the knowledge of the greatest Friend.

Samuel Zwemer, the apostle to Islam, spoke movingly of the great prayer of the father of Ishmael, in which he pled with his great Friend to let his son live before him. This impassioned plea arose from the heart of the friend of God. His very being had become totally enmeshed in his 13-year-old son. Abraham's Friend hushed his turbulent emotions with, "I will bless him, just as you have asked me to do."

Our dogmatic proclamation, our Western methodology, and our development projects must be permeated with the incarnate Christ. Let us draw near to share their grief and speak to them. We are not Christians preaching to Muslims; we are not westerners trying to communicate with easterners; we are not the developed seeking to lift the undeveloped. We are fallen men and women embracing fallen men and women. We share their grief so they will share the joy of God's presence.

Reference

Jones, Bevan. 1932. *People of the Mosque: An Introduction to the Study of Islam with Special Reference to India*. Republished 2005. Whitefish, Mont.: Kessinger Publishing, LLC.

Section 5

Evangelistic Methods
& Church Planting

AT THE END OF THE DAY, the gospel has not been fully shared until it has been done so verbally. We cannot sacrifice proclamation for deeds alone. But how do we go about that in a way that is both effective and compassionate? Similarly, how do we go about church planting in areas and among peoples hostile to Christians and Christianity in general? What does an effective church-planting strategy look like? In this concluding chapter we seek to equip you to fulfill your evangelism calling to Muslim friends.

Mark Terry (1996) says that approaches to Muslim evangelism fall into five major categories: confrontational, traditional evangelical, institutional, dialogical, and contextual. **Phil Parshall** (1998) writes that instead of using confrontational debate, missionaries to Muslims should emphasize prioritizing a "classic" approach. **Ralph E. Brown** (1971) encourages missionaries to continue to witness to Muslims in dialogue and proclamation, faithfully, with self-giving love, believing prayer, and in humility, always learning. **Bruce Thomas** (1994) asks, "Has there been something missing in our understanding and preaching of the gospel so that we fail to reach the Muslim at his or her point of deepest insecurity?"

Knowing we cannot overlook the deeply spiritual element in ministry to Muslims, **Jerry Otis** (1980) shares principles for missionaries working in animistic areas. **Randal Scott** (2008) says that a biblical understanding of dreams can facilitate a contextual approach to reaching Muslims with the gospel. **Ken Peters** (1989) believes that very little is said about what methods or approaches are best suited for Muslims who practice Islamic mysticism.

Turning to church planting among Muslims, **Dan Brown** (1997) gives a description of Frontiers' successful Seven Phases of Church Planting among Muslims. **Steven Downey** (2008) writes about a 2006 conference that allowed ministries in Muslim areas to discuss training, community development, and partnership in church planting. **David Greenlee** (2002) shares case studies of twelve churches in resistant areas that have continued to thrive in difficult areas.

Finally, **Tony Lynn** (2002) reflects upon how God used a Muslim chief to get their first church building established.

April 1996

Approaches to the Evangelization of Muslims

Mark Terry

Approaches to Muslim evangelism fall into five major categories, including confrontational, traditional evangelical, institutional, dialogical, and contextual models.

THE LEADER OF THE MUSLIM TONG-GAN people of Kyrgyzstan has invited the Great Commission Center (Lewisville, Tex.) to send as many as twenty medical, development, and educational specialists. Short-term workers will establish clinics and water treatment systems and will teach computer use, Chinese, and other subjects. The 300,000 Tong-Gan people of Kazakhstan and Kyrgyzstan were driven from China a century ago. "This is a ministry of pre-evangelism; it requires love, kindness, patience, compassion, and a high degree of sensitivity. This is a very rare opportunity for Chinese Christians to serve among Muslim people of our own kindred," Thomas Wang of the Great Commission Center stated. "In my lifetime, this is the first invitation of its kind that I have witnessed."

• As part of a strategy called "Pillars of Hope," local Christians and workers with the Christian and Missionary Alliance have started a church of Muslim converts in western Cote d'Ivoire. Two Lebanese missionaries are working among Middle Eastern Muslims in Abidjan, while four couples have been assigned to work through twenty Alliance churches to reach out to Muslims in Bouake.

• "A combined mission umbrella organization in Cote d'Ivoire has called its first ever conference of 150 converts from Islam for mutual encouragement," WEC International reports. "When people were invited to stand together by people groups or regions, it was discovered that over the whole country Muslims are coming to Christ." WEC says a committee was formed to help those who lose everything when they convert.

• Members of the international Yemen Prayer Fellowship (YPF) report continuing spiritual interest in that civil war-battered country on the Gulf of Aden. At one undermanned hospital, YPF says, "A vital witness continues and signs of hunger for the truth are evident." A broadcasting agency says it received 134 letters responding to broadcasts in April, compared to a monthly average of thirty-three during 1994. Christ Church in Aden, "almost totally destroyed at the end of the war" in 1994, has appointed a new chaplain to oversee the church, the planned rebuilding, and the establishment of a clinic. YPF also states that some of the fifty thousand Iraqi refugees in Yemen have turned to Christ.

• A major evangelistic effort in Spain, uniting local churches with specialized missions and organizations, takes place every summer. In July and August, the highways fill with 800,000 Moroccans and Algerians who are either going on, or returning from, vacation. The Muslims are concentrated in Alicante, Almeria, Malaga, and Algeciras. According to the Bible Society, in 1994 workers distributed 3,374 Bibles, 188,179 New Testaments, 399,970 Gospels, 131,450 Bible portions, 22,542 audio and video cassettes, and 5,544 books.

• There are about four hundred known Christians meeting in ten or more small groups in Morocco, according to Arab World Ministries. "There are groups of Christians in all major cities and new people meeting the Lord almost everywhere," a ministry source reports. In addition, about 150 Christian tentmakers work in the country.

Christianity has confronted Islam since the age of Muhammad. From the time of Raymond Lull (thirteenth century), missionaries have sought to win Muslims to Christ. Generally, this has been a difficult, discouraging task, but as the reports above show, there are some encouraging signs.

Models of Muslim Evangelism

The many different models or approaches to Muslim evangelism fall into five major categories.

1. Confrontational. In the eighteenth and nineteenth centuries some missionaries—Henry Martyn, Karl Pfander, and St. Clair Tidall, for example— tried to win Muslims by public debate. They also preached in the bazaars and produced apologetic and polemical literature in English and the vernacular. Their approach was never very successful in terms of converts, and it often aroused increased Muslim antipathy toward Christianity.

This approach is not widely used today. First, most Muslim countries do not allow it. Those earlier missionaries often worked under the protection of colonial governments. Second, today's missionaries prefer to emphasize the positive nature of the gospel, rather than expose objectionable elements in Islam. Finally, this method is not usually successful. Occasionally a Muslim intellectual is convinced, but the debates do not move the masses.

2. Traditional evangelical. Samuel Zwemer (1867-1952), the "apostle to the Muslims," was the pioneer of this method. During his early years (1890-1916), he tended toward confrontation. In his books, *The Disintegration of Islam* (1915) and *Muhammad or Christ* (1916), he called for "radical displacement," a complete rejection of Islam by its adherents. However, later in his career he followed a more anthropological and Christocentric approach. He wrote empathically of Muslims as seekers after God, although he still maintained that only Jesus could satisfy their needs (Vander Werff 1982, 191).

Zwemer believed that evangelism must emphasize the incarnation, atonement, and mediation of Christ. The evangelist must call Muslims to repentance, to submission to Christ, and to involvement in the church. Zwemer, in later years, advocated witnessing to individuals and small groups. He advised his students to engage in friendship evangelism. He believed the human personality was the best bridge for conveying the gospel (1982, 195). Zwemer was a prolific writer and evangelicals have followed his example. They have produced innumerable books and tracts. They have distributed the scriptures as widely as possible. They have propagated the gospel by means of radio and Bible correspondence courses.

The traditional approach has resulted in Western-style churches. Missionaries have told their converts to break with Islam and publicly identify with a church. Zwemer rejected the idea of allowing a convert to remain in Islam as long as possible so as to influence other Muslims (Zwemer 1941, 261). The main criticism against the traditional approach is simply that it has not been very effective. Critics also say it is too Western. But defenders say the approach is biblically sound. They see themselves as sowing seed that will bear fruit in time. They admit meager results, but attribute this to political, historical, and social barriers beyond their control. They continue to sow faithfully, hoping for more favorable results.

3. Institutional. Several denominational missions have used this model. For example, Presbyterians and Congregationalists have tried to win Muslims through hospitals, schools, and orphanages. The Foreign Mission Board of the Southern Baptist Convention has operated three hospitals in Arab countries, as well as schools and orphanages in Lebanon, Jordan, and Israel (for Palestinians). The assumption is that demonstrations of love, compassion, and humility will break down the walls of prejudice. Some missiologists say we should send more teachers, doctors, nurses, and agriculturalists, because their deeds will speak louder than their words (Fry and King 1980, 133).

The institutional model continues to be valid. Institutions are a good way to overcome prejudice and win a hearing for the gospel. However, institutions face difficult times. For one thing, governments are taking over many of their services. Also, inflation makes it hard to maintain them. Nevertheless, in some countries—Yemen, for example—institutions are the only Christian presence allowed.

4. Dialogical. The dialogical approach was pioneered by Temple Gairdner (1873-1928) and developed more fully by Kenneth Cragg. Dialogue is motivated by a sincere love that seeks to reconcile Muslims and Christians. It has four purposes: (1) to learn what Muslims believe and to appreciate their beliefs in relation to their culture; (2) to seek to establish both contact and rapport on the basis of sincere, honest friendship; (3) to learn how to witness to them; and (4) to bring them ultimately to salvation in Christ (Register 1979, 11-12).

This approach must not be confused with the syncretistic, universalistic dialogues sponsored by some ecumenical groups. The missionary does not surrender his or her convictions. Rather, he or she affirms them in a way that permits him or her to grow in his or her understanding of Muslims.

5. Contextual. In this approach missionaries try by every possible way to become like Muslims so they can present the gospel in religious and cultural forms that Muslims can identify with. This model does not forget "the offense of the gospel," but seeks to avoid objectionable factors (Massih 1982, 1-8). It calls for changes in missionary lifestyle, worship forms, theological terms, and strategy.

Proponents argue that missionary strategy for Muslim evangelism needs a major overhaul, including:

a. The missionary should make initial contact with Muslim leaders. Even if they do not become Christians, the missionary can reduce the possibility of overt opposition by befriending them.

b. People on the fringes of society should not be the focus of witness, but rather opinion leaders of the community.

c. Families, relatives, and groups of friends should be the initial conversion goal rather than individuals.

d. In the beginning only basic theological concepts should be presented.

e. We must allow adequate time for change to take place (Parshall 1980, 92-93).

f. It is best not to encourage converts to repudiate Islam. Instead, it is better to allow them to "remain in the state in which (they were) called" (1 Cor. 7:20). This way they can influence their peers.

g. In many cases, baptism should be postponed, so converts will have a greater opportunity to win other Muslims. Confession of faith should be open, but baptism is seen as a political act in some countries.

h. Missionaries should study animistic practices among Muslims to discover areas of felt need. These may provide useful points of evangelistic contact (Anderson 1976, 295-299).

Conclusion

The institutional model will have to be used in Arab countries where no other ministry is permitted. The dialogical model provides a way to approach Muslims in different settings. The church-oriented emphasis of the traditional model is biblical and should be stressed. The contextualization model has drawn on the insights of anthropology to suggest long-needed reforms that will lead to truly indigenous churches. I have tried to incorporate elements from all the models, bearing in mind that Muslims vary culturally from place to place. One strategy does not fit all situations. These are some general rules that should characterize a strategy to evangelize Muslims:

Any model must be church-oriented. As Cragg said, "No man comes into a churchless Christ" (Cragg 1959, 143). However, the church must be contextualized. Any model that does not bring new converts into a nurturing church is sure to fail.

The successful model will emphasize worship. Worship should be designed to meet the needs of the people. The forms will be different in Africa and Asia, but here again contextualization is the key. Missionaries should use certain passages from the Qur'an as a springboard for explaining the gospel. They should feel free to use the names *Allah* and *Isa* (Jesus). Missionaries in Muslim countries will have to adjust their lifestyles for the sake of the gospel. Mission agencies would do well to give candidates special tests to see if they are psychologically fit for service among Muslims.

New missionaries should be given several years to study the language and culture of their assigned country, as well as Islam itself. Intensive preparation and reasonable expectations will reduce missionary dropouts and enhance productivity.

Missionaries need to adapt their preaching to the culture of their people. Storytelling may well be more effective than sermons. We should increase our use of the media. Radio, television, and literature could all be used more fully. Programming and writing must be contextualized. Drama would be more effective than the traditional hymn and sermon format.

Above all, **whatever model we use, it must be characterized by love and prayer for Muslims.** A Muslim convert wrote:

It is stimulating to think that cases of conversion through sheer reasoning between dogmas of two religions are very rare, perhaps nonexistent. In cases of conversion where prosperity, social status, security, vengeance against native society, emotional experimentation and the like are not the motives, the change of faith is motivated perhaps more frequently by love for charming virtues, of a magnetic person, or love for a group of lovable associates, than by cold religious arithmetic. (Khair-Ullah 1975, 824)

References
Anderson, John D. C. 1976. "The Missionary Approach to Islam: Christian or Cultic?"*Missiology* 4: 295-299.

Cragg, Kenneth. 1959. *Sandals at the Mosque.* New York: Oxford University Press.

Fry, C. George and James R. King. 1980. *Islam: A Survey of the Muslim Faith.* Grand Rapids, Mich.: Baker Books.

Khair-Ullah, Frank. 1975. "Evangelism among Muslims." In *Let the World Hear His Voice.* Ed. J. D. Douglas, 824. Minneapolis: World Wide Publications.

Massih, Bashir Abdol. 1982. "Incarnational Witness to Muslims: The Models of Jesus, Paul, and the Early Church." *World Pulse*, September 12, 1-8.

Parshall, Phil. 1980. *New Paths in Muslim Evangelism.* Grand Rapids, Mich.: Baker Books.

Register, Ray G. Jr. 1979. *Dialogue and Interfaith Witness with Muslims.* Fort Washington, Pa.: Worldwide Evangelization Crusade.

Vander Werff, Lyle. 1982. "Our Muslim Neighbors: The Contribution of Samuel Zwemer to Christian Mission." *Missiology* 10: 191.

Zwemer, Samuel M. 1941. *The Cross above the Crescent.* Grand Rapids, Mich.: Zondervan.

January 1998

Other Options for Muslim Evangelism

Phil Parshall

Instead of using confrontational debate, missionaries to Muslims should emphasize prioritizing a "classic" approach. The author offers five ways to reach Muslims.

(**Editor's note:** *This article is in response to "Courage in Our Convictions: The Case for Debate in Islamic Outreach" by Jay Smith in the January 1998 issue of* EMQ. *See page 103.*)

J AY SMITH'S PROVOCATIVE POSTULATE is not a new paradigm. Rather, it is a rehash of that which has been tried, tested, and found wanting. Even in contemporary times, we have had Anis Shorrosh boldly taking on Ahmed Deedat in a debate provocatively entitled, "The Qur'an or the Bible? Which is God's Word?" Some twelve thousand people, mostly Muslims, gathered in Birmingham, England, on August 7, 1988, for this highly animated face-off. Shorrosh took off his kid gloves and sought to academically undermine Qur'anic authority.

Perhaps he was too "successful." For in July 1990 Shorrosh journeyed to Deedat's home turf in South Africa only to be met with a wildly antagonistic and even violent response from the local Muslims. An article in the Durban newspaper headlined the story, "Controversial Christian Theologian Leaves the Country after Death Threats." Both England and South Africa are nominally Christian countries. Even so, Muslims were highly offended by being forced to endure a type of harsh criticism of their revered holy book. This, in spite of the fact that Deedat has long been the master of scorn and ridicule aimed so provocatively against our Bible.

Do we have a trade-off? Are there specific conversions emanating from the Smith-Shorrosh polemical approach? Both men have been engaged in their ministries of undercutting Islam for some years. To my knowledge, neither of them has seen Muslims come to Christ, at least not in any significant numbers. Conversely, a great deal of antagonism has been generated. If this is where all of this leads, it is only fair to seriously question the validity of their strategy.

Are there alternative methodologies? The following are some suggestions, most of which have been tested in varying contexts.

1. Interaction, Not Confrontation

"Will you come and participate in our Muslim-Christian interaction?" The intelligent, young Filipino convert from Seventh-day Adventism to Islam put this unique proposition to me. He requested I simply give a 20-minute testimony of what Christ means to me. After being assured that this would not be in a debate format, I accepted the invitation. Once before, I had observed the group's interaction in which only about forty people attended.

On the appointed evening I approached the band shell in Rizal Park. To my considerable consternation, I was confronted with a sea of seven hundred, almost all Muslim, faces. Many were in full Islamic dress. On the well-lit platform were two posters proclaiming, "Dr. Phil Parshall—special speaker on the subject, 'Is the Bible the Word of God?'" As I walked up I heard a young Filipino at the microphone forcefully explaining why he, as a Baptist pastor, had renounced Christianity and become a Muslim. Quite an introduction for me. I had been duped!

Nevertheless, I proceeded to give a clear testimony of my conversion and the rationale for my biblically-based faith. Microphones had been set up in the audience and for the next two hours. Muslims questioned me regarding biblical authority and other "easy" issues like the Trinity and how the crucifixion can affect humanity today. When the audience didn't appreciate my answer, the cry of "*Allahu Akbar*" (God is great) rolled over the band shell!

My presentation was a positive affirmation of my Christian faith. Somehow, I managed to be gracious to my Muslim host, even though I admit to a bit of anger against him for his duplicity.

At the end, several Muslims came up and said they had never heard Christianity explained in such a manner. The next day, a Pakistani and a Saudi who had been in the meeting came to my reading center. They were most gracious and concluded our time together by purchasing a Bible, which the Saudi assured me he would be taking with him back to his homeland. In my talk, I never once denigrated Islam.

My presentation was a positive affirmation of my Christian faith. Somehow, I managed to be gracious to my Muslim host, even though I admit to a bit of anger against him for his duplicity. Perhaps this format could be successfully utilized in a public setting. One word of warning: some Filipino pastors have engaged in these interactions and done very poorly. Only those trained in Christian theology and in Islamics should attempt this method of evangelism. The Muslims have been schooled in Deedat-style argumentation and know how to play hard ball.

2. Bookrooms

During the mid-1970s, I had the privilege of being part of a team which pioneered a contextualized approach to evangelism in a Southeast Asian country. As a result, thousands of Muslims have become Christians. This outreach is still being utilized by many different groups within that country. One of our most successful venues for making contacts with Muslims was through bookrooms or reading centers. In 1980, my wife and I were part of a team of four couples who went to work in a district of 1.5 million Muslims. To our knowledge, there had never been a convert in that area. Our team rented small rooms in rural village markets where the people would congregate weekly to buy and sell goods.

The centers were set up to be religiously attractive to Muslims. Scripture verses in Arabic were hung on the walls. We wore clothes appreciated by Muslims. Sitting on mats on the floor, we projected an image of a "holy man" or a religious teacher. Contextual literature was shared with the visitors. At first Muslims would drop in out of curiosity. But soon meaningful conversations took place. Within six months, we began to harvest the first fruits of our labors.

Today, there are over five hundred baptized Muslim Background Believers in just that one area. For the past thirteen years I have had a bookroom bordering the Islamic community in inner-city Manila. This "reading center" is likewise attractively decorated with Islamic art decor. But, as is appropriate in the city, simple chairs and stools are provided. I show the *Jesus* film in Muslim dialects four afternoons a week. Two tables of literature are set up on the sidewalk just outside the center.

Hundreds of Muslims have watched the film. Many have been deeply touched, especially by the crucifixion reenactment. A great deal of literature has been distributed. Visible fruit has been minimal, although perhaps the number one witnessing convert in all of the Philippines commenced her spiritual pilgrimage as she stepped into the center and was befriended by an OMF missionary lady who led her to Christ and discipled her.

In restrictive Islamic countries it may not be possible to have a bookroom outreach. But among minority Muslim populations and in more open societies like Pakistan, Indonesia, and a number of South Sahara countries, such centers are a valid option. This would be true throughout Europe as well. Each context would call for a unique approach that would be appreciated by the target community.

3. Tentmaking

The major impact in mission to Muslims in the new millennium will be, of necessity, related to tentmaking strategies. By the year 2000 few Islamic nations will be granting visas to openly declared missionaries. In extreme fundamentalist countries, even Christian lay missionaries who are overt in witness will find themselves declared persona non grata, or worse yet, as with Filipinos in Saudi Arabia, some will end up with extended prison terms.

Yet, the nature of the Great Commission demands an inclusion of the world's 1.2 billion Muslims. Political and religious barriers must be looked upon as a challenge rather than the last word as closed doors. There will always be "means" to somehow penetrate even the most difficult of Islamic lands. Many evangelical missions have now launched departments similar to SIM's "alternative ministries," which address the need for creative entry strategies into Muslim countries.

Frontiers has fielded probably the largest force specifically targeting the world of Islam. Its team-based approach has given maximum flexibility in professional options. Minimal bureaucracy within Frontiers has had a compelling appeal to the younger generation of Xers and Boomers. Few of their secularly well-trained personnel have had extensive preparation in theology and Islamics. Yet, in Frontiers' fifteen years of existence, over five hundred staff have been fielded, and scores of small Muslim Background Believer fellowships have come into being.

Islam, in its early years, was propagated through the influence of a dedicated network of laypeople. Members of this army of traveling businessmen took every opportunity to share their faith with those they met. This is why Asia today embraces almost two-thirds of the Muslim population of the world. The tentmakers were amazingly successful. It is now time for Christians to implement a similar strategy. These approaches will need to be characterized by a spirit of innovation and flexibility.

4. Radio

We have not begun to adequately experiment with contextual radio programming for the Islamic world. Much of the present effort is wrapped in Western dress and filled with Christian clichés unintelligible to the average Muslim listener. Felt needs are not a focus.

Sensitive programming could include talk shows on issues relevant to Muslims, health hints, poetry, scripture quizzes, reading from dramatic books, a soap opera with a compelling, emotional presentation, biographical drama, chanting of the Arabic Bible, talks on moral issues, discussion of the spirit world, farming information, nutrition helps, relevant indigenous music (both vocal and instrumental), question and answer interaction, relaying of personal messages, marital counseling, on-site interviews of interesting people, and finally, the offer of a free Bible correspondence lesson for all who request it. Most of these ideas could be incorporated into a low-key, one-hour daily program presented in a Muslim dialect.

One health worker, in cooperation with FEBC and SIM, is developing a radio program which assists rural people with their health needs. Considerable potential for such programming exists in the Muslim world. Where medium-wave broadcasting is not allowed, shortwave is always an option. Some entrepreneurs are considering using television to present Christ to Muslims. I can only hope the programming will be culturally and religiously relevant to the Muslim mind. I fear it might be but a rehash of Western Christian television presentations. That would be sad indeed.

5. Spiritual Dynamics

The Western missionary specializes in methodology. We have our gurus like Ralph Winter, who is perhaps the world's greatest living missiologist. And we pay him due respect for his amazing innovation and productivity. But what about a missionary guru known solely for spirituality? Can there be a consensus that such a man or woman exists? Oh, yes, we may have our individual nominations, but I doubt that anyone would garner over fifty votes. There appears to be no living missionary in the lineage of a spiritually-intense Hudson Taylor or Adoniram Judson.

Why? Have our families, churches, Bible schools, and even missions misdirected our steps? Why all the emphasis on statistics and success? Is this now what drives our mission community? "Doing" has somehow overshadowed, and in some cases obliterated, "being." Does this possibly explain our general impotence as we stand before a nearly impregnable Islam? Recently, Jim Plueddemann, general director of SIM, called together the mission leadership in London. The most pungent part of that consultation was the morning hours when Jim led us into a time of deep spiritual soul searching. On our knees, we sought the living Lord for forgiveness, humility, purity, and empowerment. It was a time few of us will ever forget.

Bill Bright, in his seventh decade of life, issued a call for Christians to be involved in a forty-day, juices-only fast and time of prayer. He has set a personal example by keeping this fast for the past three years. In 1996, thirteen of us in the Philippines who are involved in Muslim evangelism also followed this style of fast. Our two-fold focus was personal holiness and a breakthrough in Muslim evangelism. We fasted during the 30-day Ramadan fast and then for an additional ten days. Each of us testified to a new spiritual sensitivity as a result of self-deprivation. A few had a major revolution in their personal walks with the Lord. There were some gains in Muslim outreach as well.

I realize the brief confines of this article do not allow for a thorough presentation of all of the missiological options for Muslim evangelism. Others can fill in the blanks. But I would conclude by emphasizing the absolute imperative of prioritizing a "classic" approach to a revitalization of spiritual reality among us missionaries who are called to be light and salt to the "Sons of Ishmael."

Winter 1971

How Dialogue Can Be Used to Witness to Muslims

Ralph E. Brown

We must continue to witness to Muslims in dialogue and procla-mation, faithfully, with self-giving love, believing prayer, and in humility, always learning.

SOME YEARS AGO, IN THE CITY OF SHIKARPUR, West Pakistan, a blind Christian evangelist and I were invited to meet with some of the Muslim religious leaders in the courtyard of a neighborhood mosque. My Pakistani co-worker was a convert from Islam. The motive of the mullahs was to win my blind friend back to Islam. Our motive was to give witness to our Lord Jesus Christ. We sat in the mosque courtyard with our shoes at the door, in the midst of a zealous but friendly Muslim group, and with a silent audience peering over the mosque wall. As we sipped sweet tea, we listened and talked, asked questions and an-swered questions, and from the Bible sought to proclaim Christ to our Muslim friends. This was only one meeting, but to us it was an experience in dialogue.

Dialogue is a key word in the study of the world mission of the Church. R. Pierce Beaver tells us that "dialogue is the `in' word today. Everybody is for di-alogue, both in mission circles and in academic theological quarters" (1968, 113). In many areas, this is a day of tolerance, leading to open discussion and interaction between people of different religions, philosophies, and opinions. "The age of dialogue is with us whether we like it or not, right or wrong" (Cov-ell 1969, 3).

But what is dialogue? Theologians, missionary statesmen, and missionaries themselves differ considerably in their understanding of what dialogue is and what it involves. Robert L. Slater writes: "Dialogue means conversation. It is a term used, for example, with reference to what the characters in a novel say to each other as distinguished from what they do" (1964, 2). Although the Greek word *dialegomai* portrays the idea of debate or argument, the English word "di-alogue" concerns conversation.

Harold Lindsell believes that dialogue means "to exchange ideas" (1967, 205). The exchange is between people. "Strictly speaking... there is no such thing as a dialogue between religions, for the engagement is not between ab-stractions but between believers" (Slater 1964, 2). Thus it is more proper to refer to the Christian-Muslim dialogue rather than the dialogue between Is-lam and Christianity.

The World Council of Churches' statement drawn up at the Kandy Consultation in 1967 attempts to define the fundamental nature of dialogue as "...this genuine readiness to listen to the man with whom we desire to communicate" (Hayward 1967a, 53). But if our concern is only to listen, we are simply on the receiving end of a monologue. Further on, the Kandy statement does say, "We recognize that readiness to listen to each other may justly be coupled in both of us with a desire to proclaim to each other" (1967a, 74).

Some confine dialogue to ecumenical study centers, such as are found in several Muslim countries, where there is "a structured colloquium with a panel of experts politely exchanging views" (Beaver 1968, 116). But dialogue cannot be limited to the academic sphere, if there is to be genuine communication between Christians and Muslims. Only friendly conversation will not necessarily produce witness. But the object of any attempt at dialogue should not be solely to win an argument. Beaver reminds us: "Dialogue is not disputation, which is a verbal attempt to conquer a foe. Arrogance and pride always enter into disputation and real communication becomes difficult" (1968, 117).

Dialogue must of necessity concern not only mutual understanding and the comparison of ideas, but also the grappling with religious truth.

Dialogue must of necessity concern not only mutual understanding and the comparison of ideas, but also the grappling with religious truth. R. M. Speight questions whether any dialogue can be carried on in an atmosphere of complete objectivity in any realm—cultural, political, or religious (Speight 1965, 194). Hendrik Kraemer believes that in the interest of straight thinking, it is quite impossible to escape controversy and mutual cross-questioning (1960, 362).

Dialogue is a meeting of minds and hearts and voices. It presupposes right attitudes. In the words of the 1964 Bangkok statement of the East Asian Christian Conference: "True dialogue with a man of another faith requires a concern both for the gospel and for the other man. Without the first, dialogue becomes a pleasant conversation. Without the second, it becomes irrelevant, unconvincing or arrogant" (Schmidt 1967, 4). Beaver goes so far as to say that dialogue is "an evangelistic necessity" and "the only alternative to a religious `cold war'" (1968, 55).

The danger in dialogue is that the biblical teaching of proclaiming, persuading, and inviting men to come to Christ as the only Savior may be so diluted in the dialogical encounter that the Muslim sees no need of coming to Christ in repentance and faith. One certainly is benefited and stimulated by the profound scholarship and gracious attitudes of the great Islamic scholar, Dr. Kenneth Cragg.

I personally owe him a great debt. But in reading Dr. Cragg's writings, one gets the impression that in his fairness to and understanding of the people of Islam, he weakens the biblical emphasis of repentance toward God and faith in our Lord Jesus Christ. Cragg's contribution to a sympathetic understanding of Islam does not seem to be balanced with a clear call to Muslims as sinners to consider the claims of Christ. In a sermon written for Muslims, Dr. Cragg builds on the theme of the Qur'anic injunction to seek forgiveness, but fails to clearly state that only through Christ and his cross is there God's forgiveness (Cragg 1966, 91-101).The only Christian scripture referred to in this sermon based on a Qur'anic text is 2 Corinthians 5:19, and a vague reference to the atonement is made. The approach is to the Muslim scholar, but nevertheless, there is a lack of Paul's appeal, "Be reconciled to God."

Dr. Cragg's concern for dialogue with Muslims has led him to advocate "careful occasions of inter-worship" (1968a, 376).This seems to lead dangerously toward religious confusion, a denial of the mediatorship of Christ, and syncretism. In all fairness, it should be mentioned that Dr. Cragg in some of his writings speaks out against syncretism and compromise. For instance:

Sympathy with Islam and its meanings does not involve a diluted Christianity. On the contrary. It is out of the fullness of the truth of the divine Lover that we may live in the power of his love for men. We shall not the better penetrate into the ends and meanings of Islam for getting apologetic or diffident about the incarnation and the cross. (1964, 236)

L. J. Swidler, in writing on the subject of Christian dialogue with non-Christians, seems to present the thinking of many ecumenical Christians:

They (Christians) must come to the other religions, which have been on the earth for hundreds and even thousands of years, with a humility that seeks to learn what roles they play in God's providence, in what ways they manifest God to man, how they lead man toward salvation. (1968, 128)

This ecumenically oriented view of dialogue which dilutes the gospel de-emphasizes the must of personal conversion and rejoices that an age of aggressive missionary activity is hopefully at an end (1968, 9). Swidler suggests that in a certain sense it may be the task of a Christian in a Muslim land to help ignorant Muslims become better Muslims (1968, 129). But is not our mission to witness to the love of God in Jesus Christ and to plead with Muslims to come to him? The approach should certainly not be with an attitude of superiority, but with the conviction of the uniqueness of Jesus Christ as Savior and God incarnate. John MacQuarrie of Union Seminary rejects this approach when he writes:

There can be creative dialogue, to use Tillich's expression, among great religions only if Christians frankly abandon claims to superiority. This means that there must be an end to proselytizing, and to the imperialistic dream of a single religion for all the peoples of the earth. (1964, 44)

In commenting on MacQuarrie's position, Earl Herbert Cressy points out how unrealistic it is:

Today several religions are coming to envisage themselves as world religions and superior to all others. To think that the Christian can dissuade them merely by giving up his own convictions and inviting them to engage in dialogue is unrealistic. Should the Christian request his opposite number to divest himself of his own religious faith and enter into dialogue on even terms? (1966, 256)

Roman Catholic thinkers differ in their view of dialogue. The Vatican II decrees seem to stress that the Church has a mission in dialogue, but there are some strong statements which seem to be very universalistic (Van Straelen 1966, 173). R. Avens writes, "The Christian faith is radically universalistic. Every human being is under God's grace and can be saved; every world religion is under God's grace and can be a way of salvation" (1968, 69).

But there are Roman Catholic conservatives who even question the validity of dialogue and are asking themselves questions such as, "How is it justified? What connection has it with the question of salvation? For it is beyond dispute for a Christian that the only Savior is Jesus, and that the only basis of salvation is faith in Jesus the Savior" (Jomier 1966, 444). The evangelical must reject any ideas of dialogue which dilute the gospel, destroy the uniqueness of the Christian message, and deny the Christian the joy and blessing of sharing Christ with the people of Islam. Dialogue need not be reduced to a mere anemic inter-religious contact, but can, and should be "an evangelistic tactic" in spite of the rejection of this term by the ecumenists at Kandy (Hayward 1967b, 73).

Granted, there may be different approaches in dialogue, but the fundamental concept that the claims of Christ must be shared when dialogue with Muslims occurs would be accepted by all evangelicals, and by some who may not be considered as thorough-going evangelicals. In his dialogical encounters at Ephesus as he met Jews and Greeks both in public and from house to house, Paul declared, he taught, and he testified the basic message—repentance to God and faith in our Lord Jesus Christ (see Acts 20:20-21). And although the word "controversy" seems to be obsolete today when it concerns witness to Muslims, there is New Testament evidence to suggest that Paul engaged in controversy with a dialogical spirit. The word *dialegomai* is translated "argue" in the Revised Standard Version in Acts 17:2, 17; 18:4, 19; 19:8, 9; and 24:25.

The evangelical Christian living among Muslims believes that he or she can engage in dialogue as he or she endeavors to be true to his or her evangelistic mission. Lindsell points this out:

Dialogue does not mean that concessions have been or will be made to the standpoint of those with whom dialogue takes place. The notion that even to engage in dialogue is to make a concession is false, nor does dialogue presuppose that either party will change his mind. From the outset the evangelical is a propagandist in the best sense of that abused term. He is an evangelist. His purpose is to change the mind of the other person. He does not engage in dialogue simply to find out what the other person is thinking. He listens and talks so that he can answer error and convince the other person that the Christian faith is true. (1967, 206)

Although evangelicals believe in dialogue, we insist that it is not synonymous with evangelism, but only one method of evangelism. And in witness to Muslims, it is an important one. Speight is concerned about the confusion on this point:

It sometimes appears that the word "dialogue" has replaced the word "evangelism" in the vocabulary of the church elite. Dialogue as a replacement for evangelism involves some great changes in concept as well as a verbal alteration....Such a substitution of dialogue for evangelism does not seem to be legitimate....When dialogue serves Christian missionary ends, it does so only as a part of the whole endeavor, and gives way ultimately to proclamation and apologetics. (1965, 194)

Dialogue is not without its dangers. It cannot serve only as a friendly academic or philosophical confrontation. Thomas McDormand shows the dangers to witnessing:

Much that passes for dialogue...is interested in questions but resents and rejects answers. All the while, the Christian gospel offers answers, redemptive answers, to the most fundamental questions hard-pressed humanity can ask. The Christian witness must confidently and humbly offer answers. It must have a sympathetic appreciation of the difficulty many have in accepting the Christian answers, and it must realize that seeking love is very patient. (1965, 21)

Another danger is that in a dialogical encounter the Muslim may be convinced of the truth of Christianity on an intellectual plane, but he or she still needs a personal, dynamic relationship with the living Christ. Georg F. Vicedom stresses this: "In the mission, it is not a question of proof of a better religion. It is a matter of witnessing to the living Christ so that he may find entrance among men. Men should be offered the salvation of God" (1963, 152).

Dialogue with Muslims is not just inviting them to a bargaining table, or to a friendly exchange of views, nor is it mere Christian presence among them. It is going to them in love, with a sympathetic understanding of their beliefs, convictions, and practices, but in proclamation that they are sinners who need Christ, even as we are sinners who have found Christ. The Christian is "an ex-beggar giving another beggar the same kind of bread that saved his life" (Lindsell 1967, 205). In fact, evangelical Christians "must aggressively reach out to initiate dialogue. They have been sent to others, not commanded to wait for them to come. They are to go out, not to remain at home in their pleasant isolation from the world" (Lindsell 1967, 208).

Dialogue has to do with attitude as much as method, but the goal must be kept in view—the goal of witnessing, proclaiming, declaring the truth of the gospel. Speight, who is strong on apologetic, believes that dialogue is a preliminary to apologetic:

> Having endeavored, as objectively as possible, to understand and enter into sympathy with the Muslim through study and dialogue, the missionary turns to his apologetic...the ultimate, though often not the immediate, aim of this apologetic is conversion. (1965, 196-197)

We, as evangelicals, are compelled by the command of Christ, the prompting of the Holy Spirit, and the very nature of the gospel to witness to Muslims in dialogue and in proclamation. "So we say yes to presence; but no to presence without proclamation. We say yes to dialogue; but no to dialogue without decision" (Ford 1967, 208).

It is difficult to understand how true and effective dialogue can occur if one party refuses to converse. This is, unfortunately, very often the case in the Christian-Muslim confrontation. Bishop Stephen Neill comments on this problem of Muslim interest:

> But it takes two to make dialogue; the most disappointing factor in the present situation is the almost total failure so far of the Muslim scholar to approach Christianity with that reverence and open-mindedness which he rightly demands of the Christian scholar in his approach to Islam. (1961, 61)

Neill goes on to quote Dr. Charles Malik, who has candidly said, "There isn't a single Moslem scholar in all history, so far as I know, who has written an authentic essay on Christianity" (1961, 61).

If there are very few scholars who show interest in really understanding Christianity, what can be said of the *mullah* or the average Muslim? Fortunately, the modern, often Western-oriented intellectual, and the student community, are considerably more open to the possibility of dialogue than the religious leaders and the common man. A Muslim scholar came to Robert L. Slater at the Center for the Study of World Religions at Harvard and said, "The majority of Muslims know little or nothing about Christian thought; nor are they likely to give much heed to books written by Christians" (Slater 1964, 8).

Perhaps one reason that many Muslims are not interested in dialogue is that of fear. "Moslems are not fully confident that the new Christian approach signals a genuine willingness for an authentic dialogue. They are afraid that dialogue is nothing but a new form for converting Moslims to Christianity" (Habib 1969, 111). There is a distrust on the part of many Muslims of one with a missionary motive. Beaver tells of one learned Muslim historian of religion who "would exclude all people from dialogue who have a missionary motive" (1968, 116).

Some books written by Muslims reflect little of the dialogical spirit. For example, Maryam Jameelah, a former Jewess, dedicates her book, *Islam versus Ahl al Kitab Past and Present*, "for those who want to combat the menace of Zionism and Christian missionary activity in Muslim lands" (1968, 1). She concludes her book with:

> On what foundation can a lasting reconciliation between Muslims, Jews, and Christians be based? We must realize that under the existing circumstances, no friendship is possible. Jewry and Christendom have joined hands to destroy us and all we cherish.... It would be sheer folly to kiss the hands that are beating us....Peaceful relations and mutual respect among us can only be achieved through strength. (1968, 320)

Ismail Raqi Al Faruqi speaks out in support of dialogue with Christians, but he condemns the Christian mission to Islam and suggests that "the mission chapter of Christian history, as we have so far known it, had better be closed, the hunt called off, the missionaries withdrawn and the mission arm of the Catholic Church and of the World Council of Churches liquidated" (1968, 51). In the light of the general Muslim disinterest, it appears that Christians living in Muslim lands must take the initiative in seeking those who will respond to some sort of dialogical meeting and pray for more response on the part of the ulema and the average Muslim to sit down and talk in an atmosphere of genuine love and mutual respect.

Barriers to Dialogue

Aside from the Muslim disinterest in dialogue, there are historical, contemporary, theological, and practical barriers to the Christian-Muslim dialogue.

1. The religion of Islam is post-Christian and from its inception has challenged the basic doctrines of Christianity. Cragg writes:

> Islam is the only major post-Christian religion...only with Islam is Christianity antecedently formative of doctrines which disallow it and of judgments that contest its convictions. Only in the Qur'an is there a definitive scripture which has a consciously "Christian" pre-occupation in its themes and emphases. (1968, 118)

Theologically, Islam is Christianity's most skillful competitor and the Muslim faith challenges the finality of the gospel because it is "the only universal faith which claims to have surpassed and superseded Christianity" (Fry 1967, 9).

2. Islam, a missionary religion, is Christianity's greatest missionary competitor. "Islam has also been the only world religion to win great numbers of converts from Christianity" (Fry 1967, 10). Muslims are aggressively competing with Christians for the souls of men. Fry reminds us that "in its very inception, Islam stands as a judgment on the Church of the seventh century for its failure to evangelize Arabia; by its continued existence, it testifies to the most tragic failure of the Church's evangelistic mission in the successive ages" (Fry 1967, 10).

3. The minority status and the ghetto complex of Christians in Muslim lands is another barrier to dialogue. Fearful of losing their identity, Christians are often considered inferior by the majority community and exhibit a depressed people image. Referring to Christians in the Middle East, Fry remarks:

> Cut off from the larger community by custom, conviction, conscience, and social

class (sometimes also by language), the ethnic churches became passive, pessimistic, and introverted. They neither sought nor welcomed converts from the Muslim world; indeed they were frequently forbidden to do so. The churches were isolated from society. (1967, 11)

Much of this description is applicable to the churches in Pakistan and India as well. Dialogue is virtually impossible when there is such ghetto-type isolation.

4. The remembrance of the political and military clashes of past centuries, especially the Crusades, has been a serious barrier. Forgiveness comes very slowly and Christianity is still considered by most Muslims as an aggressive religio-political movement. There has been tension for a thousand years between Dar-al-Islam and the Christian West, with faults on both sides. "To us, the Crusades are very ancient history; to the Muslim they are as though they had happened yesterday" (Neill 1961, 58).

5. Western Christian behavior has not always been exemplary in Muslim countries. The impression left by some soldiers, hippies, and tourists has been that Christians have no spiritual or moral convictions. "The Christian world, by failing to exemplify the faith it confesses, has given a poor witness to the world of Islam" (Fry 1967, 11).

6. Christian missionaries and national Christians residing in the Muslim world have often revealed, through impatience, unloving attitudes, and insensitivity to the beliefs and practices of Muslims, that they themselves are a barrier to true dialogue. We are convicted by the words of Cragg:

It is just that fact that it is "our" gospel which makes it so profoundly suspect and suspected. That "we" are its messengers is its deepest discredit. For the white and Western world, with which for most of men Christianity is so closely, even irretrievably, associated, has given most of men so much cause to distrust both it and what it bears. Imperialism, race, apartheid, exploitation, sheer insensitivity...the frequent failure to respond to the unqualified desire of mankind to love and be loved—all these grimly overshadow the loving-kindness of what we announce about God. (1967, 60)

Only a Christian who has lived in a Muslim environment can understand how often we fail in communicating the love of Christ to inquirers, friends, neighbors, and other members of the Muslim community. A more sanctified missionary and Christian community would most certainly contribute to more effective dialogue in witness to Muslim peoples. His statement may be intemperate and inaccurate, but we can learn something from Al Faruqi's stinging indictment of Christians when he says, "The Western world knows of no Christian who, moved by the Sermon on the Mount, came to live among Muslims as a native, who made their burden his burden, their hopes and yearnings his hopes and yearnings" (1968, 50).

7. Both Christians and Muslims are negligent in reading each other's literature. It is true that Christian minorities are often faced with the vitriolic writings of the majority community, while on the other hand many of the classic Christian apologetic works are banned by government action. Nevertheless, both sides need to read what the other is writing with a desire to understand.

8. Roman Catholics, such as Alex Zanotelli, a young Roman Catholic missionary in the Sudan, believe that the divisions among Christians are a very real and serious barrier to dialogue. Many Protestants share this view. Zanotelli writes:

> There is good evidence for suggesting that the Christian disunity has enabled Islam to spread so quickly. Was it not the encounter with a bitterly divided Christendom, torn asunder by Christological disputes, that made Muhammad look with ridicule on Christianity? (1967, 44)

Evangelicals agree that disunity in the Church is a barrier, but more particularly division caused by sin, strife, church politics, and deviation from the great evangelical truths of God's word. Muslims who have their own movements can understand denominational differences much more than divergent views of major Christian doctrines.

9. The greatest barrier to dialogue is spiritual. Our Muslim friends are blinded by the god of this world to Christ and his truth. There is a wide gulf in the Christian and Muslim understanding of sin. The offence of the cross is ever present. As Neill so aptly suggests, "That which we ask him to look for in Jesus is in itself a cause of grave offence to Muslim pride. We suggest—we cannot do otherwise—that he find a Savior. The Muslim affirms that he has no need of any such thing" (1961, 68).

The Approach We Can Take

Earlier missionaries to Muslims are often categorized as controversialists who had no interest in dialogue, only in forthright proclamation. One gets the impression that the analysis of the old-time approach is sometimes overcritical. Certainly it is difficult to accuse Samuel Zwemer and W. H. T. Gairdner, both displaying considerable controversy in their writings, of not loving the Muslim people to whom they gave their lives.

But there is some truth to the claim that "Christian approaches to the Muslim, with certain notable exceptions, have been carried out on the basis and in the spirit of polemic" (Neill 1961, 59). Polemics is not synonymous with Spirit-filled witness. Witness sometimes involves controversy, but our primary mission is to witness to the saving grace of Christ, not to argue on a doctrinal level. What approach can we take in seeking to win Muslims to Christ and his Church?

1. We must proclaim Christ in faithful witness. Whether through monologue or dialogue, the people of Islam need to be continually exposed to the gospel as it is presented in faithful witness. As J. H. Bavinck has said, "This message has only one powerful weapon, namely, that its messengers know that if they bring it obediently and honestly, trusting in God's help and in his Spirit, it will somehow touch the heart of man" (1966, 206). A positive, articulate, and faithful witness to Jesus Christ means to engage by the power of the Holy Spirit in both dialogue and proclamation. Some ecumenists, like those at Kandy, declare that "dialogue is proclamation," a most ambiguous statement. The evangelical stress in witness to Muslims should be proclamation in dialogue.

The way of dialogue which Bishop Neill calls "the better way" seems to be the most favorable approach for the evangelical Christian as he seeks to faithfully witness to Christ in the context of the contemporary Muslim world (1961, 59). In many towns and cities, bazaar-preaching may be passé (although literature distribution is not), but "any missionary or fraternal worker whose love and humility can be sensed by other persons, who can listen as well as speak, and who is a seeker after truth as well as a witness to truth can find half a dozen opportunities for dialogue in the normal contacts of every day" (Beaver 1968, 115). Is not this way of dialogue, in an evangelical sense, linked closely to personal evangelism?

2. We must proclaim Christ in love. This is the virtue that validates our faith. The world of Islam needs, in the words of Eric Bishop, "an explosion of friendliness....Ordinary people want friendship, the only cogent antidote to the bitterness, disillusionment and antagonism that have vitiated the Christian approach to the Muslim peoples" (1965, 356). Agape love is the sum total of all the Christian virtues and attitudes which are needed in our relations with Muslims: sensitivity, humility, patience, gentleness, kindness, forgiveness. This is the Christian presence which is so necessary in the Muslim world today. To witness to God incarnate, the missionary himself must seek by God's grace to be love incarnate. Dr. Daud Rahbar, a convert from Islam, writes:

> The basic qualification for a missionary engaged in dialogue with Muslims is the quality of his personal presence....His inability to speak with faultless accuracy about the historical traditions of Islam and Christianity will be amply compensated by his personal radiance and graciousness....the primacy belongs not to the amount of factual information but to the transparency of love; though learning is an immense advantage. (1965, 353)

3. We must proclaim Christ with knowledge. An experiential knowledge of Christ and a thorough knowledge of our faith are vital, but it also means that we need to try to know and understand the Muslim and his faith. Jean Corbon suggests how to get out of the present impasse in the Christian-Muslim encounter: "Our first effort should be directed towards remaking the acquaintance of the other, getting to know him afresh, discovering him with unprejudiced eyes: `being born with him' as he is" (1965, 73).

Getting to know the inner spiritual vitality of the Muslim is referred to by Speight as identifying with him in "interiority." He feels that this is a basis for the Christian apologetic to Islam (1965, 200-201).This suggests the possibility of genuine dialogue on such subjects as knowing God, knowing yourself, prayer, the conscience, inner spiritual struggles, etc. There is a great need today for thorough evangelical missionary scholars who can seek to know the Muslim mind and faith, and can share their evangelical insights with others. But even the average Christian worker in Muslim lands needs to diligently study the language, culture, and religion of Muslims to be well-equipped for witness.

4. We must proclaim Christ with earnest, persevering, believing prayer. Brian Fargher believes that if we are going to meet the challenge of "the reproach of barrenness" in the world of Islam, we need unique workers, unique faith, and unique prayer backing (1966, 96-103). Missionaries need to rededicate themselves to the primary task, that which the early apostles gladly assumed, "But we will devote ourselves to prayer and to the ministry of the word" (Acts 6:4). A praying church and praying proclaimers are indispensable in our approach.

We must continue to witness to Muslims in dialogue and proclamation, faithfully, with self-giving love, believing prayer, and in humility, always learning. Our witness is primarily positive, in the power of the Holy Spirit. "The real Christian concentration is not: `we have the revelation and not you,' but pointing gratefully and humbly to Christ: `It has pleased God to reveal himself fully and decisively in Christ; repent, believe, and adore'" (Kraemer 1956, 97). Christ's love for us and for the Muslim compels us to witness. We need not only to be willing, but eager to preach the gospel to Muslims. In the words of Bishop Stephen Neill, "Our task is to go on saying to the Muslim with infinite patience, `Sir, consider Jesus.' We have no other message" (1961, 98).

References

Al Faruqi, Ismail Raqi A. 1968. "Islam and Christianity: Diatribe or Dialogue?" *Journal of Ecumenical Studies* 5(1).

Avens, R. 1968. "The Other Dialogue: Christianity and Non-Christian Religions." *Catholic World.*

Bavinck, J. H. 1966. *The Church Between Temple and Mosque.* Grand Rapids, Mich.: William B. Eerdmans Publishing Co.

Beaver, R. Pierce. 1968. *The Missionary Between the Times.* New York: Doubleday and Co., Inc.

Bishop, Eric F.F. 1965. "The Reasonableness of Christ." *Muslim World* LV, October.

Corbon, Jean. 1965. "Islam and Christianity: Impasse or Hope of Dialogue?" *Student World* 58(1).

Covell, Ralph. 1969. "Dialogue—Friend or Foe." *Evangelical Missions Quarterly* 6(1): 3.

Cragg, Kenneth. 1964. *The Dome and the Rock.* London: SPCK.

_____. 1966. "Man and Empire—God and Forgiveness." In *Sermons to Men of Other Faiths and Traditions.* New York: Abingdon Press.

_____. 1967. "The Credibility of Christianity." *Study Encounter* 3(2).

_____. 1968a. "Common Prayer." In *Union Seminary Quarterly* XXIII(4).

_____. 1968b. *Christianity in World Perspective.* New York: Oxford University Press.

Cressy, Earl Herbert. 1966. "Christian Missions Today." *Religion in Life,* Spring.

Fargher, Brian. 1966. "Taking Away the Reproach of Barrenness." *Evangelical Missions Quarterly* 2(2).

Ford, Leighton. 1968. "Presence vs. Proclamation." *Evangelical Missions Quarterly* 4(4).

Fry, C. George. 1967. "Christianity's Greatest Challenge." *Christianity Today* XIV(3).

Habib, G. 1969. "Possibilities of Christian-Moslem Dialogue." Excerpts from an interview in *Christian Century*, January 22.

Hayward, Victor E. W., ed. 1967a. "Christians in Dialogue with Men of Other Faiths," a statement drawn up at the WCC Consultation in Kandy, Ceylon, in *Study Encounter* 111(2).

_____. 1967b. "Theological Tensions Behind Points in the Kandy Statement." *Study Encounter* III(2).

Jameelah, Maryam. 1968. *Islam versus Ahl al Kitab Past and Present*. Lahore, West Pakistan: Mohammed Yusuf Khan.

Jomier, J. 1966. "Roman Catholic Thinking Concerning the Christian-Muslim Encounter." *International Review of Missions* LV(220).

Kraemer, Hendrik. 1956. *The Christian Message in a Non-Christian World*. Grand Rapids, Mich.: Kregel Publications.

_____. 1960. *World Cultures and World Religions*. London: Lutterworth Press.

Lindsell, Harold. 1967. "Attack Syncretism with Dialogue." *Evangelical Missions Quarterly* 3(4).

MacQuarrie, John. 1964. "Christianity and Other Faiths." *Union Seminary Quarterly Review* XX.

McDormand, Thomas. 1965. "Dialogue or Witness." *Christianity Today* X(5).

Neill, Stephen. 1961. *Christian Faith and Other Faiths*. London: Oxford University Press.

Rahbar, Daud. 1965. "Christian Apologetic to Muslims." *International Review of Missions* LIV(215).

Schmidt, William J. 1967. "Ecumenism and the Problem of Religious Syncretism." *Occasional Bulletin of the Missionary Research Library* XIII(5).

Slater, Robert L. 1964. "The Coming Great Dialogue." In *Christianity: Some Non-Christian Appraisals*. Ed. David W. McKain, 2. New York: McGraw Hill Book Co.

Smith, Wilfred Cantwell. 1969. "Participation: The Changing Christian Role in Other Cultures." *Occasional Bulletin* XV(4).

Speight, R. M. 1965. "Some Bases for a Christian Apologetic to Islam." *International Review of Missions*, April.

Swidler, L. J. 1968. "Christian Dialogue with Non-Christians." *Journal of Ecumenical Studies*, Winter.

Van Straelen, Henry. 1966. *The Catholic Encounter with World Religions*. Westminster, Md.: The Newman Press.

Vicedom, Georg F. 1963. *The Challenge of the World Religions*. Philadelphia: Fortress Press.

Zanotelli, Alex. 1967. "A Letter to the Ecumenist." *The Ecumenist* 5(3).

The Gospel for Shame Cultures: Have We Failed to Reach Muslims at Their Point of Deepest Insecurity?

Bruce Thomas

The author asks, "Has there been something missing in our understanding and preaching of the gospel so that we fail to reach the Muslim at his or her point of deepest insecurity?"

I HAVE DISCOVERED THAT ONE OF THE MOST DIFFICULT ASPECTS of evangelizing Muslims is getting them to appreciate their need for a Savior. I have found the Islamic doctrine of God and humans to be such that Muslims tend to be unaware of their sinfulness and inability to save themselves (Schlorff 1981, 24). As a result, convincing a Muslim to embrace Jesus as the blood sacrifice for his or her sins usually requires considerable time and pre-evangelistic effort.

In observing one particular culture, I have noticed a curious thing. While my Muslim friends and neighbors do not worry much about "little sins" like lying and cheating, their daily lives and religious rituals seem to revolve around something which I would consider to be even less significant, namely their ceremonial purity. The intensity of this insecurity has caused me to consider that defilement might be a basic human problem as serious to some as sin is to others.

One day, our helper told us that when she was a little girl she had a friend who used to feel her mother's hair in the morning to see if it was damp. Her friend did this so that she could tell if her mother, who was divorced, had been messing around. According to Islam, you are unclean after you have had sex and must take a complete bath, including washing your hair, in order to be clean again.

When asked why her friend's mother would bother to take the bath if she was already committing adultery, our helper responded that no one would dare think of not taking the ritual bath after having had sex. Such a person would be a curse and the ground they walked on would be cursed. In other words, a prolonged state of ritual uncleanness following sexual intercourse was more unthinkable than adultery.

Interpretations

Suddenly a lot of things made sense. It had always puzzled me why Muslims make such a big thing out of not eating pork, not getting licked by dogs, and keeping the fast, when sins like lying, cheating, and stealing are treated so superficially. Few Christians seem to comprehend, for instance, the seriousness of eating pork. Dwell for a moment on the revulsion you feel when you think about a Stone Age tribe eating human flesh, and you will begin to understand something of the degree of disgust most Muslims have for the idea of eating pork. It is probably not a sin issue, but an issue of ceremonial cleanness. Thus, because eating pork is the worst possible state of defilement, and more attention is given to ceremonial purity than moral purity, the pork eater (George W. H. Bush) is worse off than a murderer (Saddam Hussein).

In the light of this perspective, I began to consider that perhaps the greatest need felt by Muslim people is not for assurance of salvation from sin, but for deliverance from the tyranny of being in a near constant state of defilement. Every element of their daily lives is ordered by this insecurity: the direction to face when falling asleep; the Arabic words uttered when beginning a task,

> **I began to consider** that perhaps the greatest need felt by Muslim people is not for assurance of salvation from sin, but for deliverance from the tyranny of being in a near constant state of defilement.

speech, or greeting; even the way to blow one's nose or wipe one's bottom.

Defilements come in various levels and for each level there is an appropriately matched cleansing. Burping and passing gas is one level of defilement. Touching your private parts is another. Touching semen, urine, feces, or menstrual flow is getting pretty serious—serious enough that a woman's prayers will not be heard during her period. I wonder if there is a more relevant way to present the gospel under these circumstances. Perhaps we could communicate more effectively with a gospel message addressing one's defilement as well as, or as part of, his or her depravity.

An Application

Before furlough a year ago, a friend asked me quite sincerely why we Christians insist that Jesus is God and that he was crucified. My answer moved him visibly. Instead of beginning by saying all have sinned and that the wages of sin is death, I waxed eloquent on what he knew better than me—that all flesh is defiled. He nodded knowingly as I affirmed that from the day we are born we continually carry inside us the very substances from which we need to be cleansed.

He squirmed as I illustrated the futility of ceremonial rituals for such internal cleansing, and concluded that human flesh cannot cleanse itself for either God or heaven any better than darkness can make itself light. *He was still as attentive when I climaxed by saying that just as a candle drives the darkness from a room by entering it, God drives defilement from human flesh by becoming it.* In other words, the very thing Muslims object to most in Christianity, *syirik*— the identification of God with his creation—is the solution to humanity's most basic problem as perceived by these Muslims.

If I'd thought of it at the time, I would have gone on to show how the nature of Jesus' miracles—healing blindness with his spit and leprosy with his touch—proves who he is. I didn't forget to answer the second part of his question by pointing out that Jesus touched and destroyed the most serious consequence of our defilement—death. Finally, I concluded by saying that our only hope lies in appropriating the once-and-for-all cleansing from defilement and victory over death that Jesus offers to those who believe in him, and by saying that baptism is the symbol of this appropriation.

Foundations

It took months and considerable reflection for me to realize the possible implications of what I had stumbled into. Do general and specific revelation teach something about the defilement of humans? Is our defilement an integral part of our sinfulness? Is shame related to defilement the way guilt is related to sin? Does Christ's death atone for our defilement as well as our sin? Is the apparent lack of attention to this area related to Christianity's predominance in the West, which is more guilt and performance oriented as opposed to the East which is more shame and being oriented? Have we missed some important concepts in our commentaries and in our English translations of the original languages?

In cultures where defilement is a bigger issue than depravity, have our converts been discipled into a healthy maturity, or are they still wrestling with unaddressed and misunderstood insecurities?

I believe the answer to the above questions may be yes. When Adam and Eve sinned, the first thing they felt was shame, not guilt. Before the fall, "The man and his wife were both naked [*arowm*] and they felt no shame" (Gen. 2:25). After the fall, "The eyes of both of them were opened, and they realized they were naked [*eyrom*]; so they sewed fig leaves together and made coverings for themselves" (Gen. 3:7). But with the coverings they were still naked. "I heard you in the garden, and I was afraid because I was naked, so I hid" (Gen. 3:10). Interestingly, and perhaps symbolically, it is God who suitably provides for Adam's nakedness. "The Lord God made garments of skin for Adam and his wife and clothed them" (Gen. 3:21).

More than Death

The consequence of Adam's sin was death. "But you must not eat from the tree of the knowledge of good and evil, for when you eat of it you will sure-ly die" (Gen. 2:17). The concept of death includes spiritual separation from God, but I wonder if it includes something more. That the resultant awareness in chapter 3 is of nakedness and not separation, and that the word for *naked* takes different forms before and after the fall, may indicate a situation of de-filement as well.

The progression in Genesis 3 is also interesting. Adam and Eve hid after they sinned because they were afraid, and they were afraid because they felt naked. Interestingly, shame over nakedness, which preceded feelings of fear, alienation, and separation, appears stronger than shame over the sin of dis-obedience.

No wonder the Old Testament is full of images showing humanity's defile-ments integral to our depravity. As a lasting ordinance for the generations to come, Aaron and his sons were to wash their hands and feet whenever they entered the tent of meeting or approached the altar, otherwise they would die (Ex. 30:17-21). Blemished or defective animals were not permitted to be used

Jesus himself, when he challenged the Pharisees in their use and understanding of cleansing and dietary laws, affirmed that humans are unclean (Mark 7:20-23).

for sacrifices. Items used for worship had to be anointed or consecrated. Un-clean animals could not be eaten, and even circumcision probably had some connection to ceremonial cleanness, as the illustration in Colossians 2:11-13 indicates by relating the foreskin with the sinful nature. Finally, Jesus himself, when he challenged the Pharisees in their use and understanding of cleansing and dietary laws, affirmed that humans are unclean (Mark 7:20-23).

Makes Depravity Sensible

The concept of original defilement makes total depravity more sensible. There is no one righteous, not even one (Rom. 3:10) and all our righteous acts are like filthy rags (Isa. 64:6), because we are defiled. Sin is not inherited, but stems from our being. We are unclean and everything we touch or do, even with good intent, becomes contaminated. The Muslim who understands that the ground is cursed wherever he or she steps if he or she has not bathed after having had sex is showing an understanding of how bondage to unrighteous-ness stems from defilement. This defilement may form the basis for shame, in-security, and a felt need for the gospel in shame cultures.

A New Paradigm

Niels Mulder says, "Shame is the feeling of anxiety about one's presentation, about being criticized or laughed at, for short, a feeling of embarrassment and fear for the eyes, ears, and opinions of others" (1989, 26). Gailyn Van Rheenen quotes Jacob A. Loewen saying, "While shame is the response to disapproval of one's own peers, guilt is the self-condemnation resulting from the violation of internalized convictions of right and wrong" (1991, 282). To all that has been written on guilt and shame, I would like to add that guilt is a feeling and/or a condition occurring when one has broken or not kept a divine or human law, while shame is a feeling and/or a condition stemming from a shortcoming in one's state of being either before God or peers.

This definition creates for shame the same real and imagined distinctions that exist for guilt. Just as there is legal guilt whether it is felt or not, and there can be felt guilt whether there is an infraction or not, so there is a tangible condition of shame whether it is felt or not, and there is a felt condition of shame whether it has an objective basis or not.

Both Paul (Rom. 9:33) and Peter quote Isaiah on the subject. "See, I lay a stone in Zion, a chosen and precious cornerstone, and the one who trusts in him will never be put to shame" (1 Pet. 2:6). If shame is limited to a subjective feeling in the face of one's peers without any objective condition, then how could this promise be true?[1] What about all the saints and prophets who got ridiculed? If, on the other hand, shame in this verse refers to an objective condition, then the one who trusts in the cornerstone laid in Zion (Jesus) has the objective basis for feeling shame permanently removed, whether he or she gets ridiculed or not.

We talk about how sacrifice for forgiveness of sins is no longer necessary because Christ has provided the ultimate sacrifice, but what is our excuse for setting aside the Levitical dietary and cleansing laws? When Jesus declared all foods "clean" (Mark 7:18-23), he was not setting these laws aside but challenging added traditions by pointing out that the issue of cleanness was in humanity's basic condition and not in the food.

Could it be that the purpose of these laws was to draw attention to humanity's defiled condition in the same way that the sacrifices drew attention to our sinful condition? Could it be that these laws are no longer adhered to because Jesus' work on the cross once and for all removed our defilement like it removed our sin?

The blood of goats and bulls and the ashes of a heifer sprinkled on those who are ceremonially unclean sanctify them so they are outwardly clean. How much more, then, will the blood of Christ, who through the eternal Spirit offered himself unblemished to God, cleanse our consciences from acts that lead to death, so that we may serve the living God. (Heb. 9:13-14).

Implications

I have never heard a presentation of the gospel which addresses human defilement and shame as well as our guilt and sin. I wonder what kind of gospel we have been taking to the Muslim world when we neglect the issue of our na-kedness? Jesus not only bore our sins; he bore our shame. As the "author and perfecter of our faith, he endured the cross, scorning its shame" (Heb. 12:2).

What did it mean for "him who had no sin to be sin for us, so that we might become the righteousness of God" (2 Cor. 5:21)? Did he become depraved, or defiled? Could he have conquered our defilement by assuming it? Christ was not only "pierced for our transgressions" and "crushed for our iniquities"; he "took up our infirmities and carried our sorrows" (Isa. 53:4-5). The atone-ment is not just the simple matter of someone taking our punishment, a con-cept which Muslims find extremely distasteful. There seems to have been an assumption of our defiled state resulting in the destruction of our contamina-tion which was the foundation of our depravity. If this is so, there would be no need for an assumption of our depravity, so that some theological constructs involving imputed sin and imputed righteousness may have to be reevaluated.

Something Missing

Has there been something missing in our understanding and preaching of the gospel so that we fail to reach the Muslim at his or her point of deepest insecurity? Does the Muslim's preoccupation with endless cycles of ritualis-tic cleansing point to another human problem as basic as sin? Do we need an approach to evangelism, discipleship, and contextualization which will meet people at this other point of need? Could such an approach revolutionize out-reach and church planting in some of the most resistant parts of the world? Someday, I hope we have answers to these questions.

Endnote

1. "Never" translated from *ou me*, "the most decisive way of negativing something in the future." William F. Arndt and F. Wilbur Gingrich. 1957. *A Greek English Lexicon of the New Testament and Other Early Christian Literature*. Chicago: University of Chica-go Press, 519. Other future indicative uses include: Matthew 16:22; 26:35; John 4:14; 6:35; 10:5; and Hebrews 10:17. "Shame" translated from *kataischuno*, "as in the OT, of the shame and disappointment that come to one whose faith or hope is shown to be vain" (Ibid., 411).

References

Mulder, Niels. 1989. *Individual and Society in Java: A Cultural Analysis*. Yogyakarta, In-donesia: Gadjah Mada University Press.

Schlorff, Samuel P., ed. 1981. *Discipleship in Islamic Society*. Marseille, France: Arab World Mission, Ecole Radio Biblique.

Van Rheenen, Gailyn. 1991. *Communicating Christ in Animistic Contexts*. Grand Rap-ids, Mich.: Baker Books.

October 1980

Power Encounter: The Way to Muslim Breakthrough

Jerry Otis

Principles for missionaries working in animistic areas.

IF YOU CAN CAST OUT THE DEVIL from the woman, we will truly believe and embrace immediately the faith in Jesus Christ." This was the challenge issued to Ahmad by a number of people in a small Muslim fishing village in the southern Philippines. The scene was thus set for a power encounter between Jehovah and animism, after the manner of Elijah's encounter with the priests of Baal.

God's "Elijah" in this case was, from our Western Christian perspective, a highly unlikely instrument. By his own testimony, Ahmad was eighty-five percent illiterate, grade five being the extent of his schooling. He was untaught in the deeper truths of the word of God and admits that when he submitted to water baptism, after being led to faith in Christ, he did not really understand its meaning. But because he took the step seriously and obediently, the Holy Spirit dealt with him in a most unique way in the days to follow. An evangelical perfectionist undoubtedly could have picked Ahmad's personal life to pieces and declared him a vessel unfit for the Master's use.

"Mt. Carmel" is a small Samal fishing village in the southern Philippines. The Samal have been pretty much untouched by the onslaught of progress. Small frame houses on stilts over the sea are still the order of the day. For centuries now, the people have adhered to a curious mixture of animistic and Muslim beliefs. While observing certain tenets of Islam, a typical villager's life revolves around attempting to manipulate the supernatural, either through Muslim or animistic ritual, usually both.

The "priests of Baal" are, in a real sense, all the inhabitants of the village, and Ahmad could quite honestly say, "I am the only one of the Lord's prophets left, but Baal has 450 prophets" (1 Kings 18:22). A difference should be noted here. In the Old Testament account, Elijah issued the challenge to the prophets of Baal. In this modern encounter, the "prophets of Baal" challenged the man of God. Need we wait for the forces of evil to instigate the battle? Do we lack faith to take the battle to the enemy?

Ahmad accepted the challenge and the time was set for the confrontation. Ahmad knew that, humanly, he was alone in this venture and prayed earnestly for wisdom, power, and the presence of the Holy Spirit. As he approached the home of the demon-possessed woman, he was aware that the Holy Spirit was controlling his words and actions. Without hesitation, he confronted the woman in the name of the Lord Jesus Christ.

Words flowed from her lips indicating the battle to come. "You are nobody to me, I can eat you alive," a voice from within the woman said. "The only one I'm afraid of is that Holy One within you," the voice continued. With every eye focused on Ahmad, he commanded the demon to depart in the name of Jesus Christ the Savior. The demon again spoke, "Yes, I will go away." After a time of jerking and struggling, which rendered her seemingly lifeless, the woman awoke fully sober and sane, totally free from the chains of Satan.

Results of the Encounter

As in Elijah's day, the omnipotence and authority of God were clearly demonstrated and the confession, "The Lord, he is God," flowed from the lips of those present. The following day, those who had issued the challenge made good their promise. They came to Ahmad's house, confessed, repented, and surrendered to the Lordship of Christ. They forsook their superstitious beliefs and parted with long-valued fetishes and amulets.

This demonstration of the power of God has resulted in the only known people movement among Muslims in the Philippines. From this small fishing village, a church of sixty adults and one hundred children was born between January 1977 and December 1978. These Samal fishermen, while continuing their livelihood, are now fishing for men. Two sorcerers, upon witnessing the power of the Lord, confessed and surrendered to him. Relatives far beyond the boundaries of this village and the island on which it is located have been touched, and faith in Christ has been born in these new areas.

A new group of Samal Christians has been established on the island of Simunul in the southern Philippines. This island is thought to be the place where Islam first entered the Philippines, perhaps as early as 1380 A.D. This new group came into existence through the efforts of Ahmad and his congregation. Miracles continue to characterize the movement. Early in 1979, Ahmad prayed for a new believer who was concerned that he was illiterate and could not read the word of God. After prayer, the man was able to read. What unbelievers see is enough to convince them of the saving knowledge of Jesus Christ.

The services in the new congregation are characterized by a simple exposition of the Word. How to apply the Word to everyday life is of great importance. Much stress is laid on prayer, healing, and claiming Christ's power against the demons. Having come out of a spirit-dominated culture, it is obvious that the gospel needs to speak to this felt need.

The new quality of life manifested by the Samal Christians has drawn favorable comment even from some Muslims. One Muslim leader, observing a new Christian return money which he had found, remarked that this man was truly changed, for he had been a sorcerer and thief before.

There is still strong opposition from some, so the young church does its witnessing low key, usually by praying for the sick when so invited. Some of the congregation has moved to other areas and other groups are springing up through their witness. A Samal living in Sabah, Malaysia, who had been sick for a number of years, returned to his home in Silompak to die. He was healed through prayer and eventually returned to Sabah. He has since returned to the Philippines, bringing a number of Muslim converts for baptism.

An Analysis

To dissect such an obvious working of God seems almost sacrilege. In the final analysis, one can only bow humbly before the sovereign Lord and give praise to him. Yet a number of principles stand out that are important for missionaries working in animistic areas. Some of these are applicable to any situation.

1. God's instruments are not always the ones we would choose. Perhaps we haven't learned very well the truth that God's ways are not our ways. Our society stresses the wise, the strong, the trained. We have been taught to despise the small, the common, the ordinary, but God used such to display his majesty in the southern Philippines.

2. Faith to believe the Lord for an observable power encounter should be sought. While any genuine conversion implies a change of allegiance from one authority to another, it would seem only natural that in animistic areas, where the spirit world is so real, a more visible demonstration of the authority of the Lord over the spirits is necessary. Ahmad's simple faith, unspoiled by Western biblical reflection, which often questions if signs and wonders are possible or even allowable today, was equal to the task. Ahmad believes that any substantial movement of Filipino Muslims to the Lord will require miracles and, in the light of what has happened through his ministry, can his statement be refuted? It will take unquestioning faith in the Lord to demonstrate forcefully that "The Lord, he is God."

3. Favorable response of a sizeable number of people at one time, or over a short period of time, is extremely desirable. Societal pressures to revert can be withstood better by a group than an individual. Pressure to conform in Muslim areas, even animistic Muslim areas, is immense, and one-by-one conversion against the tide is extremely difficult. In the movement to Christ noted above, about forty adults made a decision for Christ during the initial two or three-month period. These then stood as a group against rising opposition.

4. Growth through web relationships characterized the movement initiated by Ahmad. It is known that relatives sought out other relatives both on the island and other islands. Relatives as far away as Davao (some seven hundred miles to the east) were won to the Lord. The new group of believers on Simunul Island is a result of web relationship evangelism.

Without a doubt, God has done a new thing in a Samal fishing village in the southern Philippines. It is interesting to note that, in the midst of the supernatural manifestation of his power, a number of spontaneous church growth principles emerge that we dare not lightly brush aside. What has happened may be only the first chapter of God's working among Muslims in the Philippines, and many more exciting chapters may follow for his glory.

April 2008

Evangelism and Dreams: Foundational Presupposition to Interpret God-given Dreams of the Unreached

Randal Scott

A biblical understanding of dreams can facilitate a contextual approach to reaching Muslims (and those of other faiths) with the gospel.

W HEN I FIRST MOVED TO THE MIDDLE EAST I found it fascinating how neighbors, merchants, and friends would readily tell me their dreams, especially their dreams of Jesus. I would listen intently but was a bit lost as to how to proceed.

Unfortunately, I had no training in this area and didn't know anyone who did. And to be honest, I wasn't alert enough to see the relationship between extraordinary dreams and evangelism. I was content to leave the practice of interpreting dreams to fortune tellers, New Agers, and psychologists...and keep to more familiar and conventional opportunities to share the gospel with Muslims. I was unaware how a biblical understanding of dreams could facilitate a contextual approach to reaching Muslims (and those of other faiths) with the gospel.

In the years that followed I met more and more Muslim-background followers of Jesus. In hearing their testimonies, I noticed that at least fifty percent of them had an extraordinary dream as part of their pilgrimage of faith. By this time, I was also studying the dreams of the Bible and was beginning to see the connection between God-given[1] dreams and evangelism. In response to what I sensed God was already doing, I tried to equip myself to help my Muslim friends respond to the God-given dreams they were receiving. Now, after living in the Middle East for twenty years, it seems to me that the prophetic words of Joel continue to be fulfilled in our day: "In the last days, God says, I will pour out my Spirit on all people. Your sons and daughters will prophesy, your young men will see visions, your old men will dream dreams" (Joel 2:28; see also Acts 2:17).

Today, we have more empirical data about dreaming than at any time in human history. We know, for example, that everyone dreams—even those who think they don't. In fact, around ten percent of our lives are spent dreaming. By the time we are thirty, we will have spent three solid years dreaming. This article, however, is not about the clinical research done on dreaming; it is on how dream interpretation can facilitate evangelism.

Credential as an Interpreter

Although dreams have a mysterious nature, those who believe in the inspiration, authority and sufficiency of the Bible can approach the subject of dream interpretation with presuppositions that others cannot. I make two presuppositions here.

1. The interpretation of God-given dreams (and visions[2]) is a ministry for followers of Jesus. I would argue that no one has the credentials to interpret God-given dreams to non-believers[3] except followers of Jesus. Followers of Jesus have been appointed ambassadors of God and made members of his royal priesthood (2 Cor. 5:19-20, 1 Pet. 2:9). If the ambassadors and priests of God are not qualified to help people respond to their God-given dreams, then who is? As ambassadors of Christ, we can embrace this ministry with humble confidence. Indeed, a major reason God gives dreams to the unreached is to help facilitate the spread of the gospel. It is one of his many signs of love and mercy. God is in the business of revealing mysteries (Dan. 2:28) and it remains a mystery to the unreached that God is passionately in love with them.

2. God-given dreams are vehicles by which he communicates his personal love and mercy to the unreached. Fatma told me how she had seen Jesus in a dream. Before the dream, she was not particularly religious or interested in the things of God. The dream changed her life. Fatma's dream took place at a time when her youngest daughter had an undiagnosed illness and was close to death. In Fatma's dream, a figure dressed in white appeared to her and told her not to worry and that her daughter would be healed. She intuitively understood that the figure in her dream was Jesus. That week, her daughter mysteriously recovered from her illness and Fatma began to search for someone who could tell her more about Jesus. This dream required no interpretation, but it did require a believer to explain the gospel to Fatma. She asked my wife and me to tell her more about Jesus. A few months later Fatma and most of her family were baptized.

Through the dream, Fatma began to realize God loved and cared for her. This theme is present in almost every God-given dream I have encountered. It is the key characteristic I look for when listening to an extraordinary dream.

Sometimes, the love-message of a God-given dream can be unclear to an unbeliever. It is true today and was true in biblical times. Meanings of dreams were often revealed to non-believers in two or three distinct phases.

A God-given dream is frequently a very personalized form of revelation. The dream is the deliver-vehicle for a message from God to the dreamer. There are often three phases to the revelation if the message of the dream is not immediately understandable: the mystery phase, the meaning phase, and the response phase. If the meaning of the dream is understandable from the beginning, then only the second and third phases are part of the process.

Phase 1: The mystery phase. In this phase, the message of the dream remains a mystery until the meaning of the dream is revealed. If the dream remains a mystery to the dreamer, it is like receiving a letter but not opening the envelope or like hearing a parable without knowing the meaning. In most cases, the dreamer will stay in phase 1 unless he or she proactively seeks the meaning of the dream. Interpretation can bring a dream from the mystery phase to the meaning phase. Interpretation answers the question "What does this dream mean?"

Phase 2: The meaning phase. In this phase, there is a good or complete understanding of what the dream means. In some way, the message "God cares for me" is being revealed. In Fatma's dream, the meaning was not veiled in symbolic language or metaphor—and required no interpretation. It launched Fatma on a search to learn more about Jesus. But the dream was personal. It touched her personal situation. In the meaning phase, we see God tangibly revealing his love in a way the dreamer can receive it. The personalized nature of the dream makes it a powerful communicator of God's love.

Phase 3: The response phase. In this phase, the dreamer is called to take action. This phase answers the question of how to respond to God's love revealed in phase 2. It typically requires a conscious act of the will or an observable proactive step of faith. In my experience, more often than not, the response asked of the dreamer has something to do with following Jesus. In other words, the dreamer is invited through his or her dream to take a step of faith toward Jesus. This might be to believe something else about themselves, others or God. It might be to forgive, reconcile or help someone. It might be to change the person's mind or overcome a prejudice that is keeping him or her from obeying God. Unfortunately, it is not uncommon for the non-believer to ignore or disobey the dream even though he or she understands the meaning.

Biblical Precedence of the Three-phase Process

We know from scripture and other ancient literature that dream interpretation was commonly practiced in many cultures throughout history. Each society seemed to have had its own dream lore and interpretation specialists. In ancient Egypt and Babylon, for example, magicians, diviners, astrologers and wise men practiced the art. In the biblical record, the interpretation of God-given dreams seems to have been the domain of God's people.

This is most clearly seen in the account of Pharaoh's dream in Genesis 41 and in Nebuchadnezzar's dreams in Daniel 2 and 4. Neither the magicians of Pharaoh's court nor the diviners of Nebuchadnezzar's court were able to interpret their masters' dreams. Certainly these astrologers and diviners of the royal courts were the most gifted and highly esteemed dream interpreters of their day. They knew the symbolic language of dreams and were masters of their craft. Yet for these mysterious God-given dreams, their interpretation skills were ineffective. Why?

In each of these scenes God orchestrated events in such a way so as to introduce followers of Yahweh onto the stage. These believers were brought in to interpret the God-given dreams and/or tell how to respond to them. This happened no fewer than four times in the Old Testament. The same pattern was also found in the New Testament where Ananias was sent to Saul in Damascus and Peter was sent to Cornelius in Caesarea. In both cases, God sent visions to people and then orchestrated events to allow followers of Jesus to explain the gospel. Notice that in the NT examples, the believers were not needed to interpret the God-given visions but rather to explain how to respond to them. (See chart on page 239.)

Applying the Three-phase Process in Ministry

This process has also been present in most of the God-given dreams I have encountered or heard about over the years. By understanding that God-given dreams often have three phases, we can be better prepared to know our role in helping the dreamer respond correctly. Being equipped to help people correctly respond to their God-given dreams is a function of at least three factors:

1. Our foreknowledge of God's predisposition toward people (particularly the unreached).

2. Our ability to discern how the Kingdom of God is being revealed to the dreamer.

3. Our ability to discern an appropriate response (through a working understanding of the Bible).

Let's start with the first factor, our foreknowledge of God's predisposition toward people (particularly the unreached). We know God is "not wanting anyone to perish, but everyone to come to repentance" (2 Pet. 3:9b). The Bible has given us the foreknowledge of God's loving and compassionate heart for the unbeliever. We know God is eager to reveal his love for the dreamer in a way the dreamer will receive.

Correctly understanding God's predisposition toward unbelievers is foundational in being able to correctly help them understand and respond to their God-given dreams. Knowing that God is lovingly predisposed to the unreached is always a fundamental presupposition when helping non-believers understand and respond to their dreams. We are not starting with a blank slate but with definite presuppositions that point us to possible meanings and responses.

The other two factors are forms of discernment. Discernment is informed and developed by a working understanding of scripture. While God's love for the non-believer is perfectly clear, the manner (or technique) in which God communicates or personalizes his love may not be. Somehow in the mystery of the dream, God is personalizing a message to the dreamer that will speak to his or her soul, catch his or her attention, warn the person of danger, turn the individual from sin, etc.

As ambassadors and priests, we should have a humble confidence that we can discern God's voice in the dream on behalf of the non-believer. In this way, the follower of Jesus is validated as God's spokesperson in the eyes of the dreamer. But how God is personalizing his love through the dream can often only be known if God reveals it. In my experience, sometimes God reveals it through intuition (or by a thought coming to mind). Frequently, it is

Examples of Believers Interpreting God-given
Dreams & Visions of Non-believers

Dreamer (non-believer)	**Phase 1** (Mystery Phase)	Inter-preter (believer)	**Phase 2** (Meaning Phase)	Did Dreamer Obey?	**Phase 3** (Response Phase)
Cupbearer and Baker Genesis 40:1-23	Cupbearer dreamed of vines and wine; baker dreamed of birds eating bread.	Joseph	The cupbearer was restored and the baker was executed.	n/a	These dreams fore-told the future of the cupbearer and baker. The cupbearer forgot about Joseph.
Pharaoh Genesis 41:14-43	Dreamed of cows and stocks of grain.	Joseph	Seven years of bounty will be followed by seven years of famine.	Yes	Pharaoh was told to prepare for the famine. Thus, thou-sands were saved from starvation and Joseph was promot-ed from obscurity to prominence.
Nebuchad-nezzar Daniel 2:1-49	Dreamed of enormous dazzling statue.	Daniel	Predictions of future kingdoms and their glory.	Yes	Nebuchadnezzar re-sponded in praise to God and promoted Daniel from obscu-rity to prominence.
Nebuchad-nezzar Daniel 4:10-37	Dreamed of a large beautiful tree that was cut down to a stump.	Daniel	The tree represented Nebuchad-nezzar.	No	Nebuchadnezzar was to humble himself and act justly. He refused, became insane, and lost his kingdom for a time.
Belshazzar Daniel 5:1-30	Fingers appeared on a wall and wrote mysterious words.	Daniel	Pending judgment for wicked-ness.	n/a	There is no record of Belshazzar's re-pentance. Judgment came immediately.
Saul of Tarsus Acts 9:1-26	Experienced a vision of Jesus. Blinded in vision.	Ananias	Told to go to Damas-cus and wait for in-structions. Ananias explained the gospel.	Yes	Saul was called to re-pent and believe the gospel. He repented from persecuting fol-lowers of Jesus and became one himself.
Cornelius Acts 10:1-48	In a vision, Cornelius was told to fetch a man name Si-mon, but didn't know why.	Peter	Peter explained the gospel.	Yes	Cornelius and family responded in faith to Peter's message and became followers of Jesus.

a cognitive (non-mystical) process of connecting aspects of the dream with my knowledge of scripture. And sometimes I draw a blank... as if God isn't revealing anything.

If no interpretation is readily apparent to me, I might find myself prayerfully in a "reverse engineering" mode—starting from my presuppositions and working backward to bring greater clarity to the dream. I ask myself, "How is God revealing his love for this person through this dream?" I may also ask myself, "How is God inviting this person to follow Jesus?" There are many possibilities to both of these questions and therefore we must have discernment and God's grace.

I am NOT asking myself, "How can I get this person to pray and ask Jesus into his or her life?" Rather, I am trying to interpret (discern) how the Kingdom of God is being revealed to the dreamer. It typically requires me to ask many questions of the dreamer, listen carefully, and pray. All the while, I am looking to partner with God in facilitating the proper response.[4] If, after following this process, I still have no clarity, I have several options: (1) assume

Suggestions for Interpreting God-given Dreams

Practically all the dream literature on the market is written from a non-biblical worldview. Even books authored by Christians can tend to go beyond what the scripture teaches or promotes. So be cautious...but not timid. Never seek guidance through dreams. Never try to induce dreams. Always filter what you read through your knowledge of scripture. Below are four suggestions for those who want to be better equipped to interpret God-given dreams in evangelism.

1. Recruit a group (a dream team) of people who are interested in this topic. Together study scripture (see #2 below) and read books (see #3 below) on the topic. Do evangelism together (see #4). Journal your dreams and discuss them to help make you alert to your own dream life. To do this, keep a pen, notebook and flashlight next to your bed.

2. Study and take notes of all OT and NT references regarding dreams and visions. Be very familiar with what the Bible says about dreams. Discuss what you are learning with your study group.

3. Study other books and resources about dreams. Unfortunately, evangelicals have written very little on this subject. However, below are three places to begin:

• *Understanding Dreams from God* by Scott Breslin and Mike Jones. 2004. Pasadena, Calif.: William Carey Library. This is the English edition of an evangelistic tract for Muslims who are having extraordinary dreams. It introduces people to dreams of the Bible and points them to Jesus as God's most complete and important revelation. This booklet demonstrates an approach to evangelism using dreams.

that I am not the right person to help the dreamer respond to the dream and recommend/introduce someone else I know, (2) assume the dream was not God-given, or (3) be discouraged and/or ashamed that God did not use me.[5] Even if I cannot offer the dreamer an interpretation of the dream, I will ask to pray for the dreamer. I have never been refused. Among other things, I will pray for the blessings of Jesus upon the dreamer and his or her family. I will also ask the dreamer if he or she wants to hear more about the person and teachings of Jesus.

Final Comments

The process I use for interpreting God-given dreams has little to do with understanding the symbols and imagery of dreams and more to do with discerning how the Kingdom of God is being revealed to the dreamer (and what he or she should do about it). I am not an advocate of the practice of interpreting dreams through a "knowledge" of symbols and metaphors. This goes beyond my comfort zone. I do not see that the Bible commands or encourages that

---

- *More Than Dreams* is a DVD that dramatizes the true story of how five people (an Egyptian, Turk, Indonesian, Nigerian and Iranian) came to faith in Jesus through dreams. It is designed to be used as an outreach tool for Muslims, but it also testifies to what God is doing throughout the world with dreams. It can be ordered at www.morethandreams.org.
- *God, Dreams and Revelation* by Morton Kelsey. 1991. Minneapolis, Minn.: Augsburg Fortress. This is a scholarly study of a Christian worldview of the importance of dreams. Kelsey was a scholar and Episcopal clergyman with a high view of scripture. Be aware of a Jungian psychological perspective that is also present in parts of his book. Nonetheless, I believe the discerning reader can gain many useful insights from *God, Dreams and Revelation*. Kelsey documents how dreams have been a highly valued aspect of church life from the days of Polycarp through the 1600s. He also presents a compelling argument as to why dreams have been neglected in the Church today.

4. Experiment. You have nothing to lose—and the dreamers have much to gain. If possible, bring a co-worker with you and work as a team in the interpretation process. Listen thoughtfully and prayerfully to the extraordinary dreams of non-believing friends and neighbors. Ask God to give you wisdom and discernment. Does it strike you as a possible God-given dream? If so, try to get a sense of how the Kingdom of God is being revealed to the dreamer and what the dreamer is supposed to do about it. If you cannot (in good conscience) suggest how the dreamer should respond to the dream, don't worry or be perplexed. Simply pray aloud for the dreamer. Ask the dreamer if he or she would like to hear more about Jesus. Later, when you are alone with your co-worker, debrief together. Discuss what happened, what went right, how it could have gone better, and what you would do differently.

practice. Interpretations come from God—not by studying dream interpretation dictionaries. In scripture, it appears that the meanings of dreams were "revealed" and not translated or decoded.

Therefore, I see no biblical precedence for trying to decode or interpret symbolic images in dreams. In my experience, mature followers of Jesus who know their Bible (it also doesn't hurt to have a spiritual gift of discernment, wisdom or evangelism[6]) have the God-given equipment to help non-believers interpret God-given dreams.

Finally, I want to remind the reader that faith comes from hearing the word of God (Rom. 10:17)—not by dreams. Dreams prepare people to believe and repent; however, they never (in my experience) contain a clear gospel message. God uses followers of Jesus to explain the gospel so that dreamers can believe and repent. It will always take people equipped with the gospel to help a dreamer become a follower of Jesus. It becomes a divine partnership. God-given dreams (or visions) are only one part of the evangelism process. Human agents (like you and I) are necessary to consummate the process.

Endnotes

1. I use the term *God-given dreams* throughout this article but never define the term because, frankly, I am not sure how to…nor do I think it is prudent to try. In essence, a *God-given dream* is a dream sent to a person by God and not sourced from somewhere else. We can say with certainty that all dreams are not from God. Scripture clearly recognizes there are many sources of dreams and visions. Some of these include: anxiety (Ecc. 5:11), chemical imbalances (Prov. 23:31-33), delusions of the mind (Jer. 23:23), and evil spirits (Matt. 4:1-11; 2 Cor. 11:14). There are also false dreams (Jer. 23:32). A God-given dream will not conflict with the teachings of the Bible.

2. Visions are extraordinary dreams that happen when we are awake. Visions share the same characteristics as dreams and for this discussion are treated as virtually identical to dreams.

3. The terms *non-believer* or *unbeliever* are admittedly awkward. They do not mean that the person has no faith in God. In this article, as in the New Testament, these terms can refer to a religious person whose faith is incomplete and/or misinformed. It can also refer to both seekers and to those estranged from God. In one sense, it refers to any person who does not yet believe in God's passionate love for him or her as demonstrated by sending Jesus to die for his or her sins.

4. A proper response answers the following two questions: (1) How is God revealing the Kingdom of God to the dreamer? and (2) What does God want the dreamer to do about it?

5. I suggest that those who most clearly identify with option 3 are not ready to start this ministry until they overcome the personal insecurity, misunderstandings, and issues of faith that are at the root of such thinking.

6. I propose that the gift of evangelism is best measured by fruitfulness rather than boldness. We too often mistake the prophet (who boldly shares the same message to all audiences) with the gifted evangelist (who skillfully tailors each message for each audience).

Touching the Mystical Heart of Islam

Ken Peters

Very little is said about which approaches are best suited for Muslims who practice Islamic mysticism, a simple Islam of the heart, which is based as much upon their tribal traditions as upon the Qur'an.

I WAS TALKING WITH AN ORTHODOX MUSLIM, one of the mosque leaders in the northern Sudan village where I was doing development work. He was friendly and spoke English well. I had gone to his home to find out more about Islamic mysticism which I had seen in Sudan. When I mentioned Sufism, he knew exactly what I was talking about. Deadly serious, he described what he called the "errors" of Sufism and how widely it was practiced. During our conversation, a huge truck packed with excited, festive school children rumbled out of the village toward the desert.

"Do you know where those children are going?" he asked. I didn't know, so he told me. "They're going to a shrine where they will pray to a Sufi leader buried there, so they will do well on their exams. Is that Islam? Is that Islam?"

"No," I said, and he emphatically agreed. What I meant was that it wasn't textbook Islam, orthodox according to a strict interpretation of the Quran and the traditions of Muhammad. Rather, it was the popular Islam of those school children, and their parents, and of the people in this village, and the next, and the next.

As we continued to talk, I wondered how much Christian missionary work among Muslims corresponds to popular Islam, what I call *Islamic mysticism*. It occurred to me that most of what I've heard and read about reaching Muslims applies only to the minority in Islam who are literate and well-schooled in Islamic orthodoxy. Very little is said about what methods or approaches are best suited for Muslims who practice a simple Islam of the heart, which is based as much upon their tribal traditions as upon the Qur'an. Consequently, I've developed some ideas that I think will help us to be more effective in communicating the gospel to Muslims.

The Hunger of the Heart

Since the founding of Islam, many Muslims have reflected a strong desire to know God personally and to find acceptance with him. The traditional view of God in Islam, together with oppressive rules, leaves little room for a mystical experience with God. But that has not thwarted the attempts of those who through the centuries have sought a deeper, more emotional expression of their faith. That fact, it seems to me, opens the door to our witness about Jesus Christ.

Jesus Christ must become the great *Sheikh* of all Muslims, their spiritual guide, their intercessor, and the bestower of God's blessings. This is the redemptive analogy in Islam that could be used to invite Muslims to Christ. Having found it, we must learn appropriate ways to use it. For me, that means through power encounters with the *sheikh*s of Islamic mysticism.

By Islamic mysticism, I mean the subjective rather than the objective side of Islam. It stresses an intimate relationship with Allah, rather than doctrine and worship based upon tradition. Mystical Muslims emphasize the immanence of Allah rather than his transcendence. Mysticism is the longing for God, the love one feels for God. Today, over 1,300 years after the birth of Islamic mysticism, about seventy percent of all Muslims are being influenced by it in one form or another. That means there are more than 600 million Muslims who teach and

Beneath the surface of what often appears to the West as a solid phalanx of truth, there is a seething ferment among millions of people whose deepest spiritual aspirations orthodox Islam cannot meet.

practice forms of Islam and place unorthodox experience over orthodox theology. How can such a tension exist in Islam without serious outbursts against the movement's leaders?

In Islam, where men are judged by their actions, mere heterodoxy cannot as a rule be effectively penalized, and however sharply the truth of mysticism may clash with the law of religion, nothing very serious is likely to occur so long as the mystic continues to worship with his fellow Muslims. Beneath the surface of what often appears to the West as a solid phalanx of truth, there is a seething ferment among millions of people whose deepest spiritual aspirations orthodox Islam cannot meet. That not only explains the appeal of mysticism, it also points the way for our evangelistic approaches to Muslims.

Beliefs and Practices

The basic beliefs and practices of Islamic mysticism arise from common human psychological and spiritual needs, among them: fear of evil, the future, the unknown, and a hope for better things. Popular among Muslims are such animistic beliefs and practices as witchcraft, sorcery, spells, amulets, and fetishes.

Muslim mystics do not abandon Islam's theological foundations. Most of them cling to Islam's five pillars, but apply them through the sieve of mystical experiences. While fear of evil and the unknown is a powerful motivator, a stronger influence among Muslim mystics seems to be their love and longing for God. To be nearer to Allah, and, ideally, to be united with him, casts out all fear and brings bliss and ecstasy. Therefore, in their practices we see some designed to cast out fear and evil on the one hand, but, on the other, they do things designed to bring them closer to Allah. Although these practices carry significance for missionaries, the one that intrigues me the most is veneration of Islamic mysticism's spiritual leaders.

The mystics' spiritual leaders are commonly called *sheikhs*. Highly esteemed in their villages, they are the only ones who know how to make mystical contact with Allah. Mystics assume that the *sheikh*s are friends of Allah who intercede with him on their behalf. *Sheikh*s reveal the path to blessing and bestow Allah's blessings. The s*heikh* has traveled the road to Allah and has found the highly desired mystical union with him. The *sheikh* is the *logos* of Islamic mysticism, because he has reached the point of being perfectly one with Allah. In fact, the *sheikh* is often described as actually being Allah himself.

On his mystical journey to Allah, the *sheikh* grows more virtuous and takes on the character of Allah. His goal is to find perfect goodness, liberality, knowledge, and other such qualities.

The *sheikh* who achieves this goal is called at times Guide, Beacon, Mirror of the World, Mighty Elixer, *Isa* (Jesus) and Raiser of the Dead. He is believed to have perfect knowledge of Allah and to have supernatural powers himself. In fact, one of the things that leads people to believe in the *sheikh* is his power to work miracles. Healing the sick, flying in the air, traversing long distances in a moment, walking on water, talking with inanimate objects, and predicting future events have been attributed to *sheikh*s. Although scattered within Islam, they are a powerful, influential group.

The *sheikh*s are at the same time a barrier against and an opening toward Christ. That's why missionaries must work with them and not behind their backs. If a *sheikh* were to turn to Christ, he would exercise powerful influence on his followers to do the same. The greater his influence in the community, the better for our witness. In effect, the *sheikh*s could become the pastors of newly-formed clusters of Christian believers, thus preserving their status in the community.

The Great *Sheikh*, Jesus Christ

Of course, the key to my vision is the approach to the *sheikh*s and their followers. To me, it's the redemptive analogy of Jesus Christ being the greatest of all *sheikh*s. For example, David Shenk describes the time he was speaking to Muslim mystics who told him they venerated their *sheikh* because he achieved answers to their prayers. Then he told them about the *sheikh* Jesus, who also answers prayers.

There are many parallels between the *sheikhs* and Jesus. *Sheikhs* are said to answer prayers by interceding before Allah on behalf of people, not just while they are alive, but even after they die. They work miracles and are gentle, kind, humble, submissive, and generous. They are given many titles that Jesus has earned. They are to be intimately joined with their devotees, even to the point of sharing pain vicariously. No man could be all that a *sheikh* is thought to be by Muslim mystics, but Jesus can be and is, plus a lot more. Missionaries must go to Muslim mystics with the message that Jesus Christ is the greatest of all *sheikhs*, doing so with unusual care and sensitivity.

Don Richardson explains that when using a redemptive analogy, one needs the Holy Spirit's wisdom to discern the analogy's validity in a given context. The Holy Spirit's love is needed to unveil Christ as the analogy's fulfillment and to drive out all anti-redemptive aspects that may surface.

Signs and Wonders

My second key is the supernatural enabling of the Holy Spirit. Missionaries must not be reluctant to join the spiritual battle on the deepest levels. Because Muslim mystics believe in signs and wonders, we must confront them with the power of the true and living God.

For example, if the *sheikhs* can prophesy, we must challenge their wisdom through prophecies from the wisest of all *sheikhs*, the Lord Jesus. If they can heal, we must enter power encounters and ask Jesus to heal as well, showing his power compassion. If we wish to convert *sheikhs* operating with demonic powers, we must cast out the demons who control them. By exercising the power and authority of Jesus, missionaries will gain credibility and success with people who have been exposed to the powers of darkness.

On the Field Today

While I was in the Sudan, it was amazing to see how much of what I learned about mysticism from the local mosque leader confirmed what I had read about beforehand. Because I spent a relatively short time in development work, I was not able to try out my evangelistic theories. However, I have since consulted with veteran missionaries to Muslims, such as Phil Parshall and David Shenk, to get their reactions. I wanted to find out if any missionaries are doing what I propose here.

In a nutshell, the answer is yes, especially in West Africa and Asia. Shenk told me that in Indonesia "power encounter is the normal manner in which the church is growing. Several significant Muslim leaders have been converted and this has dramatically influenced the profile of the Christian-Muslim encounter. Divine healings and exorcism are part of the normal Christian witness in Indonesia."

Those who responded agreed that there is a need in many Muslim countries—although not all of them—for missionaries to emphasize power encounter in Muslim evangelism. They also affirmed the effectiveness of targeting the leaders first. For example, to cite one story among many I've been told, one entire West African Muslim village turned to Christ in the footsteps of several leaders' conversions.

Certainly, we must be wise and sensitive to the Holy Spirit in deciding the appropriate and most effective approach to Muslim mystics. Our strategies must be tailor-made to fit the local cultural context. The steps I'm proposing here could be thought of as one of many suits missionaries should be prepared to wear to reach Muslims. To follow that analogy, at times our "suits" must be taken in or let out in various places, so as to achieve the best possible fit for a given village.

Our Opportunity

I believe we could achieve positive results if we placed more emphasis on reaching the large number of Muslims influenced both by animism and mystical Islam. It is time for our meetings with Muslims to take on a mystical as well as an apostolic flavor. What we have seen happen in Indonesia and in West Africa can be duplicated elsewhere. Through signs and wonders and victorious power encounters with the forces of darkness, great numbers of Muslims who follow their *sheikhs* can be turned to the Great *Sheikh*, our Lord Jesus Christ.

April 1997

Is Planting Churches in the Muslim World "Mission Impossible"?

Dan Brown

A description of Frontiers' Seven Phases of Church Planting among Muslims.

TWO HALF-TRUTHS: (1) church planting among Muslims is an impossible task and (2) God must intervene in a special way to reveal how to do it. First of all, in a sense it is impossible. When you consider all that's stacked up against seeing a movement of Muslims coming into the kingdom, it seems almost ludicrous. Second, who can debate that without the miraculous work of the Holy Spirit in a person's heart, no one's eyes are opened. Yet in our brief experience, Frontiers' ninety-one teams across North Africa, the Middle East, Central Asia, South Asia, and Southeast Asia are seeing churches planted. God is forming his Church out of Muslim Background Believers (MBBs) in nearly every country. So is it impossible? No.

God does not expect us to make this up from scratch. Sure, we depend upon him to lead in specific ways and to provide the keys that will "unlock the doors" in each location. But we now see that he has already revealed in the Bible most of what we need to know about getting the job done. Much of it comes down to a steady aim. We see a strong correlation between the narrowness of a team's objectives and its eventual effectiveness. When a team goes into a Muslim city with the singular aim of planting a church among the Muslim majority—and is committed to doing nothing else except what will lead to that goal, and having some clearly understood stages in mind—then usually MBB fellowships emerge.

Where teams go in with broad multiple goals, having only a vague notion of how to get there—and conflicting views on strategy within the team—then usually there are little or no results. When you see a church among an unreached people group, it's like finding a turtle upon a fence post: clear intentionality from an outside party was involved.

Our "Seven Phases of Church Planting" has grown out of such a context. While some may object that there is no magic plan in the Bible for church planting, we believe that in fact there are definitive stages indicated in the New Testament. Common sense tells us that before you can have a church, you probably first have a gathering or fellowship of believers that may not yet have the minimum New Testament characteristics of "church." Before that you must have at least one from the target group who has come to Christ, and into whose life you are building the faith. And that presumes you have been evangelizing. So it's no surprise that we find these basic stages (with some variation) in each of Paul's church-planting situations.

Multistage church-planting models are not new (for example, David Hesselgrave's "The Pauline Cycle"). Other models have certainly influenced our seven phases, which have been contextualized to our Muslim church-planting teams and agency ethos.

To illustrate, Frontiers' teams (including those in pre-field preparation) are currently at these phases:

Phase 1, "Launching the Team"—19 teams
Phase 2, "Preparing to Sow"—16 teams
Phase 3, "Sowing"—9 teams
Phase 4, "Discipling Begins"—12 teams
Phase 5, "Beginning the Church"—26 teams
Phase 6, "Training Leaders"—4 teams
Phase 7, "Reproducing and Exiting"—5 teams

This shows a healthy movement up the ladder. Also, our sister agencies who are likewise working to plant churches in the Muslim world are seeing similar progress. It's been our privilege to cross-pollinate with them and share resources, and therefore we rejoice together.

Promoting and using the seven phases widely in our organization has proven invaluable. Some examples:

• When a team has a clear picture of what the next one or two steps are, it is able to work with greater confidence and intentionality (e.g., language learning). Simple tools work best, and much time can be saved from always needing to figure out the next step.

• When a new team is formed in Frontiers, it is linked with 90-plus other teams working at the various phases 1 through 7. This provides a great milieu for peer-to-peer coaching, and faith is energized that the new team, too, will eventually be at Phase 5, 6, or 7, by God's grace.

• One of the biggest causes of conflict and ineffectiveness on field teams is mismatched ideas about goals, strategy, methods, time allocation to specific tasks, etc. The "Seven Phases of Church Planting" provide a common vehicle that the team can use to discuss all those crucial aspects of team planning. Using it reduces conflicting expectations, and individual team members can more readily see where they fit into the bigger picture.

• The seven phases also give us a common language across the whole organization to identify progress levels, strategy, and activities.

What the Church-planting Phases Are Not

They are not a cookbook. "Just do A, then B, then C, add 3 pints of Bible, then *voila!* You'll have a church." In seeking to establish communities of believers in some of the most hostile, unreached, and dangerous places of the world, nothing is so easy or automatic. Of course, there is spiritual battle, persecution, ingrained sin, false conceptions of God, falling away, and betrayals. And it never goes as you expect it to. Our teams still require help and course corrections from leaders and coaches.

Likewise, they are not a precise road map. There remains great need for the team's creativity and Spirit-led ingenuity. As someone has said, church planting is an art, not a science. Frontiers comprises wide diversity in evangelical theology, philosophy of ministry, and ideas about "church."

That's okay, as this is certainly not intended to be a cookie-cutter approach to missions. The seven phases are intended to encompass a variety of church-planting models. For example, one team intends to plant house churches. Another a cell church. Another team will plant a large traditional or normative-type church. Specific philosophies of ministry have been kept to a minimum for the sake of broad applicability.

What the Church-planting Phases Are

They are a good tool to show where a team's work is at, where it needs to go, and to give many specifics on what the team should work on in each phase. Each phase has four parts.

1. The Phase Title. E.g., Phase 5 is "Beginning the Church."

2. Definition. A brief thumbnail of what the phase is. E.g., Phase 2 is "Learning the language, adjusting to the culture, becoming 'belongers' in society."

3. When Begun. One of the crucial aspects of the seven phases is to differentiate between one phase and another, so that a given team can unambiguously know which phase members are in—like a mark on a yardstick, to clearly distinguish between 35 3/4 inches and 3 feet. E.g., in Phase 4, "Begin regular discipleship with an MBB of the target group (regardless of how he/she came to Christ)."

4. Activities. Very specific objectives or tasks that should be accomplished during the given phase. However, let me hasten to clarify that these are suggestive only. Not every activity needs to be done in each situation.

Specific activities and styles are going to vary greatly from ministry to ministry. For example, Activity #19 in Phase 4 is "Disciple the new believer to become familiar with God's plan for the extension of the kingdom, from the book of Acts." That may be perfect. Or it may be that the discipler has a different way to teach those truths. Also, they're not comprehensive, as other things will usually come up that are not anticipated in our list.

Real-life Examples

We have a team of three families in a large Indonesian city. Having started a growing MBB fellowship, they are in Phase 5. The fellowship has around twenty adult believers, plus children. A spiritually mature, middle-aged MBB couple gives primary leadership within the group. The expatriate team leader and wife are very close to this couple and are discipling them, now focusing largely on ministry and church matters—a fine example of 2 Timothy 2:2.

But the situation is far from being one-dimensional. Various team members must work hard at discipling MBBs, training other leaders, learning the language further (especially for newer members), or carrying out the necessary governmental work related to projects and other logistics. Also, some of the team members are not highly involved in the MBB group, as the cultural dynamics don't allow for too much of an expatriate presence. So they focus mainly on evangelism and training some Christian background believers in Muslim evangelism.

All the while the team needs to pay attention to its own life and growth. So under the Phase 5 umbrella, they still remain active in many facets of previous phases (e.g., language learning, evangelism, discipling, etc.). Nonetheless, this team needs to move toward Phase 6 (later aspects of work just prior to full "church-ship," such as majoring on leadership development) and also keep an eye on Phase 7 (appointing elders, ensuring a mode of reproduction, and exiting). Keeping these two later phases in view prevents the team from straying into cul-de-sacs or nice ministries that don't contribute to the main thing: church planting.

A very large team in Kazakstan has planted a large MBB church and some satellite groups in other cities. As in the previous example, lots of work remains, with much variety, so that team members can operate in areas of their gifts, whether they be teaching the Bible, discipling, evangelizing, serving, counseling, leading, music, youth work, administration, etc. Being at Phase 7, the work concentrates on multiplication—starting new fellowships and churches.

Another team has worked for years in a major Arab capital. After experiencing many setbacks and waves of opposition from the government, the MBB fellowship they started has grown in size and maturity. This church is comprised of around twenty adults plus children, and two MBB men have been recognized as elders through their active leading and teaching. However, one of these elders, highly gifted as a church planter, is yearning to move his family to a new city and start afresh. So this ministry must focus on both Phase 6 and Phase 7 priorities.

Diversions

Phases 2 and 3 in particular are difficult to persevere in. There's usually a strong temptation to give up. More commonly there's the danger of getting diverted into other good things: heavy tentmaking involvement, working with ethnic Christians, creating media, "computer work," lots of team activities, or simply spending time with Muslim friends, but never challenging them to a decision point for Christ. All these may be worthwhile pursuits, but which do not really lead toward planting a church. Therefore the seven phases are a constant reminder and discipline to pull them back toward the main thing, and hopefully give some good ideas of what to do within Phases 2 and 3.

Finally, Frontiers has several teams at Phase 5, that is, they have started and are giving leadership to an MBB fellowship in their target city. But some are tempted to conclude, "Great, we've accomplished what we came here for. We're done. Praise the Lord." The seven phases force them back to realize that in fact the work is not at all done. Much is still required if they are to leave their work in a similar ecclesiastical condition as Paul and Titus left the churches in Crete, i.e., as real "churches" under a plurality of qualified elders in each place.

Three Signs of a Church

This begs the question, "What is a New Testament church, and how do we know when we've planted one?" Such an issue is beyond the scope of this paper. However, I believe that by New Testament examples and criteria, three things must be true for the church planter to be able to walk away and say, "I planted a church there":

1. There must be some "critical mass"—in other words, some minimal size and social makeup. A group of three single men is not a church. A fellowship of fifteen adults plus children may be. The New Testament doesn't give us a magic number, and that's probably because what is a minimal critical mass will vary from one situation to another.

2. There are two or more men who meet the qualifications for eldership and are willing to serve as such. I say two because I believe the New Testament teaches a plurality of elders in a given church; and again, no number is given. Three or more is usually a whole lot better than two.

3. These elders are installed and assume the leadership authority and responsibility. If the believers are still looking to the foreigners to call the shots, the church planting is not yet done.

As we stand near the close of two millennia of the Church's efforts in obeying the Great Commission, clearly the task remains unfinished. Yet the signs are that God is pouring out his mercy on more and more unreached people groups, and pioneer church-planting teams are seeing results that in many cases are unprecedented. We believe that the main thrust of the Church's work to extend the gospel to "those who were not told about him, and those who have not heard" needs to be church planting. Tools such as the "Seven Phases of Church Planting" can aid in this task.

July 2008

What Are Best Practices of Church Planting among Muslims?

Steven Downey

A 2006 conference allowed those serving in Muslim areas to discuss training, community development, and partnership in church planting.

(**Note:** *Due to the sensitive nature of this conference, no locations, names, or ministries could be identified, except by country.*)

IS THERE ANY HOPE IN REACHING MUSLIMS for Christ when there are so many obstacles?" A participant who attended a "Best Practices of Church Planting in an Islamic Context" conference asked this question. The Indonesians provided an answer with a case study on probably the most amazing and significant turning to Christ in the history of Islam: the conversion of twelve million Javanese Muslims. This case study came at the end of a day which began with a devotional on Matthew 16:18—"I will build my Church, and the gates of Hades will not overcome it"—from an Indian working among Muslims in Kashmir. (Note: Only weeks after the conference, the first convert of this Kashmiri outreach was martyred.)

Certainly the promise of Matthew 16:18 seems to apply to the movement of God among the Javanese. According to the case study, major growth began around 1930 when baptized Javanese numbered about 30,400. Today, unofficial estimates report that Javanese Muslim Background Believers (MBBs) number nearly twelve million.

While Partners International sponsored the gathering in Europe in November 2006, the conference was held at the request of non-Western indigenous leaders who wanted to share successful ministry models at work in Muslim-majority countries. The sixteen participants were experienced practitioners who welcomed a forum where they spoke directly with ministries like their own. Together, their agencies have about 530 ministry workers.

None of the participants claimed to be seeing large numbers of Muslims coming to Christ. One leader noted that of every ten Muslims who become Christian in his country, eight will return to Islam within two years because of family pressure, social ostracism, or job loss. In one town, where the number of Christians has doubled in ten years, many more people in the same period were born into Islam.

No one pretended that ministry among Muslim-majority people groups is easy. "How do you build bridges to Islam when Muslims do all they can to avoid Christians?" asked a Malian church leader. Another leader admitted that five years passed before their ministry saw the first baptism. But all the indigenous ministry leaders, representing ten countries, recognized that even though militant Islam gets most of the media's attention, they still find Muslims receptive to open dialogue about Christ. What works in winning Muslims to Christ is the same that wins anyone to Christ: having an authentic, personal relationship. "The power of Christian love is the single biggest factor in people coming to faith, even among Muslims," said one participant.

But how does one enter that relationship when the Muslim and Christian communities often live apart from each other—or even actively avoid each other? One Indian missionary couple, who purposely moved into a Muslim area to minister, discovered that one of their greatest challenges was convincing local Christians that Muslims will actually respond to the gospel. According to this couple, more than one thousand Indian missionaries are sent out annually; however, fewer than one hundred out of twenty thousand Indian missionaries reach out to Muslims.

There is no single, monolithic, Islamic world. Reaching people groups dominated by syncretistic folk Islam requires a different approach from reaching nominal Muslims.

The danger with "best practices" is to think that there are techniques that will quickly enhance a ministry's effectiveness. What skills are needed? What competencies? What strategies? What training? Fortunately, one devotional leader began the conference by saying that the first question is not the "how" of ministry but the "why." What is your motivation? What is your calling? "The shaping of one's heart is more important than the skill set," he said. "Once the character issues are worked out, you can move on to competence, training, and strategy."

The other widely acknowledged truth is that there is no single, monolithic, Islamic world. Reaching people groups dominated by syncretistic folk Islam requires a different approach from reaching nominal Muslims. How one defends or presents the gospel in rural Mali differs from that of urban Dakar. Ministering to wealthy Muslims in the Gulf States is a world apart from the destitute of Hyderabad. Nevertheless, participants were stimulated by the different models they saw, and while no one is likely to jettison what they already do in favor of a new model, many are sure to allow those models to influence and modify their existing practices. The various conference presentations can be summarized around three themes: training, community development, and partnerships.

Training

One of the most impressive training models presented was from Indonesia, a model born out of hard lessons learned. The ministry chose several years ago to focus on the most resistant Muslim unreached people groups, but discovered, to their dismay, that ninety percent of their church planters left the ministry within five years. While many factors accounted for this hemorrhaging, one was the recognition that seminaries prepared students for church ministry but not cross-cultural ministry among Muslims. The ministry developed a training philosophy centered on several principles, including:

- seventy percent of the training must be field experience
- trainees need to be mentored by an experienced church planter
- trainees learn best when role-playing real situations

The training shows students the types of rituals, customs, and beliefs that are part of Muslim life so that future church planters can better understand and relate to their audience.

The first step of a comprehensive seven-stage church-planting process became the most important: personal and team preparation. Originally, teams of two or three were sent out; however, these often failed because interpersonal conflicts would paralyze the team. Now, with larger teams going out, creativity, accountability, and gifting come together more effectively to plant churches. The other critical preparation piece is for church planters to create a respected, accepted, and if possible, even indispensable, identity within the community. Examples include: teachers, nurses, small business owners, and mechanics. Team members learn how to live next to Muslims and gain their respect. In addition, the training addresses more standard fare:

- principles of cross-cultural communication
- contextualizing the gospel
- developing relationships with community leaders
- spiritual warfare and praying for the sick
- using the Qur'an in evangelism
- creating sacraments and special services appropriate for the community
- caring for the poor
- identifying and training potential leaders

While these subjects may be considered standard today, their introduction to the Indonesian missions community at the time was groundbreaking. A different, but also effective, training model is used by a ministry reaching out to

North Africans. This agency provides its expatriate missionaries two to three days of orientation, but then places them with Muslim families for the first five months of service. This immersion experience is a language and cultural juggernaut that crushes any illusions about the challenges ahead. The ministry has found that it can take up to three years before a missionary effectively shares the gospel and up to five years to start a Bible study group or small church—not a calling for the faint of heart.

Community Development

Everyone agreed that training is essential. The role of community development, however, was more controversial. Christians criticize Saudi Arabia, Libya, and other Islamic governments for providing funds to other nations for those who become (or remain) Muslim. But Muslims criticize Christians for evangelizing under the guise of community development. Would Christians do community development if it did not lead to conversions? Some Christians would answer an emphatic, "Yes! We do community development whether or not it makes disciples, because ministering to the whole person is what Jesus modeled." Other Christians seem to engage in it only as an effective way to make disciples.

Conference attendees did not address this issue directly; however, the discussion brought out the distinction between community-driven development and church-driven (or evangelistically-motivated) development. In other words, who determines the agenda?

Does the church or Christian agency come in with what it thinks the community needs—or are the solutions coming in response to the expressed needs of the community? Perhaps a water well is a good thing for a community, but do they really want a school? A medical clinic may be important, but do community leaders want an irrigation system? And once the project is completed, is it run by the church as a favor to the community, or is it truly community-owned and operated? Can a Christian-built school, for example, hire Muslim teachers?

Partnerships

The topic of partnerships was especially relevant, because working together in some highly sensitive Muslim-majority nations is far different from working together in Mexico or Haiti. For example, bringing North Americans to some places risks exposing the confidential nature of an indigenous ministry's discreet outreach.

Two partnership types were examined: North-to-South and South-to-South. The conference itself was an example of a South-to-South learning exchange. Partners International, the only Western organization present, played mainly a facilitating role. All but one of the ministry model presentations originated from indigenous ministries. Partners International hopes to be a catalyst for more South-to-South gatherings that could spawn South-to-South partnerships. For example, an Indian leader now wants the leader of a ministry in the Gulf States to train congregations in India to demonstrate that reaching Muslims is possible. And the head of training for an Egyptian ministry wants an Indonesian brother to share his training model in Egypt. This potential for "cross-pollination" was one of the main purposes behind the conference.

But North-to-South partnerships are not going away anytime soon. In fact, with greater ease of travel and many high-tech communication tools available, interaction between Northern and Southern churches is not only going to grow in frequency, but is already happening outside of formal organizational channels. How do we balance the desire of the North to help the South with the actual needs of the South? Northern churches love to send short-term teams to Southern churches, but how appropriate is this in Muslim countries where public witness is restricted and foreign faces could raise suspicion?

The North American bent is for practical service (e.g., building churches,

The North American bent is for practical service (e.g., building churches, sending medical teams), but one conference participant asked, "Will a team come for two weeks just to pray for us?"

sending medical teams), but one conference participant asked, "Will a team come for two weeks just to pray with us?" Another one pointed out, "Even if a team comes for the short-term, for us it is a long-term relationship, not just the week or two that they are there. For us it is a process, not a one-time event."

It was acknowledged that hosting short-term teams can be a ministry to westerners, but one church leader has refused teams because it takes so much time to orient them to appropriate cultural practices and set up introductions to the local community. "It takes away from ministry time," said the leader, "and teams don't know the context of our work. The ministry needs to tell the outsiders what is needed. And sometimes those needs cannot be met in a week or two, but over several months."

Without a doubt, providing orientation and training before trips was a *sina qua non* for those going to the field. Another non-negotiable was that the needs had to be field-, not donor-, driven. Leaders desired a relationship that would continue after the team has left. "We want to know what they do with their experience after they return to the USA," said one leader, making clear that true partnership goes both ways.

The other side of the North-to-South equation is what might be called

"South-to-North"—how do we get the North to see they have much to receive from the South? "Do westerners want to receive from us, not just give?" asked a participant. Another wondered, "Why don't churches in the North invite groups from the South? Would a North American church want to learn at the feet of an Arab pastor?"

Someone observed that there is a Somali immigrant population in Seattle, Washington. Instead of a church sending a short-term team to East Africa to build a well in a Somali village, why not have an East African ministry teach the Seattle church how to reach their Somali neighbors? "It seems we spend a lot more time thinking about what the Northern church can do for the South than the other way around," said Carlos Calderon, Partners International's vice-president of international ministries. "How do we get the North to see that they have as much to receive from the South as they have to give?"

The conference only scratched the surface of a myriad of issues facing Muslim ministry. Participants left wanting more. Any future gathering needs to be based on two cornerstones that made this one a successful start: an indigenous ministry-driven agenda and a genuine spirit of "What can I learn from my co-workers in the gospel?"

Growing Churches in Resistant Areas

David Greenlee

*Case studies of twelve churches in resistant areas reveal charac-
teristics of why "vigorous" churches have continued to thrive in
difficult areas.*

HOW DO CHURCHES GROW? From Paul's basic, yet profound, explanation
(1 Cor. 3:6) to Christian Schwartz's statistical studies (1996), many have
attempted to explain the principles that effect the growth of churches, and
wondered how they could foster greater growth in and of the Church.

Many books have been written born from research in regions such as India (McGavran 1955) and sub-Saharan Africa (Braun n.d.). Less attention has
been paid, at least in terms of formal research, to the recently emerging churches in the Muslim world. Greg Livingstone (1993) provided a global survey, but
indicated the absence of research on conversions from Islam to Christianity
(1993, 154). My dissertation (Greenlee 1996) was an attempt to start bridging
that gap. In early 1997, a regional church development working group asked
what could be learned from existing churches to benefit those planting new
churches of Muslim Background Believers (MBBs). Those discussions led to
the collection of case studies of twelve churches in the region. Analysis of the
cases points to certain tendencies and patterns among the churches.

These findings, we should remember, arise from descriptive studies; we
must be very careful in moving from them to prescriptive statements. What
I have written is true about these churches. As you read, I encourage you to
bracket these findings with a question mark and allow them to stimulate reflection on your own ministry setting.

Categorizing the Churches

Case studies were provided for twelve churches. *Church* refers to a group of
Christian believers who regularly meet for fellowship, teaching, worship, and
the sacraments. Eleven were located in a setting dominated by Islam and with
no significant Christian presence in recent centuries. The remaining church was
in a neighboring country with a historic Christian presence, but these MBBs had
virtually no contact with Christianity except through a small number of Western
expatriate missionaries or other national MBBs. Eight of the churches continue
to function today; one ceased in the 1980s and three in the 1990s.

Of the eight churches functioning today, I have classed five as *vigorous*, two
as *plateau*, and one as *struggling*. These groupings are based upon the case

studies themselves, not on an external scale. Although admittedly somewhat subjective, the factors affecting my categorization include numerical growth, vitality of fellowship, response to opposition, and strength of national leadership. At least two of the churches which have ceased meeting, at one time, could have been called vigorous. In looking at the case studies, I tried to learn lessons from those ceased groups when they were at their best, as well as the factors leading to their decline.

Burden Bearing

Galatians 6:2 gives practical instruction on how to put John 13:34-35 into practice: bear one another's burdens. My earlier work on individual male believers in one country revealed a disturbing lack of commitment to "burden bearing" (Greenlee 1996, 159-61). In this study, it is encouraging to find that all of the vigorous churches report a strong sense of community demonstrated in specific instances of burden bearing. Caring for the sick, helping the unemployed, and encouraging those in various struggles were some of the examples reported.

The two plateau churches referred to burden bearing, but it seemed to have occurred more in the past. The struggling church gave no indication that burden bearing was a part of the fellowship. Of the ceased churches, one had gone through a vigorous phase in which it did have a time of significant burden bearing. The only other reference among the ceased churches to burden bearing was to the absence of this practice in one group before its demise. The informant reported that the decline of the church "might have been that everyone was exhausted with some people always giving and not being able to give any more while others were always receiving and not willing to give."

Evangelism and Welcome of New People

Missionaries should evangelize! But the vigorous churches tend to be those in which the national believers have taken on an active role in evangelism. Schwartz argues that, although "it is indeed the responsibility of every Christian to use his or her own specific gifts in fulfilling the Great Commission ... the gift of evangelism applies to no more than ten percent of all Christians" (Schwartz 1996, 34).

How then does a church characterized by evangelism emerge? Much, it seems, depends on the founder, or a leader who has come in at a time of revitalization. Robert Coleman's classic work (1993) points to eight principles Jesus followed beyond simply evangelizing. He produced evangelists through selection, association, consecration, impartation, demonstration, delegation, supervision, and reproduction.

Of the two vigorous churches most strongly characterized by evangelism, the founder of one and the revitalizing leader of the other clearly exemplify the principles Coleman presents. Their own commitment to evangelism, close association with a select few, training, and demonstration have led to several others being equipped and involved in evangelistic ministry.

What should be done with seekers and new believers in an environment where betrayal may bear serious consequences? Welcoming new people to the church is a critical issue. Several churches had experienced negative repercussions from welcoming an insincere person; most of the rest were fearful of what could happen. Various strategies were adopted by the vigorous churches, but it is clear that finding some plan to welcome seekers and new believers, a workable plan which the church as a whole adopts, is very important.

Spiritual Gifts

It is not surprising that the vigorous churches indicate that the members are, in one way or another, using their spiritual gifts. Some churches which were weaker, or ceased, also made such reports, although the reports tended to indicate this had to do with teaching and not a broader range of spiritual gifts that contribute to the life of the body.

Two of the ceased churches were characterized by the unwillingness of some to get involved, leaving a heavier load on a small number. This contributed directly to the demise of these churches.

Leadership Transitions

Leaders are vital. Finding qualified national leaders is very important to long-term growth. How those leaders are appointed appears to be crucial. In the countries of these twelve churches, national politics is characterized by a strong, central figure. Where an attempt has been made at free elections, the result has been years of civil unrest. The people tend to accept the situation but when crops fail or the economy turns sour, tension on the streets can become acute.

Intercultural relations expert Geert Hofstede (1997) describes the countries of this region as having a very high power distance. That is, in this region inequality is accepted, hierarchy is needed, superiors are often inaccessible, and power-holders have privilege. Having visited most of these countries myself, I would agree with Hofstede's description of society as a whole. But what applies to successful national politics and social structure does not apply within these churches. In fact, it could be that two sets of values are competing— those described by Hofstede and a more biblical, egalitarian, servant-leader approach to Christian community.

All of the vigorous churches have made a transition to national leadership. For some, it was a bumpy process as leaders failed in one way or another, leading to a turbulent period. Failure in the leadership transition contributed to the decease of two groups and is a continuing problem for one which is struggling. In one setting, an expatriate who had helped found a church appointed a leader with apparently adequate gifting. When the expatriate left the country the church fell apart. The others in the church did not place confidence in the new leader and were not in agreement with his appointment. In other cases, appointing people to leadership prematurely, or taking leadership back out of their hands, were reported as negative influences on church development.

Our cases do not provide definitive answers for this thorny issue of transition from an expatriate founder to national leadership. It appears, though, that a consensus-building approach to decision-making and leadership issues is helpful. Having leadership gifts alone is not enough; building trusting relationships is vital. The failure of leaders to develop relationships and build consensus run counter to the health of the church. On the other hand, good leadership must be complemented by the rest of the church sharing the load, using their spiritual gifts and bearing one another's burdens.

Persecution

Persecution, as experienced by these churches, ranged from the general social pressures and intimidation from family and employers to harassment and, at times, torture at the hands of the police. The only specific death threat reported was directed at an expatriate by friends of a fundamentalist who had come to faith. Perhaps the most common characteristic among the churches was the problem of fear of what might happen.

Among the twelve churches studied, the only pattern I find linking the cases is that persecution tends to push the believers inward, to curtail witness, and to cause them to be cautious in relationships. The specifics of their responses vary greatly. Some struggle with fear, while at least two of the vigorous churches want to avoid unnecessary trouble, and so have measured their (somewhat) open evangelistic activity accordingly.

The demise of the church which ceased in the 1980s was, in part, a result of severe police intimidation and arrests of several believers. Another church seemed to be growing well, but fear linked to one man's open evangelism led to division and eventual break-up of the group. In another short-lived church, quite strong police intimidation helped prevent the group from being solidly grounded, leading to its demise.

Since the cases were gathered, I have been aware of serious police intimidation of two of the vigorous churches. The believers made it clear that they were Christians, making no attempt to emulate Muslim religious practices (cf. Green 1989). I have been informed that, when the intimidation subsided, both groups saw significant numerical growth or multiplication in the formation of other groups.

Singles or Families?

One mission agency's definition of an autonomous, functioning local church includes the presence of Christian families in the fellowship (Livingstone 1993, 170). Although doubtless we all long for the incorporation of entire families in the churches, no clear pattern emerged linked specifically to the question of singles-only churches.

One group started by two single men, involving just single men, thrived and eventually, through marriage of the members, included families. Another similar group struggled. A group started by couples involving singles eventually fell apart as a result of police intimidation and inadequate leadership transition when the expatriates had to pull out of participation. At the same time, presence of families in a church was no guarantee of the church's vigor.

It is evident that families can add a measure of stability to a church, but single men at times give the needed leadership and evangelistic drive to a church made up of singles and families together. At other times, the married man (and his wife) provide leadership as well as a secure place to meet. Study of the roles of Philemon, Onesimus ,and Epaphras among the New Testament churches in the Colossae-Laodicea-Hierapolis triangle may help to illuminate this point further.

One important finding is a confirmation of the role of single missionaries as church planters in the Muslim world. One of the older churches was blessed for many years through the ministry of a godly single woman missionary who, perhaps due to her age and longevity in ministry, held the respect of both men and women. Another of the vigorous churches was planted by two single men. As singles, the two did not attempt to bring in women but when a church member married, followed some time later by the marriage of one of the missionaries, the group was able to transition to mixed membership in the church.

Place

It seems that having a secure, regular place to meet which is identified more with nationals than missionaries is an aid to growth. Too much dependence on the missionaries for a place to meet appears to be unhealthy.

Alternatively, it seems that the weaker churches tended to be dependent upon the missionaries for a place to meet, or that the meetings took place outside the normal environment of the national believers. One exception is a house that has been known as a Christian place for decades and has been somehow tolerated by the authorities (although with waves of persecution over the years). Another vigorous church comprised of singles did meet initially in the single missionaries' apartment. Its location and the lifestyle of these men, however, reflected their close bonding to the local culture.

Conferences and Special Events

Mathias Zahniser (1997) suggests the importance of symbol and ceremony in the cross-cultural discipling process. In an Islamic setting, MBBs may struggle with their response to Ramadan and the various Islamic feasts, all the while wondering how to incorporate such Christian celebrations as Christmas and Easter.

The case studies I have considered remind us again of the importance of special events in building up the church. Summer Bible camps, Easter and Christmas events and other opportunities to gather believers for celebration, fellowship, and teaching make a major, positive contribution, especially among the vigorous churches. Even some reporting on churches that have now ceased, in looking back at better times, consider these gatherings of great importance.

Conclusion

There is no simple key, no recipe, for planting thriving churches of MBBs. Suggested success principles and practices developed in countries with significant freedom for open church life may not prove relevant to our setting. Schwartz's excellent work must be applied with care since his extensive surveys involved few churches in settings dominated by Islam (1996, 19). We may even find that practices developed in one region of the Islamic world are irrelevant among MBBs elsewhere. Joshua Massey (2000, 12-13) helps us understand the reason for this by reminding us of the diverse attitudes Muslims hold toward Islam, not just their diverse theologies.

The research project giving rise to this paper grew out of the disquiet of a group of MBBs and missionaries concerned to see churches growing and thriving in their region. Broader research might help us refine these findings and extend the range of their validity. The hard work will not be further studies, surveys and analysis; the real challenge is in creatively, contextually bringing these principles to life in ourselves and in the people entrusted to our care and training.

References

Braun, Willys K. n.d. *Evaluating and Escalating Church Growth in the Third World.* Kinshasa, DRC: International Center of Evangelism.

Coleman, Robert E. 1993. *The Master Plan of Evangelism.* 30th anniversary edition. Grand Rapids, Mich.: Fleming H. Revell.

Green, Denis. 1989. "Guidelines from Hebrews for Contextualization." In *Muslims and Christians on the Emmaus Road.* Ed. J. Dudley Woodberry, 233-250. Monrovia, Calif.: MARC.

Greenlee, David. 1996. "Christian Conversion from Islam: Social, Cultural, Communication and Supernatural Factors in the Process of Conversion and Faithful Church Participation." Ph.D. diss. Deerfield, Ill.: Trinity International University.

Hofstede, Geert. 1997. *Cultures and Organizations: Software of the Mind.* New York: McGraw-Hill.

Livingstone, Greg. 1993. *Planting Churches in Muslim Cities: A Team Approach.* Grand Rapids, Mich.: Baker Books.

Massey, Joshua. 2000. "God's Amazing Diversity in Drawing Muslims to Christ." *International Journal of Frontier Missions* 17(1):5-14.

McGavran, Donald A. 1955. *The Bridges of God.* New York: The Friendship Press.

_____. 1970. *Understanding Church Growth,* 3rd ed. Ed. C. Peter Wagner. Grand Rapids, Mich.: William B. Eerdmans Publishing Co.

Scharwz, Christian A. 1996. *Natural Church Development Handbook.* British Church Growth Association.

Zahniser, A.H. Mathias. 1997. *Symbol and Ceremony: Making Disciples across Cultures.* Monrovia, Calif.: MARC.

A Church Built by Muslims

Tony Lynn

The author reflects upon how God used a Muslim chief to get an area's first church building established.

A S THE MUSLIM CHIEF AND I stood beside my white Toyota wagon, the traditional African gestures and greetings were exchanged. The scorching Saharan sun was beating down on all of us. Men greeted the chief and then turned to me. All of us were shaking hands and gesturing to our own hearts and foreheads, showing that no ill will or thoughts stood between us. A symphony of common greetings filled the air while sparkling smiles beamed from everyone's faces. I could see by the expressions on the faces of the adults and the children that they felt as if they were greeting a celebrity. The men shook the strong hand of the chief, then glanced with pride at one another to see if anyone had noticed.

The African chief had a stoic expression on his face when he spoke. He beamed with a firm but warm authority. It appeared that he was selecting every word with great care. His tight white curls on his face and head barely covered his milk chocolate colored skin. The wrinkles on his weathered face were more than old age—they were marks of tender wisdom.

The chief was not speaking to me; instead, he was speaking about me. The chief, whom I had affectionately learned to call *Chief Chameleon*, was addressing the ever-growing multitude of people. The residents of the crowded African neighborhood had started gathering from the first moment they had observed the chief and me driving around the neighborhood in my small car.

I could tell that the people liked the chief. At the same time, they seemed to have a deep respect for him. The chief moved gently through the crowd. He walked slowly enough that he seemed to float from person to person in his long colorful Muslim robe of indigo blue. His brimless Muslim prayer cap was a complementary sky blue with splashes of startling hues embedded throughout the fabric. The people appeared to be in a trance as the chief took control of the crowd with his commanding presence.

The chief spoke on my behalf, not his own. He said, "This man with me today is named Tony. He is a friend of mine. He is a good man and a religious man. He is not a Muslim but he is a teacher of the Bible and Christianity. From now on, you must treat him as you would treat me."

The chief added, "You know Tony has been preaching on the streets of our neighborhood these past two months. Many of you have heard the good things he has said about God. All of our children and we need to hear these lessons that he and his wife, Jamie, are teaching. You know, as I do, that many of our adult children do not follow the ways of Islam. I would rather my children follow the way of Christianity than to not follow any way at all."

Then the venerable old chief shocked the crowd and me when he said, "I want all of you to know that I am loaning this property upon which we are standing to Tony and his church. They will use this property freely and for the benefit of our community. What is more, all of you will be here next week to help build his church when he comes with the materials to build a thatch and wood shelter for his meeting place."

The chief paused, then panned the crowd with a careful survey and asked for a response, "Do you understand? You will help build this church!" To which the crowd replied, "Yes. Yes. We will help if Allah wills." I stood stunned and in awe, reflecting on how God had used a Muslim chief to get our first church building established. In a matter of minutes, our first building project was under way in Africa and its construction was in the hands of Muslims. Later that evening, during my prayers, I thanked the Lord for allowing us to see so much of his power in the lives of our people.

How It All Started

Almost nine months earlier, Jamie and I vividly remember meeting Boubacar the first day we arrived in Africa. The very moment we had moved away from the customs inspectors at the airport, a slender dark hand was there to take my bags from me. I looked up to meet Boubacar who was there to greet us along with the missionaries. Boubacar quietly introduced himself to me.

He leaned close to my ear and in his best and slowest English he whispered, "My name is Boubacar. I am a Christian. I have been praying with the missionaries for the safe arrival of you and your family. It is my prayer that God will use you to reach my tribe for Christ." I was so deeply moved that I have never forgotten those words and the emotions of that day.

During the next six months of language acquisition, my wife and I learned an African tribal language on top of our one-year of French study. We loved learning from our tutor, but we also enjoyed practicing the language as quickly as we could use it. We spent many days and evenings visiting with Boubacar and his wife Biba.

While the four of us spent time together, we learned that Boubacar was a good Christian man, but that he had the heart of a lamb when it came to witnessing for his faith. He was reluctant to witness openly because ninety-eight percent of his countrymen were not Christians. The vast majority of the population was Muslim and the remainders were animists. Most mingled the two religious ways of Islam and animism together. Boubacar was justifiably afraid of the persecution he would bring upon himself and his family. While we spent time getting to know one another in those early months, we challenged each other to grow in the Lord and to stretch our faith to more completely trust God.

After six months of language learning, Jamie and I were longing to share the gospel in the heart language of our people group. We had observed the open exhibition of Islam throughout the country, especially in the capital city where we lived. Muslims stopped anywhere they wanted when the call to prayer was issued from the minarets that filled the skyline of our sprawling metropolis. Homes had prayer areas just outside the walls of their compounds on the edge of city streets. We wondered if we could practice our religion with the same openness as the Muslims.

We approached Boubacar about the opportunity of street witnessing, suggesting that we tell the major stories of the Bible from a chronological plan. The idea was to witness and teach the Bible from a designated area just outside of Boubacar's compound. We would place a mat on the street at a certain time of the week and, with singing and Bible stories, we would share our Christian faith. He was excited about the prospect but he was also timid about the endeavor.

After we spent some days in prayer and reflection, we knew exactly what needed to be done. Three types of visits came to mind. First, we knew that we needed to stop by the local police station and explain what we were doing.

After we spent some days in prayer and reflection, we knew exactly what needed to be done. Three types of visits came to mind.

Only two years earlier, the government of our West African nation had voted to become a free democracy. Islam was no longer the official religion of the country. We didn't want them to think that we were starting trouble; rather, we were simply exercising our religious freedom. We went to the district chief of police with a gift of cola nuts and a Bible. The cola nuts were a local custom of friendship and the Bible was our introduction. We merely explained to the chief of police that we wanted to practice our religion much like they had been doing for centuries. Since he had never seen Christians worshipping before, he accepted our explanation of practicing our religion as the Muslims did on the side of the street. He gave us his approval to gather in his district.

The second visit was as important as the first. We knew that we needed to visit the unofficial chief of the neighborhood. Every district of the city had an unofficial chief to whom everyone had to answer. Normally, he was a highly regarded man in politics, business or religion. That was the occasion when I met Chief Chameleon.

He was a retired colonel from the military. He had been on the president's cabinet during the last administration. Chief Chameleon actually had a very long and illustrative name. He told me his real name during our first meeting when I gave him a Bible and a small bag of cola nuts. It was obvious though that he preferred his nickname given to him by his closest friends. He was so named because he had four wives who were from four different tribes in the country. The tint of the skin of each of his four wives was distinctly different, from a Mediterranean cream to a dark black. Therefore, all of his twenty-one children were different in appearance and color and thus the name Chief Chameleon.

My anxiety was the highest when I went to visit the chief. I didn't know what to expect. The visit ended up being my most rewarding encounter. I learned more about the transition of the government and the culture during our half-day conversation than I had learned in months of language study. After I had openly explained our intentions to evangelize in the neighborhood, the chief replied with an unexpected but pleasant reaction.

The chief said, "Tony, when I was a colonel in the army I traveled to many parts of the world. I have seen Rome, Paris and Washington, D.C. I have seen in those great places mosques standing next to churches and synagogues. I want

Two men outside the door demanded that Boubacar come down to the neighborhood mosque to have a conversation with the local priest after evening prayers.

my country to become a great place too. My nation will only be great when we allow each person the right to choose his own religion." I marveled at his national pride and I was so relieved when I understood that his nationalism was opening our way to start a church in his area.

The chief went on to say something more personal, "My adult children do not practice Islam. I wish that they did. But if they will not be good Muslims perhaps they will make good Christians. You have my approval to meet in the streets of our district."

Later in that same conversation, I shared my testimony and I witnessed to the chief about my faith while we were alone underneath the shade of a tree. His response was heart wrenching. He thoughtfully replied, "It is too late for someone my age to change his ways. I may be like a chameleon because of my many wives but I cannot see myself changing my religion. I will die a Muslim." He then wrapped up our conversation by saying, "If you can help my children to become Christians then do it. I have no problem with that."

The third type of visit required a great deal of time. Before setting out to simply start witnessing, my wife and I realized we had to establish relationships with Boubacar and Biba's neighbors. During our initial visit we started with Biba and asked her to take us next door to meet the family. Within minutes and with Biba's introductions we were greeted, invited in, and offered a glass of water.

Three times a week, we went to homes in the same neighborhood. Each time we started with the last family that we had visited the time before. On each occasion we asked them to introduce us to their neighbors and we would spend one hour visiting with the family, getting to know their names, and sharing about ourselves. Whenever they asked why we were in their country we openly explained that we were followers of Christ. We explained that we were there to teach whoever was interested the words of the Bible. We told the hosts and hostesses that we would begin our Bible teaching on a certain day in September. We invited them to join us and left after praying for their family.

The response to our Bible studies went way beyond our expectations. The first week we had thirty guests. The second week we had sixty attending. At one month, we had over 120 people of various ages listening to us teach and sing in their tribal language. The whole process was so simple and so moving. It continued for two months without incident.

Trouble Starts

It was at the end of those two months of bliss that we then learned that a local Muslim priest, who lived down the road from Boubacar, was not happy with our success. One Sunday morning after services had started, three men came to chase away their family members from our gathering. While the services were going on, the men threw stones at their wives and children. The men were warning everyone to flee from our meeting. One man even pulled off his shoe and repeatedly threw it at his wife while she fled in embarrassment.

That night, just after Boubacar had put out the lantern in his home and settled into bed next to Biba, a loud pounding on the door of his home caused him to leap from his bed. His two infants were startled by the noise. Boubacar stood at the door with nothing on but his shorts.

Two men outside the door demanded that Boubacar come down to the neighborhood mosque to have a conversation with the local priest after evening prayers. One hour later, Boubacar was sitting in the shadows of the mosque with the priest and his two messengers. Boubacar informed me the next morning about the ten-minute conversation with the priest. The Muslim priest warned Boubacar that having me preach in front of his home was a mistake. He then threatened that if I continued preaching, Boubacar might lose his rental home. He also informed Boubacar that it was not the business of the chief to give us permission to preach in the community. Then, with a mocking tone of concern, the Muslim priest said, "Do you think I want to see any harm come to you, your wife or your children?"

It was at that moment, when the Muslim priest was awaiting his reply, that something grew in Boubacar's chest. He said that courage filled his heart and it gave strength to his bones. He responded in a low tone but a raised voice, "My life is in the hands of God, not yours. It is time for you to realize that you are not the Lord over the people in this country. Jesus Christ is Lord!" With that declaration, Boubacar rose up from where he had been sitting face to face with the priest and pushed his way past the two men at the door of the mosque. Boubacar said that at the door he turned back to look at the priest still sitting on his mat and he yelled, "Do what you must and I will do what I must do!"

A Prayerful Solution

It was at breakfast time the next morning that Boubacar was at my door. He joined me for the meal and we reviewed the previous night's misadventure. I felt too many feelings all at once. I was angry with the priest. I was frightened for my new friend and his family. At the same time, I was exhilarated by the spiritual battle that had begun. What were we going to do?

Together, before the dishes were removed from the table, we decided to spend three days praying over the matter. It was only Monday morning. We knew there was time to consider all of the possibilities before the next Sunday morning's gathering.

Thursday, Boubacar and I met together with Jamie and we all came up with the same conclusion. We decided that I would go to see Chief Chameleon by myself. I would inform him of the priest's nighttime invitation to Boubacar and inform him of the conversation, especially the criticism of the chief himself.

I went by the chief's home on Friday and he wasn't there. Nevertheless, the family greeted me warmly. They visited with me for a few minutes and informed me that they had already heard about the disruption of the meeting last week. Some of them had even been there. They invited me back on Saturday to see the chief.

Saturday morning when I arrived back at the chief's home, he was sitting out in front as if awaiting my arrival. When I approached him, he ordered one of his sons to bring something from inside the house. He took the package from his son's hands and placed the gift in mine. It was a pair of handmade well-crafted sandals. He told me it was my turn to receive gifts. I was touched by his generosity and thoughtfulness.

The chief asked about the new church work. I was elated to tell him about the tremendous growth, but I was reluctant to tell him about last week's nightmare. Speaking about the bad news seemed to rob our conversation of its joy. The chief listened to every detail with great interest. He asked for the exact words that the priest had spoken. It was apparent that he was angered by the remarks about himself. At the end of the account, Chief Chameleon spoke calmly and said, "I don't go to that priest's mosque. He listens to the extremists. He is not a good Muslim. His feet do not follow his words." Those were the only harsh words I had ever heard from the chief.

It was that day that Chief Chameleon asked for a ride in my Toyota station wagon. I wasn't certain what was going to be done. I had already apologized for causing a disturbance in his neighborhood, to which he replied that it was the priest who was guilty of causing the trouble, not me. While we were getting into the white wagon and rolling away from the chief's home, one of his wives was reminding him that he had another friend waiting to speak with him when we were finished. His only reply was, "I'll return when I'm finished."

The chief directed me as I drove. He told me to slow down and to take my time. As we were driving, he showed me three places that would make wonderful meeting places for our church. One of the meeting places was at the end of the road where Boubacar, his family and the priest lived. I informed the chief that we were not in a position to buy any property. He answered with, "That's not a problem." He offered no further explanation and I asked for none.

What I enjoyed the most during the drive was surprising. We passed the Muslim priest's home twice. The priest was out front and he easily noticed our

I stood to the side and watched a miracle of God. My wife and three children were also watching the divine event unfold before their very eyes. Muslim men were building our first church building in Africa.

passing. Each time he stared at the chief and me in total disbelief. The priest even stood so near to the car as we passed the second time that I felt compelled to wave to him. The chief and I had been waving to the many others who were watching us from the side of the roadways. The chief, it seemed to me, deliberately ignored the priest and continued his gaze straight ahead. Later, I concluded it was a subtle but strong African message from the chief to the priest. It was after that final pass in front of the mosque in which Boubacar had been threatened that we stopped in front of the throngs of people and on top of the future site of our new church.

Muslims Built Our Church Building

It was then, as it was at the beginning of this article, that the venerable old Muslim chief shocked the crowd and me when he said, "I want all of you to know that I am loaning this property upon which we are standing to Tony and his church. They will use this property freely and for the benefit of our community. What is more, all of you will be here next week to help build his church when he comes with the materials to build a thatch and wood shelter for his meeting place." I stood stunned and in awe, reflecting on how God had used a Muslim chief in order to get our first church building established. In a matter of minutes, our first building project was underway in Africa and its construction was in the hands of Muslims.

Sunday, the next day, our services went well as we met on the street in front of Boubacar's home. The chief even asked me to come by and to pick him up so that he could attend our service. We did just that. While we met, sang, and celebrated, the priest and a few of his friends watched from the safe distance of the mosque. The crowd was as big as ever, Boubacar counted two hundred people that day. At the end of the service, we announced that we would be at the new site on Saturday with construction supplies to build a meeting place. Everyone seemed as happy as we were.

The following Saturday we pulled up to the new site at midmorning. The materials and tools were unpacked. I couldn't keep my hand on a shovel, axe or even a rope. Dozens of men joined in the construction. Everyone refused to let me help build the thatch and wood structure. They wanted me to watch and to supervise. They asked me how large I wanted the structure and which walls I wanted left open so the air could cool the congregation.

I stood to the side and watched a miracle of God. My wife and three children were also watching the divine event unfold before their very eyes. Muslim men were building our first church building in Africa. Muslim women were looking on. Boubacar was there working alongside his Muslim neighbors. Our language tutor and first convert, Sekou, was there watching in disbelief. He had only been a Christian for two months. All of us were watching the handiwork of God and praising his holy name.

After the construction was done and the last mat was tied down, we asked everyone to join us in prayer. I led in prayer with the best tribal language I could muster. With the noise quieted and everyone still, they listened with rapt attention as I spoke to God in their tribal language. At the end of the prayer, everyone joined as instructed and said, "Amen."

That building site proved to be the beginning of many great undertakings for our mission. The ministry of the church became the model for the remainder of our efforts. Our converts tested themselves in ministry at that site. Some gave testimonies. Some prayed aloud. Some preached and others led the music. Everyone that wanted to learn to stand up for Christ was given the opportunity. Many conversions and baptisms came from the new work, and one final report added further proof of the faithfulness of God. The first Sunday we met together under our newly built church building, three hundred people were in attendance. The entire miracle happened because of God's gracious ways and because Muslims built our first church building in Africa.

Continuing Impact of the Church Built by Muslims

The radical impact of this new church start jarred the region in five obvious ways.

1. The church took on a tribal name, meaning the "Good Way Church."
The congregation selected the name from John 14:6. Within a year of its own

birth, the church flourished and multiplied into two additional church ministries. The leadership of the Good Way Church had proven that if church starting techniques were indigenous and easily reproducible, then new congregations could easily be formed.

2. Almost immediately potential leaders became evident within the new church groups. Seminary extension became mandatory if the churches were going to develop properly. I taught one session a week in the French language with students who were literate. Later that same day, I taught the same material to the preliterate students who could only understand in their tribal language of Zarma. I never had a total of less than twelve students under my care.

3. The Good Way Church shook up the region in the realm of missions. The seminary students were making great strides developing in their theological knowledge, but they lacked practical ministry skills. The early church leaders needed an environment in which they felt less danger while sharing their faith. Consequently, I took them on mission trips into the bush, three and four hours outside the capital city. On a weekly basis, I would load up the land cruiser with my brothers in the Lord and we would set out for villages where I introduced them to an unreached people group of a different tribe. During those years of training, I went from being the main mission leader to being nothing more than a chauffeur escorting a team of African missionaries. Developing those leaders were some of the best years of my life. The young men quickly learned to share their faith with boldness regardless of their location.

4. The gospel penetrated the Muslim country in unparalleled ways. There were two remarkable indications. First, during our inaugural national Bible conference we surveyed the attendees, and we discovered that we had more than eight hundred known converts in the region supporting the work of eighteen reported Bible studies and churches. Second, those mission trips into the bush established a vibrant ministry to another unreached people group called the Gourma people. Even now, news continues to pour out of the country that many of the mission agencies working with the Gourma people feel there is such a strong response to the gospel that a church growth movement is under way. Both of these miraculous milestones started within three years of the establishment of the church built by Muslims.

5. A Zarma edition of the *Jesus* film was produced. The film was a joint endeavor between four mission agencies and Campus Crusade for Christ. Jamie enlisted volunteers from our early churches to do the voices. We can still remember the looks of astonishment on the faces of our friends, their family members and their neighbors as they saw the film for the first time. One African woman who was converted at the film's debut said: "I never believed that God spoke my language because I had been following the way of Islam. I now believe that God does hear me and that he does love me, just as the Christians have been telling me for years."

It is marvelous to see what God can do when he fulfills his promise written in Matthew 16:18, "I will build my Church and the gates of Hades will not overpower it." Even in the sub-Saharan world of Africa, God is the designer and builder. But if he so chooses, his construction team for the church building can be a construction crew of Muslims.

Three Lessons We Learned

1. God uses those who are lost to accomplish his will. Satan was trying to use one priest to stop our efforts. All the while, God was using an army of unredeemed Muslims to accomplish his perfect will. His holy will cannot be stopped.

2. The priority of prayer makes a big difference during the large challenges. During the two-month planning stage of this endeavor at street evangelism, broad prayer support was enlisted in the US and among the missionaries in the host country. Many people voiced their fears about such a bold endeavor, yet they kept on praying. Their confidence in God made the difference.

3. Penetrating the layers of relationships in the Muslim-African world can make the difference between victory and defeat. When undertaking any effort at evangelism among Muslims and Africans, the missionary must initially take the responsibility of orienting the entire community toward the gospel. There are many with whom you have to deal. Americans think individually. Most other cultures think collectively. Missionaries must be willing to risk moving an entire community toward accepting the ways of Christianity over and against their traditional ways. That can never be forgotten.

EPILOGUE

Muslim Ministry in the Days Ahead: Two Fault Lines, Two Favorable Winds

Gary R. Corwin

Envisioning what the future will hold is never an easy task. In fact, in a pure sense, it's impossible. What is possible, however, is to learn the lessons of the past, to discern the patterns of the present, and to project the likely scenarios for the future.

I**T WILL COME AS NO SURPRISE** to most of you who have already read the preceding sections of this book that both the fault lines and the favorable winds have much in common with the emphases that have gone before. The perspectives and passions reflected in those articles reveal many lessons of the past, describe many patterns of the present, and provide the raw material for speculating about the future. To those speculations we now turn.

Fault Line #1: Reluctance on the part of believers to obey Christ by demonstrating sacrificial love toward Muslims.

"'Teacher, which is the great commandment in the Law?' And he said to him, 'You shall love the Lord your God with all your heart and with all your soul and with all your mind. This is the great and first commandment. And a second is like it: You shall love your neighbor as yourself. On these two commandments depend all the Law and the Prophets.'"—Matthew 22:36-40

"You have heard that it was said, 'You shall love your neighbor and hate your enemy.' But I say to you, Love your enemies and pray for those who persecute you…" —Matthew 5:43-44

Two powerful sets of circumstances will almost certainly make the challenge of sacrificially loving our Muslim neighbors a particularly daunting one. First, *there are the continuing attacks by the forces of militant radical* jihadism *on the West and on more moderate forms of Islam.* To the extent this remains, it will continue to be one of the most significant drags on mobilizing and energizing effective Christian outreach to Muslims.

Second, *there are the demographic patterns of relative birthrate and immigration that suggest a rapid growth in the percentage of Muslims in the populations of most Western nations and many African ones.* Terms like "Eurabia" and "Londonstan" have become part of the common media parlance in discussing the issue.

The impact of this in ministry calculus has been to increase fear and to reduce the desire on the part of many to be friendly or in proximity to Muslim populations, let alone seek to evangelize them. This is the present and it will likely be the future unless the case for evangelizing Muslims moves from compassion to obedience.

How can these fault lines be overcome? On one level, the answers seem especially hard to discern, not least because there is so little any individual can do to alter the circumstances. What can be done, however, and what is so very important from the point of view of God's kingdom, is to take seriously the admonitions to love quoted above. And only heart commitment energized by the Spirit's power can make it possible.

But part of the battle ministry leaders must wage is to assist believers to understand that only a minority of Muslims are radical militants, and that even those who may be are not beyond the reach of God's grace. The status of Christians as "infidels" singled out for hatred by Muslim radicals does not negate our responsibility and privilege of communicating the power and love of the gospel to them. God has ordained governments as part of his common grace to us all for dealing with those who would commit evil acts and oppress the weak; that's a part of his plan that believers should be grateful for and support, but it's not the believers' singular task. That task is to love; and love, if it means anything, means living sacrificially and sharing the gospel of grace with our Muslim neighbors.

Fault Line #2: Confusion over the limits of contextualization that are biblically appropriate in light of who Jesus Christ is and what he requires of his followers.

"In the beginning was the Word, and the Word was with God, and the Word was God."—John 1:1

"And the Word became flesh and dwelt among us, and we have seen his glory, glory as of the only Son from the Father, full of grace and truth."—John 1:14

"Whoever believes in him is not condemned, but whoever does not believe is condemned already, because he has not believed in the name of the only Son of God."—John 3:18

This fault line is a big one. The number of passionate articles committed to this subject over the last decade or so bears ample witness to that. This book contains a large number of them, and there are many additional ones that have been published elsewhere.[1]

I must confess I am a partisan in this debate; hopefully not one who misses what is worthy in the arguments and practice of those with whom he disagrees, but a partisan nonetheless. Why so? What difference does it all make?

And why can't we all just forget our differences and focus on introducing Muslims to the Savior? What follows are my personal answers to these questions.

1. Our passion for Muslims to know the Savior will mean little if we hide the reality of the Savior, who he really is, and what he requires of his followers.

2. The debate between C4 and C5 advocates is not about culture or the need to fully contextualize to accommodate all the cultural nuances that are not prohibited by the Bible. The debate is about theology: discerning and being faithful to those things that cannot be biblically accommodated.

3. Because the differences are theological and concern issues that are primary to the meaning of the gospel, it is not possible to simply split the difference. The result therefore, unless things change radically, will almost certainly be division. The signs of it are already evident among the churches, among and within agencies, and even within broad-based cooperative forums that have otherwise functioned well for decades.

4. Unless broad agreement can be reached on the limits of appropriate, biblically permissible levels of contextualization, the aggressive and sometimes secretive recruiting efforts of radical insider movement activists will create a

Bible translation efforts that prioritize eliminating biblical emphases and wording that offends Muslims above faithfulness to the text will create division in historic Christian communities.

serious divide between them and churches and agencies that believe long-term commitment of believers to maintaining Muslim identity dishonors Christ and confuses critical issues concerning his person and work.

5. Bible translation efforts that prioritize eliminating biblical emphases and wording that offends Muslims above faithfulness to the text will create division in historic Christian communities, confusion in newer Christian communities, and anger among Muslims smelling deceit in such actions.

6. The issue in question is not, as C5 advocates so often assert, the genuineness of faith of believers who continue to identify themselves as Muslims. There have always been such on the pathway from little understanding of the gospel in Christ to a more complete understanding based upon solid biblical teaching and Spirit-led reflection on the Word.

7. The core issue is the advocacy by some of the idea that believers in Christ should continue in an open-ended way to identify themselves as Muslims (including in matters of faith that are essential to being a Muslim), and continue with practices that many believe affirm false doctrine and contradict biblical commands.

8. A primary example is the recitation of the Creed (*Shahada*), the most important and essential declaration of Muslim identity. It affirms "There is no God but Allah, and Muhammad is his messenger." The intent of the creed is not just to assert Muhammad is one messenger among many, but the final and ultimately authoritative one. (Check out "Law of Abrogation" in any of the many Google listed sources on the subject.)

9. The bulk of the hardcore advocacy comes from outsiders who traverse the earth to win converts to their cause, at times through highly secretive meetings in which dissent is not welcome. Believers of Muslim background, on the other hand, are generally simply sorting their way through a new understanding of God and what he requires of them, and what it will mean for their relationships in their local context.

10. Those who express concern regarding the unbiblical affirmations of Islamic doctrine inherent in C5 practice are often dismissed as slaves to the dichotomistic Hellenistic Christianity dominant in the West. It is asserted that if they only better understood the more Hebraic Christianity of the first century, they would find the parallels in Muslim practice and teaching so much more palatable. It all sounds very enlightened, but at its core it reflects a subtle challenge to the equal authority of all parts of God's revelation in the Bible.

Our God is a God of infinite variety.

The ways and means he uses to draw people to himself are almost as varied as those he calls.

11. The sole choice with regard to insider movements is not between a C5 approach and a Western transplant one. There is a whole spectrum of approaches, and among them the C4 approach seeks to do everything that is biblically permissible to honor the traditions and mores of the believer's family, community, and people, even where these have Islamic roots. And contrary to C5 advocate suggestions otherwise, the C4 approach has produced equally significant, if not superior, results in many places.

12. Where C4 approaches draw the line, however, and where C5 advocates are much less careful to draw the line, is at identity with Islam as a system of belief. To declare "I am a Muslim" is to declare that I believe in its core beliefs regarding God, Jesus, salvation, and the Bible. That, many of us would contend, is not biblically permissible. On the other hand, to declare oneself a Muslim and not follow Islam's teaching in these matters is to fulfill the centuries-old accusation that followers of Christ are deceivers.

The issue, in short, represents a divide so serious and potentially destructive to Christian unity that one can only hope and pray that it will soon be resolved—and that the long-term impact to gospel penetration among Muslim peoples will not be hindered by doctrinal confusion and worse.

Favorable Wind #1: The Sovereign God is drawing Muslim men, women, boys, and girls to himself—sometimes through extraordinary means, and sometimes through more common ones. There is no reason to think this will change.

"And I, when I am lifted up from the earth, will draw all people to myself."—John 12:32

"No one can come to me unless the Father who sent me draws him. And I will raise him up on the last day."—John 6:44

"And they sang a new song, saying, 'Worthy are you to take the scroll and to open its seals, for you were slain, and by your blood you ransomed people for God from every tribe and language and people and nation.'"—Revelation 5:9

Our God is a God of infinite variety. The ways and means he uses to draw people to himself are almost as varied as those he calls. The articles that have gone before highlight a great many of them. But whether the immediate stimulus is radio, television, literature, the Internet, a dream, an act of mercy, or a conversation, almost always there is a personal relationship involved somewhere. The need for believer proximity, therefore—whether that person is a family member, friend, co-worker, acquaintance, fellow citizen, or cross-cultural worker—is huge. It always has been, and it almost certainly always will be so.

Two of the above stimuli that require at least a bit more comment are the Internet and dreams; the former because it has become so ubiquitous and powerful in such a short time, and is likely to remain so, and the latter because it is such an ancient and marvelous example of God's direct and personal involvement in the lives of individuals. While it would not be wise to go into detail on even a smattering of the many Internet and other social networking endeavors reaching out to Muslims, it is important to acknowledge the great creativity that is being modeled to make this medium as effective as possible. It is also important to note again the importance that is normally placed on the high-touch element of the equation (i.e., a personal human-to-human engagement with inquirers and new believers, either through correspondence or in person).

As far as dreams and other "special" means God often uses to draw Muslims to himself, I would highly recommend David H. Greenlee's 2006 book, *From the Straight Path to the Narrow Way*. The descriptor for the book states:

A group of nearly fifty missionaries and practitioners [from over 20 countries] gathered to consider how Muslims are coming to faith in Jesus Christ. They shared an interest in understanding how God is at work in drawing people into the faith journey from the way of Islam to faith in Jesus Christ. From the *Straight Path to the Narrow Way* is a compilation of papers presented at this consultation. The contributors point to the various ways in which God is at work in the lives of Muslims. While the papers reflect diverse global settings, three core factors seem to repeat: a demonstration of God's love, a sign of God's power, and an encounter with the truth of God's Word.

It is these core and common factors that unite the love role of the servant with the power, love, and truth of God.

Also helpful in providing insight into the interrelationship between fallible human work and witness, and the unique and powerful work of God directly in the lives of Muslims, is the 2008 book *From Seed to Fruit: Global Trends, Fruitful Practices, and Emerging Issues among Muslims*, edited by Dudley Woodberry. Its descriptor states:

> *From Seed to Fruit* presents the most recent worldwide research on witness to Christ among Muslim peoples, using biblical images from nature to show the interaction between God's activity and human responsibility in blessing these peoples.

It grew out of the insights shared and subsequently analyzed from a consultation of workers in the spring of 2007. Both of these resources, and others like them, provide abundant evidence that the God of history is the God who does not change, but acts on behalf of his people and his purposes to achieve all that his Word has promised. The favorable wind of God's faithfulness should never be underestimated or distrusted to achieve his good purposes, including the wooing of Muslims to gospel faith.

Favorable Wind #2: The Sovereign God is overseeing the affairs of nations and peoples in such a way that his purposes will be accomplished. This too will not change.

> *"The king's heart is a stream of water in the hand of the Lord; he turns it wherever he will."*—Proverbs 21:1

> *"Many are the plans in the mind of a man, but it is the purpose of the Lord that will stand."*—Proverbs 19:21

> *"Behold, the nations are like a drop from a bucket, and are accounted as the dust on the scales; behold, he takes up the coastlands like fine dust."*—Isaiah 40:15

> *"For as the rain and the snow come down from heaven…so shall my word be that goes out from my mouth; it shall not return to me empty, but it shall accomplish that which I purpose, and shall succeed in the thing for which I sent it."*—Isaiah 55:11

One of the things that always amazes me in debates about mission methodology is the generally short shrift given to God's sovereign work in the affairs of humans. As the above verses suggest, few errors could be more detrimental to a true understanding of our role. God hasn't called us to invent new methods, although there is certainly room at the margins for discerning new vehicles to apply what he has instructed us in his Word. He has called us to faithfully apply what he has shown us, and to keep a sharp opportunistic eye out in order to get in sync with what he is doing in a special way at any particular place and time. Unfortunately, we often expend the bulk of our energy trying to discern or invent new "golden keys" to winning the world.

The debate in recent years about contextualization in Muslim ministry is a case in point. As important as the issues related to it are, our preoccupation with them has often left us incapable of really seeing what God is doing around us. Some of the most dramatic and substantial movements of Muslims to the gospel in modern times have had practically nothing to do with the fine points of contextualization that we debate today. Unfortunately, we often miss them because they are works of God with which we have had practically nothing to do!

One might go all the way back to the first decade of the twentieth century, and the Sialkot Conferences associated with the name of John "Praying" Hyde; this brought thousands into the kingdom in what is today Pakistan. Or, the great movement of the Spirit in Indonesia in the 1960s that brought over

The recent emergence of reconciliation
ministries to build bridges between Muslim and Christian populations carry with them both promise and pitfalls.

a million to faith in Christ. Or the great work of the Spirit in a nation of western Asia where two hundred believers grew to tens of thousands over the last thirty years under the thumb of a most tyrannical Islamic theocracy. Or the tens of thousands of Berbers in a most unlikely nation of North Africa who have recently embraced the Savior, largely in reaction to hundreds of years of second-class citizenship under the rule of the majority population's Arab national leadership. The fact is that God has often used the affairs of nations and peoples to open the door to great kingdom advances.

Two other developments that deserve at least a brief mention because of their potential impact in the years ahead are *reconciliation ministries* and the *shifting sands of political and economic leverage in the sphere of global energy*. The recent emergence of reconciliation ministries to build bridges between Muslim and Christian populations carry with them both promise and pitfalls; the former if they can move beyond political correctness and geo-political and theological naivety, the latter if they cannot.

With regard to energy, conditions regarding international sources and consumption are changing rapidly and could result in decreased global leverage for the petroleum producers of the Middle East. This could have a dramatic impact on the stability of autocratic regimes, in turn impacting access to the gospel, potentially for both good and ill.

Conclusion

One of the great dilemmas in Muslim ministry, as in so many crucial spheres, is the confusion caused by starting with the wrong questions. We end up in the wrong place if we begin with the assumption that everything exists for and revolves around us, rather than for God's glory and purposes. We also end up in the wrong place if we assume that the only important question is what it will take to turn Muslims from unbelief to belief with regard to the person and work of Jesus Christ. Pragmatism is great for deciding which way to walk to the store, but it is terrible for maintaining theological faithfulness.

It is clear from the things we have discussed that certain patterns of present Muslim ministry and the contexts in which they take place, both troubling and terrific, are likely to continue well into the future. How could it be otherwise when they reflect the constancy of both God's grace and human frailty? We have discussed some of these, as well as some possible futures based upon historical precedent and a seat-of-the-pants guess on where current events might be leading. Hopefully, some of them may be helpful in and of themselves, or at least inspire others to deeper insights that better explain what the future may hold.

Endnote

1. Two sources include the *International Journal of Frontier Missiology*, which has overwhelmingly published in support of a C5 insider approach, and *St. Francis Magazine*, which has overwhelmingly published in opposition to it.

References

Greenlee, David H. 2006. *From the Straight Path to the Narrow Way*. Milton Keynes, U.K.: Authentic.

Woodberry, Dudley, ed. 2008. *From Seed to Fruit: Global Trends, Fruitful Practices, and Emerging Issues among Muslims*. Pasadena, Calif.: William Carey Library.

Appendix

Preparing Spiritually for Ministry in Muslim Contexts: Receiving Prayer for Healing of the Heart

John Travis

I WILL ADDRESS ONLY ONE ASPECT of spiritual preparation for ministry in Muslim contexts: receiving prayer for healing of the heart (similar terms for this kind of prayer are inner healing, deep level healing, and listening prayer). Other vital aspects of preparation, such as assembling a strong prayer team, fasting, scripture study, worship, and accountability, will not be touched upon here.

Our hearts are the "wellspring" of our lives, and must be guarded (Prov. 4:23), as they are easily wounded and can succumb to bondage. This may happen because of what is done to us, and also what we do in response, often beginning when we are very young. As we grow in our faith, many of these wounds and bondages are healed. Yet often there are areas of our hearts that need a special touch from God, so that we can more deeply experience his love and find freedom from weights such as rejection, anxiety, demonic oppression, anger, or condemnation.

It is likely that certain unhealed areas of our hearts will become more pronounced as we take up residence in the unfamiliar places where we are called. For example, we may have strong emotional reactions and find our relationships with others affected. The challenge of language learning, the strain of understanding the rules of a new culture, and the stress of starting efforts from scratch may highlight our own need for healing.

Certain areas of bondage in our hearts can make us vulnerable to spiritual attack, coming in forms different from what we experience in our home countries. When difficulties come into the lives of Muslims, many engage in "folk" practices such as using amulets and visiting shamans. They hope for a good outcome, yet unknowingly are inviting demonic activity. In addition, our presence could be threatening to certain people who may pronounce curses in our direction. Direct attack from evil spirits is common in areas where the gospel has never before entered and the ground is still very hard. The increased intensity of spiritual warfare will highlight our own need to know our authority in Christ, and learn to actively appropriate it.

There are many different models of prayer (see Kraft 1993; Taylor and Taylor n.d.; Payne 1989; and Sandford and Sandford 1982) for issues of the heart.

Most include these two important aspects: healing of wounds and freedom from bondage. By purposely seeking this type of prayer, we become more able to experience the loving presence of God, and more practiced in the use of our authority in Christ (see Kraft 1997 and 1992; Murphy 1996; Arnold 1997; Anderson 1993; and Swindoll 1995). It benefits us personally, and often later extends into our families and ministries (see Travis and Travis 2008; Kim, Travis, and Travis 2008; Colgate 2000; and Stacey 1989), as we naturally have opportunities to pray for others in the way we have received prayer ourselves.

Case Study of Heart Healing through Prayer

The following is a composite of experiences of many field workers in the Muslim world. I hope it will increase our desire for the healing of our hearts, using our authority in Christ, and seeking this kind of prayer in our lives.

Caleb was raised in a believing family, but sometimes felt unappreciated by his father. He fell in love and married Nicole, but not before he became a little too physically involved with one or two girlfriends in college. They have a solid marriage; yet once in a while, Nicole's subtle criticisms set Caleb off. Their two small children are adapting well to life in an urban Muslim neighborhood, but the older one has scary dreams every few nights.

One day, Nicole went with her neighbors to visit a young woman who appeared sick. It turned out she was in a demonic trance, and she screamed at the top of her lungs when the ladies walked in. They called for the resident Muslim spiritual practitioner, who used holy water and incantations to calm her down. The incident sparked many excellent language learning conversations over the next few months about charms, curses, and exact characteristics of various evil spirits that regularly visit the neighborhood (see Woodberry 1990; Hiebert 1982, 1989; Love 1996; and Musk 1989, 1995).

Caleb has been getting to know some Muslim men at the university, and notes that most of them feel hurt when parents favor one of their siblings. Recently, Caleb and Nicole attended a seminar on prayer for healing of the heart. When it was Caleb's turn to receive prayer, he found himself remembering scenes from childhood when his father's words had been critical. Although he hadn't thought about these for decades, after he told God exactly how he felt, he sensed the presence of God so strongly that the sting of those words disappeared, and the love of God soaked deeper in his heart than ever before. He forgave his father out loud.

When Nicole received prayer, she remembered how her mother had tried to motivate her to do better in school by telling her how well her older sister was doing. Nicole felt a heaviness, and with tears flowing, she told the Lord. Soon it seemed that Jesus was sitting next to her at her desk. The comfort she missed as a child was given to her now. The heaviness decisively left her when the person praying said, "Any evil spirit that has oppressed Nicole because of this must leave now."

Caleb and Nicole are making early attempts to pray for each other in this way. Caleb found a friend to pray with him about severing any lingering emotional ties with his previous girlfriends. Yesterday, Nicole was able to pray with their older son about something that happened to him last year. They now pray nightly for the family, canceling any curses in Jesus' name, commanding all evil spirits to stay away, and asking God to protect them with his presence and angels. Nicole wonders what she may do next time if she is with a Muslim neighbor who goes into a trance. Caleb imagines one day being fluent enough in the language to pray with one of his colleagues about childhood hurts.

References

Anderson, Neil. 1993. *Bondage Breaker*. Eugene, Ore.: Harvest House Publishers.

Arnold, Clinton. 1997. *3 Crucial Questions Regarding Spiritual Warfare*. Grand Rapids, Mich.: Baker Books.

Colgate, Julia. 2000. "Muslim Women and the Occult: Seeing Jesus Set the Captives Free." In *Ministry to Muslim Women: Longing to Call Them Sisters*. Eds. Fran Love and Jeleta Eckheart, 33-63. Pasadena, Calif.: William Carey Library.

Hiebert, Paul. 1982. "Flaw of the Excluded Middle." *Missiology* 10(1):35-47.

_____. 1989. "Power Encounter and Folk Islam." In *Muslims and Christians on the Emmaus Road*. Ed. J. Dudley Woodberry. Monrovia, Calif.: MARC Publications.

Kim, Caleb, John Travis, and Anna Travis. 2008. "Relevant Responses to Folk Muslims." In *From Seed to Fruit*. Ed. J. Dudley Woodberry, 265-278. Pasadena, Calif.: William Carey Library.

Kraft, Charles. 1992. *Defeating Dark Angels: Breaking Demonic Oppression in a Believer's Life*. Ann Arbor, Mich.: Servant Publications.

_____. 1993. *Deep Wounds, Deep Healing: Discovering the Vital Link Between Spiritual Warfare and Inner Healing*. Ann Arbor, Mich.: Servant Publications.

_____. 1997. *I Give You Authority*. Grand Rapids, Mich.: Chosen Books.

Love, Rick. 1996. "Power Encounter among Folk Muslims." *International Journal of Frontier Missiology* 13(4): 193-195.

Murphy, Ed. 1996. *Handbook for Spiritual Warfare*. Nashville, Tenn.: Thomas Nelson Publisher.

Musk, Bill. 1989. *The Unseen Face of Islam*. East Sussex, U.K.: MARC Publications.

_____. 1995. *Touching the Soul of Islam*. East Sussex, U.K.: MARC Publications.

Payne, Leanne. 1989. *The Healing Presence*. Wheaton, Ill.: Crossways Books.

Sandford, John and Paula Sandford. 1982. *The Transformation of the Inner Man*. Tulsa, Okla.: Victory House.

Stacey, Vivian. 1989. "Practice of Exorcism and Healing." In *Muslims and Christians on the Emmaus Road*. Ed. J. Dudley Woodberry, 291-303. Monrovia, Calif.: MARC Publications.

Swindoll, Charles. 1995. *Demonism: How to Win Against the Devil*. Grand Rapids, Mich.: Zondervan Publishing House.

Taylor, Albert and Elisabeth Taylor. *Ministering Below the Surface*. Accessed February 6, 2010 from http://www.soundswrite.ch/cct.

Travis, John and Anna Travis. 2008. "Deep-level Healing Prayer in Cross-cultural Ministry." In *Paradigms of Christian Witness*. Eds. Charles Van Engen, Darrell Whiteman, and J. Dudley Woodberry, 106-115. Maryknoll, N.Y.: Orbis Books.

Woodberry, J. Dudley. 1990. "The Relevance of Power Ministries for Folk Muslims." In *Wrestling with Dark Angels*. Eds. Peter Wagner and Douglas Pennoyer, 313-331. Ventura, Calif.: Regal Books.

Writer's Guidelines
for Submitting an Article to
Evangelical Missions Quarterly

A. Scott Moreau, editor
Gary R. Corwin, associate editor
Laurie Fortunak Nichols, managing editor

What We Are

EMQ (*Evangelical Missions Quarterly*) is a professional journal serving the worldwide mission community. *EMQ* articles reflect missionary life, thought, and practice. Each issue includes articles, book reviews, editorials, and letters. Subjects are related to worldwide mission and evangelism efforts and include: successful ministries, practical ideas, new tactics and strategies, trends in world evangelization, church planting and discipleship, health and medicine, literature and media, education and training, relief and development, and missionary family life.

Our Purpose

The purpose of *EMQ* is to increase the effectiveness of the evangelical missionary enterprise by:

• providing a forum for communicating new concepts, strategies, and resources

• reporting, analyzing, and interpreting significant trends in missions

• encouraging and assisting mission personnel in their personal and professional growth

• providing a platform for the discussion of important mission issues

About Our Readers

• They include: short-term and career missionaries, mission executives, mission scholars, mission professors, mission students and missionary candidates, mission pastors, lay leaders, and mission supporters.

• Over half of our readers live and work overseas.

• They serve with dozens of different denominations and sending agencies.

• They are well-educated; two-thirds of them have graduate degrees.

• They work at dozens of different missionary ministries, most of them as church planters and teachers.

• They are most interested in cultural and biblical values, Christianity and culture, church and culture, discipleship processes, evangelism methods, church planting methods, and leadership training methods.

• They do not see *EMQ* as a scholarly journal; rather, they see it as a very readable, informative, stimulating, and practical publication.

Our Editorial Philosophy

Submissions are open to individuals who have fresh ideas about anything pertaining to world missions. We are not a scholarly journal written for academics, but we do want material that is academically respectable, reflecting careful thought and practical application to mission professionals, and especially working missionaries. We like to see problems not only diagnosed, but solved either by way of illustration or suggestion.

We prefer articles about deeds done, showing the why and the how, claiming not only success, but also admitting failure. Principles drawn from one example must be applicable to missions more generally. *EMQ* does not include articles which have been previously published in journals, books, websites, etc.

Criteria by which We Evaluate Articles

1. Importance of subject to our readers
2. Freshness and creativity
3. Clarity and readability
4. Development and depth
5. Support and resources
6. Convincing arguments
7. Accuracy and validity
8. Overall treatment of a subject

How to Submit Articles and Book Reviews

1. Before sending your article or review, email: emq@wheaton.edu to ask the editor if he is interested in the subject or book. He may have a similar article on hand, he may have already assigned the book to someone, or your subject may not be on his agenda.

2. Think about your word length: 3,000 for articles; 400 words for reviews.

3. Submitted articles need to be formatted to *EMQ* editorial standards (see "Editorial Guidelines for Submitted Articles" below).

4. Send copy by email to: emq@wheaton.edu with the subject line reading "Article submission."

Editorial Guidelines for Submitted Articles

In an effort to offer our readers clear references for future research, *EMQ* follows the Turabian Style (author, date system) for references both within articles and in reference lists at the end of articles. To make the editorial process easier, we ask that submitted articles be formatted as follows:

If referencing a source within an article, the quote, idea, or fact should be followed by: author's last name, year and page number (e.g., Thomas 1992, 34).

All reference materials should be included in the reference list at the end of the article. For books in reference lists, the format is: Last name, first name, year, book title, where published, and publisher.

For journals in reference lists, the format is: Author's last name, first name, year, article, journal name, editor (if available), date of journal, issue number, page number.

For information found on a website, the format is: author's last name, first name, year, name of article, name of publication, date of publication, date of access, website URL.

How We Treat Articles and Reviews

1. We give a prompt acknowledgment that we received your piece.

2. We may make suggestions for improvements and return it to you if we are interested in your subject.

3. Typically, we are scheduled a year or more in advance for a publication and may not be able to give you a prompt decision.

4. If we do more than routine copy editing, we normally return our edited version for your approval before we print it.

5. We pay $50 upon publication for articles.

What We Look for in *EMQ* Book Reviews

1. A sparkling opening to grab the reader; state the central problem or issue in a broad mission context.

2. A succinct overview of the contents. Do not try to cover everything. Strip it down to its essence.

3. Author's contributions that are new. We want fresh insights. How does he or she help us solve a problem or grow?

4. Succinctly state anything you think the author has missed or stated wrongly. No nit-picking, please.

5. A lively style and tone. Be upbeat. Keep sentences short. Use short, simple words. No academic, technical jargon.

6. Add two or three related books as a separate item at the end. Include title, author, city of publication, publisher, date of publication.

7. Overall length: 400 words. (That's one page in *EMQ*.)

How to Submit Photos

We welcome photo submissions after an article is accepted for publication. We accept black and white or color photos. If emailing photos, send photos as attachments at 300 dpi in tiff or jpeg files under two megabytes (total email size). If sending hard copy, preferred photo size is at least 3x5. Include a caption and photo credit, and specify the article which the photo accompanies. For more information on submitting photos or to submit photos, email: emq@wheaton.edu.